Keeping the peace explores the new multidimensional role that the
United Nations has played in peacemaking, peacekeeping and peacebuilding over the last few years. By examining the paradigm-setting
cases of Cambodia and El Salvador, and drawing lessons from these
UN "success stories," the book seeks to point the way toward more
effective ways for the international community to address conflict in the
post-Cold War era. This book is especially timely given its focus on the
heretofore amorphous middle ground between traditional peacekeeping
and peace enforcement. It provides the first comparative, in-depth
treatment of substantial UN activities in everything from the demobilization and reintegration of forces, the return of refugees, the monitoring of human rights, and the design and supervision of
constitutional, judicial, and electoral reforms, to the observation and
even organization and conduct of elections, and the coordination of
support for economic rehabilitation and reconstruction of countries
torn by war.

Keeping the peace

Keeping the peace

Multidimensional UN operations in Cambodia and El Salvador

Edited by

Michael W. Doyle
Ian Johnstone
and Robert C. Orr

CAMBRIDGE
UNIVERSITY PRESS

PUBLISHED BY THE PRESS SYNDICATE OF THE UNIVERSITY OF CAMBRIDGE
The Pitt Building, Trumpington Street, Cambridge CB2 1RP, United Kingdom

CAMBRIDGE UNIVERSITY PRESS
The Edinburgh Building, Cambridge CB2 2RU, United Kingdom
40 West 20th Street, New York, NY 10011–4211, USA
10 Stamford Road, Oakleigh, Melbourne 3166, Australia

First published 1997

Printed in Great Britain at the University Press, Cambridge

Typeset in Plantin 10/12 pt

A catalogue record for this book is available from the British Library

Library of Congress cataloguing in publication data
Keeping the peace: Multidimensional UN operations in Cambodia
and El Salvador / edited by Michael W. Doyle, Ian Johnstone, and
Robert C. Orr.
       p.   cm.
Includes bibliographical references and index.
ISBN 0 521 58185 0. – ISBN 0 521 58837 5 (pbk.)
1. United Nations Armed Forces – Cambodia.
2. Cambodia – Politics and government – 1975–
3. United Nations – Armed Forces – El Salvador.
4. El Salvador – Politics and government – 1992–
I. Doyle, Michael W.   II. Johnstone, Ian, 1960– .
III. Orr, Robert C. (Robert Cameron), 1964– .
JX1961.P7K4   1997
341.5′84–dc21   96–39891   CIP

ISBN 0 521 58185 0 hardback
ISBN 0 521 58837 5 paperback

To Patricia McDonald and Bre-Ann McDonald, who should have had the opportunity to enjoy peace – Michael Doyle

To my wife, Pam McKee, for her spirit and constant encouragement – Ian Johnstone

To Bonnie and Jack Orr for teaching what matters – Robert Orr

Contents

Preface

This volume is the product of the International Peace Academy's research program, one of the key program areas that IPA has developed over the last twenty-five years. Today the core activities of the IPA program fall into five areas.

IPA plays a facilitating role by bringing together parties in conflict to explore – informally and often off the record – ways to promote political settlements. In the past we have played this role in relation to conflicts in Central America, Southern Africa and Cambodia. We are now engaged in developing this facilitating role into a major program on preventive action.

Over the last three years IPA has worked closely with the Organization of African Unity (OAU) to develop ways of enhancing the capacity of the OAU to respond more effectively to the dramatic situation of conflicts in Africa. These efforts have culminated in adopting a new OAU mechanism devoted to the prevention and management of conflicts in Africa. We are now working with the OAU Secretariat on the challenge of translating this new mechanism into an operational instrument that can make a difference on the ground.

From its inception, IPA played a pioneering role in organizing training seminars for peacekeeping. These have now evolved into policy seminars for senior officials (diplomatic and military) as well as members of the UN Secretariat. The principal objective of the policy seminars is to deepen the participants' understanding of critical policy issues of the day on peacekeeping and peacemaking. The policy seminars have also served the related purpose of providing a setting for networking among senior officials responsible for peacekeeping from different parts of the world.

IPA also directs a wide-ranging program of activities designed to build broader awareness and understanding of peacemaking and peacekeeping trends and issues within the international community at large. These include the IPA Roundtable Series, IPA Global Forum, and the IPA Internship Program.

Last but by no means least, the research program has been at the heart of IPA's unique contribution to the development of an intellectual community in support of international peace and security. IPA monitors peace processes in action, with a view to assessing their effectiveness and drawing lessons for the future. It also produces timely policy briefs on issues before the international community. *Keeping the peace* is the concluding product of IPA's Research Program on Peacemaking and Peacekeeping 1993–1995. Some of the concepts and strategies presented here first appeared in two IPA occasional papers: *UN Peacekeeping in Cambodia: UNTAC's Civil Mandate* (Lynne Rienner, 1995) by Michael Doyle and *Rights and Reconciliation in El Salvador* (Lynne Rienner, 1995) by Ian Johnstone. The next phase of our program will concentrate on assessing the effectiveness of the strategies employed in peace-building.

This volume is also the first, large step in an extended IPA program of research designed to take stock of fifty years of UN experience in peacekeeping and peacemaking, and to examine measures necessary to strengthen multilateral peace operations into the twenty-first century.

The evolution of UN peacekeeping thus far may be divided into three distinct, though closely related, phases. In the first phase the UN developed and practiced traditional peacekeeping with its emphasis on consent and cooperation; ceasefire; impartiality; and the non-use of force, except in self-defense. Traditional peacekeeping, which applied mainly in inter-state conflicts, dominated UN practice in the period from 1948 to about 1988.

In the aftermath of the Cold War and with the proliferation of deadly internal conflicts, a broader, more ambitious, and intrusive notion of peacekeeping emerged that is the focus of this volume on multi-dimensional peace operations. This evolution highlighted the second phase which has been marked by increasing UN engagement in a broad range of intra-state conflicts undertaking some aspects of national political reconstruction, including supervision and observation of elections; the growth and evolution of humanitarian action; the graying of the zone between peacekeeping and enforcement action; and new questions concerning the issue of impartiality. This phase gained universal currency with the publication by the UN Secretary-General, Dr. Boutros Boutros-Ghali, of his seminal paper, *An Agenda for Peace*, in June, 1992.

After several years of extensive engagement and experimentation in multidimensional peacekeeping, the UN has successfully conducted several major operations, such as those in Namibia, Cambodia, El Salvador, and Mozambique. At the same time, the organization has experienced some tragic failures, as evidenced by Somalia, Rwanda, and the earlier operation in Angola. Meanwhile, some operations, like that in former Yugoslavia, ran up against a terrible impasse. The UN was overwhelmed by escalating demands that could not be met; undermined by the lack of resources and capability; and perplexed by the complexity of some of these internal conflicts.

Already there are signs that the UN may be entering a third phase of peacemaking and peacekeeping, a phase that could be marked by a reduced measure of ambition and optimism, a reassessment of the scope of engagement, and a renewed emphasis on the imperative of preventing conflicts before they degenerate into full-scale violence. It is not yet clear if these signs of retrenchment are a passing phenomenon, an inter-regnum marking the present period of great uncertainties, or whether we are witnessing an enduring wave of the future.

As we look ahead, what measures will be necessary to improve and strengthen peacekeeping and peacemaking in general? The authors of *Keeping the peace* look back at the UN operations in Cambodia and El Salvador, hallmarks of the cruicial second phase of multidimensional peacekeeping. They highlight what the UN has done well and what the UN will need to do better, if the organization is to continue to play a central role in promoting peace as we enter the twenty-first century.

For their financial support, the editors, authors, and IPA's Research Program on Peacemaking and Peacekeeping would like to offer their thanks to the Ford Foundation, the MacArthur Foundation, the Pew Charitable Trust, the Tinker Foundation, and Foreign Minister Ali Alatas. IPA's Research Program also benefited from the thoughtful advice of its Research Advisory Committee consisting of Ambassador Richard Butler, Ambassador Nabil Elaraby, Professor Robert Keohane, Ambassador Razali Ismail, Professor John Ruggie, and Sir Brian Urquhart. We received valuable suggestions at various stages in the work from David Holiday, Stephen Marks, Steven Ratner, and the reviewers of Cambridge University Press. The research assistance of Marisa Angell, Marc Bennett, Larry Borowsky, Danny David, Neal Higgins, Mallika Krishnamurthy, Laurence Pearl, Ayaka Suzuki, Elisabeth Uphoff, and Carole Wulff contributed greatly to IPA's project. Special thanks go to Florence Musaffi for her indefatigable assistance and patience throughout the project. The editors thank Hilary Scannell for expert copy-editing and Katharyn Dunham for the index. The editors are also grateful for the advice and support of colleagues F. T. Liu, Dent Ocaya-Lakidi, George Sherry, and Tim Wilkins. The UN Publications Board of the Department of Public Information permitted us to reproduce the two maps. None of this research would have been possible without the cooperation of numerous participants in Cambodia, El Salvador, and New York – citizens and officials, civilians and military – who shared with us their time and wisdom. Many of the interviews were conducted on a "not for attribution" basis. The research as a whole enjoyed the assistance of the UN's Department of Peacekeeping Operations, UNTAC, ONUSAL, and particularly Mr. Kofi Annan, Mr. Marrack Goulding, Special Representatives Yasushi Akashi and Dr. Augusto Ramirez-Ocampo, Mr. Alvaro deSoto, Mr. Iqbal Riza, and Miss Hisako Shimura.

OLARA A. OTUNNU
President of International Peace Academy

Contributors

MICHAEL W. DOYLE is Professor of Politics and International Affairs in the Politics Department and Woodrow Wilson School of Princeton University. He is currently a Senior Fellow and was formerly Vice President of the International Peace Academy. His publications include *Ways of War and Peace* (W. W. Norton), *Empires* (Cornell University Press), *UN Peacekeeping in Cambodia: UNTAC's Civil Mandate* (Lynne Rienner), two other books, articles, chapters in books and occasional essays including "Kant, liberal legacies, and foreign affairs: Parts I and II," in *Philosophy and Public Affairs* (1983). He is North American Editor of *International Peacekeeping* and a member of the Committee of Editors of *World Politics*.

IAN JOHNSTONE is Second Officer in the Executive Office of the Secretary-General of the United Nations. Formerly he was Senior Associate for Research of the International Peace Academy, and has also served as a legal officer in the Office of Legal Affairs of the UN. His most recent publications include *Rights and Reconciliation: UN Strategies in El Salvador* (Lynne Rienner, 1995), *Aftermath of the Gulf War: An Assessment of UN Action* (Lynne Rienner, 1994), and "Treaty Interpretation: the Authority of Interpretive Communities," reprinted in *International Law Anthology*, edited by Anthony D'Amato.

ROBERT C. ORR is Associate for Research of the International Peace Academy and Fellow of the Princeton Society of Fellows, Princeton University. He is formerly Research Fellow in the Foreign Policy Studies Program at the Brookings Institution, Washington, DC. His publications include, "Democracy Promotion and US Foreign Assistance in Africa" in the *Journal of Public and International Affairs* (1992), "The democracy for which they died: the Chinese popular movement of 1989" in the *Journal of Public and International Affairs* (1990), and a number of reports on peacemaking and peacekeeping.

GRACIANA DEL CASTILLO wrote her chapter when she was Senior Officer at the Executive Office of the Secretary-General of the United Nations and Adjunct Associate Professor of Economics at Columbia University. In early 1996, Dr. del Castillo joined the Western Hemisphere Department at the International Monetary Fund where she works on Colombia. She holds a Ph.D in economics from Columbia University and has been the author of numerous articles in books and journals such as *Foreign Policy* and the *Journal of International Money and Finance.*

DAVID CHANDLER is Professor of Southeast Asian history, Monash University, Australia. Recently he served as a visiting professor at the University of Paris and as a resident fellow of the Woodrow Wilson International Center in Washington DC. He has also served as a consultant to the United Transitional Authority in Cambodia (UNTAC), the United Nations High Commissioner for Refugees (UNHCR), and Amnesty International. In the 1960s he worked as a US Foreign Service Officer in Phnom Penh. His major publications include *A History of Cambodia, The Tragedy of Cambodian History: Politics, War and Revolution since 1945* (Yale), and *Brother Number One: A Political Biography of Pol Pot* (Westview).

CHERYL M. LEE KIM is a recent masters degree graduate of Princeton University's Woodrow Wilson School of Public and International Affairs. Formerly she served as Project Officer for the US Agency for International Development (USAID) in Nairobi, Kenya.

MARK LEVINE is Adjunct Professor at Hunter College, City University of New York and Program Coordinator of the Foundation for Ethics and Meaning in New York city. He is in the process of completing his doctorate in the Department of Near Eastern Languages and Literatures at New York University. His writings have been published in the *Christian Science Monitor,* the *Arab Studies Quarterly,* and *Tikkun Magazine.*

DAVID MCCORMICK is an associate of McKinsey and Co. He received his Ph.D. from Princeton University's Woodrow Wilson School of Public and International Affairs. He is a former US army officer. Prior to his arrival at Princeton, he served with the US Rapid Deployment Force in the Persian Gulf. Mr. McCormick is a 1995 Earhart Fellow and holds a Masters degree from the Woodrow Wilson School and a graduate of the United States Military Academy at West Point.

MARK METRIKAS is an Australian army officer, currently serving in the Headquarters of the Australian Defense Forces as staff officer on the

Joint Exercise Planning Staff. He is a graduate of the Royal Australian Air Force Staff College. He has served as a Military Observer in Iran with the United Nations Iran–Iraq Military Observer Group (UNIIMOG), as Director of Peacekeeping at the International Peace Academy, and as Assistant Military Advisor to the Australian Mission to the United Nations.

JIN SONG is Director of Congressional Affairs at the Korea Economic Institute in Washington, DC, where she works on trade and multi-lateral investment issues related to the Asia Pacific region, including Korea, Japan, China, and the ASEAN countries. She has previously worked at the East-West Center in Honolulu, Hawaii, and briefly for the US Department of State in Seoul, Korea.

NISHKALA SUNTHARALINGAM is Legal Officer with the UN Observer Mission in Liberia (UNOMIL). Formerly she served as Legal Officer with the United Nations Angola Verification Mission II and III in Luanda, Angola. She is author of "Temporary protected status in the United States: an assessment of a new humanitarian remedy," Lawyer's Committee (1992), and co-author with Michael Doyle of "The UN in Cambodia: lessons for multidimensional peacekeeping," *International Peacekeeping* (1994).

EDELBERTO TORRES-RIVAS is Professor of Social Sciences in the Graduate Program on Central America at the University of Costa Rica and Professor Emeritus of the Facultad Lationoamericana de Ciencias Sociales (FLACSO)-Ecuador. From 1985 to 1993 he was Secretary General of FLACSO. He has taught at prestigious universities in Chile, Argentina, Mexico, Brazil, the United States, Spain, and the Netherlands. His most recent publications include *History and Society in Central America* (University of Texas), *El tamaño de nuestra democracia* (Istmo), *El desorden democratico* (Istmo-DEI).

ELISABETH UPHOFF KATO is currently a consultant with the World Bank working in Cambodia on reconstruction and development. Previously she worked with Cambodian refugees in Thailand. She is author of two books in Khmer on contemporary Southeast Asian history, as well as *Intellectual Property Protection and US Relations with Indonesia, Malaysia, Singapore, and Thailand*.

TIMOTHY WILKINS is an attorney at Cleary, Gottlieb, Steen and Hamilton in New York City where he maintains a broad practice of international corporate law and public international law. He is a graduate of Harvard University's JD/MBA program, served as a resident law tutor of Harvard's Eliot house, an editor of the *Harvard*

International Law Journal, and a Ford Foundation Fellow in Public International Law. He is author of "Title VII protection for US citizens working overseas" in the *Harvard International Law Journal* (1992).

BRIAN WILLIAMS is Project Manager of the Democratic Initiatives and Governance Project with the US Agency for International Development (USAID) in Kigali, Rwanda. Formerly he served as Acting Provincial Officer for CARE Cambodia's refugee repatriation program, as well as Director of Administration and Finance for CARE Zaire/Burundi. He has also worked with the Peace Corps in Kyrghyzstan, CARE in Afghanistan, and the International Rescue Committee in Pakistan.

Abbreviations

ARENA	Nationalist Republican Alliance
ASEAN	Association of Southeast Asian Nations
BCU	Border control unit
CARERE	Cambodian Area and Rehabilitation Project (UNDP)
CGDK	Coalition Government of Democratic Kampuchea
COPAZ	Comisión Nacional para la Consolidación de la Paz (National Commission for the Consolidation of Peace)
DK	Democratic Kampuchea
DNI	National Intelligence Directorate
EAS	Existing administrative structure
ERP	People's Revolutionary Army
FAES	Armed Forces of El Salvador
FAPU	People's United Front for Action
FDR	Democratic Revolutionary Front
FMLN	Farabundo Marti National Liberation Front
FUNCINPEC	National United Front for an Independent, Neutral, Peaceful and Cooperative Cambodia
ICK	International Conference on Kampuchea
ISTA	Instituto Salvadoreño de Transformación Agraria
KPNLF	Khmer People's National Liberation Front
MCTU	Mine Clearance Training Unit
MINUSAL	Mission of the United Nations in El Salvador
MMWG	Mixed Military Working Group
MNR	National Revolutionary Movement
NADK	National Army of Democratic Kampuchea
ONUC	UN Operation in the Congo
ONUCA	UN Mission in Nicaragua
ONUMOZ	UN Operation in Mozambique
ONUSAL	UN Observer Mission in El Salvador
PCN	National Conciliation Party
PDK	Party of Democratic Kampuchea
PNC	National Civil Police

PRK	People's Republic of Kampuchea
PRTC	Workers' Revolutionary Party of Central America
PRUD	Revolutionary Democratic Unification party
QIP	Quick impact project
RN	National Resistance
SEATO	Southeast Asia Treaty Organization
SIU	Special Investigative Unit
SOC	State of Cambodia
UDN	Nationalist Democratic Union
UEA	Special Anti-Narcotics Unit
UNAMIC	United Nations Advance Mission in Cambodia
UNAVEM III	UN Angola Verification Mission III
UNHCR	United Nations High Commisssioner for Refugees
UNITAF	Unified Task Force
UNO	National Opposition Union
UNOSOM	UN Operation in Somalia
UNPROFOR	UN Protection Force
UNTAC	United Nations Transitional Authority in Cambodia
UNTAES	United Nations Transitional Administration for Eastern Slavonia, Baranja, and Western Sirmium
UNTAG	United Nations Transition Assistance Group for Namibia
USC	United Somali Congress/Somalia National Alliance
WFP	World Food Programme

1 Introduction

Michael W. Doyle, Ian Johnstone, and Robert C. Orr

Since the end of the Cold War, the community of nations has struggled to redefine the relation between those issues that fall within the realm of a state's sovereignty and those that represent a legitimate concern of the international community. The expanding scope of collective intervention, by coercive means, under chapter VII of the United Nations Charter is one manifestation of this struggle. From the Gulf crisis ceasefire resolution in 1991 to the US-led intervention to restore Haitian President Aristide, the United Nations Security Council has employed an increasingly broad interpretation of what constitutes a threat to international peace and security, authorizing action that would undoubtedly have been seen as unlawful interference in sovereign affairs only a decade ago.

But setbacks encountered in Somalia and the former Yugoslavia have highlighted the difficulties of collective intervention by force. Limited forcible intervention, for humanitarian purposes, remains a viable and often necessary task – although even these operations have been most successful when "contracted out" to multinational coalitions – but efforts to impose peace on recalcitrant parties have either failed or been abandoned before completed. The result has been a retreat from "peace enforcement," though not a retreat from globalism or UN activism. The future of UN peacekeeping, it seems, lies between the extremes of forcible intervention and absolute respect for sovereignty. That is, the future of UN peace operations lies in "multidimensional peace operations."

Multidimensional peace operations

The outlines of the middle ground between forcible intervention and absolute respect for sovereignty are readily apparent in the first group of multidimensional operations – those recently completed in Cambodia, El Salvador, and Mozambique, and those underway in Haiti, Angola, and Croatia. These operations, though firmly based on consent, have

1

embodied a novel relationship between the international community and the states in question. In some instances the UN has closely monitored the state, in others it has become involved in renovating and rebuilding – or building for the first time – the basic structures of the state, while in yet other cases the UN has even substituted for the state. These very new tasks have required the UN to deploy civilian and police components to complement the traditional "blue helmets."

In the paradigm-setting multidimensional operations in Cambodia and El Salvador, the UN undertook a threefold mission: it served as a peacemaker facilitating a peace treaty among the parties; as a peacekeeper, monitoring the implementation of complex agreements that go to the roots of the respective conflicts; and as a peacebuilder, supporting the political, institutional, and social transformations necessary to overcome deep-seated internal animosities and strife. The goal of the UN was not merely to create conditions for negotiations between the parties, but to develop strategies and support structures that would bring about a lasting peace. In practice this meant that in Cambodia and El Salvador the UN undertook virtually all of the activities identified by the Secretary-General in his "Supplement to *An Agenda for Peace*": "the supervision of cease-fires, the regroupment and demobilization of forces, their reintegration into civilian life and the destruction of their weapons; the design and implementation of de-mining programmes; the return of refugees and displaced persons; the provision of humanitarian assistance; the supervision of existing administrative structures; the establishment of new police forces; the verification of respect for human rights; the design and supervision of constitutional, judicial and electoral reforms; the observation, supervision and even organization and conduct of elections; and the coordination of support for economic rehabilitation and reconstruction."[1]

Understanding multidimensional peace operations is not only important because of the vast range of new activities undertaken, and what this represents in terms of the relationship of the UN to those countries in crisis, but also because consent-based multidimensional operations appear to be a viable option for addressing future conflicts. In fact, among the three broad categories of peace operations – traditional peacekeeping, multidimensional peace operations, and peace enforcement[2] – consent-based multidimensional operations like UNTAC and

---

[1] "Supplement to *An Agenda for Peace*: position paper of the Secretary-General on the occasion of the fiftieth anniversary of the United Nations," para. 21, in Boutros Boutros-Ghali, *Agenda for Peace* (New York: United Nations, second edition, 1995).

[2] "Traditional peacekeeping" is a shorthand term to describe many but by no means all peacekeeping operations established during the Cold War years – UNFICYP in Cyprus and the three Middle East operations (UNDOF, UNTSO, and UNIFIL) being current

ONUSAL are the growth industry for the UN. To understand why, it is worth considering briefly why the other two categories, traditional peacekeeping and peace enforcement, are less likely to shape the UN agenda in the years ahead.

In traditional peacekeeping operations, unarmed or lightly armed UN forces are stationed between hostile parties to monitor a truce, troop withdrawal, and/or buffer zone while political negotiations go forward. They were devised by the UN as a practical mechanism to contain armed conflicts and facilitate their political settlement by peaceful means.[3] They are based on consent and must be completely impartial, using force only in self-defense and as a last resort. Their success depends on the cooperation of the parties and the ability of the peacekeepers to resolve problems by negotiation rather than coercion.

Traditional peacekeeping operations are normally deployed in situations of inter-state conflict. They were possible during the Cold War years either because the superpowers had no interest in the conflicts, or because they had a mutual interest in ensuring the conflicts did not escalate. They provide transparency to the parties through an impartial assurance that the other party is not violating the truce. They also raise the costs of defecting from, and the positive benefits of abiding with, the agreement by various means: the threat of exposure; the potential resistance of the peacekeeping forces; and the international legitimacy of UN mandates. Their deployment is meant to calm the military situation while a political settlement is pursued. As the thirty-year operation in Cyprus illustrates, however, the deployment of peacekeepers does not necessarily signal an urgent desire among the parties or the international community to achieve a comprehensive settlement.

Times have changed to the point where traditional peacekeeping no longer addresses the challenges of either managing or resolving many complex civil crises. The UN will continue to have a role to play in the monitoring of ceasefires between states, as it is now doing very

examples. "Multidimensional peacekeeping" describes post-Cold War operations such as those in Cambodia, El Salvador, Mozambique, and Angola, though the term might also include the four-year Congo operation in the early 1960s that had many of the characteristics of more complex current UN missions. "Peace enforcement" refers to post-Cold War operations such as that in Somalia that were undertaken under chapter VII of the UN Charter. These three categories are often called "first, second, and third generation" operations respectively, but this terminology is not used here because it implies a sequential, linear development that recent events have increasingly called into question. For a cogent analysis of the types of peacekeeping operations, see Marrack Goulding, "The evolution of United Nations peacekeeping," *International Affairs*, vol. 69, no. 3, 1993. For a description of the post-Cold War qualitative changes in peacekeeping operations, see "Supplement to *An Agenda for Peace*", paras. 8–22.

[3]   F. T. Liu, *United Nations Peacekeeping and the Non-Use of Force*, IPA Occasional Paper (Boulder, Col.: Lynne Rienner, 1992), p. 11.

successfully on the Golan Heights between Israel and Syria. But today conflicts are increasingly within rather than between states. They are typically fought between regular armies and irregular forces, or among irregular forces. Many involve more than two parties, with shifting alliances and allegiances. They are often accompanied by humanitarian emergencies, systematic human rights abuses, and the breakdown of law and order.[4] In the most extreme cases – influentially described by two commentators as "failed states" – no functioning government exists at all.[5] The demands upon and dangers to the peacekeeper are considerably greater than those faced by military personnel deployed along a well-defined front line between two states. The UN usually refuses to deploy a force in these circumstances until a negotiated settlement has been reached, or at least until the contours of one are visible. When the UN does deploy a force, the range of tasks it is asked to perform are extensive and complex, combining military, police, and civilian elements.

Peace enforcement operations range from low-level military missions to protect the delivery of humanitarian assistance, to full fledged enforcement action to roll back aggression. Undertaken under chapter VII of the United Nations Charter, their defining characteristic is the lack of consent to some or all of the UN mandate. Militarily, these operations seek to deter, dissuade, or deny success to acts of aggressive force.[6] By using collective force to preclude an outcome based on the use of force by the parties, the UN seeks to persuade the parties to settle the conflict by negotiation.

The operations in Somalia and Bosnia, both having elements of peace enforcement, were inspired by a global sense of duty (albeit weak and inchoate) to address humanitarian emergencies when they occur. A new-found sense of vigorous capacity in international institutions recently freed from the gridlock of the Cold War made it appear as though the global capacity to intervene could meet the demands of these crises. The dangers and limitations of these new commitments, however, became painfully evident in the streets of Mogadishu and the not-so-safe areas of Bosnia.

In Somalia, the inability of UNOSOM I to stem the humanitarian crisis engulfing the country prompted the Security Council to authorize

---

[4] "Supplement to *An Agenda for Peace*", paras. 12–13.

[5] Gerald Helman and Steven Ratner, "Saving failed states," *Foreign Policy*, vol. 89, 1992–3, pp. 3–20.

[6] See John G. Ruggie, "The United Nations: stuck in a fog between peacekeeping and enforcement," in *Peacekeeping: The Way Ahead?*, McNair Paper 25 (Washington, DC: Institute for National Strategic Studies, National Defense University, 1993). See also John MacKinlay and Jarat Chopra, *A Draft Concept of Second Generation Multinational Operations* (Providence, RI: Watson Institute, 1993).

UNITAF, a chapter VII, US-led operation, to create a secure environment for the delivery of humanitarian assistance. When the USA was ready to withdraw UNITAF, the back of the famine had been broken but the factions were still fully armed and the environment was far from secure. The Secretary-General therefore recommended, and the Council agreed, to endow UNOSOM II with chapter VII enforcement powers to prevent a resumption of violence and disarm the parties, among other objectives. UNOSOM II's vigorous pursuit of its mandate turned General Aidid's United Somali Congress/Somali National Alliance (USC/SNA) faction against the UN, resulting in an attack on a Pakistani battalion that left twenty-five dead. The Security Council responded with a resolution affirming the right to take "all necessary measures" against those responsible for attacks on UN personnel, including the power of arrest and detention. Several months of intensive efforts to capture Aidid and his aides culminated in the disastrous raid on a USC/SNA stronghold by US Rangers, under US command, in which eighteen Americans died. US troops were withdrawn shortly thereafter, as were other Western contingents, and UNOSOM II essentially reverted to functioning as a humanitarian relief operation, coercive methods having been abandoned. As an effort to impose peace, the UN operation in Somalia had failed.[7]

An almost opposite dilemma emerged in Bosnia, where the UN was criticized for employing too little force. A peace operation with enforcement powers, UNPROFOR was tasked with monitoring a "no-fly-zone", protecting relief convoys and deterring attacks on "safe areas" for Bosnian civilians. But with almost half the population in UN-PROFOR-protected areas directly dependent on UN convoys for vital supplies of food and medicine, military action against the predominantly Serb aggressors would be met by a complete cut-off of humanitarian assistance by those same Serbian forces, who maintained control of the vital access routes. General Sir Michael Rose's reluctance to cross what he called "the Mogadishu line" captured the dilemma well. Determined to maintain the neutrality of the peacekeepers, and ill-equipped for

---

[7]   This is not to say that the UN effort as a whole failed. In late 1992, 3,000 men, women, and children were dying of starvation daily – a tragedy that the international relief effort ended. Two major conferences on national reconciliation were held, both of which continue to serve as a frame of reference in discussions of a political settlement. The UN helped to establish a number of district and regional councils, which may facilitate rehabilitation and development when the security situation permits. The UN also administered a police training program and a judicial training program. For a thorough internal assessment of UNOSOM's achievements and setbacks, see Report of the Secretary-General on the Situation in Somalia, March 28, 1995 (S/1995/231). See also Eric Schmitt, "Somalia's first lesson for military is caution," New York Times, March 5, 1995.

major military action, UNPROFOR went to great lengths to avoid the use of force. And as long as no major outside power was willing to do more militarily than support pinprick NATO airstrikes, UNPROFOR could only muddle along by providing as much protection as possible without getting drawn into the war. This fragility of this position was dramatically highlighted in May and June 1995, when 370 UN peace-keepers were taken prisoner by Bosnian-Serb forces. Another round of airstrikes by NATO in late August and early September 1995 eventually did help drive the Serbs to the negotiating table where the Dayton Agreement was produced. However, care should be taken not to overestimate the precedent-setting value of NATO's actions in Bosnia.[8] By mid-1995, the successful Croatian government offensive in the Krajina had dramatically altered the balance of military power in the region, prompting the USA to launch a major diplomatic offensive to secure a comprehensive peace agreement. Meanwhile, the fall of the safe areas of Srebrenica and Zepa, and the inability to find troop contributors for Gorazde, virtually eliminated the risk of hostage-taking.

Somalia and Bosnia have painfully exposed the limitations of peace enforcement. Forcible intervention may help overcome humanitarian emergencies, but typically only in short, sharp actions. At the same time, however, neither the UN nor any other outside body is in a good position to impose a peace on recalcitrant parties or reconstruct failed states. Even short-term humanitarian interventions – demand for which is likely to continue to increase – may be beyond the current capacities of the UN if they are likely to require significant military force. Thus in recent cases the Security Council has "contracted out" chapter VII actions, not only to the USA in Somalia and Haiti, but also to the French in Rwanda and the NATO-led Implementation Force in Bosnia.

In Haiti, the Council again authorized "all necessary means" to create a secure environment, this time to permit the return of democratically elected President Aristide. Fortunately, the intervention succeeded with barely a shot fired, and in January 1995 the UN took over. Unlike Somalia, however, the US-led intervention force withdrew only when it and the Secretary-General had certified that a secure environment had been created and a UN peacekeeping operation could safely take over. In the peacekeeping phase of the Haiti operation, despite the concerns about the capacity of the local forces to control violence, force was used only in self-defense, not to disarm the parties, maintain law and order, or rebuild the state. Although the circumstances in Haiti are unique, the case does suggest a pattern that may be replicated in the future: a

---

[8] Shashi Tharoor, "Should UN peacekeeping go 'back to basics?'," *Survival*, vol. 37, no. 4, 1995–6, p. 58.

"contracted out" enforcement action to end the violence followed by a consent-based UN operation to consolidate peace.

Multidimensional, chapter VI operations are a substantial step beyond traditional peacekeeping and a significant step short of peace enforcement. They are based on the consent of the parties, but the nature of and purposes for which the consent is granted are qualitatively different from traditional operations. Complex peace agreements cannot possibly provide for every contingency, nor completely define the scope of UN involvement. Implemented over an extended period, gaps in the accords materialize, problems of interpretation arise and circumstances change. The original consent granted, therefore, is open ended and in part a gesture of faith that later problems can be worked out on a consensual basis. Within the framework of the agreement, international norms, and the degree of commitment of the parties, the UN acts as an independent agent, helping to bring about extensive social and political transformations.

Cambodia and El Salvador, the first comprehensive cases of multidimensional peacekeeping, proved to be fruitful laboratories for the unprecedented tasks the UN was asked to perform. Having recently been terminated, these missions also provide a timely yet sufficiently "complete" view of multidimensional peacekeeping, from which lessons can be learned concerning the roots of success and failure.

War and peace in Cambodia

Settling the Cambodian conflict required the participation of local, regional, and global actors and the participation of the UN in a crucial implementing role. Following years of Cold War deadlock, it took three years of negotiation and a number of false starts before the Paris Agreements of 1991 were finally agreed upon as the best route for pursuing peace.

Following the devastating bombing Cambodia suffered during the Vietnam War and the deaths of as many as a million Cambodians at the hands of the Khmer Rouge, the conflict entered a new stage in December 1978 when, responding to repeated provocations, Vietnam invaded Cambodia. As David Chandler explains in his chapter "Three visions of politics in Cambodia," Vietnam's installation of the Heng Samrin–Hun Sen regime in 1978–9 gave rise to a guerrilla movement of the three major resistance groups: Prince Norodom Sihanouk's party – National United Front for an Independent, Neutral, Peaceful and Cooperative Cambodia (FUNCINPEC) – Son Sann's Khmer People's National Liberation Front (KPNLF), and the Party of Democratic

Kampuchea (PDK, or the Khmer Rouge). Each of the four, including the Hun Sen regime itself (later called State of Cambodia, or SOC), contested the others' claims to legitimate authority over Cambodia. In 1982, at the urging of the Association of Southeast Asian Nations (ASEAN), the United States, and China, the three groups opposing the Hun Sen regime formed the Coalition Government of Democratic Kampuchea (CGDK), headed by Prince Sihanouk.

The conflict was shaped by the collapse of the legitimacy of the Cambodian state following the "auto-genocide" inflicted by the Khmer Rouge between 1975 and 1979 and the ensuing installation of the Heng Samrin–Hun Sen regime by the Vietnamese. The regime developed an effective (albeit dictatorial) authority over more than 80 percent of the national territory.[9] What it lacked was legitimacy, international recognition outside the Soviet bloc, and voluntary domestic support.

For the Hun Sen regime and its Vietnamese and Soviet backers, the conflict was a counter-insurgency waged against a genocidal opponent (the Khmer Rouge). For the CGDK and its ASEAN, Chinese, and US supporters, the conflict represented an armed international intervention and occupation of a sovereign country by Vietnam. Conflicting claims to authority between CGDK and the Hun Sen government created problems of recognition for the international community. Cambodia's internal conflicts were compounded by each faction's external allegiances. The United States had supported a military coup in 1970, the Chinese backstopped the Khmer Rouge, and the Vietnamese installed the Hun Sen regime in 1979 (finally withdrawing their military forces in 1989). Though the UN seated the CGDK delegation as the representative of the legal government of Cambodia, the Hun Sen faction controlled the country.

From the very beginning the UN was involved in the search for peace. The Secretary-General's envoy, Rafeeuddin Ahmed, in consultations with the Cambodian parties and regional states between 1982 and 1985, developed the outlines of a comprehensive solution that would engage all four factions, establish a ceasefire, supervise the withdrawal of all foreign forces, guarantee Cambodia's independence and neutrality, repatriate refugees, demobilize military forces, provide for genuine national self-determination through free and fair elections, and institute a human rights education program to help insure "a non-return of the policies and practices of a recent past" (the diplomatically polite code

---

[9] For background on these issues, see Ben Kiernan and Chantou Boua (eds.), *Peasants and Politics in Kampuchea 1942–1981* (London: Zed Press, 1982), and Michael Vickery, *Kampuchea: Politics, Economics and Society* (Boulder, Col.: Lynne Rienner, 1986) and David Chandler's chapter in this volume, "Three visions of politics in Cambodia."

words for the Khmer Rouge's actions which led to the death of more than a million Cambodians).[10] By this point, however, the UN had moved far ahead of the parties themselves. It was not until December 1987 that Prince Sihanouk and Hun Sen informally met, and the Cambodian factions began to demonstrate a willingness to discuss peace.

Following the encouragement of the Secretary-General, regional actors – and particularly Indonesia's foreign minister Ali Alatas – began to take the lead. In July 1988, all four Cambodian factions were brought together for the first time, joined by Vietnam, Laos, and the states of ASEAN. At that meeting and another in February 1989, the participants succeeded in identifying the need for an international control mechanism to supervise the transition to peace, but they could not reach an agreement on how such a mechanism would operate. Thus French foreign minister Roland Dumas joined Mr. Alatas to co-sponsor the first Paris Conference on Cambodia in July 1989. Eighteen countries attended, including the five permanent members of the Security Council (the P5), plus the Secretary-General. Progress was made on a number of key issues, but the sticking point proved to be the interim control mechanism. Disappointing the expectations of the co-chairs, the Hun Sen regime rejected Khmer Rouge participation in an interim quadripartite government.[11] Regional talks resumed among the four factions and various alternatives to "power-sharing" were proposed, the most ambitious of which came from US representative Stephen Solarz, who called for a trustee-like authority for the UN in Cambodia during the period between a political settlement and the installment of freely, democratically elected leaders.[12] With the withdrawal in September 1989 of Vietnamese forces and the failure of the peace process, however, war resumed.

Beginning in January 1990, the P5 took the initiative by convening a series of monthly meetings alternating between Paris and New York. Working with drafts from Gareth Evans, Australia's foreign minister, and papers of the UN Secretariat, the P5 steadily crafted the outlines of a comprehensive settlement featuring a strong controlling role for the UN. When they reached a consensus, they asked the co-sponsors of the Paris Conference (France and Indonesia) to convene an informal

[10] See Report of the Secretary-General, *The Situation in Cambodia*, UN Document A/40/759, October 17, 1985, para. 13. Ahmed's informal negotiations leading to the 1985 report came to be called the "Cocktail Party" talks.

[11] See Tommy T. B. Koh, "The Paris Conference on Cambodia: a multilateral negotiation that 'failed'," *Negotiation Journal*, vol. 6, no. 1, 1990, pp. 81–7.

[12] Stephen Solarz, "Cambodia and the international community," *Foreign Affairs* vol. 69, no. 2, 1990, pp. 99–115.

meeting of the four factions in Jakarta. There, on September 10, 1990, the four accepted the framework and announced the formation of the Supreme National Council, consisting of all four factions and embodying Cambodian sovereignty during the transition process. Eleven months later, the framework was turned into a workable accord, known as the Paris Agreements.

The notable aspects of the Paris Agreements included the comprehensiveness of the settlement plan; the identification of the Supreme National Council as the "unique legitimate body and source of authority in which, throughout the transitional period the sovereignty, independence and unity of Cambodia are enshrined"; and the unprecedented civilian role of the UN in the settlement process.[13]

In the Paris Agreements, the parties agreed not only to the terms of a ceasefire and the disarming of the factions, but also to the maintenance of law and order; the repatriation of refugees; the promotion of human rights and principles for a new constitution; the supervision and control of certain aspects of the administrative machinery by a UN body; and the organization, conduct, and monitoring of elections by the UN. UNTAC was required to assume traditional peacekeeping responsibilities (monitoring the ceasefire and withdrawal of foreign forces, and supervising the cantonment and demobilization of local forces), as well as new civilian duties (controlling and supervising civil administration, organizing elections, coordinating refugee repatriation, promoting human rights, and facilitating economic rehabilitation). It was not successful in every area – the military forces did not abide by the ceasefire or disarm – but considering the fundamental lack of cooperation between the main antagonists in Cambodia, the Vietnamese-installed government, and the radical Khmer Rouge, UNTAC's achievements were remarkable. Most significantly, the UN went beyond monitoring – which it has done many times before – to organize a nationwide election from beginning to end, in which 90 percent of the Cambodian electorate voted in the face of intimidation and violence.

FUNCINPEC won 45.5 percent of the vote in the May 1993 elections, followed by Hun Sen's CPP, with 38.2 percent. The two agreed to form a coalition government, sharing the prime ministership and dividing the ministries, with Prince (now King) Sihanouk reigning

[13] For valuable background on the new features of the UN mandate in Cambodia see Steven Ratner, *The New UN Peacekeeping* (New York: St. Martin's Press, 1995); Trevor Findlay, *The UN in Cambodia* (Stockholm: SIPRI, 1995); Jarat Chopra, *United Nations Authority in Cambodia* (Providence, RI: Watson Institute, 1993); and Janet Heininger, *Peacekeeping in Transition: The United Nations in Cambodia* (New York: Twentieth Century Fund, 1994).

as head of state. The Khmer Rouge did not participate in the elections, planning to hold out for a negotiated seat in the future coalition. In fact, they were not given a seat and the government has pursued a policy of interdiction ever since. The Khmer Rouge have weakened steadily but, as of early 1996, remain a force to be reckoned with. Meanwhile, UNTAC withdrew in September 1993, leaving behind a small human rights center and various UN development agencies to help consolidate the fragile peace.

During 1994 and 1995, Cambodia continued to experience significant progress in the consolidation of civil society, but the coalition government was charged with complicity in a series of attacks on opposition political parties, restrictions on the freedom of the press and interferences with the privileges of the National Assembly. Leading ministers – including Sam Rainsy, the finance minister, and Prince Sirivuddh, the foreign minister – were forced to resign after they accused the government of financial corruption and the government accused them of subversion. Much of the government's efforts went into a continuing military offensive against Khmer Rouge forces. As of early 1996, the Khmer Rouge have weakened substantially, but small forces remain in arms in the remote areas of the western provinces. Major challenges to the principles of "liberal pluralism" embodied in the Paris Peace Agreement lie in economic and social development where progress, stymied by the continuing civil war and governmental strife, has been extremely slow.

War and peace in El Salvador

As Edelberto Torres-Rivas explains in his chapter, "Civil war and insurrection in El Salvador," the roots of the eleven-year civil war in the Central American nation date back at least to the last century.[14] A program of state intervention in the economy at that time led to substantial economic growth, based mainly on the production and export of coffee. In the mid-1800s the government decreed that an ever-increasing proportion of land should be devoted to coffee, and by the end of the century the best land was concentrated in the hands of the wealthiest "fourteen families." Most of the presidents of the country during the period – who were generals prior to their elections – came

---

[14] For thorough discussions of the background of conflict in El Salvador, see Tommie Sue Montgomery, *Revolution in El Salvador: From Civil Strife to Civil Peace* (Boulder, Col.: Westview Press, second edn., 1994); Christopher C. Coleman, *The Salvadoran Peace Process: A Preliminary Inquiry* (Oslo: Norwegian Institute of International Affairs, Research Report no. 173, 1993); Terry Lynn Karl, "El Salvador's negotiated revolution," *Foreign Affairs*, vol. 71, no. 2, 1992, p. 147.

from that oligarchy. By 1931, the social cost of this concentration of wealth and power had precipitated a series of peasant and worker uprisings, culminating in an attempted insurrection led by Augustín Farubundo Martí. The uprisings were brought to a bloody end in December 1931 by a number of young military officers who seized power in a coup d'état.

By the end of 1932, the military was firmly in control. It ruled to preserve its own position and to serve the interests of the oligarchy – goals that were often, but not always, compatible. The years 1932 to 1979 were characterized by cycles of repression and reform, dominated by the army and the oligarchy although, after 1960, the church and popular organizations began to make their presence felt.[15] These new actors wielded more influence after the election of 1972, which by all accounts was stolen from the Christian Democrat José Napoleon Duarte.[16] The period of repression that ensued throughout most of the 1970s was fertile ground for the growth of so-called "political-military organizations," who came increasingly to believe in the necessity of armed revolution. Four of these organizations were formed in the 1970s and, joined by the communist party of El Salvador, they united in 1980 to become the FMLN. By this point, full-scale civil war had already erupted.

Throughout the 1980s, a number of presidential, legislative, and mayoral elections were held, but political developments were determined more by what happened on the battlefield than at the ballot box. Salvadoran society was militarized, with civilian rule constrained and undermined by widespread right-wing violence, military will, and active US government involvement. Acts of political violence by right-wing "death squads" increased dramatically, and untold human rights abuses were committed.[17] In the end, over 75,000 lives were lost and more than 1 million people – almost one-quarter of the population – had been displaced.

Regional peace efforts in Central America began in 1983, when the members of the Contadora Group (Columbia, Mexico, Panama, and Venezuela) initiated a series of consultations with five governments of the region. What has been called the "official birth" of the Central American peace process did not come until August 1987, however, when the presidents of the five nations signed the Esquipulas II

---

[15] Montgomery, *Revolution in El Salvador*, p. 79.

[16] Ibid., pp. 62–5; Coleman, *The Salvadoran Peace Process*, p. 11.

[17] See Report of the Commission on the Truth for El Salvador, *From Madness to Hope: The 12-Year War in El Salvador*, S/25500 (1993), p. 27 (hereinafter, Truth Commission report).

Agreement.[18] In it, they requested all governments concerned to terminate support for irregular forces and insurrectional movements in Central America, and reiterated their commitment to prevent the use of their own territories to destabilize their neighbors. The Security Council endorsed the Agreement in July 1989, and lent its full support to the Secretary-General's good offices efforts.

The first UN operation to be deployed in the region was ONUCA, in November 1989, with a mandate to monitor compliance with Esquipulas II by patrolling the borders of the five countries. Meanwhile, in September 1989, the government of El Salvador and the FMLN agreed to a dialogue to end the armed conflict. Given the rapprochement that was taking place between the USA and the USSR, it seemed that real progress was possible. However, following the murder of a key trade union leader at the end of October 1989, the FMLN launched a major offensive, which for the first time brought the war to the capital of the country.

The parties fought to a stalemate, becoming convinced that a military victory was impossible.[19] With the backing of the five Central American presidents, they separately requested diplomatic intervention by the Secretary-General. His personal representative, Alvaro de Soto, spent the next three years helping to hammer out a series of six accords between the parties, culminating in the Chapultepec Agreement signed in Mexico City on January 16, 1992.

The cumulative effect of the six agreements was a profound transformation of Salvadoran society, what the new Secretary-General Boutros Boutros-Ghali called "a revolution achieved by negotiation." In a nutshell, the accords brought an end to the war by drawing the FMLN into the political process in exchange for extensive institutional and legal reforms designed to "demilitarize" Salvadoran society. The overarching objectives of the negotiations were set out in the framework agreement reached in Geneva in April 1990: to end the armed conflict by political means; to promote the democratization of the country; to guarantee respect for human rights; and to reunify Salvadoran society. One month later, an agenda and timetable for the negotiations were agreed upon in Caracas, identifying seven substantive topics for negotiation.

The San José Agreement on Human Rights was the first substantive agreement reached by the parties, in July 1990. It set out a number of rights both sides had to respect and, most importantly, provided for the

[18] *The United Nations and El Salvador 1990–1995* (United Nations Department of Public Information, 1995), p. 9.
[19] Ibid., p. 12.

establishment of a UN human rights verification mission, intended to take up its responsibilities after a ceasefire was achieved. For various reasons, however, the parties subsequently requested the deployment of the verification mission in mid-1991, before negotiations on other issues were completed and the ceasefire was in place.

Meanwhile, almost a year after the San José Agreement was signed, the parties agreed in Mexico to a set of constitutional reforms relating to the armed forces, the justice system and the electoral system. The reforms were approved by the outgoing National Assembly, whose term ended on April 30, 1991, and ratified by the new Assembly shortly thereafter. The Mexico Agreement also provided for the establishment of a Truth Commission to investigate "serious acts of violence that have occurred since 1980 and whose impact on society urgently requires that the public should know the truth."

The fifth accord, the New York Agreement, was signed in September 1991. Its key elements were the creation of the National Commission for the Consolidation of Peace (COPAZ), and agreements in principle to the reduction, doctrinal reform, and "purification" of the armed forces. Because the FMLN was represented on COPAZ, the insurgent group had a channel to participate in overseeing implementation of the agreements even before it became a political party. The agreement on reform of the armed forces – the most difficult issue in the negotiations – did not cover all details, but the principle of "purification" pointed the way to a final settlement. Finally at midnight, December 31, 1991 – the last hour of Secretary-General Pérez de Cuéllar's term – the parties reached agreement on all outstanding issues, including the cessation of armed conflict. The final Peace Agreement was signed in Chapultepec two weeks later.

ONUSAL's success rate was higher than UNTAC's, although not surprisingly so, given the less ambitious mandate and the greater willingness of the parties to make peace and cooperate with the UN. The human rights situation in El Salvador has vastly improved: a new police force has been created, a large portion of the senior military establishment has been removed, and the FMLN won the second largest number of legislative seats, in elections which, though flawed, were fair enough to have been deemed acceptable. On the other hand, the reform of the judiciary and the police are not complete. In particular the new civilian police force has begun to manifest a host of serious problems, including alleged assassination and membership in illegal armed groups within the ranks. In addition, the ongoing crime wave – especially the increase in drug trafficking, organized crime, and the proliferation of street gangs and illegal armed vigilante groups – has prompted the government to use the military to patrol rural areas in contravention of the constitutional procedures established under the peace accords.

Similarly, the Salvadoran peace process has done little to meet the economic and social grievances of the people at large.[20] Although never intended to directly redress El Salvador's deep social inequities – for example, patterns of land ownership – it was expected that through institutional and political reforms disadvantaged groups would gain a greater say in decisions that affected their lives. Indicative of the frustration felt by many who did not benefit from the peace process, in late 1995 peasants took part in at least seventeen different land occupations in the western region of the country, demanding that the government investigate landowners who continued to own lands in excess of the 245-hectare constitutional limit. Even providing ex-combatants and "squatters" with the land and wherewithal to reintegrate into civilian life has proven to be very difficult. As late as January 1996, only 36 percent of the potential recipients eligible for land under the peace accords had received their registration and fully completed the land transfer process, though 87 percent of the land had been transferred.

Despite these problems and others, the Security Council terminated the ONUSAL mission in April 1995, confident that the peace process in El Salvador was irreversible. On the Secretary-General's recommendation, a small political office, MINUSAL, was left behind to provide good offices and follow through on implementation of the outstanding obligations, in cooperation with UN agencies and other donors.

Plan of the book

In this volume, each dimension of the respective cases is treated independently. The chapters are largely self-contained analyses of each step in the peace processes, developed in parallel fashion for the two cases, with comparative lessons drawn systematically in the conclusion.

The chapters by David Chandler and Edelberto Torres-Rivas, on Cambodia and El Salvador respectively, trace the roots and development of the two conflicts. In the former, Dr. Chandler posits three contending visions of politics in Cambodia, each of which were ascendant at various times in the country's recent past but none of which ever firmly took hold. The source of conflict in El Salvador, according to Dr. Torres-Rivas, was the long history of exclusion – from political, economic,

---

[20] On the economic and social challenges facing El Salvador, see James K. Boyce et al., *Adjusting Toward Peace: Economic Policy and Post-war Reconstruction in El Salvador* (San Salvador: UNDP, 1995).

social, and other aspects of public life – experienced by large sections of the population. A proper understanding of how these internal sources were exacerbated by external factors, particularly during the height of the Cold War, helps clarify why, after so many years of conflict, the situations were "ripe" for UN involvement – or at least close to it.

The chapters by Jin Song and Mark LeVine examine peacemaking in Cambodia and El Salvador respectively, focusing on the role of the UN and its interaction with other intermediaries. In Cambodia, the role of the UN Secretary-General and his representatives, though prominent at the start, gave way to regional actors and eventually the permanent five members of the Security Council, three of whom (China, the USSR, and the United States) were finally able to cooperate in settling a conflict that had engaged their contending interests for many years. Similarly, the end of the Cold War had a profound influence on peacemaking in El Salvador, facilitating the de-escalation of US military involvement, and allowing regional actors to hand over their peacemaking role to the UN Secretary-General. In both cases the parties were ready to make peace, but only on terms that were so complex that the impartial involvement of the UN was necessary to motivate the process and guarantee compliance with agreements reached. In both cases, the UN had to innovate, most notably by relying on the "Friends" mechanism which joins states in support of the Secretary-General's efforts to negotiate and manage peace.

The chapters by Nishkala Suntharalingam and Timothy Wilkins analyze the two sets of agreements from a legal perspective, providing the standard against which success and failure in their implementation can be measured. The Paris Agreement, the all-encompassing product of four years of negotiations, charged the UN – for the first time in its history – with the political and economic restructuring of a member state. It "enshrined" the sovereignty of Cambodia in the Supreme National Council, a creation of the accords, but gave the UN extensive authority and responsibility for implementing the agreed peace. The El Salvador accords, a series of agreements negotiated over the span of two years, ceded less authority to the UN, but mapped out an important, if different type of transformation of Salvadoran institutions and society. Comparing the two cases, it is striking to note ONUSAL's very active peacebuilding role, despite its limited verification mandate, and UNTAC's limited achievements in institution-building, despite its much broader mandate.

In post-Cold War peacekeeping missions, military and police components have performed a number of functions, from monitoring local security forces and training new recruits, to dismantling old forces and creating new ones, and in the most ambitious case, actually performing public security functions by maintaining law and order. To varying degrees, all of these functions fell within the mandates of UNTAC and/or ONUSAL, as the chapters by Mark Metrikas/Cheryl Kim and David McCormick illustrate. In Cambodia, the pivotal role of the military and/or police components proved to be the creation and maintenance of an environment conducive to free elections – no mean feat in view of the Khmer Rouge's decision not to disarm as contemplated by the Paris Agreement. Less noticed and less successful was the power of arrest and detention given to UNTAC, the first time the UN was given such powers and, in light of the unhappy experience there – and later in Somalia – perhaps the last. ONUSAL was not tasked with providing security or maintaining law and order, responsibilities that remained firmly with the government. It was, however, called upon to oversee the dissolution of the FMLN as a military force, the reduction and reform of the government armed forces, and the creation of a new police force. The strategies employed by UNTAC and ONUSAL in carrying out these unprecedented tasks, and the capacity of both to adapt as circumstances on the ground changed, provide a particularly rich source of lessons for future UN efforts.

The chapters by Michael Doyle and Ian Johnstone focus on the key civilian functions of UNTAC and ONUSAL respectively. Michael Doyle examines UNTAC's civilian mandate, which included not only civil administration and the national election, but also human rights, civil police, rehabilitation, and information. Although all were affected by the continuing civil war and the defection of the Khmer Rouge from the peace, the two key areas of responsibility – the control of civil administration and the organization of the national election – experienced very different results. The first, Doyle shows, was overall a failure, while the second was overall a success. He then explains the general factors that can account for their varying outcomes, highlighting the important role that direct organization by UNTAC played in the success of the national election in May 1993. Ian Johnstone's analysis of the civilian functions of ONUSAL focuses on human rights, described by one UN observer as the "spinal column" of the peace accords. Protecting and promoting human rights involved more than simple observance: ONUSAL's "active verification" entailed investigating cases, pressuring low-level officials to respond, uncovering structural defects in the administration of justice, recommending remedies, and pressuring high-level officials to make the whole system work better. Moreover, three investigative commissions were established by the parties themselves, none of which constituted a full fledged tribunal but

[margin handwritten note: UNTAC's mixed success.]

which together represent an important experiment in striking the delicate balance between securing rights and promoting reconciliation.

The chapters by Brian Williams, Elisabeth Uphoff Kato and Graciana del Castillo cover the humanitarian, economic, and social dimensions of the respective peace processes. Brian Williams examines the largely successful repatriation of 360,000 Cambodian refugees to that country. He questions how voluntary that repatriation was and calls attention to the large risks that the UN took in repatriating the refugees before a new government was in place, as well as in promising more than it could deliver in terms of providing land to returning refugees. Elisabeth Uphoff Kato analyzes the rehabilitation process in Cambodia, noting that it was successful insofar as important financial and administrative reforms were put in place and disasters such as hyperinflation, rice shortages, and government bankruptcy were averted. At the same time, however, aid did not reach the rural, disadvantaged people as mandated, nor was much local capacity built in a sustainable manner. In addition, UNTAC had the unexpected negative side-effects of price distortions, increasing geographic and income disparities, corruption, and the spread of AIDS. Graciana del Castillo examines one of the most complicated features of the Salvadoran peace process: the agreement to transfer both land and other means for ex-combatants and the occupiers of land to rejoin civil society. Turning warriors into citizens is critical to the consolidation of peace in the aftermath of any conflict, but is unfortunately an area in which the international record is poor. Realizing this danger, the Salvadoran parties made provisions in the peace accords for the people who actually fought the battles. But carrying through on that agreement has proven to be one of the most difficult and explosive aspects of the post-conflict environment.

Conclusion

Given the limited function of traditional peacekeeping and the acknowledged difficulties of peace enforcement, the UN's future as a peace-keeper for internal conflicts seems to reside in multidimensional operations. While variants of traditional operations involving interposition of "blue helmets" and monitoring will likely continue, the very complexity of internal conflicts – where various subnational actors are involved and the polity itself is often in question – will demand a much more holistic response if international intervention is to have any chance of success. In the wake of relatively successful efforts in Cambodia and El Salvador to engage in what the Secretary-General called "comprehensive efforts to identify and support structures which will tend to consolidate peace," these types of operations appear to offer a way forward.

UNTAC and ONUSAL embody two different options for future multidimensional operations. Where UNTAC was massive and intrusive, ONUSAL was modest and largely monitorial. Constrained by a persistent financial crunch at the UN, and an international community which has become less sanguine about large transformative projects, the greatest possibilities for the future seem to lie closest to the relatively modest, "monitoring plus" type of operation as exemplified by ONUSAL. This operation involved a judicious combination of traditional monitoring functions, more aggressive human rights monitoring and supervision, repeated diplomatic intervention, and modest institution-building and reform. While future efforts will undoubtedly be comprised of different mixes of activities, the active, yet relatively "hands off" facilitating style of the Salvador operation appears promising.

In some cases, however, where a sufficiently grave situation demands attention, and where state functions and capacities are severely limited or highly contested, the international community may choose to engage in an operation more like the intrusive, large-scale UNTAC operation in Cambodia. Though the cost of such operations combined with their difficulty mean that they will not be common, where at least one major state has interests at stake (as various did in Cambodia), or where a situation is so horrendous as to jolt the international community into action (as is potentially the case in Burundi), such operations may be possible and desirable. The United Nations "transitional administration" in Eastern Slavonia (UNTAES), though much smaller than UNTAC, has many of its same characteristics.

While very different in many respects, UNTAC and ONUSAL shared one very important feature in common – they were based on negotiated agreements. As such they did not face the sort of military dilemmas that plagued UNOSOM in Somalia and the UN forces in Bosnia before Dayton and Croatia before the Basic Agreement between the government and the Serbs was signed. Making the agreements stick, however, entails no fewer challenges. Civil wars rarely give rise to disciplined, prudent factions prepared to take a statesman-like view of long-term interests. Instead, factions tend to be fluid, driven by deep hatreds, caused in many cases by the civilian casualties each side has inflicted. Multidimensional operations come about when the parties are ready to make peace – or at least say they are ready – but cannot agree on its precise terms and need the active involvement of the UN to facilitate, support, and guarantee the agreements they reach.[21] At every stage – peacemaking, peacekeeping and post-conflict peacebuilding – the UN must work creatively to identify, nurture, and often expand upon the initial consent of the parties.

A number of central themes run through this book. The first is the complex character of success and failure in multidimensional operations. Neither success nor failure comes in one package. Dimensions succeed or fail separately, with for example, the ambitious effort to conduct a national election succeeding in Cambodia and the equally ambitious effort to control civil administration largely failing. In El Salvador the success of the Ad Hoc and Truth Commissions in purging the military stands in some contrast to the painfully slow effort to reform the judiciary. Moreover, the very concept of success and failure is ambiguous in these complex operations. It can signify the successful implementation of the mandate detailed in the initial Secretary-General's report. It could also mean the successful implementation of the peace agreement which shaped, but may not be identical to, the mandate the Secretariat drafted. Success can also be measured against the fundamental purposes – long-term peace, democratization, human rights, the rule of law, social and economic development – which may be reflected in the peace agreement. But even if those principles are not specifically reflected in the treaty, there are underlying purposes of the United Nations itself that should govern the actions of the peacekeepers who wear the UN blue. And lastly, success may be measured against much more pragmatic standards: did the peace operation reduce the pre-existing level of violence, promote a modicum of stable centralized government, permit citizens to return to something resembling their pre-war lives? Sometimes, achieving success along one measure may require bending another. We will try to be clear as we discuss success and failure in each instance, but we aware that there is more than one standard against which these difficult operations should be measured.

In determining success or failure in the challenging environment of civil strife, the UN faced a daunting task requiring both conceptual and strategic innovation. Transforming societies, however much desired and supported by the signatories to accords, was and is bound to meet with resistance from other elements that have a stake in – and capacity to

---

[21] Ian Johnstone, *Rights and Reconciliation: UN Strategies in El Salvador*, International Peace Academy Occasional Paper (Boulder, Col.: Lynne Rienner, 1995), p. 86. See also C. William Maynes, "Relearning intervention," *Foreign Policy*, vol. 98, 1995; Mats Berdal, *Whither UN Peacekeeping?*, Adelphi Paper 281 (London: Brassey's for the IISS, 1993); Thomas Weiss (ed.), *The United Nations and Civil Wars* (Boulder, Col.: Lynne Rienner, 1995) and I. William Zartman (ed.), *Elusive Peace: Negotiating an End to Civil Wars* (Washington, DC: Brookings Institution, 1995).

disrupt – complex peace processes. In these circumstances, peace cannot be imposed by force. Even less coercive forms of pressure, such as official censure or the glare of publicity, are often resisted. Less threatening and more subtle means of challenging entrenched interests and institutions must be employed, a host of which were attempted in Cambodia and El Salvador – some successfully, some not, and some ongoing.

Two key innovations, which we highlight in this volume, often made the difference. The first means was a subtle and dynamic redefinition of the evolving notion of sovereignty, by which the parties agreed to UN involvement in areas long thought to be the exclusive domain of domestic jurisdiction – from the reform and abolition of military forces, to the protection of human rights and organization of elections, to the creation of new institutions for the maintenance of law and order. The parties in effect were persuaded to cede a major role to the UN in transforming the political and institutional landscape, in the interest of securing peace.

The second means employed was a political strategy of "enhancing consent," which took three forms.[22] The first was pressure, whether diplomatic or otherwise, to negotiate a peace, including the formal and informal mobilization of interested states with a recognized role as guardians of the peace, the so-called "Friends of the Secretary-General." The second involved the creation of new legal mechanisms to embody and sustain the consent once granted, which ranged from consultative bodies, as in El Salvador, to recognized institutions that embodied the sovereignty of the nation in transition, as in Cambodia. Third was the active involvement of the UN in building peace upon that consent in ways the parties did not specifically ordain and may not have even intended. This book develops those themes and examines the whole range of UN activities in these two complex operations with a view to drawing lessons about the underlying conditions and strategies that lend themselves to success in this new era of peacekeeping.

[22] Michael Doyle, *UN Peacekeeping in Cambodia: UNTAC's Civil Mandate* (Boulder, Col.: Lynne Rienner, 1995).

Cambodia

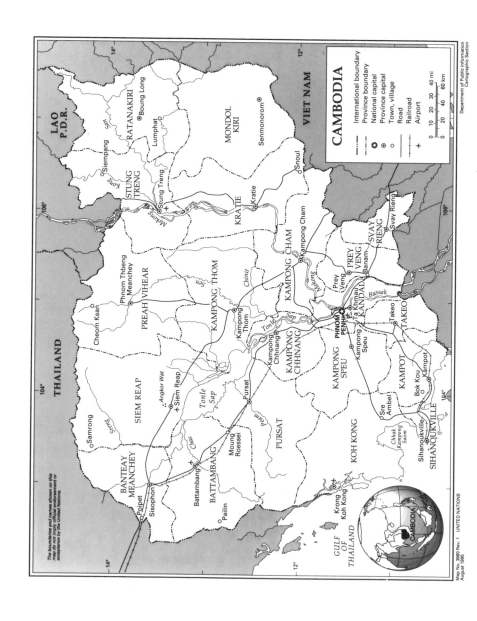

CAMBODIA

International boundary
Province boundary
National capital
Province capital
Town, village
Road
Railroad
Airport

0 10 20 30 40 mi
0   20   40   60 km

LAO P.D.R.

THAILAND

VIET NAM

RATANAKIRI

Boung Long

Lumphat

Siempang

MONDOL KIRI

Senmonorom

Snoul

STUNG TRENG

Stung Treng

Kratie

KRATIE

Kampong Cham

Phnom Thbeng Meanchey

Cheom Ksan

PREAH VIHEAR

KAMPONG THOM

KAMPONG CHAM

PREY VENG

SVAY RIENG

Svay Rieng

Prey Veng

Banam

Ta Khmau

KANDAL

SIEM REAP

Angkor Wat

Siem Reap

Kampong Thom

Kampong Chhnang

KAMPONG CHHNANG

PHNOM PENH

Kampong Speu

KAMPONG SPEU

TAKEO

Takeo

Samrong

BANTEAY MEANCHEY

Poipet

Sisophon

Battambang

BATTAMBANG

Pailin

Moung Roessei

PURSAT

Pursat

Chhas

Tonle Sap

Sre Ambel

KOH KONG

Chhak Kampong Saom

Sihanoukville

SIHANOUKVILLE

Bok Kou

KAMPOT

Kampot

GULF OF THAILAND

Krong Koh Kong

Mekong

Sen

Chinit

Sap

Pouk

Srepok

Kong

Sang

Mekong

Bassak

CAMBODIA

The boundaries and names shown on this map do not imply official endorsement or acceptance by the United Nations.

Map No. 3860 Rev. 1 UNITED NATIONS
August 1996

Department of Public Information
Cartographic Section

104° 106° 108°

14° 12°

2   Three visions of politics in Cambodia

David Chandler

Introduction

At the end of 1993 Cambodia began a new phase of its history. Equipped
with a new constitution, a refurbished monarchy and a 120-member
National Assembly split between royalist, republican, and former
socialist parties, the country is a contradiction in terms that seems to be
working. Political actors from the past crowd the stage, or lurk in the
wings. The country's poverty is abysmal, with per capita GDP estimated
to be 50 percent lower than it had been in 1966. The future is impossible
to predict, but the political and social history of Cambodia since World
War II helps provide insight into the current situation.[1]

In the twilight of the French colonial era, in 1945, an independent
Cambodia emerged briefly when it was given independence by Japan,
only to revert to French control at the beginning of 1946. Since then, its
political history can be described as a struggle among factions and
visions of order. Three of these visions – royalism, parliamentarianism,
and socialism – have competed for power and allegiance. The visions
have been shared and contested by different sectors of Cambodian
society and supported from time to time by foreign powers. Parliaments
and socialism have shallow roots in Cambodian history, while royalism
is a primordial institution that has been in place for over a thousand
years.

Royalism, embodied by King Norodom Sihanouk (1922–) held sway
between 1946 and 1970, when Sihanouk, then chief of state and a
former king, was replaced against his will by a parliamentary regime. A
new phase of royal government began in September 1993, when
Sihanouk agreed to become a constitutional monarch. His paternalistic,

I am grateful to Susan Chandler for her comments on drafts of this chapter. The discussion
that follows benefits from conversations over the years with Kate Frieson, Stephen Heder,
Ben Kiernan, Serge Thion, and Michael Vickery among many others.
[1] For a detailed political history of Cambodia between 1945 and 1979, see David P.
Chandler, *The Tragedy of Cambodian History: Politics War and Revolution Since 1945*
(New Haven, Conn.: Yale University Press, 1991).

authoritarian rule honored what he perceived as Cambodia's status quo, with modernizing elements. Over the years, he attracted support from many nations, most systematically from France and China and in his years in exile from North Korea. The regime that succeeded him, led by a mystically oriented general named Lon Nol (1916–86), based its legitimacy on its republican credentials and on a poorly defined and ill-fated alliance with the United States. From 1975 to 1992, two socialist parties – one Maoist, its successor oriented to Vietnam – governed Cambodia, and experimented with Maoist – and Vietnamese-inspired social, political, and economic programs. In May 1993 UN-sponsored elections set in place a coalition regime composed of royalist, parliamentary, and formerly socialist elements. For the time being, civil war has been replaced by a combination of compromise, good will, and gridlock.

Pluralism, even of this bewildering variety, is generally welcome in Cambodia for the time being. Its future is clouded, however, by the absence of a pluralist tradition, and by the fact that the royalists and (former) socialists are split among themselves into factions, while the parliamentarians, electorally the weakest of the three, have never developed a coherent strategy or an appealing, cohesive set of leaders.

A major difficulty as these lines are written is that so many actors remain on stage or in the wings and insist on declaiming their lines. These include King Sihanouk himself, 73; the communist Pol Pot, 67, who remains at the head of the once awesome Khmer Rouge; and Son Sann, 84, whose parliamentary faction, once popular among Cambodians living abroad, has lost much of its credibility in recent years. The gray eminence of the anti-Pol Pot socialists, Chea Sim, 66, has been active in the communist movement since the 1950s. Younger politicians, including Sihanouk's son Prince Rannaridh, 51, and Chea Sim's colleague Hun Sen, 42, Cambodia's co-prime ministers, have been fighting each other for over a decade. None of these men, except possibly Prince Ranariddh, has shown much interest in sharing genuine power with his opponents. With so many recycled actors, history is set to repeat itself as the players jockey for position.

Developments in Cambodia must be understood in an international context. For almost half a century, Cambodia, like Laos and Vietnam, has been buffeted by its neighbors and by the Cold War. A Cambodian proverb, often cited by Sihanouk, makes the point succinctly: "When elephants fight, the grass is trampled." In the 1950s, Sihanouk's neutralist foreign policy stance was opposed by pro-American, anti-communist regimes in Saigon and Bangkok. Following historical precedents, Sihanouk sought help from his "enemies' enemies" in the communist bloc. The republican regime that overthrew him was a satellite of the United States, while Pol Pot's Democratic Kampuchea pursued Maoist policies with Chinese encouragement. With China's support Pol Pot waged war against Vietnam (just as Lon Nol had done, spurred on by the United States). When Pol Pot was overthrown, Cambodia became the last, forlorn battlefield of the US–Vietnam war, with the United States, Thailand, and China backing a government in exile while Vietnam and the Soviet Union supported an impoverished pro-Vietnamese government in Phnom Penh.

These years were painful for Cambodia, which was cut off from UN system and Western development assistance. The economic blockade, questionable from the beginning, made even less sense once the United States, China, and the Soviet Union stopped confronting one another. The Paris Accords of 1991 allowed these larger powers a chance to dissolve alliances with Cambodian factions and to retreat from the responsibilities of patronage while appearing to save face. The "free and fair" elections of 1993 celebrated these arrangements, and delivered the country into the hands of a range of former clients, recently set free and enjoined by their increasingly indifferent patrons to be friends.

In Cambodia today, the three political visions, springing from the past and pointing to the future, are competing for allegiance, power, and attention. Under the 1993 constitution, royalism has been revived, and parliamentary government of a sort has been reintroduced. Real power, in the meantime, remains in the hands of those (former) socialists who have held it since 1979, and a genuine if diminishing threat is posed by the Khmer Rouge who tore the country apart between 1975 and 1979.

The potential outcomes of the struggle between current factions and their corresponding visions are illuminated by an examination of the various eras of modern Cambodian history in which each faction held a dominant position. To this history we now turn.

Royalism in the French colonial era

While it is possible to imagine a communist revolution taking place in Cambodia without Pol Pot, or a pro-American regime without Lon Nol, Cambodian political history between 1945 and 1970 is impossible to reconstruct without taking account of Norodom Sihanouk (1922–). For nearly half a century, as king, prime minister, chief of state and now as king again, Sihanouk has seen himself, and has been seen by many, as the embodiment of Cambodia and the father of his people.

As a child, Sihanouk never expected to be king. When his grandfather, King Sisowath Monivong died in 1941, however, France had recently been defeated by Germany in Europe, and by Thailand in a smaller war.

The French were hanging onto their Asian empire fearfully and with reduced resources. The governor-general of Indochina, Admiral Jean Decoux, chose Sihanouk to be king, expecting him to be a pliable instrument of French policy. Decoux's assessment has generally proved correct. Sihanouk has never quarreled on substantive issues with the French, and the French, in turn, have always been careful to identify him as the personification of the state.

While the French designated a ceremonial role to Sihanouk, this did not diminish the status or power of royalty in the eyes of the Cambodian people. The impotence of Cambodian kings, after all, had been produced by exterior forces (Vietnam and Thailand in the nineteenth century, the French thereafter) rather than by consensus, or by an anti-royalist revolution. The institution, although weak, remained unquestioned.

For several years the young king politely followed French advice. The first opportunity to do otherwise occurred in March 1945 when the Japanese armed forces occupying Indochina interned French authorities and informed local rulers, such as Sihanouk, that their countries were independent. The young king's response was cautious, but he soon was working comfortably alongside Cambodian patriots like Pach Chhoeun and the prime minister, Son Ngoc Thanh (1909–76), who hoped to free Cambodia from France. Nonetheless, already a gifted student of realpolitik, he acquiesced swiftly when the French returned in force in October 1945 and arrested Son Ngoc Thanh. Over the next few months, he allowed the French to dictate the terms of Franco–Cambodian relations. The alternative would have been to follow Son Ngoc Thanh and Pach Chhoeun into prison.

These new arrangements included French permission for political parties to form and for Cambodia to have a constitution of its own. These concessions papered over French determination to grant their possessions in Indochina as little independence as possible, and as slowly as they could.

A parliamentary experiment

In 1946–52 Sihanouk gradually came to identify himself with the state at the expense of other political visions which attracted people's attention at the time. Communism became a powerful force in the region in the context of the first Indochina war (1946–54). By 1950 armed resistance to the French in Cambodia, where perhaps 10,000 guerrillas were involved, was almost entirely controlled by the Vietnamese-dominated Indochina Communist party, led by Ho Chi Minh (1890–1969).

Sihanouk's hostility to parliamentarianism, fueled by his conservative advisors and by the French, focused on the Democrat party, founded in 1946 by a group of Cambodian intellectuals, and headed by Prince Sisowath Yuthevong (1912–47) a minor member of the royal family who had spent sixteen years as a student in France. Support for the Democrats was widespread among school-teachers, Buddhist monks, and in the middle ranks of the bureaucracy – precisely those parts of society where there was considerable anti-French sentiment, and, somewhat ironically, where French-republican ideals of progress, democracy, and independence flourished. Many Democrats were mildly anti-royalist, believing that Cambodia's kings had sold out Cambodia to France.

As part of their mild program of reforms, the French allowed national elections, the first in Cambodia's history, to take place for a constituent assembly in 1946. In form, the elections foreshadowed those for a similar body in 1993. The elections were orderly, and the Democrats' easy victory reflected their popularity with newly enfranchised voters. The Democrats won fifty-five of sixty-seven seats; the remaining twelve were won by the French-financed Liberal party, which attracted votes from ethnic minorities, large landowners and the rural population in eastern Cambodia. Democrats in the Assembly, which convened at the start of 1947, set about drafting a constitution.

The text that evolved received Sihanouk's approval. It was based on the recently promulgated constitution of the Fourth Republic in France. Both documents called for a ceremonial chief of state and a relatively strong National Assembly. The Cambodian text said nothing of independence. While some of Sihanouk's advisors opposed the Democrats, others suggested that he approve the constitution and work alongside people who were, after all, the best and brightest people in the country – even after Prince Yuthevong had died unexpectedly soon after the constitution took effect.

By selecting a document modeled on the French constitution, the Democrats probably hoped to finesse opposition from the colonial authorities and to set in place a parliamentary government which they hoped to dominate. By allowing the king's residual powers to remain so poorly defined, however, the Democrats signed their own death warrant.

Elections in 1947 installed a Democrat-controlled National Assembly, but economic and military power in Cambodia – as in Laos and Vietnam – remained in French hands. Two years later, the French granted a measure of independence to all their possessions in Indochina. By that time, many senior members of the civil service, like Sihanouk himself, had grown restless with Democrat power, and uneasy about Vietnamese involvement in Cambodia's armed resistance. Some of these men, including a lackluster police official named Lon Nol, formed splinter parties to contest the 1951 elections.

None of the leaders of splinter groups had an alternative vision for Cambodia. They were distressed by communism, annoyed by the Democrats' "dictatorship," and disconcerted by what they saw as the erosion of local patronage networks. Many were opportunists. Nearly 600 candidates contested seventy-eight seats in the 1951 election. None of the splinter parties fared well and the Democrats won their third victory in a row. Nonetheless, the new parties gained tens of thousands of votes, indicating to Sihanouk that the Democrats were more vulnerable than they looked.

In 1952 the king staged a coup d'état against the elected government (eerily foreshadowing an elected government's coup against him, eighteen years later). He dismissed the Democrat cabinet, and promised to deliver independence to Cambodia within three years. The French had helped him pull off the coup d'état by secretly bringing troops to Phnom Penh to reinforce it, but were astonished by his subsequent proposal. For the remainder of the year he consolidated support, mobilized the leaders of disaffected political parties, appealed to ordinary people to take up arms against France, and threatened to mobilize world opinion behind his cause. Emboldened by the Democrats' failure to resist (they were unarmed), Sihanouk dissolved the Assembly in early 1953, and proceeded to govern the country by decree. At the time, he remarked to a French correspondent: "I am the natural ruler of the country . . . and my authority has never been questioned."[2]

Taking advantage of the disarray of other political factions and of his own control of the police, Sihanouk waged a vigorous campaign to gain independence for his country and political power for himself. The Democrats had no forum where they could challenge him, and were upstaged. The communist resistance, similarly deprived of outlets, was nonplussed by his vigor and sincerity, and continued to refer to him as a "feudal puppet." Leaders of smaller parties sensed correctly that going along with Sihanouk would bring them rewards.

As Sihanouk emerged onto the world stage in 1953–5, alongside a range of post-colonial figures, he gave an impression of pluckiness and courage that mixed nicely with the exoticism that suffused his faraway little country in the eyes of other people.

Sihanouk constructed "Cambodia" as he went along, pleased by people's affection and by the absence of questioning or resistance. Under his pressure, and because the unpopular war in Vietnam was

---

[2] Ibid., p. 66.

going badly, the French granted Cambodia its independence at the end of 1953, ahead of Laos and Vietnam – a fact that gave Cambodia added freedom of maneuver at the Geneva Conference, convened in 1954 to settle the first Indochina war. In effect, the agreements reached at Geneva lowered the profile of the Cambodian communist movement, and handed Sihanouk a personal triumph.

He was already supremely confident of his abilities. In June 1954, on the eve of the Geneva Conference, Sihanouk told a high-ranking French official that "those favoring democracy in Cambodia are either bourgeois or princes ... The Cambodian people are children. They know nothing about democracy, and they care less."[3]

Cut off from "bourgeois and princes," Sihanouk embraced his "children." Basking in their affection, he abdicated the throne in 1955 to become an "ordinary citizen," though retaining his pre-coronation princely title. Soon afterwards, he founded a national political movement, the Sangkum Reastr Niyum or Peoples' Socialist Community in an attempt to achieve consensus in Cambodian politics once and for all. Political parties survived for a time, but members of the Sangkum were not allowed to belong to them. This provision, and Sihanouk's exuberant sponsorship of the movement, meant that other kinds of pluralism and political dialogue were doomed.

The funeral of parliamentarianism was celebrated in the September 1955 elections. These provided the last opportunity before 1993 for Cambodians to choose among royalist, parliamentarian, and communist candidates – the latter concealed behind a front party, the Krom Pracheachon, or Peoples' Group. Saloth Sar (known twenty years later as Pol Pot), recently returned from France, where he had become a communist, worked in secret for the Pracheachon. Because Sihanouk controlled the police, dominated the media, and wanted so badly to win, non-Sangkum candidates, and Democrats in particular, were harassed and intimidated. Many were imprisoned and some were killed. When the votes were counted, Sangkum candidates were declared to have won all the seats, although evidence suggests that the Democrats won at least three seats but were denied them in the final count. The Pracheachon's 30,000 votes nationwide indicated that the communists retained a reservoir of dedicated supporters. The poor showing, however, persuaded Saloth Sar and his colleagues to abandon electoral adventures.[4]

The size of the Sangkum victory told Sihanouk what he wanted to

---

[3]   Ibid., p. 72.
[4]   On the Democrat seats, see David Chandler, *Brother Number One: A Political Biography of Pol Pot* (Boulder, Col.: Westview Press, 1992) p. 204, note 16. The information was generously supplied by Justin Corfield.

hear – namely, that party politics were dead and that all Cambodians belonged to one happy family. Unfortunately, suppressing opposition and closing off debate left a residue of bitterness among the losers – communists and Democrats alike – that they took underground, where the resentments smoldered, only to re-emerge in the 1970s in altered form, either as republican under Lon Nol or Maoist under Pol Pot. It seems likely that Sihanouk's high-handed repression of opponents drove them deeper into opposition than if they been allowed to operate in the open and perhaps wither on the vine.

The Sihanouk years

Even though Sihanouk was no longer king, the period 1955–70 extended the royalist phase in Cambodian politics. The prince was regarded as a king, and was genuinely popular. His programs, stressing expanded education, better health care, and the achievements of the Sangkum, induced a new sense of self-confidence among ordinary people, and led painlessly to the trappings of modernization, although rice yields remained low, technology was limited, and per capita income lagged behind that in the rest of Southeast Asia. Foreign aid poured into the country, and foreign visitors found much to praise in Sihanouk's regime. They looked favorably, as Sihanouk did, on what they perceived to be the deep conservatism of most Cambodians, their good manners, and their *joie de vivre*. Bad news was unwelcome and never published. "Cambodia," in fact, came to resemble a musical extravaganza, with Cambodia's five million agricultural workers forming a compliant chorus, and Sihanouk as the star, librettist, and impresario.

It is natural enough, reading back from the March 1970 coup that removed Sihanouk from power, or through the chaos of the years that followed the civil war, to search for events, forces and personalities that foreshadowed or "led to" Sihanouk's collapse. In fact, these are hard to find before the late 1960s. At that time opposition arose due to Sihanouk's missteps, his opponents' moves, and perhaps most importantly, to pressures from abroad. Indeed, after 1955 it is impossible to study Cambodia in isolation. Much of Sihanouk's behavior, and the conduct of those opposed to him, was conditioned by the Cold War and the concomitant pattern of alliances and antagonisms that formed in Southeast Asia during the 1950s. One might even say that without the Cold War, and the Vietnam war that was being waged as part of it, Sihanouk would not have been overthrown when he was, and the Khmer Rouge might never have come to power.

The partitioning of Vietnam in 1954, with a communist regime taking office in the north and an anti-communist one in the south, led the United States to commit itself to "saving" what was left of France's Asian empire – southern Vietnam, Cambodia, and Laos. In the late 1950s, US activities included sponsorship of the anti-communist SEATO alliance, headquartered in Bangkok, perennial plots to support conservatives in Laos, and patronage for the harsh regime of Ngo Dinh Diem in South Vietnam. In Cambodia, Sihanouk tried hard to preserve his country's independence. The United States was reluctant to accept his neutral stance in the Cold War, interpreting it as a "pro-communist" policy that offended America's allies in Bangkok and Saigon. Toward the end of the Eisenhower presidency, the USA was involved tangentially in a series of abortive plots against Sihanouk concocted and paid for by Thai and Vietnamese officials. These hardened Sihanouk's animosity toward the United States.

With Washington, Bangkok, and Saigon arrayed against him, Sihanouk edged closer to the Sino-Soviet bloc, and especially towards China whose leaders, Mao Zedong and Zhou Enlai, had always treated him politely. Prudently, he retained US military and economic aid as well as relations with a range of other countries. Although he pursued an anti-communist policy at home, Sihanouk's foreign policy became, in the view of overseas communists, correct. For this reason the Vietnamese communists, up to the late 1960s, discouraged their Cambodian clients from antagonizing the prince. Instead, Cambodian communists were encouraged to engage in "political struggle," a recipe for lying low or, if they spoke up and emerged from hiding, for being put in jail. In the 1950s, the movement came close to disappearing.

In 1957 the Democrat party formally dissolved. The communist Pracheachon ran one candidate in the 1958 elections, gaining only 350 votes. For the next twelve years, Sangkum candidates were unopposed and Sihanouk was confident about his position. Nonetheless he worked hard to maintain his popularity, criss-crossing the country by car and helicopter, and delivering marathon speeches in which he encouraged, cajoled, praised, threatened, and amused his "children" while celebrating what he perceived as Cambodia's incomparable homogeneity and capacity to share the pleasures of everyday life. The prince believed fervently in education, and much less fervently in social change. Unfortunately for his vision of Cambodia, educated Cambodians were increasingly reluctant to accept his dictatorial, eclectic style, and began thinking of progress in political as well as economic terms. This meant that many of them became disgruntled and a few drifted in secret toward the left.

In late 1963, encouraged by France and China, Sihanouk rejected further military aid from the United States. He broke off diplomatic relations in 1965. At that point he allied himself with the Vietnamese communists – openly on the diplomatic front and secretly in military terms, allowing the Vietnamese to station troops on Cambodian soil and to pass through the country on their way to battle in south Vietnam.

Sihanouk had formed this alliance on the assumption that the Vietnamese communists were poised to win in South Vietnam, as indeed they were, on the eve of massive American military intervention. He was encouraged to form the alliance by his former patrons in France, where President de Gaulle, whom Sihanouk idolized, had adopted an anti-American stance, and by his friends in China. Domestic opposition to the alliance was limited to a handful of pro-Americans in the elite, so for Sihanouk, seeking short-term benefits, the decision to ally himself with the communists was relatively easy. At the same time, by allying himself with them Sihanouk was playing with fire, not only because the alliance would bring the war closer to Cambodia, but also because many Cambodians were fearful of Vietnamese intentions.

By this time, the Cambodian communist movement had all but collapsed. After forming a central committee at a secret meeting in 1960, the party remained in hiding. Its secretary Tou Samouth was killed by Sihanouk's police in 1962, and was replaced by his assistant Saloth Sar who fled the capital in 1963, fearing arrest. Rural networks of the party had broken down by then, and communists in the capital were frightened and inactive. For the next two years Sar found refuge in Vietnamese communist encampments on the border – a humiliating period of his life that he never mentioned later.

Summoned to Hanoi in 1965, he was berated by high-ranking Vietnamese communist officials for the naiveté of his political program, which stressed class warfare and paid scant attention to international factors. The diatribe lasted for an hour. According to an eyewitness, Sar said "absolutely nothing" in reply. He lingered on in Hanoi for several months. In early 1966 he traveled to Beijing on the eve of the Cultural Revolution. Sar seems to have been discreetly encouraged by Chinese radicals to carry on with his "autonomous" revolutionary ideas. His alienation from Vietnam began widening at this point. For the time being, he did nothing to arouse Vietnam's suspicions. He returned to Cambodia via Hanoi, arriving at his jungle headquarters in the middle of 1966. From then on, isolated in Cambodia's northeast with a handful of associates, Sar developed extreme ideas about Cambodian society, and harsh remedies for widespread corruption, injustice, and inequality. No longer constrained by Vietnamese advice or by contact with outsiders he worked out a voluntaristic, secretive, and uncompromising ideology.

Overtly, Sar rejected foreign models. He wanted to wage a totally Cambodian revolution. His ideas about "Cambodia," however, were often unconnected or at odds with those of ordinary people, on whose behalf the revolution was ostensibly being waged. Another problem which the movement faced was that it still needed Vietnamese assistance. Trapped by this dependency, which the leaders of the party resented, the Cambodian communists, dubbed "Khmer Rouge" or "Red Khmer" by Sihanouk, believed that they were surrounded by enemies. Their paranoia made them more reclusive, which in turn made them more confident than ever.[5]

At the same time, fissures had begun to develop between Sihanouk and the Cambodian officer corps, and also between Sihanouk and the commercial class, concentrated in Phnom Penh. Tensions in the army sprang partly from budgetary considerations; Sihanouk's break with the United States in 1963 meant that the wages of the armed forces, previously paid by US aid, now had to be found from Cambodian resources. Equipment provided by the United States had started to run down. Many officers were also distressed by the presence of Vietnamese communist troops on Cambodian soil, in spite of profitable commercial dealings that the Cambodian army had with them. Others were favorably impressed by the personal fortunes being made by colleagues in South Vietnam, who had "turned on the faucet of US dollars." Finally, the military coup against President Sukarno in Indonesia in 1965–6 and the massacre of half a million alleged communists that accompanied it may well have drawn the attention of some Cambodian officers, grown tired of a similarly "pro-communist," narcissistic chief of state.

Lon Nol, a senior military man described by some as being "silent as a carp," bided his time and husbanded his ambitions. Apparently slavishly loyal to Sihanouk, who was contemptuous of his abilities, he was deeply respected by his troops. Privately, he saw himself as a gifted and messianic leader. This led him to take power in 1970, supported by a wave of anti-Vietnamese feeling and parliamentary discontent. He took office with a well-documented contempt for pluralism and parliamentary procedures.

Discontent among the Sino-Cambodian commercial elite in Phnom Penh was also rooted in the Vietnam war. In late 1963, defying his conservative advisors, Sihanouk had nationalized the import–export

---

[5]   See Ben Kiernan's path-breaking study, *How Pol Pot Came to Power* (London: Verso, 1985). On Pol Pot's trip to Hanoi and Beijing, see Chandler, *Brother Number One*, pp. 73–5. For information about Pol Pot's confrontation with Vietnamese authorities, I am grateful to Christopher Goscha and J. Thomas Engelbert, who shared the results of their research in Vietnamese archives.

sector, placing it in the hands of a few favored cronies who proceeded to mismanage it. Nationalization alienated many Phnom Penh traders from Sihanouk's eclectic "socialist" policies, which prevented them from finding markets for Cambodian goods. As exports fell, tax revenues on exports – a major source of government income – also declined. In the ensuing confusion, informal trade with the Vietnamese communists drew more than 20 percent of Cambodia's rice surplus out of normal export channels.[6]

In the late 1960s, the national pro-Sihanouk consensus, crafted by the prince, began to come apart. In the elections of 1958 and 1962, Sangkum candidates for the National Assembly had been hand-picked by Sihanouk, and ran for election unopposed. In 1966 too many people applied to the prince for selection, and he impulsively threw open the election to anyone who wanted to run, provided that they were members of the Sangkum.

With hindsight, the 1966 elections revealed that Sihanouk's grip on the political process, which had worked so well for a decade or more, was loosening. At the time, however, he remained buoyant. He did not feel threatened by the Assembly, which since 1955 had served as a rubber stamp; but, ominously for the prince, several assemblymen whom he had attacked for "disloyalty" won their seats with increased majorities in 1966. More generally, the open election favored wealthy candidates with local interests rather than people chosen on the basis of other criteria by the prince. The National Assembly, while remaining ineffective, began to drift out of his control, and it was this body that voted him out of office four years later.

In 1966 the prince's choice of the anti-communist patriot Lon Nol as prime minister pleased conservatives, but worried radical students, among others, who had been subject for some time to intimidation by the army and the police. No observers of Cambodia in 1966–7, however, remarked that Sihanouk's days as chief of state were numbered.

In early 1968 a series of events unnerved the prince, and alienated him from what was left of his radical allies. The Vietnamese communist Tet offensive, the inauguration by the Cambodian communists of armed struggle and the ongoing Cultural Revolution in China led the prince to renew his ties with the United States. Diplomatic relations were restored in 1969. By that time US air force bombers, without the knowledge of the American people, had begun bombing targets inside Cambodia, along the border with Vietnam. The raids continued for over a year. The

---

[6] See Laura Summers, "The sources of economic discontent in Sihanouk's Cambodia," *Southeast Asian Journal of Social Science*, vol. 14, 1986, pp. 16–33.

Americans may have had Sihanouk's permission, and were expected to kill Vietnamese rather than Khmer. The US military aid that Sihanouk may have hoped for was not forthcoming. As things got worse, Sihanouk backed away from politics, and spent his time producing expensive, mediocre films. Sensing the possibility of a power vacuum, his opponents among the elite and in the army began to gather strength.

Over the years, in the eyes of these opponents, Sihanouk had undermined the royalist vision by turning the revered institution of kingship into a cacophonous concert by a one-man band. A parliamentary alternative had been stifled by his heavy-handedness and his disdain. Although the prince himself was financially honest, and never amassed a fortune, many of his cronies were corrupt. By the late 1960s, the Cambodian economy was dead in the water. Hundreds of political prisoners languished in jail, without being formally charged. To many young Cambodians, appalled by endemic corruption and unable to find jobs, "communism"– and they were often uncertain what was meant by this – seemed to offer an alternative. Sihanouk himself, after all, frequently praised communist governments overseas for their energy and apparent lack of corruption.

Because the Cambodian party was underground, many of these young people had no place to go. After inaugurating armed struggle in early 1968, the communist movement gained several hundred new recruits. These were not enough to staff a revolution but provided the basis for its later infrastructure. Some of these men and women, recruited as guerrillas, had already fought the French in the 1940s and 1950s. One of these veterans, Chea Sim (1928–), re-emerged as a powerful politician in Cambodia in 1979. Others were new recruits, drawn in because the Khmer Rouge offered a detailed agenda for equity and social change. To many young people in the 1960s in Cambodia and elsewhere, communism was the wave of the future. Except to initiates, however, the Khmer Rouge concealed their communist affiliations, and posed as patriotic Cambodians supporting Sihanouk and opposed to the United States. This stance altered after the Khmer Rouge inaugurated armed struggle, and their propaganda began to target "feudal" elements in Cambodian society while remaining opposed to the United States.

In January 1970 the prince left Cambodia, as he often did, for medical treatment in France. He was worn out. Many who saw him leave said years later that they were convinced that he was fleeing the country in despair. He certainly lacked the allies he needed to suppress dissatisfaction among the elite, the officer corps, and ordinary people suffering from underemployment and a protracted drought. His experiments with socialism had failed. His short attention span and his impatience with advice had tripped him up. Cambodia could no longer be dealt with single-handed. His alliances with Vietnam, China, France, and now the United States had not saved Cambodia from bloodshed. The quasi-royalist experiment, aimed at holding the country together, had largely failed. Sihanouk had walked a tightrope, domestically and overseas, but the tightrope had begun to sway, and there had never been a safety net.

The Khmer Republic: a parliamentary vision deferred

The roots of parliamentarianism in Cambodia, such as they were, can be traced to the 1940s, and the early success of the Democrat party. Representative bodies are almost non-existent in Cambodian history, but the presence in the 1940s of so many respected authority figures – monks, school-teachers, and civil servants – in the ranks of the new party convinced voters that the Democrats would deliver something more equitable. The French notions of liberty, equality, and fraternity, adopted by the Democrats, seemed wholesome and exciting. Behind these concepts, and the parliamentary framework in which they were expressed, lay a vision of independence.

By 1950, however, the Democrats had lost much of their élan. Some of the difficulties were difficulties of leadership. Their two most important leaders, Yuthevong and Ieu Koeuss, died prematurely and another inspiring figure, Son Ngoc Thanh, remained under house arrest in France until the end of 1951. Moreover, because the National Assembly, where the Democrats were concentrated, had so little authority, factionalism quickly developed, and many founders of the party, including patriots like Sim Var, wearied of parliamentary government and supported Sihanouk's Sangkum movement in 1955. Over the years, several of these same people (including Sim Var) drifted away from the prince but could find no alternative political base.

Enthusiasm for a republican form of government (i.e. one without Sihanouk at the helm) was kept alive outside Cambodia by Son Ngoc Thanh, who had lived in exile in Thailand and South Vietnam after failing to gain power in the elections of 1955. Thanh presided over an anti-Sihanouk movement, the Free Khmers (Khmer Serei), financed by the regimes in Bangkok and Saigon, with the full knowledge of the United States. Support inside Cambodia for a republic or even for more than one political party, however, was weak and rarely voiced, partly out of fear of opposing the prince, but even more out of widespread apathy.

In March 1970 the National Assembly voted Sihanouk from power and placed its speaker, Cheng Heng, in office as a ceremonial chief of state. This was the assembly's last courageous act. The prime mover in the coup was Sihanouk's cousin, Sisowath Sirik Matak (1913–75), an astute bureaucrat who had become estranged from the prince on economic issues. Matak's high school friend Lon Nol, the prime minister, was brought into the coup at gunpoint. His support neutralized what little opposition there was in the army. Lon Nol quickly formed an alliance with the United States, and promised to drive Vietnamese "unbelievers" from Cambodian soil. Unfortunately, he chose to embark on a crusade at a time when the Vietnam war was consuming the rest of Indochina. The United States, withdrawing its troops from South Vietnam, was eager to secure Vietnam's western flank. Lon Nol was the instrument chosen by Washington to insure America's orderly departure from the region.[7]

Sihanouk was in Beijing when these events occurred. He was soon persuaded by the Chinese and Vietnamese prime ministers to form a government in exile, supported by Hanoi and Beijing. His impulsive gesture, hardly the first in his career, plunged Cambodia headlong into the Vietnam war.

In Phnom Penh, where opposition to Sihanouk had always been most intense, the coup was popular at first, and pro-Sihanouk demonstrations in rural areas, often organized by local communists, were brutally suppressed. In a quixotic gesture, Lon Nol ordered Vietnamese troops to leave the country "within 48 hours." None of them did. The new government's first weeks were marred by massacres of unarmed Vietnamese civilians around Phnom Penh, military incompetence, and factional bickering. Freed from Sihanouk's embrace, the country's new leaders had inchoate, liberated feelings, but no precedents for self-government. Lacking a clear idea how to proceed, the new leaders stripped Sihanouk of his citizenship and sentenced him to death in absentia.

In May 1970 a joint US–South Vietnamese force invaded Cambodia. Lon Nol had not been informed beforehand. The invaders remained in the country for a month, and succeeded mainly in pushing Vietnamese communist forces deeper into the Cambodian countryside. Later in the year, Lon Nol's best units, conducting an ill-advised offensive and encouraged by the United States, were cut to pieces by these Vietnamese troops. The defeat was re-enacted a year later, on the same terrain, and after 1972 Lon Nol's forces ceased offensive operations.

On October 1971, during the first offensive, Cambodia became the Khmer Republic, officially turning away from over a thousand years of

---

[7] See Ben Kiernan, "The American bombardment of Kampuchea, 1969–1973," *Vietnam Generation*, Winter 1989, pp. 4–41; and Kiernan, *How Pol Pot Came to Power*, pp. 351–7.

royal politics. The move to a republic, though, was poorly thought out, hastily put together, and ineptly marketed. Most Cambodians had no idea what had happened, and could perceive few if any advantages in the supposedly revolutionary change. Son Ngoc Thanh returned home to become a powerless prime minister, and the National Assembly, ignored by Lon Nol, was immobilized by factionalism.

Lon Nol, the single dominant political figure of this period, was a pious but poorly read Buddhist who saw himself as Cambodia's savior. He did not believe that the Khmer Rouge were authentic or important. Instead, he considered the Vietnamese to be the only enemies he faced, the "unbelievers" (*thmil*) against whom he could lead the once glorious Khmer "race" in a holy war. He paid little attention to technology (ignoring the telephone in favor of personally delivered messages) and more than he should have done to astrologers and mystics who came up with many of his half-baked ideas. Reassured by blandly worded letters of encouragement from US President Nixon and by fawning hangers on, Lon Nol believed that the war was winnable, that Nixon was his personal friend, and that the United States' support for the republic was deep, sincere, and open ended. He was wrong on all three counts.

Although leading a supposedly parliamentary regime, Lon Nol thought of the state in familial and ethnic terms. He conceived of politics in terms of patronage, and was impatient with elections, parliaments, or consultation. After the middle of 1971, he operated at reduced capacity, following a crippling stroke. Leaning on a cane, and listening to astrologers, he limped through a twentieth-century war, waged against the experienced Vietnamese and later against the well-equipped, highly motivated Khmer Rouge. Drifting out of touch, he showed no interest in relinquishing office. From time to time, overwhelmed with the difficulties he faced, he would burst uncontrollably into tears.

The Khmer Rouge in the meantime benefited from the aggressiveness of Vietnamese communist units, from Vietnamese weapons and training, and from disordered conditions in rural areas. Although in 1971 they abandoned their pro-Sihanouk propaganda, the Khmer Rouge drew many young people into the movement under the illusion that they would help the prince return to power. One such recruit was Hun Sen, then a high school student in Kompong Cham. In a related development, several hundred Cambodian communists who had been exiled to North Vietnam in the 1950s now returned home, ostensibly to help the revolution. Because they were so highly trained and because their loyalties seemed uncertain, they were distrusted by the less experienced and naturally suspicious Khmer Rouge.

The Cambodian communists believed less in training their followers than in political indoctrination. Readings were seldom in Marxist-Leninist classics. Instead, students in Khmer Rouge zones were required to memorize short, hortatory texts prepared by the party's leaders. Some of these told party members how to behave toward other people, emphasizing politeness, fervor, and cooperation. Others emphasized the injustices of Cambodia's "feudal" society. The texts were used to expand the revolutionary consciousness of those who memorized them. They emphasized the supposed autonomy of the Cambodian revolution, and said little about the party's historic dependence on Vietnam. The documents claimed that the Khmer Rouge, rather than the Vietnamese, had defeated Lon Nol's forces in 1970 and 1971. By 1972, party schools had been organized throughout the country. Following Chinese precedents without admitting it, the Khmer Rouge claimed to favor practice over theory, a stance that fitted with the anti-intellectual image which Saloth Sar and his colleagues had been projecting in the forest for several years.

Practice, however, did not mean learning how poor Cambodians worked together, or drawing political tactics from the rural world. Instead, it meant whatever the party's leaders had in mind at a given time: class warfare, collectivization, or war with Vietnam. Practice also meant proper revolutionary behavior, a bizarre mixture of violence and good manners, of secrecy and "storming attacks," of voluntarism and unquestioning obedience. "Counter-revolutionaries" were literally and figuratively moving targets. An important effect of these contradictions was to allow the leadership, who remained in hiding, far more freedom of maneuver, and far less accountability, than those they led.

In late 1972 the Vietnamese communist delegation to the peace talks in Paris agreed to sign a ceasefire affecting their troops in South Vietnam. The South Vietnamese and the United States planned to join in the ceasefire. The Khmer Rouge were consulted, but refused to go along, fearing that Sihanouk would capitalize on an armistice to seize power in Phnom Penh and finesse the revolution. They also believed that without continuing violence and unquestioned party control the revolution would lose momentum. Finally, Saloth Sar and his colleagues distrusted the Vietnamese, and felt that the ceasefire was in large part a US–Vietnamese conspiracy intended to destroy Cambodia. When the Vietnamese withdrew their troops from Cambodia in late 1972 following the ceasefire, the Khmer Rouge secretly began purging the cadre who had come down to help them from Hanoi. In party briefings, Vietnam replaced the United States as the party's "number one enemy."

The Khmer Rouge's refusal to stop fighting attracted America's wrath. Between March and August 1973, when it was halted by the US

Congress, the United States conducted sustained saturation bombing campaign in Cambodia ("the only war in town," in one US official's mordant phrase), intending to deny the Khmer Rouge a military victory as long as the anti-communist regime in Saigon remained relatively intact. During this time, 250,000 tons of high explosives were dropped on Khmer Rouge positions and troop concentrations in the provinces around Phnom Penh. The number of casualties has never been assessed. Perhaps as many as 10,000 Khmer Rouge troops were among the dead. Civilian casualties were obviously higher. Several hundred thousand survivors, fleeing the bombing, became refugees in Phnom Penh where, over the next two years, thousands of them died of malnutrition and disease.

Tactically, the bombing was a success as it relieved Khmer Rouge pressure on Phnom Penh for the time being. Without the bombing, it is conceivable that the capital would have been taken and Lon Nol forced to surrender. Politically, the bombing postponed the end of the war, discredited the Lon Nol regime even further, and to an extent played into the hands of the Khmer Rouge, whose cadre were able to blame the Lon Nol "puppet" regime, rather than the United States, for the bombing. Scattered evidence suggests that the Khmer Rouge were able to gain hundreds of recruits among people enraged by the bombing campaign.[8]

The civil war lasted for two more years, with republican and communist forces locked in combat, neither strong enough to win or weak enough to lose. Tens of thousands of soldiers and civilians were killed. Conditions in Phnom Penh, except for the rich, became unbearable as services broke down, people starved, and the Khmer Rouge launched indiscriminate rocket attacks. In the "liberated" zones the first steps were taken to collectivizing agriculture in 1973, probably to insure that sufficient food reached the fighting forces, but also to accelerate the pace of the revolution that the communists planned to achieve. By 1974, the Khmer Rouge controlled 70 percent of the country, and almost half the population.

On New Year's Day 1975 communist forces blockaded the Mekong, cutting off supplies to the capital. Soon afterwards, they launched their final assault. By mid-April, Lon Nol had been driven into exile, eighty-two Americans remaining in the capital had been evacuated by helicopter, and Phnom Penh was running out of food. On what later became known as "the glorious 17th of April," Khmer Rouge forces marched into Phnom Penh unopposed. Twenty-four hours later, to

[8]   Ibid.

everyone's surprise, they ordered the entire population – perhaps as many as 2 million people – to evacuate the city at once, so as to start new lives as agricultural workers. Cambodia was liberated (or as most of its inhabitants would have said, fell) a month before communist forces were victorious in Vietnam.

On April 17, 1975, the so-called republican interval in Cambodian history was unceremoniously snuffed out. Because the regime had come to life during a foreign invasion and ended in a civil war, republican ideas, unfamiliar in any case, never had a chance. Even under ideal conditions it would have been difficult for pluralism or republicanism to have taken hold, given Cambodia's brief exposure to genuine parliamentarianism in the 1940s and early 1950s, and Lon Nol's monarch-like disdain for elected officials and for sharing power.

This is not to say, as the Khmer Rouge leaders had always done, that a communist victory over the republic was "inevitable." In fact, the victory, like the communist party itself, was dependent on developments in China and Vietnam and on foreign support. Being dependent on Vietnam angered the Khmer Rouge leaders (a sentiment encouraged by China), and fueled the Khmer Rouge military adventures against Vietnam that ultimately brought the communist government down. Ironically, ideas of innate Khmer superiority and Vietnamese weakness were inherited from the regime the Khmer Rouge overthrew. Its irrational nationalism, like Lon Nol's, sustained the movement for a time and then destroyed it.

Democratic Kampuchea: the socialist vision at work

When Khmer Rouge spokesmen proudly declared that with the liberation of Phnom Penh "2000 years of Cambodian history had ended," they were referring to the social arrangements that in their view had ruined the country for two millennia. These included deference, hierarchies, private property, individualism, and the demands placed on people by family life.

The royal, Sangkum, and republican phases of Cambodian politics had washed across Cambodia without challenging these underlying notions, which were for the most part rural, village oriented, and family based. The civil war of the 1970s, to put it mildly, destroyed people's illusions and disrupted rural life, and for some Cambodians prepared the ground psychologically for revolution; but the fighting by itself did not break down the primordial values shared by all Cambodians.

Despite instigating dramatic revolutionary experiments such as the depopulation of Phnom Penh, Cambodia's new rulers represented more continuity than was immediately apparent. The communist takeover, after all, was essentially a coup d'état. The Khmer Rouge treated those "below" them with the same indifference and contempt as previous governments. While in theory they set out to put an end to centuries of exploitation, in practice, one group of exploiters – formerly the poorest of the poor – simply replaced another. To be sure, society was overturned in the process. Those who had held power, the rich, and people with advanced education, were brought low. As power relations sorted themselves out, the poorest of the poor, now honored by the party, often became the only ones who had enough to eat. They were also the only ones allowed to bear arms. The psychic and material costs of the experiment for all but a few Cambodians were enormous. To the Khmer Rouge leaders the costs were irrelevant, because, they thought, the revolution responded to inexorable laws of history.

The early stages of the Khmer Rouge period were traumatic for the so-called "April 17" people evacuated from the towns, but had less impact on the rural population, who welcomed an end to the fighting and were accustomed, as many from the cities were not, to back-breaking agricultural work. To be told that subsistence agriculture now served a higher cause was taken by most peasants with a grain of salt, but many rural Cambodians probably enjoyed being told that the new regime had "put an end to all oppression." At first, the new government moved cautiously, inviting Sihanouk back as a powerless chief of state and concealing its plans, its leaders, and information about the party from the population.

Before the end of April 1975, the Khmer Rouge set in motion a wide-ranging, utopian, and ultimately catastrophic program for the country. Money, markets, schools, books and newspapers, religious practices, postal services, and private property were abolished from one day to the next. Freedom of movement was constricted. Personal adornment even to the extent of wearing anything but black peasant work clothes, was forbidden; so was sexual activity outside marriage. The country was collectivized. Everyone became an unpaid employee of the state. Individualism and "family-ism" were condemned. Collective virtues, supposedly inherent among the rural poor, were singled out for praise. Everyone's activities, tasks, and conversations were to be monitored by an invisible body known only as the "higher organization" (*angkar loeu*), said by the terrorized population to have "a thousand eyes, like a pineapple." The organization ruled through spies, heavily armed rural children – the party's most loyal recruits – and a thoroughgoing use of terror.

In early 1976, the regime proclaimed itself Democratic Kampuchea and promulgated a constitution that collectivized "all important means of production" and placed power in the hands of the Cambodian people. In fact, all power rested in the hands of the concealed communist party apparatus. The main right of citizens bestowed by the text was the right to work.

Soon afterwards, in the wake of elections in which less than half the population was eligible to vote, a government was announced that was headed by someone called "Pol Pot," a name that no one outside the party had heard before. This was Saloth Sar, the communist party secretary, choosing to hide behind a new identity at exactly the moment when he might have been expected to step into the open and take credit for what was happening. The wholesale depersonalization of Cambodian politics in the Khmer Rouge period was a memorable innovation. Although "Brother Number One," as Pol Pot was known to his close associates, ruled the country as single-handedly as Sihanouk and Lon Nol had done, and more tyrannically than either of them, he never encouraged a cult of personality to form around himself and system-atically concealed biographical data.

In June 1976, the Khmer Rouge dismissed Sihanouk from office and placed him under house arrest. The communist leadership, fearful of Sihanouk's potential and of his foreign friends maintained him in comfort, incommunicado, for the next two years.

With Sihanouk out of the way, the regime occupied itself with smashing enemies of the revolution, carrying out a war with Vietnam, and collectivizing Cambodia's economy. Whereas Sihanouk had worked to establish a national consensus, and Lon Nol had based his regime on fighting foreign unbelievers, the Khmer Rouge deliberately imposed a conflict model onto Cambodian society that set elements of the population against each other in a life and death struggle from which a resplendent new nation was expected to emerge. As these "contra-dictions" worked themselves out, over a million people, and perhaps as many as two million, died of disease, overwork, starvation, and executions.

The vehicle chosen to collectivize Cambodia was a 110-page secret document entitled *The Party's Four Year Plan to Build Socialism in All Fields* which was to be inaugurated in 1977. The plan stressed agricultural development, and sought to earn hard currency by expanding the export sales of agricultural products, especially rice. A national target of three tons of paddy per cultivated hectare, borrowed without acknowledgment from a previous campaign in China, meant that rice production throughout the country was expected to double and even triple in the wake of a grueling civil war, without monetary incentives, fertilizer, draft animals, or tools. As they set the plan in motion, the communist leaders boasted of their lack of experience in national planning, claiming that revolutionary fervor, inspired leadership, and collective energies would be sufficient for the country to achieve its goals.[9]

The effects of this demented policy, particularly in the northwest, where over a million "April 17" people had been resettled to grow rice, were administrative chaos and thousands of deaths from overwork, beatings, and malnutrition. Cadres met production quotas by falsifying reports and sending rice intended for consumption along to the center for use elsewhere. In the ensuing confusion, thousands of people starved, and Cambodia's agricultural economy, built up over centuries, came close to collapse in many regions. Thousands of people were literally worked to death. The rest of the plan proposed industrialization and a cultural renaissance, but no increase in rights or freedoms, once agricultural production had reached its goals.

The *Four Year Plan* was never made public. By the end of 1976 Pol Pot and his colleagues had altered their priorities, and began to blame failures of their program on enemies of the revolution and more generally on the Vietnamese, although very few ethnic Vietnamese remained as residents of the country. The Khmer Rouge became preoccupied with rooting out "enemies" (*khmang*). Perhaps 15,000 of these victims were interrogated, tortured, and killed at the DK facility in Phnom Penh known by its coded designation, S-21. Written confessions of perhaps a quarter of these victims have survived, and provide harrowing glimpses of the regime's paranoia.

In 1975–6, those purged tended to be people associated with the republican regime, or Cambodians educated abroad. The pace quickened in August and September 1976, soon after the death of Mao Zedong in China. The death of their powerful patron unnerved the Khmer Rouge leaders, who feared that Vietnam would attempt to resume its guidance of the Cambodian party. They began to persecute party members who had been active in the 1940s and 1950s when the Vietnamese had been influential in the Cambodian communist movement. Soon afterward, for reasons that have never been made clear, the Khmer Rouge began vicious cross-border raids into Vietnam, which soon escalated into a full-scale, but officially unacknowledged, war between two supposedly fraternal communist regimes.

In the meantime, purges of party members gathered momentum. In

[9] See David P. Chandler, Ben Kiernan and Chanthou Boua (eds. and tr.), *Pol Pot Plans the Future: Confidential Leadership Documents from Democratic Kampuchea, 1976–1977* (New Haven, Conn.: Yale University Press, 1988), pp. 36–118.

1977, intellectuals in the party were targeted for execution, as were those in charge of areas where tens of thousands of people had died as a result of the demands placed on them by the *Four Year Plan*. In 1978 the party's baleful attention shifted to cadres in the eastern part of the country, who were alleged to be pro-Vietnamese because of Vietnamese military successes in the region. Fighting with Vietnam went badly, and Khmer Rouge military in the eastern part of the country were purged for "cooperating" with Vietnam. Some eastern zone cadres, fearing for their lives, fled into Vietnam and were harbored there as a potential government in exile. Some of these men, including Heng Samrin, Hun Sen and Chea Sim, came to power following the Vietnamese invasion of Cambodia at the end of 1978. Tens of thousands of Cambodians who did not flee to Vietnam were cut down by troops sent from Phnom Penh to purge them.[10]

Later in the year, high-ranking cadres in the party, some close to Pol Pot himself, were purged as the revolution proceeded to devour its best and brightest people. As the economy stumbled, the war went badly and the party tore itself apart, the Khmer Rouge experimented with diplomatic relations, opening up in a belated attempt to gain allies in the event of a Vietnamese invasion.

Time ran out before these alliances could have any effect. In December 1978 over 100,000 Vietnamese troops invaded the country, and Cambodia cracked open like an egg. The population did little to resist and in fact welcomed the invaders. In January 1979 Pol Pot fled to Thailand by helicopter, echoing the ignominious departure of the American ambassador and his staff in 1975. Hundreds of thousands of his followers spent several months moving slowly toward the northwest, eventually finding sanctuary along the Thai border, by which time thousands of them had starved to death.

The revolutionary era in Cambodia, like those that had preceded it, was cut short by war. Despite the Khmer Rouge claims that everything they did was unprecedented, the revolutionary era must be understood in terms of foreign patronage and in relation to previous regimes. A major area of continuity between the republican regime and the Khmer Rouge was the reluctance of leaders to see the country in terms of its genuine vulnerability rather than its supposed grandiose potential. Focusing on Cambodia and on themselves, the leaders were misled and misled their followers, ignoring the fact that Cambodia's survival

---

[10] See Ben Kiernan, *Cambodia: The Eastern Zone Massacres* (New York: Center for the Study of Human Rights, Columbia University, 1987), an invaluable analysis based in large part on interviews with survivors.

depends on retaining peaceful relations with its expansive and far larger neighbor to the east.

The Vietnamese protectorate

Between 1979 and 1989 the Vietnamese communists imposed a protectorate on Cambodia, working through a government known as the People's Republic of Kampuchea (PRK), made up of Khmer Rouge defectors and Cambodians who had spent many years working in Vietnam. The new regime pursued what its leaders – among them Chea Sim and Hun Sen – perceived as a rational, technocratic road to socialism, based on Soviet and Vietnamese models, and sustained by substantial Soviet and Soviet bloc aid.[11]

The first two years of the protectorate were crucial for Cambodia's survival. With a quarter of a million Vietnamese troops stationed in Cambodia, and the Khmer Rouge licking their wounds in sanctuaries in Thailand, the new regime set about undoing many of the painful, utopian measures that had been taken under Pol Pot. The cities came back to life and by the mid-1980s half a million people were living in Phnom Penh. Schools, markets, and Buddhist monasteries were reopened. Money was reintroduced, but for the time being no taxes were levied on the people. Collective farms were broken up, but buying and selling real estate was not yet permitted. More importantly, people were allowed to move around the country, to grow their own food and, where possible, to resume their pre-revolutionary lives.

These bold measures had mixed results. Few Cambodians wanted to stay on collective farms, growing rice under arduous conditions. Collectives were abandoned, rice surpluses, draft animals, and other foodstuffs were consumed, no new rice was planted, and hundreds of thousands of undernourished people took to the roads, looking for relatives or seeking asylum in Thailand. By allowing Cambodians to move and by retaining many socialist policies discredited under Pol Pot, the PRK lost tens of thousands of educated people who might have been persuaded to stay behind and work to rebuild their country.

Over 600,000 people had left Cambodia for good by 1981. Roughly half of these were eventually resettled in France, Australia, the United States, and other countries, while 300,000 were crowded into refugee camps administered by the United Nations. With Thai encouragement,

---

[11] The best scholarly study of this period is Michael Vickery, *Kampuchea: Politics, Economics and Society* (Boulder, Col.: Lynne Rienner, 1986). See also Viviane Frings, *The Failure of Collectivization in the PRK*, Monash University Centre of Southeast Asian Studies Working Paper, 1992.

these camps soon came under the control of royalist, communist, and parliamentarian factions opposed to Vietnam's occupation of Cambodia. The factions were led by Sihanouk (who had been allowed to flee the country just before the Vietnamese arrived), Pol Pot, and an 80-year old former prime minister named Son Sann. Although the Cambodian communist party claimed to have dissolved in 1981, its leaders remained unrepentant and in place.

The factions, receiving open support from Thailand, and more discreet support from China and the United States, engaged in ineffectual guerrilla warfare against the Vietnamese. The powers patronizing the resistance opposed Vietnam so strongly that they were willing to support the Khmer Rouge. Democratic Kampuchea retained Cambodia's seat at the United Nations, in spite of the fact that the true horrors of its years in power were now widely known to the outside world.

By 1982, it became clear that the Vietnamese envisaged a long, and perhaps even permanent occupation of Cambodia, which, as a satellite, had come to resemble the Vietnamese-protected regime in Laos. Foreign humanitarian assistance to the country ceased, and the PRK was isolated diplomatically and economically.

A government in exile

In 1982, under pressure from China, Thailand, and the United States, the factions along the border coalesced to form a government in exile that was recognized by the United Nations. To these powers, the coalition was an inspired move, which served their interests in the closing phases of the Cold War; these interests coalesced around the idea of punishing Vietnam and enhancing Thai influence in the region. These arrangements fueled Cambodian factionalism, left the country impoverished, and postponed a peaceful solution. The coalition itself was united only by the factions' hatred of Vietnam, their nostalgia for power, and their fondness for foreign assistance. These characteristics were matched or surpassed by their intense and time-consuming hatreds for each other.

In the meantime, politics inside Cambodia had evolved along Cambodian lines as Vietnamese troops gradually withdrew, Vietnamese advisors relinquished control of ministries, and non-communists were brought into some positions of authority. The fusion of party and state retained an awesome security apparatus, and no opposition politics was permitted; but behind the military shield provided by the Vietnamese army, the PRK made commendable strides in the fields of education and agriculture, which became decollectivized by 1988. The regime was sustained by infusions of aid from the Soviet bloc, amounting in the mid-1980s to US$200 million a year.

Cambodia's economic situation changed drastically in 1989 in response to the tumultuous events in Europe that brought the Cold War to an end and toppled a series of communist regimes. Soviet bloc aid plummeted to $18 million almost overnight. The Vietnamese hastened to repatriate what remained of their occupying army, some 80,000 men, a move that encouraged guerrilla opposition movements on the Thai border to seize pieces of territory in Cambodia's northwest. The collapse of the Soviet Union and its hegemony in Eastern Europe forced the Vietnamese to think of Vietnam first, and threw the PRK back onto its own limited resources. The fluid situation also encouraged the factions along the Thai border to move their troops onto Cambodian soil. What had been a stalemate threatened to erupt into a full-scale civil war.

It was at this stage that international interest began to focus on Cambodia as a problem to be solved, and as a threat to the stability of the region. In the mid-1980s, French, Indonesian, and Australian initiatives made little progress, largely because of China's reluctance to abandon its alliance with the Khmer Rouge, and because of Thai intransigence. To retain or enhance its popularity, the PRK inaugurated a series of reforms in 1989–90. These lifted restrictions on Buddhist practice, privatized state owned enterprises, and granted urban householders title to their homes. Foreign investment was encouraged. The party changed its name, altered the national flag and claimed to have abandoned Marxism-Leninism as an ideology. Market forces, restrained and atrophied for several years, came almost uncontrollably into play. Real estate and currency speculation flourished, as did corruption. Services deteriorated, and the civil war continued. In the course of sporadic fighting, millions of anti-personnel mines were laid by both sides, rendering large stretches of the Cambodian northwest uninhabitable. Well into the 1990s, hundreds of Cambodians, mostly innocent civilians, were maimed or killed every month by mines.

In 1990, the Khmer Rouge took advantage of a military vacuum to send troops into the gem-mining areas of western Battambang, where they supervised the mining, and by selling gemstones to Thai entrepreneurs soon built up a sizable war chest. Khmer Rouge units elsewhere teamed up with Thai middlemen to exploit Cambodia's timber resources, and so did troops affiliated with the other factions. The ecological effects of this free-wheeling exploitation, which continued into the 1990s, were severe but have not yet been assessed. By 1990, perhaps as much as a quarter of Cambodia's territory was no longer in government hands.

In the meantime, foreign efforts to negotiate an end to the fighting continued to be unsuccessful, producing an impasse.

Breaking the impasse

The impasse broke in 1991, when the permanent five members of the UN Security Council (the United States, the United Kingdom, France, China, and the Soviet Union) agreed to convene a conference on Cambodia that envisaged a UN protectorate over the country pending national elections. Smaller nations, notably Australia, had been active in bringing the conference about, but it would never have taken place without the concurrence of China and the United States. In effect, the Paris Agreements attempted to fasten the coalition government in exile onto the existing, and antagonistic government in Phnom Penh, in an exercise that also involved the great powers abandoning their Cambodian clientele. An almost unimaginable four-faction interim regime, which contained all four strands of Cambodia's tangled political history, was to remain in place while its members, who despised each other, competed for votes in a national election.

The United Nations Transitional Authority in Cambodia (UNTAC) phase of Cambodian history is dealt with elsewhere in this book. What is important about it from an historical point of view is that four Cambodian factions were allowed to flourish simultaneously, under UN protection. The intensity of political debate was greater than at any time since 1970–1. For the first time in Cambodian history, pluralism was openly encouraged. Unsurprisingly, the factions behaved true to form. The Khmer Rouge boycotted the process, and in a few months massacred over a hundred Vietnamese residents of the country, claiming that they were spies. The Phnom Penh government heavy-handedly used its security apparatus to cow opponents, while the royalist and parliamentary factions spent their time offering nostalgically vague scenarios for voters grown weary of the incumbent regime. None of the candidates stressed ideology as an important component of Cambodian politics. Instead, politics became re-personalized under a range of visible, talkative leaders. The absence of foreign backing for any one faction, and the closeness of the vote, forced the factions to work together, and produced compromises among them that many observers had thought impossible. More importantly, the withdrawal of foreign support seems to have spelled the end of the Khmer Rouge as a major political force in Cambodian life.

How long this fragile and contentious pluralism will survive, or whether it will grow, are questions that are impossible to answer when the government and its institutions are so young. The fragile possibility that parliamentarians, royalists, and former socialists can put their animosities and their discredited visions aside and share a view of the country's politics and society that does not include one-man rule (ending two thousand years of Cambodian history), is unprecedented and encouraging. This, combined with the fact that war with Vietnam is unlikely, offers more grounds for optimism, as far as ordinary Cambodians are concerned, than any political development in recent years.

Of course, it is perilous to predict events in Cambodia without considering Thailand and Vietnam, to say nothing of even larger powers. However, the end of the Cold War and the withdrawal of larger powers in Cambodia, heralded by the Paris Agreements, are encouraging in the sense that at last Cambodians will be encouraged to stand on their own feet.

3   The political dynamics of the peacemaking process in Cambodia

Jin Song

Introduction

After a long and arduous peace process, the negotiations for a political settlement in Cambodia finally culminated in the adoption of the Agreement on a Comprehensive Political Settlement of the Cambodia Conflict in Paris on October 23, 1991. Nineteen nations and the four Cambodian factions gathered to sign a document that would, for the first time in UN history, implement the visions of Secretary-General Boutros-Ghali's "peacebuilding" initiatives, as later outlined in his *Agenda for Peace*. Unlike the peace process in El Salvador – which was primarily a series of agreements and settlements – the Cambodian conflict was resolved through a series of informal and formal meetings on domestic and international levels, with the Paris Agreement as the multilateral product of a comprehensive set of agreements made during the lengthy peace process. The Cambodian conflict was complicated by geopolitical factors on the factional, regional, and international levels, with such regional and multilateral organizations as the Association of Southeast Asian Nations (ASEAN) and the United Nations (UN) playing a significant role.

The purpose of this chapter is to explore the political dynamics of the peacemaking process that led to the signing of the Paris Agreements in 1991. Placing particular emphasis on the diplomatic initiatives of both the regional actors and the great powers, the chapter will also explore how the ongoing civil war, the history of genocide, and powerful neighbors posed serious obstacles to peace and necessitated a solution which would require the creation of the most ambitious and expensive UN peacekeeping mission in the organization's history.

Setting the scene: regional and great power interests in the 1980s

The early and mid-1980s saw little hopes for peacemaking in Cambodia. After Vietnam's 1978 invasion of Cambodia, the People's Republic of

Kampuchea (PRK) government was established to achieve "a rational, technocratic road to socialism, based on Soviet and Vietnamese models, and sustained by substantial Soviet and Soviet bloc aid."[1] The United States seemed content to defer to ASEAN's regional initiatives and apply a passive "wait-and-see" policy, cautiously avoiding any appearance of stage-managing another country's internal process. This caution was the product of domestic pressures, the recent war with North Vietnam, and US reluctance to jeopardize its new relations with China. However, the United States was willing to provide diplomatic and military assistance to keep the non-communist resistance alive and competitive against the PRK. China, angered by Vietnam's pretensions to an Indochina Federation, began to payroll the Khmer Rouge – the genocidal regime and former government of Cambodia which had been sent running into the jungles along the Thai–Cambodian borders. The anti-Vietnamese sentiment over the invasion of Cambodia stirred the USA, China, and ASEAN to join forces and revive the exiled Cambodian factions, the Khmer Rouge (or PDK, Party of Democratic Kampuchea) and the two non-communist resistance groups – Prince Norodom Sihanouk's political party FUNCINPEC (United National Front for an Independent, Neutral, Peaceful and Cooperative Cambodia) – and former prime minister Son Sann's KPNLF (Khmer People's National Liberation Front).

At the urging of China, ASEAN, and the USA, the Khmer Rouge joined with FUNCINPEC and the KPNLF to create the Coalition Government of Democratic Kampuchea (CGDK), a semblance of a united opposition front intended to muster international support. Although ASEAN, China, and the USA perceived that a resistance government could pose as a counter-force against the imposed regime in Phnom Penh, its practical effect was to legitimate the revival of the Khmer Rouge, which was included in the resistance government because China and ASEAN viewed it as the strongest counter force to the Vietnamese. The consequences of including the Khmer Rouge, however, exacted a heavy toll from the Cambodian peace process; the faction refused to sign any agreement which it did not deem beneficial to its own interests.

Beijing was key to the peacemaking process because of its linkage with the Khmer Rouge.[2] It was essentially funding the guerrilla group's

---

The author and the editors would like to thank Steven Ratner for his exceptional advice and assistance in preparing this chapter.

[1] Michael Vickery, *Kampuchea: Politics, Economics and Society* (Boulder, Col.: Lynne Rienner, 1986).

[2] For an excellent analysis of the China relationship to the Cambodian conflict see Robert Ross, "China and the Cambodian peace process," *Asian Survey*, vol. 31, no. 12, 1991.

extreme racial hatred for the Vietnamese and its menace potential for the imposed regime in Phnom Penh. Because China's support of the Khmer Rouge was based on the Khmer Rouge's actions against the Vietnamese, China's strategy throughout the negotiations was to constantly assess the nature of the relative strengths of the Khmer Rouge and the PRK.[3] By the late 1980s, it became apparent to Beijing that the Khmer Rouge, however strong their military force and their hatred for the Vietnamese, would be able neither to force Vietnam to withdraw its troops nor to topple the PRK. Once Beijing reached this conclusion, it shifted its policy in favor of a peace settlement in Cambodia, providing the peace process with one of its most crucial players.

Factional interests

The Cambodian conflict is viewed by many scholars as a domestic problem that was solved, in large part, by an international solution – specifically, the UN's comprehensive role as the transitional authority in Cambodia prior to free and fair elections. But many of the most frustrating issues confronted in the negotiations over the peacemaking process – including UNTAC's role in the power-sharing deadlock, the demobilization of military forces, and the creation of the civilian component – were tied directly to the negotiations, or lack thereof, among the four domestic Cambodian factions.

When the three resistance factions joined together in the CGDK to fight the Vietnamese-imposed Hun Sen regime, a major cohesive factor in their alliance was each member's extreme hatred of Vietnam and nostalgia for power. Though all four factions welcomed foreign assistance, each possessed a great desire to liberate the Cambodians from foreign domination.[4] Indeed, each of the factions has ruled Cambodia at one point in its history, and the institutional memory of strength and control over the state has deterred all of them from effectively sharing power. The complexities of negotiation during the peacemaking process hinged largely on the delicate balance of power between the Cambodian factions which Sihanouk, the P5, and other interested countries constantly struggled to manipulate. However, Cambodia lacks a democratic tradition conducive to sharing power,[5] and the depth of hostility felt by the Khmer Rouge toward the Vietnamese ensured that national reconciliation would require, at the very least, that each recognized the other. Thus power-sharing would be the crucial sticking point in the process of bringing peace to Cambodia.

[3] Ibid.   [4] Ibid.
[5] Nayan Chanda, "Civil war in Cambodia?," *Foreign Policy*, Fall, 1989.

Prince Norodom Sihanouk was regarded by most interested states as the most important individual player in the negotiation for a resolution to the Cambodian conflict. His long and popular history as the only leader who had brought any modicum of stability and progress to Cambodia made Sihanouk the obvious candidate to lead the nation again. His dynamic personality, French education, and close ties with China and the US further emphasized Sihanouk's central role in the Cambodian peace process. Sihanouk views himself as the "father" of Cambodia, the Cambodians as his "children." The force of his personality and the aura of his *devaraja*, or "god-king," lent Sihanouk a legitimacy that the PRK, the Khmer Rouge, and great powers scrambled to link with their individual agendas. Although some observers have long described Sihanouk as a "mercurial" personality with erratic behavior that makes him difficult to work with – let alone predict – others consider this trait to be the sign of an extremely shrewd diplomat. In the last four decades, Sihanouk has maintained diplomatic leverage either by abruptly changing sides (or at least threatening to do so) and winning concessions from more powerful actors who, for various reasons, need his cooperation.[6] Gareth Porter claims that Sihanouk, as a strategist of weak-state diplomacy, "was – and still is – unequaled in contemporary international politics."[7] US strategy in Cambodia has even been described as "a gamble on Sihanouk," where aid to the non-communist resistance was primarily given to maintain the survival of the factions until ceasefire conditions could be achieved, at which point the battle could shift from a military struggle to a political one.[8] Appreciating the value of the legitimate authority that Sihanouk's support conveyed, China made every effort to control his activities during the early part of negotiations.[9]

As an exiled prince possessing all the legitimacy but none of the power base from which to proceed, Sihanouk believed he could only save his country by restoring himself to power, and that power could only be attained through direct negotiation with the relevant parties. Sihanouk may have felt that he was above factional politics, but he was unable to rise above the negotiating parameters set by Beijing. A mutual dependency existed between Sihanouk and the Chinese: he needed Beijing's financial support and China valued him as the unique leader

---

[6]   Gareth Porter, "Cambodia: Sihanouk's initiative," *Foreign Affairs*, vol. 66, no. 4, 1988.
[7]   Ibid.
[8]   Peter W. Rodman, "Supping with devils," *The National Interest*, no. 25, 1991.
[9]   Ben Kiernan, "The inclusion of the Khmer Rouge in the Cambodian peace process: causes and consequences," in *Genocide and Democracy in Cambodia: The Khmer Rouge, the UN, and the International Community* (New Haven, Conn.: Yale University Press, 1993).

capable of supporting China's interests via the Khmer Rouge. Even though Sihanouk was unpredictable, his foreign policy always aimed at maximizing Cambodian independence. With the Vietnamese invasion in 1978, Beijing continued to champion Sihanouk's leadership credentials, hoping to back a new, legal government under the prince's leadership.[10] Sihanouk's inability to go his own way resulted in many false starts and dashed expectations, as became more than evident at the first international conference held in Paris.

Regional interests

ASEAN believed that an acceptable peace could only be achieved if the Vietnamese were required to leave. But the Phnom Penh regime was determined not to leave, fearing that a power vacuum might invite the Khmer Rouge's return to power. The Cambodian issue helped fuel the cohesion of ASEAN. Its leading member, Indonesia, played one of the most active roles in resolving the conflict. Indonesia took the lead in 1982 by asking Washington to normalize relations with Vietnam as a first step toward removing Vietnamese troops from Cambodia; but Washington's position was just the opposite – Vietnamese troop withdrawal was the pre-condition to normalization.[11] Mochtar Kusuma-Atmadja, the Indonesian foreign minister, pushed his idea of an informal gathering, or "cocktail party," of the Khmer factions. Eventually, Prince Sihanouk agreed to meet PRK prime minister Hun Sen for "cocktails for two," near Paris in December 1987 and January 1988, leading to the Jakarta Informal Meetings, or JIM I and II regional meetings, held in Indonesia in 1988 and 1989. Indonesia's main objectives were to end the isolation of Indochina and resolve a conflict that had attracted the interests of too many outsiders. Following his tenure as Indonesian ambassador to the UN, Ali Alatas was appointed Indonesia's foreign minister and came to lead ASEAN's efforts to negotiate a peace. A globalist rather than a regionalist, Alatas strove to continue President Suharto's ambition for a "higher-profile" Indonesia.

Even though Suharto and Alatas sought to become leaders in the peace process, they nonetheless joined other ASEAN leaders in allowing Thailand to remain the primary state with the responsibility of

[10] Robert Ross, "China and the Cambodian peace process," *Asian Survey*, vol. 31, no. 12, 1991. For further analysis on China's earlier interest in Sihanouk, see Robert Ross, *The Indochina Tangle: China's Vietnam Policy, 1975–1979*, chapters 2 and 3 (New York: Columbia University Press, 1988).

[11] Michael Haas, *Genocide by Proxy: Cambodian Pawn on a Superpower Chessboard* (New York: Praeger, 1991).

containing Vietnam.[12] Thailand's policy "ran down a single track" for over a decade, as Prime Minister Prem left all of Cambodian affairs to Foreign Minister Siddhi Savetsila. Under Siddhi's leadership, Bangkok consistently refused offers to negotiate with Hanoi, even rejecting Hanoi's offer of a non-aggression pact in the early 1980s, as it seemed to imply acceptance of Vietnam's hegemony in Indochina.[13] ASEAN singled out the perceived threat to Thailand's sovereignty as its basis of contention against the Phnom Penh regime. In 1988, Prime Minister Prem retired, and Chatichai Choonhaven became the new prime minister. Thailand's policy toward Cambodia in the late 1980s and early 1990s shifted under Chatichai's leadership, dominated by its need to expand its growth into other markets in Southeast Asia. Bangkok saw itself as a future economic superpower of Southeast Asia. Thailand, already involved in such lucrative enterprises as the smuggling of retail goods and the distribution of supplies to the resistance provided by outside powers, wanted to expand its interests into the rest of Southeast Asia, especially Vietnam. By 1989, Chatichai had invited Hun Sen to Bangkok for private talks even though Thailand did not recognize the PRK – a move that greatly annoyed both China and the USA. Thailand's steadfast economic agenda created greater incentives for it to see Cambodia reach a settlement. Chatichai pledged to cut off aid to the resistance forces in an effort to move the peace process further and faster.[14]

Great power interests

China's one overriding objective since the fall of Saigon to North Vietnamese forces in April 1975 has been to contain Soviet expansion into China's southern periphery.[15] Beijing's foreign policy has been predicated on resisting Soviet regional hegemony and preventing the "encirclement" of China. When Soviet-backed Vietnamese forces entered Cambodia in 1978, Beijing focused on "rolling back" Vietnamese power in Indochina via the full withdrawal of Vietnamese forces from Cambodia. Vietnam alone was a minimal threat to China; but when backed by an international power like the Soviet Union, it could pose a formidable challenge. Furthermore, having failed to keep Vietnamese forces out of Cambodia, Beijing was determined not to agree to any settlement that would allow the Heng Samrin regime to remain as the legal government of Cambodia. In short, Beijing adopted a zero-sum policy: whatever permitted Vietnam to be strong necessarily

[12] Ibid.   [13] Ibid.   [14] Haas, *Genocide by Proxy*, p. 172.
[15] Ross, *The Indochina Tangle*.

ran counter to China's interests. The Khmer Rouge's uncompromising hostility toward the Vietnamese occupation of Cambodia was enough to assure Beijing's full support.

Moscow also saw the Cambodian issue as a major obstacle to a Sino–Soviet summit. By the mid-1980s, the Soviet Union was ready to sign an agreement resolving the problem in order to push forward other, more important bilateral concerns between the Soviet Union and China, like Afghanistan and Sino–Soviet border issues.[16] Furthermore, the financial costs of Vietnam's occupation of Cambodia were becoming more of a burden than Moscow originally intended them to be, and with Moscow's growing desire for Sino–Soviet rapprochement, the Soviets became increasingly reluctant to support Hanoi's client. Although the Soviet Union had an interest in maintaining strategic relations with Vietnam, it wanted to reduce its military and economic aid to Hanoi. While Moscow had an investment in the Hun Sen regime, and wanted to prevent any future threats to Vietnam's security, it was limited in what it could do for the regime.

While some observers have argued that the United States had a strategic interest in seeing the Cambodian conflict resolved through Sino–Vietnamese accommodation, others believed the USA wanted to see Vietnam bleed. Moscow's concentration of military forces in Cam Ranh Bay could only be diminished through a Vietnam less dependent on the Soviets and fully integrated into the mainstream of Pacific trade and investment. Unfortunately, US policy in the mid-1980s was based on a determination to avoid becoming involved. ASEAN, however, was incessant in demanding that the USA take a greater role in resolving the Cambodian conflict. During the 1984 ASEAN foreign ministers' meeting in Jakarta, the foreign ministers of Malaysia, Indonesia, and Singapore pressed Secretary of State George Shultz to pressure China to ease its hardline stance on negotiation of an agreement.[17] One ASEAN diplomat put it frankly, "Let's face it, we are only a small power. The US can have a lot more influence on the Chinese than we can."[18]

The United Nations' role

The UN's response to the crises in Cambodia had a certain predictability. While the Khmer Rouge ruled, the lack of information flowing out of the country hampered international involvement in the human

---

[16] International Peace Academy workshop paper: Frederick Brown, *Cambodia Beyond Impasse: Prospects for a Settlement.*
[17] Porter, "Cambodia: Sihanouk's initiative," p. 825.   [18] Ibid.

rights nightmare. Khmer Rouge supporters insisted that the extremist movement was simply pursuing its path to social and economic development. By 1976 and 1977, however, refugees' anecdotes and accounts prompted a group of Western states to raise the matter before the UN Human Rights Commission. After the Khmer Rouge refused to cooperate with any investigation, the Chairman of the Commission's Sub-Commission on Prevention of Discrimination and Protection of Minorities prepared a detailed analysis based on information provided by governments. Before the Commission could act on that report, however, Vietnam conquered Democratic Kampuchea, the Khmer Rouge state.

The Vietnamese invasion, however, triggered an immediate response by friends of Democratic Kampuchea, adversaries of Vietnam and the Soviet Union, and the majority of non-aligned states that viewed the aggression as a threat to small states everywhere. In the Security Council, the Soviet Union vetoed in early 1979 a resolution to condemn the invasion. In July 1981, seventy-nine states attended the International Conference on Kampuchea (ICK), including Democratic Kampuchea, represented by Ieng Sary, its second-highest official and an architect of Khmer Rouge atrocities. The Soviet bloc states boycotted it, seeing the Conference as predisposed against Vietnam, and thereby precluding any effective peacemaking. After five days, the ICK adopted a declaration that, predictably, emphasized the need to restore Cambodia's territorial integrity.[19] It also established an Ad Hoc Committee to undertake peacemaking efforts, and the Secretary-General appointed a Special Representative (Rafeeuddin Ahmed) to follow the issue.

The annual General Assembly resolutions on Cambodia reflected the opinion of most governments on the key elements of a future settlement: withdrawal of Vietnamese forces; creation of an interim administering authority; national reconciliation under Prince Sihanouk; restoration of Cambodia's independence and territorial integrity; the right of Cambodians to determine their own destiny free of outside intervention; and "effective guarantees" to achieve these ends. (As an indication of world abhorrence of the Khmer Rouge, the resolutions did not call for the restoration of the government of Democratic Kampuchea, which still held Cambodia's UN seat.)[20]

---

[19] Declaration on Kampuchea, in Report of the International Conference on Kampuchea, New York, July 13–17, 1981, ann. I, at 7, UN doc. A/CONF.109/5 (1981).

[20] Kishore Mahbubani, "The Kampuchean problem: a Southeast Asian perspective," *Foreign Affairs*, no. 62, 1983–4.

Regional attempts at peacemaking

From 1981 to 1987, a diplomatic and military stalemate prevailed in Cambodia. The Vietnamese dominated the country, except for small areas controlled by the Khmer Rouge and two smaller resistance groups – FUNCINPEC and KPNLF. Severe fighting often erupted, including a Vietnamese offensive in 1985. The Khmer Rouge accused Vietnam of encouraging large numbers of Vietnamese to colonize Cambodia. Vietnam, on the other hand, often spoke of "the genocidal crimes of the Pol Pot clique," asserting that Hanoi had in fact saved Cambodia. The PRK remained ostracized diplomatically. Diplomatic efforts by the UN Special Representative of the Secretary-General appeared to lead nowhere. The annual General Assembly resolution on Cambodia passed with increasing majorities, but no side had any interest in negotiation or compromise.

The UN role in peacemaking, managed at the regional level, dates as far back as 1982, when Secretary-General Pérez de Cuéllar appointed Rafeeuddin Ahmed as his Special Representative to Cambodia. Regional talks were, in part, the result of a set of informal discussions conducted between 1982 and 1985 by Rafeeuddin Ahmed to explore different avenues for negotiating the Cambodian conflict through regional diplomacy.[21] Ahmed and his senior advisor, Hedi Annabi, first pursued the possibilities of a peace in the region as early as 1982.[22] Pursuing these initiatives further, Ahmed and Annabi contacted the French in 1988, a month before JIM I, to develop a series of "non-paper" sketches of many of the elements which later surfaced in the comprehensive settlement presented in Paris. The most important feature outlined was a role for the UN – with a peacekeeping role that involved not only a military component, but also a civilian component, and a UN supervised election. Ahmed was asked by Secretary-General Pérez de Cuéllar to begin making contacts with the Hun Sen regime and to offer the UN's good offices. Ahmed worked with the Cambodian factions and regional states in the development of an outline that would eventually be incorporated into a comprehensive solution to the Cambodian conflict. The working proposal included all four factions, established a ceasefire, supervised the withdrawal of all foreign forces, guaranteed Cambodia's independence and neutrality, repatriated refugees, demobilized military

---

[21] See Report of the Secretary-General, *The Situation in Cambodia*, A/40/759, October 17, 1985.

[22] The following views on the early history of the UN's role in Cambodia prior to the first Paris conference is drawn from an interview with a senior UN official conducted by Michael W. Doyle, February 22, 1994. See also Secretary-General's Report A/40/759, October 17, 1985.

forces, provided for genuine national self-determination through free and fair elections, and instituted a human rights education program to help insure a "non-return of the policies and practices of a recent past," the diplomatic code for the genocide committed by the Khmer Rouge.[23] At this point, however, the parties would not welcome the possibility of either a UN role in the organization of elections or a substantial transitional authority.[24] The Vietnamese wanted no UN role in peace-keeping and the substantial transitional authority was seen as unnecessary given a true power-sharing transitional government.

By the mid-1980s there was a sense among member states of ASEAN that the regional group had attained a high level of resilience and unity and that, with US support, the ASEAN states could confidently cope with the Vietnamese threat in Cambodia.[25] The ASEAN states then saw that the peace process was ready to include the other regional actors. In 1987 Prince Norodom Sihanouk seized the initiative with a series of diplomatic maneuvers. The negotiations began as a regional effort among the four factions, ASEAN, and Vietnam. Sihanouk met with Cambodian prime minister Hun Sen in December 1987 and January 1988 in Fère-en-Tardenois, a suburb of Paris, to discuss a framework for a settlement. Although two meetings between Hun Sen and Sihanouk ensued, little concrete progress was made. Nevertheless, the two leaders did become more sensitive to the similarities and differences in their views.

The critical issue was the shape of an interim government for the period prior to a national elections. Sihanouk proposed that the PRK be dissolved and replaced by a quadripartite provisional coalition government that would hold elections under international supervision, while Hun Sen proposed that the elections be organized by "electoral commissions" with representatives from all factions, and that the coalition government be formed after the elections.[26] Phnom Penh and Sihanouk did find common ground, however, in their desire to insure that the Khmer Rouge did not return to power following a withdrawal of Vietnamese troops from Cambodia. After meeting with Hun Sen, Sihanouk went back to Beijing in late January to convince the Chinese party leader Zhao Ziyang and the Khmer Rouge's Khieu Samphan of his

---

[23] See Michael W. Doyle, "Lessons From Cambodia," presented at a conference titled *The United Nations, Peacekeeping and US Policy in the Post-Cold War World*, Queenstown, Md.: The Aspen Institute, 1994.

[24] Interview with Senior UN official, conducted by Michael Doyle, February 22, 1994.

[25] Sukhambhand Paribatra, "Can ASEAN break the stalemate?," *World Policy Journal*, vol. 3, no. 1, 1985–6.

[26] Gareth Porter, "Cambodia: Sihanouk's initiative", *Foreign Affairs*, vol. 66, no.4, 1988, p. 817.

desire for an end to the Vietnamese-sponsored regime.[27] Despite the
recent progress, Sihanouk canceled the next round of talks after China
rejected Hun Sen's proposal to disarm the Khmer Rouge.[28] Soon after,
Sihanouk gave up on the idea as being politically infeasible. He then
suggested an alternative, namely a quadripartite national army made up
of forces from the Hun Sen government, the KPNLF, the army of
Sihanouk's party, and the Khmer Rouge, which would then be in a
minority.[29] The Khmer Rouge rejected this plan as well.

Sihanouk next tried to negotiate directly with Vietnam. But Saigon
refused to talk directly with Sihanouk in order to avoid weakening the
bargaining position of Hun Sen's regime.[30] Hanoi's views on the issue of
an interim government rested largely on a comparison of the consequences of two options: a unilateral withdrawal or a negotiated
settlement. Hanoi's main problem was legitimacy: if the Phnom Penh
regime held out long enough at the bargaining table, Hanoi believed it
would be able to muster enough legitimacy from the international
community to stay in power. Hanoi hoped that maintaining a cooperative posture, opposing a return to genocide and emphasizing Phnom
Penh's progress in rebuilding Cambodian society would lead to a change
in the hearts of great power diplomats. Hanoi's final decisions on a
transitional coalition government thus would "reflect its assessment of
the relative risks and benefits of a unilateral withdrawal and of a
negotiated settlement."[31]

After Sihanouk's "cocktail party" with Hun Sen, Indonesian foreign
minister Ali Alatas convened the first Jakarta Informal Meeting (JIM) in
July 1988, followed by a second in February 1989. All four factional
leaders and representatives of Vietnam, Laos, and ASEAN attended the
talks, which were in many ways crucial to the Cambodia peace process.
First, the attempt to undertake regional diplomacy to confront the issue
of Cambodian peace was symbolically important for both Southeast Asia
and the broader ASEAN community. And while the meetings did not
reach agreement on many issues, they did lead to the discussion of the
essential elements for the establishment of a comprehensive settlement –
many of which appeared in the annual General Assembly resolution and
were later found in the final Paris Peace Agreements – including a
ceasefire, demobilization of military forces, guarantees for Cambodia's
independence and neutrality, and self-determination through free and
fair national elections.

The bargaining table, however, was criss-crossed with inflexible party

[27] Ibid., p. 819.   [28] Kiernan, "The inclusion of the Khmer Rouge," p. 196.
[29] Porter, "Cambodia: Sihanouk's initiative," p. 817.   [30] Ibid., p. 819.
[31] Ibid.

lines – Vietnam's foreign minister Nguyen Co Thach argued that the Cambodian problem had to be divided into internal and external aspects. The CGDK said there was no "Cambodian problem," pointing instead to a "Vietnamese problem," which could be solved if Hanoi simply removed itself from Cambodia.[32] Areas of consensus were reflected in a final statement signed by members of the JIM talks, and Ali Alatas announced that JIM I had agreed to form a working group composed of members from the talks to draft alternative texts for a negotiated settlement.

After JIM I, Vietnam began to consider a precise date for troop withdrawal from Cambodia. The first sessions of the working group began in October 1988, but the Khmer Rouge did not participate. Regardless, the regional negotiations plowed forward with determination, and a new tripartite coalition seemed to be emerging – minus the Khmer Rouge. Some observers believed that the "Hun Sen plus" option – joining FUNCINPEC and the KPNLF factions with the Phnom Penh government – was the best viable solution for Cambodia.[33] The plan's critical flaw, however, was its exclusion of the Khmer Rouge. The Khmer Rouge boycotted the working group sessions, and Deng Xiaoping warned Sihanouk not to sign anything without Khmer Rouge approval, while Li Peng pressured the Khmer Rouge's Khieu Samphan to take on a lesser role in an interim quadripartite government.[34] During negotiations, the prince offered his five-point plan – a definite Vietnamese withdrawal date, simultaneous dissolution of the CGDK and the Hun Sen regime, internationally controlled elections, an interim quadripartite government, and an international peacekeeping force. Increasing pressures from Beijing forced Khieu Samphan back to the bargaining table in December 1988. Although regional negotiations in 1988 witnessed Sihanouk's vehement insistence on adoption of the plan, 1989 began with a more modified Sihanouk vision, no longer asking for a dismantling of the PRK before internationally supervised elections.[35]

JIM II met in Bogor, Indonesia in February 1989, and although tensions were much more relaxed between Khieu Samphan and Hun Sen, no major breakthroughs occurred at the meeting. The meeting ended with a consensus statement which called for the four Cambodian factions to work toward a settlement that provided for "an independent, sovereign, peaceful, neutral, and nonaligned Kampuchea on the basis of self-determination and national reconciliation."[36] It also became

---

[32] Haas, *Genocide by Proxy*, p. 132.
[33] Kiernan, *Genocide and Democracy in Cambodia.*
[34] Haas, *Genocide by Proxy*, p. 133
[35] Chanda, "Civil war in Cambodia?," p. 37.   [36] Haas, *Genocide by Proxy*, p. 134.

apparent that an international control mechanism would be essential if a peace was to be achieved – although, as noted, Vietnam would not accept the idea of a UN peacekeeping operation.[37]

The issue of power-sharing

From the very beginning of the peace process, it was evident that the most divisive element of the negotiation process would be the power-sharing issue. All four Cambodian factions agreed that Cambodia should be an independent country; the crux of the problem lay in the transition to that status.[38] While China, the Khmer Rouge, and the non-communist resistance factions wanted to dismantle the CGDK and the PRK and replace it with a new quadripartite interim government, Hun Sen and Hanoi preferred a quadripartite "council" to arrange elections, while the existing PRK would handle the day-to-day affairs. The PRK essentially refused to cede to other factions an administrative power greater than what was absolutely necessary.

A comprehensive peace in Cambodia required the cooperation among the factions, the regional states, and the international actors. A ceasefire, the necessary precondition to any effective deployment of an international control mechanism for Cambodia, could not be achieved without a level of mutual trust and political will between Hun Sen, Sihanouk, Son Sann, and Khieu Samphan. Sihanouk and some regional states such as Japan, Indonesia, Singapore, and Thailand recognized this, as demonstrated by their support for a quadripartite interim government. Without an agreement on the power-sharing issue, there would be no ceasefire, and a ceasefire agreement was the precondition to the entry of any peacekeeping forces. The peace process moved forward because the USA and ASEAN insisted on a comprehensive settlement, not a piecemeal one, nor one implemented in stages. The USA and ASEAN did not want the UN deployed without an agreement on the future of the PRK because they believed that anything less than a comprehensive settlement would keep the PRK in power.

By 1989 political stalemate within the Cambodian factions and failed attempts at regional diplomacy made it clear that a comprehensive political settlement of any kind could not be reached without a more active involvement of the larger international players. As UNTAC's experiences in Cambodia would later prove, although international actors were necessary to the negotiations, their agreement for a political settlement was not sufficient for a complete resolution. Such extremely

[37] Douglas Pike.   [38] Haas, *Genocide by Proxy*, p. 131.

divisive issues as the role of the UN in civil administration, cantonment and disarmament, human rights, and power-sharing among the four factions delayed the peace process.

In addition to the distrust between the factional parties, observers suggest that a distrust among the factions extended outward to the international community, bringing to the fore serious questions about the willingness of the factions to put their fates in the hands of an international control mechanism.[39] Instead, the peace process moved into its second phase as the international powers pushed ahead. Whether the factions were in fact ready to negotiate a comprehensive settlement at this point is unclear, but the great powers led the way to the first international conference in Paris. The negotiations focused on what outside states viewed to be right for Cambodia at the time, and not necessarily what the Cambodian factions were ready to do. These outside states wanted to resolve the Cambodian problem, and the momentum of peace talks moved the process forward.

Great power diplomacy: the Paris Peace Conferences

With the Vietnamese withdrawal looming in September, the French felt pressured to call an international conference before then; after the troop withdrawal, the Vietnamese would be able to declare the Cambodian problem a purely domestic one, with no further need for international action.[40] Thus the negotiations made their way to France. The French, seeking to re-establish a role in Indochina, expressed their desire to host an international conference on Cambodia. French foreign minister Roland Dumas, along with Ali Alatas, invited the delegations to a peace conference to settle the conflict in Cambodia that was to be held in Paris in July 1989. The international conference was held by France instead of the UN because Vietnam and the PRK claimed that the UN was not an impartial forum, mainly due to the UN's critical view of Vietnam on the issue of Cambodia, and because France's good relations both with the other countries in Southeast Asia and the great powers worked in its favor.[41]

France and Indonesia attempted to forge an agreement before the conference, but achieved only superficial success – the four delegations

---

[39] Kyle A. Horst, Rapporteur's report, "Cambodia's fatigue and its implciations for a slution to the conflict," unpublished report of a conference on Cambodia in Quebec, April 10–13, 1990.

[40] Interview with senior UN official, conducted by Michael W. Doyle, on February 22, 1994.

[41] See Tommy T. B. Koh, "The Paris Conference on Cambodia: a multilateral negotiation that 'failed'," *Negotiation Journal*, vol. 6, no. 1, 1990.

would sit side by side behind a very long nameplate marked "Cambodge." The Cambodian factions were not used to sharing power, but accepted the Conference's mandate, which called for national reconciliation through an "interim quadripartite authority under the leadership of Prince Norodom Sihanouk with ... responsibility of organizing internationally supervised free elections."[42] The term "interim authority" reflected a compromise between the resistance's demand for a coalition government and the PRK's insistence on an advisory council subordinate to it. It soon became evident that an agreement over principle was easier to arrive at than defining what "authority" actually meant. There were also various disputes over the verification of the provisions of the comprehensive settlement.

Hun Sen and Hanoi ended up taking a hardline position during the negotiations in Paris, backtracking from an earlier agreement to consider the inclusion of the Khmer Rouge in an interim government. Tommy Koh, Singapore Ambassador to the USA, commented that the reason for their hardline stance in the midst of the conference was the result of the Vietnamese leadership's decision to make no concessions in Paris.[43] Encouraged by the survival of Najibullah in Kabul (the regime placed in power over Afghanistan by the Soviet Union), Hanoi's leaders believed that Hun Sen could survive against his opponents. Although the French believed there was a 50 percent chance of achieving a breakthrough, they had not counted on the hardening of Hanoi's and Hun Sen's positions.[44] The regional and factional actors simply refused to be subordinated, and a comprehensive plan depended upon resolving the issue of sharing power among the Cambodian factions. The result was a failure to reach an agreement on power-sharing. The USA, steadfast supporters of Sihanouk and the non-communist resistance, came home from Paris disillusioned with the prince's wild swings in temperament and the extent of division among the factions, as revealed during discussions over the issues of genocide and Vietnamese settlers.

Despite the failure of the international conference, major changes in regional and global interests were taking place simultaneously with the struggle to achieve a peace in Cambodia. By 1989, these shifts in regional and global power interests functioned as a catalyst for a final finish to the long and drawn-out negotiation process. The boom in Thailand's economy led Bangkok to view Cambodia, Laos, and Vietnam as potential business opportunities. With the transition to a more market-driven administration, Bangkok's prime minister Chatichai

---

[42] Organization of Work, Text adopted by the Conference at its Fourth Plenary Meeting, on August 1, 1989, Paris Conference on Cambodia doc. CPC/89/4, at p. 3.
[43] See Koh, "The Paris Conference on Cambodia."   [44] Ibid.

Choonhaven saw Thailand's strategic goals in Cambodia as to "turn the battlefield into a marketplace." Vietnam, tired and financially drained from economic isolation and diminishing Soviet support, was ready to shed its Cambodian burden. Indonesia, eager to demonstrate its capabilities as a regional leader – with foreign minister Ali Alatas at the fore – was ready and willing to broker a regional peace. After the Vietnamese occupation of Cambodia in 1979, over a hundred states joined ASEAN in opposing the PRK. With the support of both China and the USA, ASEAN was able to attract international attention and cooperation to isolate Vietnam. Now, after nine years of adamant opposition to Vietnam, ASEAN was ready to support a reconciliation that no longer leaned toward one side of the Cambodian conflict.

Post-Paris I: international diplomacy and an enhanced UN role

Confused, frustrated, and disillusioned about prospects for peace in Cambodia, the West began to rethink its strategy of support for Sihanouk and the non-communist factions. Meanwhile, the Hun Sen regime, the PRK, changed its name to the State of Cambodia (SOC) and began moderating its behavior toward the Cambodians by reinstating Buddhism and permitting forms of capitalism.

Following the failed efforts at a settlement, the factions resumed war in Cambodia. At the end of the first Paris conference, the obstacles remained the same: continued fear of the Khmer Rouge threat and the unwillingness of the regime in Phnom Penh to cede real power to anyone.[45] Nevertheless, pressures for a settlement were growing as changes in regional and great power interests converged in a consensus for an independent and neutral Cambodia. ASEAN's position regarding a political settlement remained firm: the Khmer Rouge must be allowed to participate – at least on an interim basis – because its participation was the key to convincing China to agree to stop aid for Khmer Rouge military activity. But Vietnam continued to reject the KR.[46] Verification of the withdrawal began to emerge as another critical question in the peace process. Members of the Paris conference debated an "international control mechanism" for verifying the withdrawal of foreign forces and monitoring a ceasefire, but Vietnam and the Phnom Penh government resisted the use of the UN, arguing that Cambodia's seat in the UN was taken up by the resistance coalition, which in their view made the UN a biased party.

[45] Rodman, "Supping with devils."
[46] Koh, "The Paris Conference on Cambodia."

With the failure of the (first) Paris conference still fresh in diplomats' minds, all the relevant players retreated back into their own conference rooms, hoping to pursue other avenues for peace, that could better confront the issue of power-sharing. The post-Paris I period of the peace process witnessed a gradual divergence in the patterns of regional and international diplomacy. While the great powers still pursued the comprehensive approach, Cambodian, regional, and outside players began to pursue an incremental one. Japan, eager to shape its image as a global political actor, began to participate actively in the Cambodian problem after the international conference in France.[47] After the failure of the conference, Bangkok's Choonhaven decided that the Phnom Penh regime could no longer be ignored, and began to deal directly with Hun Sen, a strategy which Japan readily agreed to support. Much to Asian frustration, Washington still denied Vietnamese diplomatic recognition, trade, and aid. Displeased with this divergence in strategy, Assistant Secretary of State Richard Solomon flew to Rome to meet secretly with the Thai premier's advisors, but the warning did not have any effect on Thailand's agenda.[48] Washington was concerned that the idea of an immediate ceasefire proposed by the Thais and endorsed by the Japanese could derail the American plan for a comprehensive settlement.

Permanent Five diplomacy

Meanwhile, in an attempt to resolve the power-sharing issue, US Congressman Stephen Solarz pushed the idea of transferring power during a transitional period to the UN, the first germ of the idea of UNTAC. Most players thought that Solarz's suggestion – which had been proposed intermittently over the latter half of the decade – to be "just impossible," and had chosen to ignore it.[49] Nevertheless, extensive discussions between Congressman Solarz and Australian foreign minister Gareth Evans in October 1989 were crucial in shaping Australia's thinking on its solution for Cambodia.[50] The idea of a "UN trusteeship" in Cambodia moved towards the forefront of talks when Evans discussed it in a speech in late 1989. Australia's proposal offered as one option that

---

[47] Nayan Chanda, "Japan's quiet entrance on the diplomatic stage," *The Christian Science Monitor*, June 13, 1990.

[48] Ibid.

[49] Telephone interview with Desaix Anderson, former Chief Deputy Assistant Secretary for Richard Solomon, on March 3, 1994.

[50] "The comprehensive political settlement to the Cambodia conflict: an exercise in cooperating for peace," Senator Gareth Evans's address to a Peacekeeping Seminar at the Australian Defence Force Academy, Canberra, May 2, 1994.

the UN itself assume "direct control of the civil administration during a transitional period enabling elections to be held, a constitution adopted and a new government formed."[51]

The crux of the proposal outlined the UN role as assuming responsibility for the administration of Cambodia during the interim period between the establishment of a new government elected through the process of free and fair elections. Australia recognized that the idea of an enhanced UN role was extremely ambitious. While the UN was experienced in traditional peacekeeping and monitoring elections, UN oversight in civil administration of one of its member states or primary responsibility for organizing and conducting elections was wholly unfamiliar, and quite unprecedented.[52] The initial response to the Australian proposal, however, was less than enthusiastic. But as the idea circulated among the participants of Paris I, it became increasingly clear that the time for an expansive UN role in Cambodia had finally come. Through an "extraordinary feat of diplomatically effective endurance" by Michael Costello, Deputy Secretary of the Department of Foreign Affairs and Trade, a series of thirty meetings with key players from thirteen countries in twenty-one days between December 1989 and January 1990 propelled the successful transition of the Australian "idea" into a fully fledged Australian "initiative."[53] The Permanent Five of the Security Council gathered in New York in January 1990 to explore the possibilities of the "enhanced role" Australia had outlined.

The P5 held six meetings alternatively between Paris and New York, during which two competing visions of a UN role emerged: the Soviet Union backed a plan that saw the UN as the monitor of the two competing governments – CGDK and the SOC – and observer of whether they were violating the right to a "neutral political environment" in which to conduct free and fair elections. The other proposal, supported by China, saw the dismantling of the SOC, and eventually the CGDK, in favor of a direct UN administration of Cambodia. Negotiations continued throughout the spring and into the summer of 1990. A sense of optimism revived the process. Gareth Evans announced confidently that the "most heartening thing ... about the Permanent Five exercise is the very active, cooperative role that China has now been playing in that process."[54] By August 1990, the Permanent Five were able to arrive at a compromise: the UN would exercise "direct control"

---

[51] Gareth Evans, *Cooperating for Peace: The Global Agenda for the 1990s and Beyond* (St. Leonards: Allen and Unwin, 1993).

[52] Koh, "The Paris Conference on Cambodia."

[53] Evans, "The comprehensive political settlement to the Cambodia conflict."

[54] News conference with Australian foreign minister Gareth Evans, August 28, 1990.

over the five areas of civilian administration – foreign affairs, defense, security, information, and finance – critical to a "neutral political environment" for a free and fair elections, as well as to supervise the other functions of the two governments.[55]

The enhanced UN role required the establishment of a transitional authority with a military component to carry out the peacekeeping aspects of the comprehensive political settlement, as well as the organization and conduct of free and fair elections on the basis of genuine and verified voter registration lists of Cambodian citizens. The Framework Document would become the blueprint for the peace accord signed fourteen months later.[56] As stated in the document signed by the Permanent Five, "the basic principle behind the Permanent Five's approach was to enable the Cambodian people to determine their own political future through free and fair elections organized and conducted by the UN in a neutral political environment with full respect for the national sovereignty of Cambodia." To this end, the Permanent Five proposed that a Supreme National Council be formed as the "unique legitimate body and source of authority in Cambodia during the transitional period . . . the embodiment of the independence, sovereignty and unity of Cambodia."[57] It would represent Cambodia externally and occupy the UN seat, but its real role was more that of a "symbolic" entity lending legitimacy to the practical authority that would belong to the UN.

Although the Khmer Rouge would have been satisfied with no Supreme National Council if the SOC were really dismantled, some observers also claim the SNC was a body created to give the Khmer Rouge an incentive to stay in the process; in effect, it was not intended to have any power.[58] There was hope, however, that the factions would begin to cooperate. The Permanent Five asked Indonesia and France to persuade the factions to accept the framework agreement and to form the Supreme National Council. The views of the Council would bind UNTAC when its members reached "consensus," if their advice was consistent with the objectives of the peace plan as determined by UNTAC. Sihanouk would have preferred to cede to the UN transitional

---

[55] UNSC Framework docs. A/45/472-S/21689 (1990).

[56] The Framework Document's proposed that the indispensable requirements for a comprehensive political settlement in Cambodia consisted of a transitional arrangement regarding the interim administration of Cambodia, military arrangements during this interim period, elections under UN auspices, human rights protection, and international guarantees to an independent and neutral Cambodia.

[57] Evans, "The comprehensive political settlement to the Cambodia conflict."

[58] Views from a seminar given by Stephen P. Marks, entitled "Cambodia: a new constitution and chances for democracy," March 8, 1994, The Woodrow Wilson School, Princeton University.

authority only "non-political and non-legislative public services, and technical administrative services," but Ali Alatas and French minister Roland Dumas implored the Cambodian factions to accept the diminished role of the Supreme National Council.[59] Dumas made it clear to the warring factions that the peace plan "can be improved, but it cannot be put into question."[60]

The main political pressure during this portion of the peacemaking process was designed to keep the Khmer Rouge and Hun Sen engaged and actively participating in the negotiations.[61] The cooperation of Beijing and Moscow was crucial to negotiations; both agreed to refuse funds and material assistance to the resistance groups who would have refused to come to the bargaining table in search of a compromise as long as supplies were still forthcoming.

Regional negotiations define the SNC and lead to Paris II

On June 5, 1990, Sihanouk, Hun Sen, and Son Sann, the leader of the KPNLF, met in Tokyo to discuss Sihanouk's own version of a plan for peace. Khieu Samphan boycotted the meeting. While there, the factional leaders agreed to a voluntary self-restraint on the use of force, cessation of armed hostilities, the establishment of the Supreme National Council, and the freezing of all military actions and forces.[62] An impasse was reached, however, over the composition of the Council. The Phnom Penh government proposed that Sihanouk become its chairman and Hun Sen the vice-chairman, with twelve places on the Council to be shared equally between the Hun Sen regime and the tripartite coalition, which meant that the Khmer Rouge would be given two seats.[63] Sihanouk's peace initiative was stalled, however, when the Khmer Rouge refused to abide by any agreement it had not signed. The failure of the Tokyo meeting clearly indicated that Sihanouk would make no progress without the cooperation of the Khmer Rouge and the full endorsement of Beijing.

The chief impediment to the formation of the Supreme National Council was the inability of the factions to agree on its composition. The Permanent Five, Australia and Indonesia believed strongly that the Framework Document had only to wait for the creation of the Council before it could be put effectively to test, so the pressure on the factions

---

[59] Kiernan, *Gemocide and Democrarcy in Cambodia*, p. 38.
[60] *Washington Post*, December 22, 1990.   [61] Ibid.
[62] Paeng-Meth Abdulgaffar, "The United Nations peace plan, the Cambodian conflict, and the future of Cambodia," *Contemporary Southeast Asia*, vol. 14, no. 1, 1992.
[63] Michael Leifer, "Power-sharing and peacemaking in Cambodia?," *SAIS Review*, vol. 12, 1992, pp. 139–53.

to resolve the membership issue soon became formidable. The main issues which plagued the creation of the Council were roles on it for Sihanouk and Hun Sen, as well as its size. The second issue would not be resolved until the summer of 1991.

In September 1990 the factions endorsed the creation of the Supreme National Council, but only to the extent that it was as a part of the wider framework agreement crafted by the Permanent Five. Composed of "indispensable requirements" for a comprehensive political settlement, the agreement defined the requisites for peace as transitional arrangements regarding the administration of Cambodia during the pre-election period, military arrangements during the transitional period, elections under UN auspices, protection of human rights, and international guarantees.[64] The proposed framework for Supreme National Council membership was a clear example of compromise in action. It ensured, on the one hand, that the Phnom Penh government would not be forced into a minority position by allocating it half the votes. But because all Supreme National Council decisions were to be made by consensus, the Khmer Rouge won veto power, a provision which was secured by China's muscle during negotiations. In addition, the agreement omitted any reference to genocide, despite demands from Hun Sen's regime that it contain at least implicit criticism of the policies of Pol Pot.[65]

Unfortunately, negotiations crumbled shortly after the agreement was reached when the factions reached an impasse in discussions over the chairmanship of the Council, a delay which stymied the peace process for the next three months. At the first meeting of the Council in Bangkok, talks collapsed over what concessions would be made to the regime in Phnom Penh if Sihanouk were allowed to head the panel. Prospects for peace began to diminish, and minor as the disputes seemed to be, Australian foreign minister Gareth Evans stated that although a solution seemed near at hand, "the window of opportunity could close." Then in late September, Sihanouk proposed a solution to the deadlock. Instead of the original plan to set up a council of twelve members – six from the Phnom Penh regime, and two each from FUNCINPEC, KPNLF, and the Khmer Rouge – Sihanouk proposed that he resign from FUNCINPEC in order to become chairman of the Supreme National Council. Almost everyone was pleased with the new idea, though obtaining the Khmer Rouge's agreement required intense pressure from Beijing.

At this point in the peace process, the Hun Sen regime was the most

[64] "Big Five reach final agreement on framework for settlement," *United Nations Chronicle*, vol. 27, no. 4, 1990, p. 25.
[65] Ross, "China and the Cambodian peace process," pp. 1170–85.

difficult faction to win over to any UN plan because it had not yet reconciled itself to negotiating away its position on the ground, having achieved hard-won territorial control over the past decade. The regime especially feared negotiating itself into a situation which provided a window of opportunity for the Khmer Rouge to return to power. In essence, the disagreement over Council membership was more concerned with the balance of future power in Cambodia, and in this regard the Phnom Penh government, which controlled almost all Cambodia, felt it had much more to lose than did the Khmer Rouge. Meanwhile, the Khmer Rouge's begrudging, yet apparent, cooperation with the Phnom Penh regime owed much to Beijing's pressure on the PDK; Beijing apparently viewed the UN plan as the most likely strategy to return the Khmer Rouge to some kind of power.[66]

Prodding the factions, outside states backed the Permanent Five's plan, which was endorsed by the Security Council in August 1990. Negotiations within the Supreme National Council continued to discuss aspects of the peace plan well into 1991. As chairman of the Council, Sihanouk was acting in an increasingly autonomous manner, a clear indication that Beijing no longer sought to "rein in" the prince. Council meetings in Beijing and Pattaya were important steps in the peace process; they marked the effective emergence of the Council and a new flexibility in Beijing's policy, which reflected the increasing value that the Chinese placed in a comprehensive settlement.

Beijing's invitation to Hun Sen to attend the Supreme National Council meeting also marked the first Chinese recognition of the state of Cambodia. Hun Sen, too, was pleased with the new attitude. As one reporter explained, "the success of the Supreme National Council meeting in Peking had given great confidence to the Cambodian people in solving the issue with the realization that the PRC has reached the stage of recognizing the State of Cambodia as one among the parties to the conflict and one which should take part in solving the problem."[67] A combination of factors – better relations with Vietnam, the costs of being associated with the Khmer Rouge and a desire to become the recognized regional leader – contributed to China's more active role. However, practical power-sharing arrangements were still not resolved, as the Phnom Penh government still insisted that it retain its constitutional position until general elections had took place. Critical disagreements, moreover, loomed over how to demobilize military forces as well

---

[66] Stephanie Gray, "Cambodia sets out on a road to peace," *Financial Times*, July 9, 1991.
[67] "Hun Sen's message on Peking SNC Meeting," BBC, *Summary of World Broadcasts*, July 25, 1991.

as how to define the UN's administrative role during the interim period.[68]

In late August 1991, at another Council session held in Pattaya, the factions agreed to reduce their forces by 70 percent and to regroup the remainder in cantonments supervised by the United Nations.[69] Deadlock occurred, however, when the Khmer Rouge demanded that the Phnom Penh government include its paramilitary police as part of the forces which were to be reduced by 70 percent. The impasse stalled the peace process yet again, but more importantly, it revealed to negotiators the fundamental distrust between the two factions. Despite the superficial successes up until this point, the factions still had a deep suspicion of each other which had dissipated little since the beginning of talks. While the Phnom Penh government wanted to keep as many of their forces as they could intact to limit the possibility of the Khmer Rouge seizing power, the Khmer Rouge sought maximum disarmament because this would mean its forces could be monitored much less readily than the Phnom Penh forces.[70] Arguments and skepticism ensued as to the UN's ability to verify demobilization of troops, since as many as 40,000 Khmer Rouge guerrilla soldiers were rumored to be hidden in the jungles of Cambodia.[71]

Negotiations which had ended in August 1991 began again in September, when the Supreme National Council represented Cambodia at the annual session of the United Nations General Assembly. As Hun Sen told one interviewer, "we expect to sign the peace agreement in the very near future."[72] All issues which stood in the way of a settlement appeared to have been solved. Nevertheless, Hun Sen expressed continued apprehension about the Khmer Rouge's role and skepticism over the demobilization arrangements negotiated in the accords. Members of the Permanent Five also felt uneasy about the plan for 70 percent demobilization, but sought to make them more specific and verifiable.[73] As the end of the peace process drew closer, diplomats felt that the crucial breakthrough in negotiations resulted from the change in

[68]   Chanda, "Civil war in Cambodia."
[69]   Final Communiqué of the Meeting of the Supreme National Council of Cambodia, Pattaya, August 29, 1991.
[70]   Chanda, "Civil war in Cambodia."
[71]   International Institute for Strategic Studies (IISS), *The Military Balance* (London: Brassey's, 1990).
[72]   Don Oberdorfer and Michael Getler, *Washington Post*, September 20, 1991.
[73]   Many of the views expressed in this portion of the chapter concerning relations between China and the Soviet Union come from Frederick Z. Brown's working paper presented at the International Peace Academy on April 10–13, 1990. The workshop was titled "Cambodia beyond impasse: prospects for a settlement," and the paper is titled "What are the interests of the external parties?"

China's attitude. It had become evident that the long-time patron of the Khmer Rouge no longer favored the faction over a comprehensive political settlement and an end to the Cambodian conflict. After suffering more than two decades of civil war and more than a million deaths from starvation and massacre,[74] Cambodia, at last, began to experience the prospect of peace.

The comprehensive political settlement agreement for Cambodia was signed on October 23, 1991, by eighteen nations and the Supreme National Council. Minister Ali Alatas proclaimed that "while the negotiating process has indeed been arduous and occasionally punctuated by misunderstandings and temporary setbacks, it has again confirmed the fundamental requirements of negotiation in the settlement of international disputes and of cooperation between the major powers and the countries of the region in the peaceful resolution of regional conflicts."[75] Furthermore, the peace process was viewed as yet another reflection of the "renewed confidence of the international community in the irreplaceable value of the United Nations as the unique, multilateral instrument in resolving the major issues of our time."[76]

A shifting context shapes negotiations

International realignments helped move the peace process forward by finally making it possible for active and cooperative involvement of the three key players, China, the Soviet Union, and the USA. In September 1989, Vietnam completed its troop withdrawal from Cambodia as the end of Soviet aid helped lead the Vietnamese politburo to conclude that the "acceptable existence of shared poverty" no longer justified the cost of maintaining forces in Cambodia.[77] Moreover, Vietnam finally recognized that China's interests in Southeast Asia could not be ignored, making the withdrawal from Cambodia into Hanoi's first attempt at Sino–Vietnamese rapprochement.[78]

Quoting from the great Chinese poet Lu Xun – "For all disasters the brotherhood has remained, a smile at meeting and enmity is banished"

---

[74] Kiernan, "Inclusion of the Khmer Rouge," *Genocide and Democracy in Cambodia*, p. 192.

[75] Agence France Presse, "Pérez de Cuéllar calls for international aid for Cambodia," October 23, 1991.

[76] Ibid.

[77] Nguyen Co Thach's phrase noted in Milton Osborne, "Return to centre stage," in *Sihanouk: Prince of Darkness, Prince of Light* (Honolulu, HI: University of Hawaii Press, 1994), p. 255.

[78] Ibid.

– Li Peng acknowledged China's hopes for new and improved relations with Vietnam. The thaw in relations between Beijing and Hanoi propelled the Cambodian peace process forward. China's policy toward Hanoi since the late 1970s had always been zero sum: it would oppose any policy that permitted Vietnam to grow stronger.[79] Partially as a result of the Sino–Soviet rapprochement that began in 1982, Beijing no longer sought to see the Vietnamese "bleed white."

Beyond changing the Sino–Soviet relationship, China had its own interests for speeding up the peace process in Cambodia. China's decision to make economic modernization a top priority led Beijing to decide that regional stability was crucial. Cross-border trade with Vietnam began to become lucrative toward the late 1980s, and normalizing relations could only improve it further. Likewise, China's extremely close security relationship with Thailand also helped to moderate Beijing's hard line toward Cambodia.[80] During the 1980s, China and Thailand developed high-level military exchanges and Thailand increased its arms purchases from China. During the decade after the Vietnamese occupation of Cambodia, Thailand served as a crucial intermediary for shipments of food, supplies, and military goods from China to the Khmer Rouge camps along the Cambodian–Thai border. By 1989, Vietnam's willingness to leave Cambodia and Thailand's willingness to join the peace process left China unable to justify its inflexibility.

As the post-Cold War era left East Asia free from superpower control, China also saw an opportunity to build its image as the legitimate regional leader. China sought to be seen as a cooperative great power by the international community, a reputation to which Beijing desperately aspired, especially after the Communist party's ruthless use of force in Tiananmen Square in 1989. Beijing also realized that its long association with the bloodstained history of the Khmer Rouge dragged down its efforts to change China's international reputation.

By the mid-1980s, both China and the Soviet Union realized that the "irritability quotient" of the Cambodian issue needed to be eliminated.[81] While both sides desperately desired a summit, Cambodia, along with Afghanistan and Sino–Soviet border issues, stood as one of the main obstacles to bilateral détente. China would agree to a summit only on the condition that it received Soviet assurance of a fixed date for Vietnam's withdrawal from Cambodia. The Soviets were expected to make good on the condition, and they delivered. In April 1989, Vietnam announced its unilateral decision to withdraw from Cambodia by

[79] Ibid.   [80] Porter, "Cambodia: Sihanouk's initiative," p. 824.
[81] See note 73.

September. In May Gorbachev and Deng Xiaoping conducted their long-desired summit.

Soviet policy in Indochina was shaped by several factors: rapprochement with Beijing, domestic preoccupation due to *perestroika*, and relations with Vietnam. Rapprochement with Beijing led the Soviet Union to turn a more benign face toward ASEAN and the rest of non-communist Asia. In addition, Gorbachev's overriding concerns with domestic *perestroika*, arms control agreements with the United States, and the developments in Eastern Europe greatly reduced the priority given to the question of Cambodia. The Soviet Union still desired to maintain a good relationship with Vietnam, despite the removal of older Soviet aircraft from Cam Ranh Bay and rapidly diminishing aid. The Soviet Union found its reputation as the sole supporter of Vietnam's imposed regime in Cambodia increasingly burdensome. At the end of the day, the Soviet Union recognized that it still had an investment in the Hun Sen regime, and it wanted to maximize the chances of survival for the regime in Phnom Penh's. Fortunately, the UN peace process provided both Vietnam and the Soviet Union with a graceful exit from their awkward position *vis-à-vis* Phnom Penh. Not surprisingly, both ultimately gave their full support to UN involvement.

The United States has long been a supporter of an independent Southeast Asia. The USA was opposed to normal relations with Hanoi until the Vietnamese forces withdrew from Cambodia. The Bush administration continued Reagan's regional policies, but with a less ideological commitment to the non-communist resistance groups.[82] By the end of the 1980s, the United States wanted to stay as far away from an active role in Southeast Asia as possible. But the disastrous outcome of the Paris conference, when Sihanouk shocked delegates by ending a ranting and confusing speech with the words "Je suis pour le génocide!" led US policy-makers to rethink their strategy of "gambling" on Sihanouk. In the late summer of 1989, Secretary of State James Baker began to realize that the peace process required an additional dose of outside diplomacy. At the annual US–ASEAN breakfast in Washington, Baker proposed a more active Permanent Five presence in the negotiations in order to move the peace process forward, a suggestion that met with ASEAN's full assent.[83]

A more active role for the United States in the Cambodian issue promoted a series of goals and interests.[84] First, domestic political

---

[82] Nayan, "Civil war in Cambodia," p. 45.

[83] Interview with Assistant Secretary Richard Solomon, by Michael Doyle, March 1, 1994.

[84] The following points in this paragraph were made by Richard Solomon, who was the

pressures responding to claims that the USA was supplying the Khmer Rouge with covert aid led to charges that US policy was "indifferent to genocide."[85] Second, there was a fear among experts that if fighting resumed after the failure of Paris I, it would inevitably spread. A confrontation between Hun Sen's regime and the Khmer Rouge could, according to Assistant Secretary Richard Solomon, easily get out of control. It was crucial for the USA to avoid this by obtaining a say in the negotiations. An expansion of civil war would have left the USA with two equally poor options with which to side: Vietnamese conquest (Phnom Penh) or genocide (the CGDK, with its Khmer Rouge). Memory of the Vietnam war made the US extremely reluctant to turn the Cambodian problem into "an American problem." Lastly, the USA realized that a multilateral process, such as a UN transitional authority, could help keep "the whole issue off the [foreign policy] agenda" and leave room for more pressing concerns like the disintegration of the Soviet Union and German reunification.

Joining with China and the Soviet Union, the USA, France and the UK were able to move negotiations ahead beginning about 1990. The UK and France remained concerned about the financial costs of the emerging transitional authority in Cambodia, and the United States feared that the UN was biting off more than it could chew. But the process took on a momentum of its own. As the Framework Document emerged in the late summer of 1990, the superpowers were determined to make it stick, and with the help of France and Indonesia, the co-chairmen of the first Paris Conference proceeded to sell the deal to the still warring factions.

Lessons learned from the Cambodian negotiating process

The lengthy process of negotiating a peace in Cambodia reveals important lessons for future UN peacemaking activities. First, unlike the involved UN role in the negotiations for achieving a peace in El Salvador, the Secretary-General's role in Cambodia was limited. Because two broad levels of the peace process were occurring simultaneously, and because the Cambodia problem was linked to a myriad of actors, the Secretary-General was unable to enjoy the autonomy he took advantage of in the Salvadoran negotiations. He was effective, however, at supporting both regional and international mechanisms. The UN had

lead US diplomat at the Paris Peace Negotiations, in an interview with Michael Doyle conducted March 1, 1994.
[85] Rodman, "Supping with devils."

been discussing a comprehensive peace settlement since the Vietnamese invasion, but the geopolitical climate was not yet ready for a settlement in Cambodia. The interests of the great powers did not "converge" enough to provide the geopolitical support which peacekeeping requires until the end of the 1980s.

Second, while the entire El Salvadoran peacemaking process was UN sponsored and mediated, there was no comparably active UN role in Cambodia's peacemaking process. Because the SOC party believed that the problem was mainly an internal one, and because it viewed the UN as a partial organization, it refused to allow the UN any significant role as a mediator. The UN was on the record as early as 1979 as anti-Vietnam and anti-PRK, and suspicions did not end until the USA and ASEAN demonstrated flexibility in 1990. In addition, Australia and the Permanent Five were the only actors in a position to promote so controversial and sovereignty-redefining an idea as UNTAC – neither the UN nor Ahmed could do it without their support. Furthermore, the backing of factions by external powers like the USA, the Soviet Union, and China until well into the negotiation process allowed the factions to remain belligerent and prolong hopes that "victory" for each party was near, if they held out at the table long enough. While the success of the negotiations in El Salvador had much to do with the "will of both parties to finally end the war," the four factions in Cambodia expressed their political will for peace only under immense pressure from the great powers and regional actors. The regional actors had economic incentives to see Cambodia achieve peace so that Southeast Asia could move forward toward economic prosperity. The superpowers had equivalent strategic incentives to improve relations and cut off costly clients.

Third, the successful conclusion of the Cambodian peacemaking process confirms the idea of "middle power diplomacy," that is, effective coalition building with "like-minded" countries to achieve a selected, realistic goal.[86] Although the Australian plan was relatively simple in concept, it required an immense amount of diplomatic effort to convince countries to see it as a way to circumvent the impasse on power-sharing. Australia's geopolitical position as a country with no immediate interests to protect and no "major power baggage," proved useful to lending credibility to the idea of an enhanced UN role.

Fourth, an important concluding lesson of the peacemaking process is the impact of "Cambodia fatigue," experienced not only by the international players, but also among the intra-Cambodian factions.[87] Sheer exhaustion, coupled with a reduction of supplies to the factions,

[86] See Gareth Evans's address.   [87] Brown, "Cambodia beyond impasse."

improved the spirit of compromise at the negotiating table. But were the concessions made at the bargaining table solid? If the compromises are artificial – the result of external pressure – the foundations of post-conflict peacebuilding initiatives are put in jeopardy. When the UN peacekeepers leave the country, superficial progress may become evident in the resumption of fighting.

Peacemaking in Cambodia, whether it is hailed for its successes or criticized for its failures, must still be studied and understood as a process. Mechanisms were built in order to resolve the fragile, complex issues which intertwined and often conflicted with one another. Although the peacemaking process has ended, Cambodia faces incredible challenges with regard to the administrative and military aspects of peacekeeping. In order for the transition from peacemaking to peacekeeping to occur smoothly, Cambodia must not forget that its fragile peace was founded upon a merging of interests between the factions, the regional countries, and the international players. While shifting alliances in the political arena are difficult to predict, the survival of Cambodia depends on its ability to insure that the four factions find the political will for maintaining peace. Power-sharing continues to be the missing link for Cambodia's long-term stability.

4   The Cambodian Settlement Agreements

Nishkala Suntharalingam

Introduction

The Cambodian Settlement Agreements[1] of 1991 provided a revolutionary blueprint for a comprehensive settlement to the twenty-year war in Cambodia, a conflict with both internal and international dimensions.[2] These agreements also gave the United Nations (UN) a unique role in the settlement and management of such conflicts. Notable aspects of the Agreements include: the comprehensiveness of the settlement plan; recognition of a Supreme National Council as a vehicle for "enshrining" the sovereignty, independence, and unity of Cambodia during the transition period; and the unprecedented role of the UN in the settlement process.

The Agreements launched the UN into a new and comprehensive role that involved not only peacemaking and peacekeeping, but also "peace-

---

The views expressed here are entirely those of the author and should not be attributed in any manner to the United Nations.

[1]   The Agreements are formally called The Agreements on a Comprehensive Political Settlement of the Cambodian Conflict, October 23, 1991, UN doc. A/46/608–S/23177; 31 ILM 183 (1992). They were signed by the Supreme National Council, as the unique and legitimate authority of the state of Cambodia, and eighteen other nations in the presence of the UN Secretary-General, Mr. Javier Pérez de Cuéllar, in Paris. The eighteen countries were Australia, Brunei Darussalam, Canada, the People's Republic of China, the French Republic, the Republic of India, the Republic of Indonesia, Japan, the Lao People's Democratic Republic, Malaysia, the Republic of Philippines, the Republic of Singapore, the Kingdom of Thailand, the Union of Soviet Socialist Republics, the United Kingdom of Great Britain and Northern Ireland, the United States of America, and the Socialist Republic of Viet Nam.

[2]   For insightful accounts of Cambodia's recent tragic history see inter alia Elizabeth Becker, *When the War was Over: The Voices of Cambodia's Revolution and its People* (New York: Simon and Schuster, 1986); Ben Kiernan, *How Pol Pot Came to Power* (London: Verso, 1985); Michael Haas, *Genocide by Proxy: Cambodian Pawn on a Superpower Chessboard* (New York: Praeger, 1991), especially pp. 211–82, and David Chandler, *The Tragedy of Cambodian History: Politics War and Revolution since 1945* (New Haven, Conn.: Yale University Press, 1992).

building."[3] The parties agreed to an active UN role not only in facilitating a ceasefire and the disarming of the factions – the traditional terrain of UN peacekeeping – but also to a major UN role in the maintenance of law and order, the repatriation of refugees, the promotion of human rights and principles for a new constitution, the supervision and control of certain aspects of the governmental administrative machinery, and most significantly, the organization, conduct, and monitoring of elections.

The significance of the Agreements lay in the international community charging the UN – for the first time in its history – with the political and economic restructuring of a member state, through which the parties would then (it was planned) institutionalize their reconciliation. The strategy of peace embodied in the Cambodian Settlement Agreements lay in the UN's stepping in to help rebuild state legitimacy, the collapse of which had helped give rise to the conflict. The Agreements provided the legal framework for the realization of this ambitious objective.

This chapter will describe and analyze the legal framework of the Cambodian Settlement Agreements. It will focus more specifically on the issue of sovereignty in the context of the Supreme National Council, as well as key aspects of the role of the UN during the transition period. The UN operation in Cambodia was perceived at its onset as providing great possibilities for the UN to carve out a new role for itself in the post-Cold War period. The UN mandate, however, did not always seem to take advantage of the scope provided for in the Agreements.

The structure of the Cambodia Settlement Agreements

The Paris Conference that began in 1989 culminated on October 23, 1991 with the signing of four documents designed to bring an end to the conflict in Cambodia under the auspices of the UN. The documents consisted of the Agreement on a Comprehensive Political Settlement of the Cambodian Conflict;[4] the Agreement concerning the Sovereignty, Independence, Territorial Integrity, Inviolability, and Neutrality and National Unity of Cambodia;[5] the Declaration on the Rehabilitation and

---

[3] Boutros Boutros-Ghali, *An Agenda for Peace* (New York: United Nations, second edition, 1995), paras. 55–60.

[4] October 23, 1991, UN doc. A/46/608-S/23177; 31 ILM 183 (1992) (hereinafter Paris Agreements).

[5] October 23, 1991, UN doc. A/46/608-S/23177; 31 ILM 200 (1992) (hereinafter Guarantees Agreement).

Reconstruction of Cambodia;[6] and the Final Act of the Paris Conference on Cambodia.[7] The two Agreements have treaty status,[8] and therefore impose binding obligations on states that are parties to them and are enforceable under international law. The Declaration and the Final Act, on the other hand, are non-binding statements by the signatories for reconstruction assistance and on a series of outstanding matters respectively. The structure of each of these instruments will be briefly outlined below.

The Agreement on a Comprehensive Political Settlement of the Cambodia Conflict

The Agreement on a Comprehensive Political Settlement of the Cambodia Conflict (Paris Agreement) was the principal feature of the Cambodian Settlement Agreements (all four of which are formally referred to by this same name). It set up the arrangements for the transitional period, the framework for a new government, as well as the reconstruction and rehabilitation of Cambodia. The parties to the Agreement created two institutions in order to implement the peace: the Supreme National Council and the United Nations Transitional Authority in Cambodia (UNTAC).[9] The Agreement defined a transitional period running from the entry into force of the Agreement to the time when an elected constituent assembly established a new sovereign government of Cambodia (anticipated at the signing of the agreement to occur around the end of August 1993).[10] The scope and implications of this agreement will be examined in greater detail later in this chapter.

The "Guarantees Agreement"

The second agreement popularly referred to as the Guarantees Agreement sets forth the legal obligations of Cambodia and the other states of

---

[6] October 23, 1991, UN doc. A/46/608-S/23177; 31 ILM 203 (1992) (hereinafter Declaration).

[7] October 23, 1991, UN doc. A/46/608-S/23177; 31 ILM 180 (1992) (hereinafter Final Act).

[8] Vienna Convention on the Law of Treaties, May 23, 1969, arts. 2(1), 26; 1155 UNTS 331, 333, 339, reprinted in 8 ILM 679 (1969).

[9] See Steven Ratner, "The Cambodia Settlement Agreements," *American Journal of International Law*, vol. 87, 1993 and his "The United Nations' role in Cambodia: a model for resolution of internal conflicts?" in Lori Fisler Damrosch (ed.), *Enforcing Peace: Collective Intervention in Internal Conflicts* (New York: Council on Foreign Relations, 1993).

[10] The new Cambodian government was created when the constituent assembly elected in conformity with the Agreement approved the new Cambodian constitution and transformed itself into a legislative assembly in September 1993.

the Paris Conference, after the transitional period. It established a series of legal commitments which, if observed uniformly by all the parties, would insure the sovereignty, territorial integrity, neutrality, and national unity of Cambodia. The Guarantees Agreement included its own enforcement provisions. These required the parties, in the event of a threat or a violation of Cambodia's sovereignty, independence, territorial integrity, neutrality, or unity "to consult immediately with a view to adopting appropriate steps to insure respect for these commitments and resolving any such commitments through peaceful means." In the event of serious violations of human rights in Cambodia, the parties agreed to call upon the competent organs of the UN to take the necessary steps for the prevention and suppression of such violations.

The Declaration on Rehabilitation and Reconstruction

Thirteen principles for the rehabilitation and reconstruction of Cambodia were identified in the Declaration. Accordingly, the principal responsibility for defining Cambodia's reconstruction needs lay with the elected government; foreigners were not to impose a development strategy on the country. The Declaration specified that reconstruction "should promote Cambodian entrepreneurship and make use of the private sector," as well as involve regional and non-governmental organizations. Particular attention was to be given to access to food, health, housing, education, the transport network, and the restoration of Cambodia's basic infrastructure and public utilities. Finally, the Declaration called for the creation of an International Committee on the Reconstruction of Cambodia to "harmonize and monitor the contributions that will be made by the international community."[11]

The Final Act of the Paris Conference on Cambodia

The Final Act outlined the history of the Paris Conference. It contained a request to take measures to foster implementation of the settlement, and included an invitation to states that had not participated in the

[11] Shortly after the establishment of UNTAC in Cambodia, a Technical Advisory Committee of the Supreme National Council was set up under the chairmanship of the UNTAC Director of Rehabilitation in order to facilitate the approval of projects by the Cambodian parties. At the Ministerial Conference on the Rehabilitation and Reconstruction of Cambodia, held in Tokyo in June 1992, the international community pledged nearly $800 million in aid to Cambodia. By the end of January 1993, over forty projects representing some $360 million had been approved by the Council. However, the actual level of disbursements by early 1993 stood at no more than $95 million, according to the Secretary-General.

conference to become party to the two Agreements.[12] The parties agreed to cooperate fully in implementing the settlement and in promoting and encouraging respect for human rights in Cambodia.

Sovereignty and the Supreme National Council

One of the innovative features of the Cambodian Peace Process was the creation of the Supreme National Council as the modality for enshrining the legal sovereignty of Cambodia. This mechanism not only provided the framework by which the UN could conduct, with the consent of the Cambodian factions, a peace operation in that country, but also created, as a byproduct, a forum in which the Cambodian factions could start the process of national reconciliation, during the transitional period.

The collapse of centralized authority in Cambodia in the late 1970s[13] and conflicting claims to sovereignty between the Coalition Government of Democratic Kampuchea (CGDK) and the Hun Sen government (State of Cambodia faction – SOC) created problems of recognition for the international community. While the UN recognized the CGDK as the legal government of Cambodia, it was the SOC that controlled more than 80 percent of the country. In the early phase of the peace negotiation process, the Cambodian factions flatly rejected the proposal that national reconciliation be achieved through an interim quadripartite government.[14] As an alternative to "power-sharing" Prince Sihanouk, in consultation with Australian foreign minister Gareth Evans, among others, proposed that since the parties could not trust each other enough to rule together, the UN take over the administration of Cambodia during the period between a political settlement and the outcome of free, democratic elections.[15]

---

[12] Portugal and The Netherlands subsequently acceded to the Agreements (conversation with a member of the UN Treaty Division).

[13] The Vietnamese invasion of Cambodia and the installation of the Hun Sen regime in 1978–9 gave rise to a guerrilla movement of the three major resistance groups: Prince Sihanouk's party, National Union Front for an Independent, Neutral, Peaceful and Cooperative Cambodia (FUNCINPEC), Son Sann's Khmer People's National Liberation Front (KPNLF), and the Party of Democratic Kampuchea (PDK or the Khmer Rouge). Each of the four, including the Heng Samrin (later Hun Sen) regime itself, contested the claims of the others to legitimate authority over Cambodia. In 1982, at the urging of the Association of Southeast Asian Nations (ASEAN) and China, the three groups opposing the Hun Sen regime formed the Coalition Government of Democratic Kampuchea (CGDK), headed by Prince Norodom Sihanouk.

[14] See Tommy T. B. Koh, "The Paris Conference on Cambodia: a multilateral negotiation that 'failed'," *Negotiation Journal*, vol. 6, no. 1, 1990, pp. 81–7.

[15] Stephen Solarz, "Cambodia and the international community," *Foreign Affairs*, vol. 69, no. 2, 1990, pp. 99–115; see also Gerald Helman and Steven Ratner, "Saving failed states," *Foreign Policy*, vol. 89, 1992–3, pp. 3–20.

However, since article 78 of the UN Charter[16] precludes the UN from adopting a trusteeship role over a member state, it was apparent that a special arrangement would be required to vest Cambodian national sovereignty during the transitional period, while the UN administered Cambodia. A legitimate sovereign entity had to delegate the required authority to the UN to indicate Cambodia's consent to the operation, enabling the UN to conduct an operation under generally accepted interpretations of the Charter as well as established practices and principles of peacekeeping. Alternatively the Security Council could have approved enforcement action under chapter VII, to restore peace and security to Southeast Asia.[17] This option never received any serious consideration owing to the Security Council's unwillingness to impose a large UN presence on Cambodia without any agreement between the factions.

During the course of the negotiations several options were suggested ranging from a revolutionary, trusteeship-like authority to be administered by the UN in Cambodia to the "Sihanouk plan" which, unlike the trusteeship model, cast the UN in a purely logistical and technical role.[18] The model finally settled upon by the Cambodian parties and the international community[19] on September 10, 1990 was the Supreme National Council. The Council was composed of representatives of the four main factions and was to serve as the "unique and legitimate body and source of authority in which throughout the transitional period, the sovereignty, independence and unity of Cambodia are enshrined."[20] In addition to Prince Sihanouk, the Council had eleven members,[21] six

---

[16] Article 78 of the Charter provides that: "The trusteeship system shall not apply to territories which have become Members of the United Nations, relationship among which shall be based on respect for the principle of sovereign equality."

[17] Article 2(7) of the Charter acts as a barrier against intervention or involvement by the UN in the domestic matters of a member state, except when authorized as a chapter VII action. See Olara A. Otunnu, "Maintaining broad legitimacy for United Nations action," in *Keeping the Peace in the Post-Cold War Era: Strengthening Mulitlateral Peacekeeping* (New York: The Trilateral Commission, 1993), at pp. 74–80 for a discussion of the broadening scope of "permissible" intervention by the UN.

[18] See Michael W. Doyle, "Lessons from Cambodia," in *The United Nations, Peacekeeping, and US Policy in the Post-Cold War World* (Queenstown, Md.: The Aspen Institute, 1994) for a discussion of these options; see also Sina Than, "Cambodia 1990: towards a peaceful solution?," *Southeast Asian Affairs* (Institute of South East Asian Studies, 1991), pp. 83–104, for a discussion of the negotiation process.

[19] The efforts of the international community were at this time channeled by the five permanent members of the UN Security Council, and an additional five, being Australia, Canada, Indonesia (which served as co-president of the Paris Conference along with France), Japan and Thailand.

[20] S/21732 (September 10, 1990), the Jakarta communiqu concerning the formation of the Supreme National Council.

[21] Later this was increased to thirteen to compensate for Sihanouk's presence as president and to maintain a balance of six members from SOC and six from the CGDK.

from the state of Cambodia faction and five divided among the CGDK. Prince Sihanouk was given authority as president of the Council, in recognition of his role as former king and prime minister, and as the only leading figure acceptable to all Cambodian parties and the permanent five members of the UN Security Council. The Security Council endorsed the formation of the Supreme National Council,[22] giving it a degree of international recognition and legitimacy which further supported its primary purpose of delegating all necessary authority needed to implement the settlement plan to the United Nations Transitional Authority in Cambodia (UNTAC).

The framework document and Security Council Resolution by characterizing the Supreme National Council as the entity that "enshrines Cambodian sovereignty," established the necessary foundation for a delegation of authority, even while it highlighted the uncertain legal status of the Council. It was not the government of Cambodia. When the Council was set up, neither the Permanent Five members of the Security Council and Australia nor the four Cambodian factions envisioned it undertaking any governing functions during the interim period. Indeed, during the negotiations, the four factions continued to assert that the government in which each participated – either the State of Cambodia or the Coalition Government of Democratic Cambodia – was the legitimate government. Nonetheless, the Council's existence provided the international community with a single entity (at least formally) with which it could interact during the negotiation process.

Under the Agreement, the Council represented Cambodia during the transitional period (prior to the installation of the newly elected government) and occupied Cambodia's seat at the United Nations.[23] Through this formulation the Council was able to delegate to the UN "all powers necessary to insure the implementation of the Agreement."[24]

The actual status of the Supreme National Council as the legitimate sovereign authority of Cambodia during the transition period remained problematic, both in design and practice. It can be best regarded as a semi-sovereign entity created by the Cambodian factions and later given a special status – a type of international recognition by the community of nations, in both a Security Council resolution and the Comprehensive Settlement Agreement. The arrangement ensured that Cambodia retained its "sovereignty" even though the UN's role meant that the Council lacked full freedom to manage its internal and foreign affairs. Nevertheless the Council, in its capacity as a semi-sovereign entity,

[22] UN SC/Res. 688 (1992).   [23] See note 1, art. 5.   [24] Ibid., art. 6.

signed several international human rights conventions which will bind successor governments.[25] The Agreement, moreover, authorized the Council to act as an "advisory" body to UNTAC. UNTAC thus had to abide by a unanimous decision of the Council, so long as it was in keeping with the objectives of the Agreement. Whenever the Council reached an impasse, Prince Sihanouk had the authority to give advice to UNTAC. The Special Representative of the Secretary-General was the final arbiter of whether a decision of the Council was in keeping with the intent and meaning of the Paris Agreement. However, the Agreement also gave UNTAC and the Special Representative wide discretion, where necessary, to act independently and to make major binding decisions whenever the Council reached a deadlock. In practice, much influence was exercised over Council decision-making by the permanent members of the UN Security Council and other interested states acting through their Phnom Penh support group of local diplomatic representatives accredited to the Council.

The Agreements granted UNTAC substantial authority over Cambodia if the Supreme National Council proved incapable of effective decision making. The structure of the agreement deliberately emphasized the authority of UNTAC based on the assumed impotence of the Council. Nevertheless, it also preserved a modicum of authority for faction leaders by requiring the UN to consider fully their advice when they all agreed. The Council was a part – indeed a symbolically vital Cambodian part[26] – of the circle of authority in Cambodia, though it lacked the resources or coherence it would have needed to have governed effectively.

The UN Mandate: United Nations transitional authority in Cambodia

The UN operation in Cambodia, like that in El Salvador, was one of the earliest to address internal conflicts by assuming a combination of responsibilities in the execution of its mandate.[27] The Paris Agreement

---

[25] The Supreme National Council signed instruments of accession to the International Convention on Civil and Political Rights and the International Convention on Economic, Social and Cultural Rights on April 20, 1992. It also acceded to the Convention on the Elimination of Discrimination Against Women, the Convention Against Torture, the Convention on the Rights of the Child, the Convention and Protocol on the Status of Refugees.

[26] The lack of even this minimally formal authority in Somalia left UNOSOM without a symbolic interlocutor that could serve to legitimate its actions. See the letter to the *New York Times* of September 15, 1993 by Issa Ahmed Nour.

[27] The UN operation in the Congo (ONUC) 1960–4, took on some multidimensional roles.

granted extraordinary power to the UN during the transition period. Aside from the precedent-setting responsibilities for controlling and supervising crucial aspects of the civil administration, and organizing, and monitoring the elections, UNTAC was also required to monitor the ceasefire and the withdrawal of all foreign forces, and to supervise the cantonment and demobilization of military forces. Additionally, part of the mandate required UNTAC to foster an environment in which respect for human rights and fundamental freedoms was ensured; coordinate with UNHCR the repatriation of the 350,000 refugees living in camps on the Thai side of the border; and encourage the social and economic rehabilitation during the period preceding the elections. The UNTAC operation, like UN operations in Namibia (UNTAG) and El Salvador (ONUSAL), thus was a multidimensional operation. It too was based on consent, impartiality, and the non-use of force.[28]

Although the UN had experience in some of these areas through past peacekeeping operations, it was the combination of these tasks that made UNTAC at the time the largest UN peacekeeping operation, requiring over 15,000 troops and 7,000 civilian personnel, and costing over an estimated $2.8 billion during the span of eighteen months, the calculated transition period.[29] Even more striking was the agreement among the four Cambodian factions and the other parties to creating "a system of liberal democracy, on the basis of pluralism."[30]

By passing resolution 718,[31] the Security Council expressed full support for the Paris Agreement and requested the Secretary-General submit a report containing his implementation plan and a detailed estimate of the cost of UNTAC at the earliest possible date. This report was finally issued on February 19, 1992,[32] by which time much of the momentum accompanying the signing of the Cambodian Settlement Agreements was lost. Nevertheless, the UN proceeded to implement the Agreements through the establishment of seven components for UNTAC: human rights, electoral, military, civil administration, civilian police, repatriation, and rehabilitation. An information division was later added to explain to Cambodians throughout the country the essence of the Cambodian Settlement Agreements and the nature of UNTAC's

---

[28] F. T. Liu, *United Nations Peacekeeping and the Non-Use of Force*, IPA Occasional Paper (Boulder, Col.: Lynne Rienner, 1992).

[29] Since then (1993), UN operations in Somalia and the former Yugoslavia have been much larger and more expensive.

[30] "Principles for a new Constitution for Cambodia," annex 5 of Agreement on a Comprehensive Political Settlement of the Cambodia Conflict at para. 4. UN doc. A/46/608-S/23177; 31 ILM 183 (1992).

[31] SC/RES 718 (1991) October 31, 1991.

[32] S/23613 (February 19, 1992), Report of the Secretary-General on Cambodia.

activities.[33] The rest of this section will look more closely at the framework behind these components.

Elections

The hallmark of the Paris Agreements was the right of self-determination of the Cambodian people through free and fair elections. Elections, thus became, for better or worse, the sine qua non of the resolution of the Cambodian conflict, one on which the parties readily concurred at least in principle. The purpose of the elections was to select 120 representatives for a constituent assembly which would draft and approve a new Cambodian constitution within three months of the elections, and which would then transform itself into a legislative assembly which would in turn set up a new Cambodian government.[34]

Elections as a mechanism for self-determination had gained new prominence in the 1990s when the UN General Assembly adopted a resolution on "Enhancing the effectiveness of the principle of periodic and genuine elections."[35] In some circles the right to vote in free and fair elections was recognized as a fundamental human right.[36] UN promotion of periodic elections was evident in the increasing number of peacekeeping operations involving an electoral component. For the first time, however, unlike UN operations in Angola, El Salvador, Namibia, and Haiti, the entire organization and supervision of the elections was left to the UN. UNTAC's responsibilities under article 13 included[37] establishing electoral laws and procedures; invalidating existing laws that would not further the settlement; setting up the voter education program; registering voters and parties organizing and conducting the polling responding to complaints; arranging for foreign observation; and certifying the elections as free and fair. The creation of laws and procedures was a critical legislative function granted to UNTAC regarding elections. This ability to draft legislation was not a power provided to UNTAC in other areas of civil administration, and signified an innovative yet intrusive role for the UN in the internal affairs of a member state.

Additionally, the Agreement specified the key requirements for the

---

[33] See S/23870 (May 1, 1992), First Progress Report of the Secretary-General on UNTAC at para. 44.

[34] See note 1, art. 12; annex 3, para. 1.

[35] UN GA Res. 45/150 (December 18, 1990), "Enhancing the effectiveness of the principle of periodic and genuine elections."

[36] Thomas M. Franck, "The emerging right to democratic governance," *American Journal of International Law*, vol. 46, 1992.

[37] See note 1, annex 1, section B, para. 4.

elections. First, the elections were to be based upon proportional representation within each province, with each political party offering lists of candidates.[38] Second, under the Agreement all persons over the age of 18 born in Cambodia or to a parent born in Cambodia, including refugees and displaced persons, were to be eligible to vote.[39] Third, the Agreement prescribed the basic rules for the conduct of the elections. Voting would be by secret ballot; the parties were to insure freedom of speech, assembly, and movement; and each party would have "fair" access to the media. The elaboration of these rights and duties was left to UNTAC to develop in its code of conduct and other electoral regulations.

Significantly, UNTAC was not constrained by the Supreme National Council with respect to elections, even if the latter spoke unanimously or through Prince Sihanouk.[40] Indeed, the mandate specifically avoided any mandatory obligation on the part of UNTAC to consult with the Council regarding the electoral process.[41] In addition, the Special Representative retained the authority to overrule the Council in the electoral processes if members of the Council had agreed among themselves on electoral procedures that furthered their own ends but corrupted the process.

The objective of the electoral component, as specified in the UN implementation plan, was to facilitate the broadest possible participation of Cambodians in the elections. In order to attain this objective, UNTAC drafted electoral laws focused on developing mechanisms which would protect the integrity of the vote, facilitating the registration process, and ensuring that freedom of speech, assembly, and movement would be fully respected. The UN implementation plan recognized the holding of elections as the "focal point of the comprehensive settlement."[42] All of UNTAC's other activities therefore were to be carried

---

[38] Ibid., annex 3, para. 2.

[39] Ibid., at annex 3, paras. 3–4. The electoral law was enacted by the Supreme National Council on August 5 and promulgated on August 12, 1992. It was later modified to restrict the franchise of Cambodians to that based on descent. It was also amended to allow Cambodians living abroad to vote (one polling station in Europe, North America and Australia). See Second Progress Report of the Secretary-General on Cambodia, September 21, 1992, S/24578, paras. 12–18.

[40] Article 13 of the agreement specifies that "UNTAC shall be responsible for the organization and conduct of these elections." Additionally, the portion of UNTAC's mandate describing its electoral functions refers only to the Election Annex, and not to that part of the mandate describing UNTAC's relationship with the Supreme National Council.

[41] The language of annex 1, section D, para. 2 provides "UNTAC may consult with the SNC ..."

[42] See S/23613 (February 19, 1992), Report of the Secretary-General on Cambodia.

out in a timely manner to insure that a climate conducive to holding free and fair elections was created.

Civil administration

One of the most notable features of the Paris Agreement was UNTAC's mandate regarding the administration of Cambodia prior to the installation of a democratically elected government. The international community for the first time empowered the UN to undertake key aspects of the civil administration of a member state. This was a major departure from traditional UN peacekeeping, since the UN had never before been entrusted with overseeing the administration of a member state.

The advocates of this enhanced UN role had no precedents[43] to work from when planning the organization and functions of UNTAC. A multilateral Peace Treaty with Italy had authorized the Security Council to approve a provisional regime and appoint a governor to administer the Free Territory of Trieste, but early Cold War rivalries prevented the appointment of a governor. The General Assembly's partition plan for Palestine had called for the creation of a *corpus separatum* for Jerusalem under a special international regime administered by the Trusteeship Council, but the Arab states and Israel ultimately rejected the plan. The General Assembly had also created the Council for Namibia in 1966, but South Africa's continuing occupation prevented it from carrying out this administration. Rather, the civilian component of UNTAG was limited to oversight and supervision of the transition to independence in Namibia, with special attention given to monitoring the South African police forces and election administrators.

The only relevant precedent for direct UN administration of any territory was the United Nations Temporary Executive Authority (UNTEA), which governed the western half of New Guinea (Irian Jaya) during its transition from Dutch to Indonesian rule. The Netherlands and Indonesia agreed by treaty to transfer administration of the non-self-governing territory to UNTEA, which would administer it until transfer to Indonesia.[44] Unlike later peacekeeping operations, the General Assembly authorized the Secretary-General to perform the tasks in the Agreement. UNTEA administered West Irian replacing Dutch officials

---

[43] See Ratner, "The Cambodia Settlement Agreements," p. 13; see also Oscar Schachter, "The development of international law through the legal opinions of the United Nations Secretariat," *British Yearbook of International Law*, vol. 25, 1948, p. 91; Rosalyn Higgins, *The Development of International Law through the Political Organs of the United Nations* (Oxford: Oxford University Press, 1963).

[44] Agreement concerning West New Guinea (West Irian) August 15, 1962, Indon–Neth. 437 UNTS 274.

with UN officials from third countries who were supplanted by Indonesian officials from October 1, 1962 to May 1, 1963. The operation though politically little more than a face-saving device for the Netherlands, was a significant success, but until the Cambodian accords no such effort had been attempted again. During the Cold War such an intrusive role for the United Nations had been unacceptable to the members of the Security Council.

The Paris Agreement provided for an expansive mandate in the area of civil administration, including UNTAC control of those aspects of civil administration necessary to achieve the "neutral political environment" that would be conducive to the holding of "free and fair" elections. The Agreement established a three-tiered system of oversight to govern the relationship between the Secretary-General's Special Representative, UNTAC and the existing governmental apparatus in Cambodia, which included the large administrative structures of the State of Cambodia, as well as the smaller structures of the resistance in the areas it controlled.[45] This three-tiered system of scrutiny was designed to permit the degree of intrusiveness that would be required in the various areas of civil administration. At the suggestion of China, the areas specified for the strictest level of scrutiny and control over *each* of the four factions were defense, public security, finance, information, and foreign affairs.[46] A lesser degree of scrutiny was required over other governmental functions like education, public health, agriculture, fisheries, energy, transport, and communications.[47] The lowest level of scrutiny was reserved for those agencies that in the Special Representative's judgment "could continue to operate in order to ensure normal day-to-day life in Cambodia."[48] These levels of scrutiny and control were anticipated as necessary to insure a politically neutral environment in which no faction (especially that of the State of Cambodia) would be able to employ state resources to tilt the electoral contest in its favor.[49]

The Secretary-General's implementation plan for civil administration largely corresponded with the parameters laid out in the agreement, the main objective being "to ensure a neutral political environment conducive to free and fair general elections." The implementation plan,

[45] UN doc. A/46/61-S/22059 annex III (Explanatory Note prepared by UN officials describing a three-tiered system and appended to the P5 Draft).
[46] See note 1, art. 6; ann. 1, §B, ¶1.
[47] Ibid., ann. 1, §B, ¶2.   [48] Ibid., ¶3.
[49] China was a strong proponent of dissolving the Vietnamese-backed Phnom Penh government (later the State of Cambodia faction) and reducing its status to that of mere "administrative agencies, bodies and offices." See Robert S. Ross, "China and the Cambodian peace process: the value of coercive diplomacy," *Asia Survey*, vol. 31, no. 12, 1991, pp. 1170–85.

however, attempted to create greater flexibility in terms of the level of control exercised. Therefore UNTAC's mandate in foreign affairs was encouraged to be carried out in close collaboration with UNTAC liaison staff exercising direct control over the area of finance. Similarly, UNTAC's scrutiny over national defense was to be carried out in close collaboration with the military component.

Under the plan, UNTAC's control was to be applied through the issuance of codes of conduct and management guidelines, though it also had the authority to issue specific discipline related directives. Additionally, UNTAC had the right to issue binding directives on an ad hoc basis. The Agreements specify this last prerogative as belonging to the Special Representative, as was the overall direction and implementation of UNTAC's mandate for civil administration. Neither the Agreement nor the implementation plan provided any further guidance on how the various levels of scrutiny and control should be exercised.

Under the Agreement the Secretary-General's Special Representative had the apparent authority to appoint UNTAC officials within the factional administrations and to remove Cambodian officials who did not respond to his directives.[50] The Special Representative's prerogatives, however, did not override the procedures governing his relationship with the Supreme National Council. The Special Representative still had to follow the guidance of the Council, when unanimously given and if consistent with the settlement, even if this detracted from his powers with respect to existing structures. The legal hierarchy, reflecting political reality, officially placed the Special Representative in deference to the Council in all areas but the elections. Therefore if the factions through the Council concurred upon a course of action, including a limitation of the Special Representative's power, he could only veto that decision by challenging it as inconsistent with the settlement. Although the Agreement did not specify the priority of the Council's directives with regard to the existing governmental entities, over that of the Special Representative, a fundamental premise of the Council's delegation of authority was that if the Council spoke with one voice in a manner consistent with the settlement Agreement, its guidance was to be fulfilled.[51]

The Paris Agreement gave considerable and specific administrative authority to UNTAC. This specificity distinguishes the Paris Agreement from the agreement on West Irian, which simply gave the head of

---

[50] See note 1, art. 6; ann. 1, §B, para. 4; the Explanatory Note, note 44 at para. 36 states that this power will only be asserted if such persons "have acted in a manner inconsistent with the objectives of the settlement agreement."

[51] Except with respect to elections, see note 1 and accompanying text.

UNTEA "full authority under the direction of the Secretary-General to administer the territory."[52] The reason for this distinction lies in Cambodia's status as a member state of the UN, which raised issues of sovereignty not applicable to non-self-governing territories.

While the UN implementation plan for the Paris Agreements tried to follow the prescriptions of the Agreement, it is also apparent from developments on the ground that the conceptual framework necessary to exercise control and scrutiny over the civil administration of a member state had not been clearly worked out. It was either naive, overly ambitious, or both to assume that the interested Cambodian parties would actually hand over key civil administration responsibilities to the UN without making their own attempts to protect their own power.[53] Another clear problem for ambitious attempts to control civil administration was the underlying resistance among senior members of the UN Secretariat to exercise such functions which bordered on UN empire building.[54] The reluctance of the UN Secretariat to exercise an intrusive role also has been observed in subsequent UN peace operations, such as Somalia, Haiti, and Angola.

Humanitarian arrangements

The humanitarian aspects of the agreement were an essential aspect to the settlement in Cambodia. While political constraints muted the provisions relating to human rights, the repatriation of refugees and displaced persons, and the release of prisoners of war, the UN nevertheless exercised a more intrusive level of participation in these areas than it had in previous operations. This section will focus specifically on the issues relating to human rights and repatriation.

The human rights provisions of the Paris Agreement were crucial to the peacemaking process, not only because of the atrocities committed by the Democratic Kampuchea regime,[55] but also due to ongoing violations by the State of Cambodia faction.[56] The United States, the

---

52 Agreements concerning West New Guinea, note 44 above, art. V, 437 UNTS at 276. But that Agreement granted UNTEA the authority to promulgate new laws and regulations and amend existing elections, it has been argued that UNTAC's authority to issue directives appears to be equivalent to the ability to impose new legislation and regulations. See Ratner, "The Cambodian Settlement Agreements", at p. 15.

53 See Michael W. Doyle's chapter in this volume, "Authority and elections in Cambodia."

54 Interviews with senior officials in the UN Secretariat.   55 See note 1.

56 See e.g. Amnesty International, *Amnesty International Report* (London, Amnesty International Publications, 1987), pp. 239–42 (reports of imprisonment without trial, torture and unfair trials).

United Kingdom,[57] and several non-governmental organizations[58] were the strongest proponents of human rights provisions in the Agreement. The difficulties of negotiating the human rights provisions are reflected in the ambiguous language of the agreements, since consensus had to be attained not only among the four Cambodian factions but also among the other parties at the Conference.

Among the more ambiguous references was the term "other relevant human rights instruments."[59] This term encompassed the full ambit of human rights conventions and declarations, many of which Cambodia was not as yet a party to. These included International Covenants on Civil and Political Rights and on Economic, Social and Cultural Rights; the International Convention on the Elimination of All Forms of Racial Discrimination; and most significantly, the 1948 Convention on the Prevention and Punishment of the Crime of Genocide.[60]

The accords, by requiring Cambodia "to adhere to relevant human rights instruments," placed the responsibility of fulfilling its duties under the Genocide Convention upon the future government of Cambodia. Similarly, the Agreement placed the primary obligation of ensuring that the policies and practices of the Khmer Rouge era and the human rights violations of the subsequent governments not reoccur, upon the elected Cambodian government. However the Agreement did not identify any mechanisms by which this could be achieved, other than through provisions in the Cambodian constitution.

The provisions relating to human rights under the Paris Agreement fell into three categories according to the actors involved. The first set of provisions referred to the obligations of the Cambodians themselves, and required Cambodia to insure respect for human rights; support the rights of Cambodians to undertake activities to promote human rights; take effective measures "to ensure that the policies and practices of the past shall never be allowed to return," and to adhere to "relevant international human rights instruments."[61] Cambodia's obligations under the Paris Agreement also encompassed the insertion of human rights provisions in its new constitution. The Agreement did not, however, call for prosecutions for past abuses,[62] given the diplomatic necessity of keeping China and the Khmer Rouge in the peace process.

The second set of obligations related to the non-Cambodian signa-

---

[57] Interview with John Griffin (UK mission).
[58] Interview with David Hawke (Cambodian Documentation Commission)
[59] See note 1 at art. 15(2)(b).   [60] Ibid.   [61] Ibid.
[62] This is different from the role of the international community in El Salvador, where an investigation into the human rights violations by leaders of that country was called for in one of the peace agreements. See the chapter in this volume by Timothy Wilkins, "The El Salvador Peace Accords."

tories.[63] These obligations of ensuring and promoting human rights were also reiterated in the Guarantees Agreement by the same parties. This recurrence highlights the significance attached to these provisions and ensures that these human rights commitments are binding for both the transitional phase and the longer term.

The third series of obligations were those of the UN. UNTAC was given the responsibility of fostering an environment in which respect for human rights and fundamental freedoms would be ensured.[64] The Agreements gave UNTAC authority to monitor human rights conditions in Cambodia, implement a human rights education program, and most significantly, investigate complaints and take "corrective action."[65] Moreover, the UN Commission on Human Rights was expected to monitor human rights in Cambodia even after the transition period through the appointment of a special rapporteur.[66]

The three-tiered series of obligations, while exclusive of each other, were designed to be mutually reinforcing. Consequently, although the Cambodians themselves had the principal responsibility of promoting and protecting human rights, the role of the states at the Paris Conference·remained crucial in exercising a checking/monitoring function upon the activities of Cambodians, not only during the transitional period, but even after the end of the UNTAC mandate.

While the human rights provisions gave the legal framework for the setting up of a proactive human rights program, the Secretary-General's implementation plan did not allocate enough resources to seemingly take full advantage of the scope offered by the provisions. The plan itself detailed UNTAC's role in promoting human rights during the transition period in three broad areas.[67] First, a human rights education program was to be set up as the cornerstone of UNTAC's activities in fostering respect for human rights and fundamental freedoms. The purpose of the program was to raise the level of awareness among Cambodians about these rights, as well as developing an understanding about protecting these rights. In setting up this program UNTAC was to work closely with existing educational administrative structures in Cambodia to insure that human rights education was appropriately included in the curriculum. Second, UNTAC was to oversee human rights compliance in all existing administrative structures in Cambodia.[68] This was to involve the production of special guidelines and materials to promote education and human rights awareness among civil servants. Third, UNTAC was to investigate any allegations of human rights abuses occurring during the transitional period; however neither the Agree-

---

[63] Note 1, art. 15(2)(b).   [64] Ibid., art. 16.   [65] Ibid., ann. 1, section E.
[66] Ibid., art. 17.   [67] S/23613 at paras. 8–22.   [68] Ibid., paras. 16 and 17.

ments nor the implementation plan provided a specific framework under which these could be conducted.

The Agreement also provided for the return of refugees and displaced persons. The years of strife in Cambodia had caused massive migration. At the signing of the accords the number of Cambodian refugees and displaced persons numbered nearly 370,000. These people fell into two categories: approximately 14,000 people eligible for refugee status under international legal standards,[69] and over 350,000 "displaced persons" who had lived since the early 1980s in camps in Thailand controlled by the factions and assisted by the United Nations Border Relief Operations, but who had not been granted refugee status.[70] The Agreement granted both groups "the right to return to Cambodia and to live in safety, security, and dignity free from intimidation or coercion of any kind,"[71] and described in an annex the guidelines and principles for their return.[72] No specific provision was made in the agreement for the 150,000 to 200,000 internally displaced persons within Cambodia.

Operational control for repatriation was the primary responsibility of the UN High Commissioner for Refugees. The Agreement required that the High Commissioner and other agencies be given access to refugees and displaced persons and encouraged the international community to provide repatriation assistance. Moreover, former refugees and displaced persons were to be free to move within Cambodia, choose their place of residence, work and own property. Under the implementation plan,[73] the UN High Commissioner for Refugees had the primary responsibility for the repatriation and resettlement of Cambodian refugees, but was to be assisted both by UNTAC, and to a lesser extent UNDP.[74] The effort included the movement of returnees, the provision of food and other immediate assistance, and a reintegration program.

Security arrangements

The objectives of the security arrangements during the transitional period were to stabilize the military situation, build confidence among parties to the conflict, and prevent the risks of a return to warfare.[75] The

---

[69] See Convention Relating to the Status of Refugees, July 28, 1951, art. I(A), 189 UNTS 150, 152; Protocol relating to the Status of Refugees, January 31, 1967, art. I(2) 60 UNTS 267, 268.

[70] See Valerie O. Sutter, *The Indochinese Refugee Dilemma* (Baton Rouge, La.: Louisiana State University Press, 1990), pp. 75–81.

[71] See note 1, art. 20.   [72] Ibid., ann. 4.   [73] S/23613 at pp. 132–49.

[74] UNDP's involvement is based on a memorandum of understanding signed between UNDP and UNHCR which concerns the reintegration program that includes a variety of development projects, at S/23613 138(c).

[75] See note 1, art. 11.

signatories of the Paris Agreement agreed to the withdrawal and non-return of foreign forces, advisors and military personnel;[76] a two-phase ceasefire to commence with the entry into force of the agreement;[77] the cessation of external military assistance to all the factions;[78] the regroupment, cantonment[79] and demobilization of the armed forces;[80] and the release of all prisoners of war and civilian internees.[81] Despite some initial reservations, the parties at the Paris Conference agreed that the UN would supervise the military aspects of the settlement. Unlike first generation peacekeeping operations, UNTAC would not merely observe a ceasefire, but like UNTAG and ONUSAL, would oversee a wide array of activities designed to end the military conflict.

The maintenance of internal security during the transitional period fell under civil administration in the agreement, but was handled separately in the implementation plan. The agreement specified that civil police was to operate under the "supervision or control" of UNTAC.[82] The level of intrusiveness with respect to civilian police was left to the discretion of the Special Representative, and judicial processes could be placed directly under UNTAC's supervision.[83] Under the implementation plan the UN opted for a less intrusive role than the agreement allowed it, forgoing "control" of the police forces by assigning responsibility for their management to the Cambodian parties. The implementation plan did, however, give UNTAC a supervisory role in order to insure that law and order were maintained effectively and impartially and that human rights and fundamental freedoms were fully protected.[84]

Under the more general security arrangements, the obligations of the Cambodian factions were to observe the ceasefire and not to resume any hostilities by land, water, or air. Additionally, the Cambodian factions were to provide UNTAC with information concerning the numbers and positions of weapons possessed by each of their forces, as well as the location of arms caches, external resupply routes and mines. Cambodia's neighbors – Thailand, Laos, and Vietnam – were to inform UNTAC of

---

[76] Ibid., art. 8; ann. 1, §C, para. 1(a); ann. 2, art. VI.   [77] Ibid., art. 9; ann. 2, art. I.

[78] Ibid., art. 10; ann. 1, §C, para. 1(c); ann. 2, art. VII. The agreement also imposes an obligation upon the Cambodian parties to stop receiving military assistance. Moreover the states bordering Cambodia must prevent the use of their territory for such aid. The Agreement's broad definition of "military assistance" prohibits all aid to the parties that can be used to prolong the military conflict. The resupply of humanitarian goods is permitted, subject to UNTAC's supervision. See note 1, ann. 2, art. VII (2)(a).

[79] Ibid., art. 11, ann. 1, §C, paras. 2–3; ann. 2, art. III–IV.

[80] Ibid., art. 11, ann. 1, §C, paras. 2–3; ann. 2, art. VIII(2).

[81] Ibid., art. 21–22; ann. 1, §C, para. 5.

[82] Ibid., ann. 1, §B, para. 5(b).   [83] Ibid., ann 1, §B, para. 5(a)

[84] S/23613 at para. 112.

the routes and means by which military assistance was provided to the factions. Moreover, UNTAC was to receive (the accords do not specify from whom) details concerning the withdrawal of foreign troops.[85]

Consequently, under the Agreement UNTAC's obligations included verification of the withdrawal of Vietnamese troops; determining the timetable for the ceasefire and monitoring it; establishing an operational timetable and detailed plan for, and then supervising the regroupment, cantonment and demobilization of the four parties, which would be followed by the demobilization of 70 percent of the factions' troops; monitoring the cessation of outside assistance along Cambodia's land and sea frontiers; interacting with neighboring governments concerning the Agreements; locating and destroying caches of weapons; assisting the Red Cross with prisoner of war exchanges; and contributing to mine-clearance operations.

While the Agreement itself incorporated specific procedures for security arrangements, much of the detail concerning the implementation of the military arrangements was left to the discretion of the UN to develop on the basis of its expertise, its assessments of the situation on the ground, and the views of the belligerents. This was somewhat unlike previous armistice agreements in which the UN had been involved where detail of demarcation lines, timetables, and deployment areas were included.[86] The negotiators presumably avoided detailed discussions on these matters in order to reach an agreement.

The UN implementation plan provided necessary details on the main and subsidiary functions of the military component. The priority of these functions was determined by the UN rather than through any specific provision of the Agreement. Among the details expanded upon in the implementation plan was the timetable for demobilization and cantonment of the military forces. The implementation plan stressed the importance of "full demobilization of the military forces of the Cambodian parties prior to the end of the registration process." Consequently, the report of the Secretary-General strongly urged the Cambodian parties to agree to complete the demobilization of their military forces prior to the end of the electoral registration process and called upon the Security Council to join him in doing so.

---

[85] See note 1, ann. 2, art. I(3), VI(1), VII(3), VIII; art. VI(1) does not specify who shall provide UNTAC with information about the withdrawal of foreign forces.

[86] See e.g. Agreement between the Commander-in-Chief, United Nations Command, on the One hand, and the Supreme Commander of the Korean People's Army and the Commander of the Chinese People's Volunteers, on the Other Hand, Concerning a Military Armistice in Korea, July 27, 1953, art. II 4 UST 234, 239 (hereinafter Korean Armistice Agreement); General Armistice Agreement, February 24, 1949, Egypt–Israel. art. II 42 UNTS 252, 254.

The success of the security arrangements depended on the positive cooperation of all the parties to the Agreements, especially the Cambodian factions. What was lacking in the Paris Agreement and in the UN implementation plan was a concrete plan of action in the event that one of the parties failed to abide by the Agreement's disarmament provisions. Instead the Agreement specified that immediate consultations should be held to rectify the situation. While the UN clearly recognized the importance of demobilizing the factions prior to elections UNTAC, like other previous peacekeeping operations, had no defined mandate to insure compliance among the parties to the Agreement. The omission of more specific enforcement provisions in the Agreement itself was due to the desire on the part of the negotiators to reach an agreement. Nevertheless, the Agreement specifically gave the UN "all powers necessary to ensure the implementation of the Agreement."[87] UN sensitivity to charges of colonialism may have hindered the UNTAC mission from interpreting the Agreements aggressively. But the determinants of the success and failure of UNTAC lay elsewhere – in the fierce political contest among the Cambodian factions. The Paris Agreement was the opening salvo in a new phase of the Cambodian war, to be waged by other means.

Democracy by agreement?

The post-Cold War era has seen the UN increasingly involved in facilitating transitions to democracy. On the one hand the gridlock of the Cold War had restrained the UN's role in promoting the purposes and principles of the Charter,[88] and on the other hand traditional notions of sovereignty hindered greater UN involvement.[89] With changing circumstances, however, the General Assembly passed a resolution in 1991 on "Enhancing the effectiveness of the principle of periodic and genuine elections," propelling the UN more readily in this direction. Prior to the UN operation in Cambodia, the UN's role in democracy promotion was confined to the supervision and verification of elections. As described above, the prescribed UN role in Cambodia went beyond the mere holding of free and fair elections. It also encompassed human rights monitoring, ensuring freedom of speech and press during elections, the control of civil administration (for purposes of transparency and

---

[87] Agreement on a Comprehensive Political Settlement of the Cambodia Conflict, art. 6, UN document A/46/608-S/23177; 31 ILM 183 (1992).

[88] Anne Marie Burley, "Toward an age of liberal nations," *Harvard International Law Journal*, vol. 33, 1992, p. 393.

[89] Michael Riesman, "Comment: sovereignty and human rights in international law," *American Journal of International Law*, vol. 84, 1990, pp. 866, 871.

accountability), and the maintenance of law and order. The UN presence was not merely a transitional mechanism, but also had the underlying purpose of instilling a greater awareness about individual rights and ensuring their protections among the people of Cambodia.

One of the Paris Accords' unique features was that the international community and the Cambodian factions agreed to a system of liberal democracy as the basis for Cambodia's constitution.[90] The Agreement specified all the elements necessary for a liberal democracy: periodic and genuine elections; freedom of assembly and association including that for political parties; due process and equality before the law; and an independent judiciary. While it remains to be seen whether the Cambodians will embrace the principles and practice of a democracy, the parties to the negotiation process (with the encouragement of the international community in general) explicitly agreed to a peace plan that required them to establish liberal democracy in Cambodia. What was significant about this process was the UN's role in guaranteeing the democracy of a member state.[91] This type of intrusion into the domestic affairs of a member state is a new departure for the UN. Since the UNTAC operation, an even more radical step in this direction has been taken in Haiti with the UN Security Council's decision to exercise chapter VII action "to restore democracy" to that country.[92]

Although the UN role in drafting the Cambodian constitution was relatively minor, it is apparent that UNTAC would have failed in an essential aspect of its mission if the provisions in the Paris Agreement concerning "liberal democracy on the basis of pluralism" were not codified into the constitution. The constitution specifies that "the Kingdom of Cambodia shall adopt a multi-party free democratic regime."[93] A series of institutions were to guarantee this "democratic process." These include the National Assembly elected by proportional representation with a direct and secret ballot; an independent judiciary; a limited monarchy, in which the king reigns but does not rule;[94] and an extensive series of civil rights, including personal freedoms and rights to property and free expression. The question now is whether Cambodia can maintain this constitutional democracy.

[90] See note 1, art. 23.
[91] In Namibia, too, part of the mandate of the UN (UNTAG) was to have the constitution of the independent Namibia adhere to a system of "liberal democracy". However, Namibia was a trust territory, whereas Cambodia was a member state of the UN.
[92] SC/RES/940 (July 31, 1994).
[93] Kingdom of Cambodia Constitution (adopted September 21, 1993).
[94] The monarchy is therefore of a symbolic nature, its purpose being to preserve the "unity and eternity of the nation." Additionally succession to the monarchy is not hereditary, rather it is subject to election by the Royal Council of the Throne.

Conclusion

Future peacekeeping challenges for the UN will no doubt, like the UN operations in Cambodia and El Salvador, occur as a result of internal conflict situations in member states. Several lessons can be (and have been) drawn from the experience of the Cambodian Settlement Agreements and the UN implementation plan to assist in future operations.

First, UN peace operations taking place in situations of internal conflict should, for the purposes of implementing the peace settlement, identify in the agreements some sort of symbolic interlocutor, consisting of the main parties to the conflict, to provide a minimalist authority for the legitimation of actions. The Supreme National Council in Cambodia, though largely acting as a rubber stamp entity, filled this vacuum as a semi-sovereign entity. The semi-sovereignty concept can be readily applied in situations of a "fractioned state" (Angola, Mozambique [before the elections in 1994], Sudan, Algeria) as well as in "failed state" situations (Somalia). The difficulty with the latter is identifying a group of representatives that would be acceptable to both the local constituents and the international actors, and also provide the requirement of legitimation. By contrast peace agreements in both Angola and Mozambique have instead delegated authority to the UN through the "enhanced consent" model,[95] through Joint Political Military Commissions for the purpose of implementing the agreements, where the UN presides over these Commissions.

Second, there needs to be greater parity between the peace Agreements and the UN mandate that attempts to implement the Agreement since one of the fundamental requirements of a peacekeeping operation is a clear mandate. Although the Cambodian Settlement Agreements gave the UN a great deal of latitude in implementing the agreements, the UN implementation plan took a more restrained approach than was perhaps warranted. This was evident with respect to UN control over civil administration, UN functions relating to law and order, civilian police, security arrangements, and human rights. Many of these responsibilities took the UN into hitherto unexplored territory, and the Agreements were not clear enough as to how the UN was to undertake those responsibilities, leaving it instead to the UN to improvise on the basis of its "past experience." Such a situation could be rectified if the UN is more actively involved in the peace process, so that the parties to a peace agreement are more aware of the legal, political, and logistical

---

[95] See the chapter in this volume by Timothy A. Wilkins, "The El Salvador Peace Accords."

constraints of the UN. Any peace agreement emerging from such a process would not create false expectations among the parties.

Third, future peace operations should in their mandate make the holding of elections contingent on the prior implementation of essential provisions of the peace agreements. Of particular importance are provisions directly relating to security arrangements and in particular demobilization and disarming of the forces, integration of the forces into a unified army, and, where specified, the establishment of an impartial police force. In this area the experience of Cambodia provides only negative lessons since the failure to disarm the factions could easily have been the recipe for disaster, as in Angola, had not the presence of the UN military and civilian police on the ground been so strong.

Fourth, every peace agreement should have a series of mechanisms for implementing the peace settlement. Such mechanisms can be either external or internal to the peace settlement itself. The framework of the agreement normally should incorporate independent and neutral arrangements for the verification, and adjudication of the process of implementation. The role of the UN in Cambodia and El Salvador provided for this, whereas the second UN operation in Angola (UNAVEM II) essentially left the verification of the Bicesse Accords to the parties themselves. Additionally arrangements like the Guarantees Agreement should, where possible, be included in the peace settlement to provide the international community with a monitoring capability beyond the immediate phase of the UN peace operation.

Mechanisms inducing the parties to abide by the Agreements also could be developed outside the framework of the actual Agreements. The establishment of incentives like economic assistance to make the peace sustainable with the rehabilitation of the country should be addressed during the negotiation process. The Declaration on the Rehabilitation and Reconstruction of Cambodia, as part of the Settlement Agreements addressed the issue of cost for the rehabilitation of that country.[96] Similarly, inducements to facilitate the demobilization of the military could be developed outside the framework of the agreements; such incentives could include the exchange of weapons for money utilized in Mozambique by ONUMOZ, or food for work programs operated in Angola by UNAVEM III, in reconstruction plans for the country.

The strategy embodied in the Paris Agreement of the UN stepping in to rebuild state legitimacy, after the parties had failed to achieve a

---

[96] See note 10 and accompanying text. A meeting of donors was organized for the purposes of implementing the peace process in Mozambique in 1993, and in Angola in 1995.

reconciliation of their own was part of the post-Cold War syndrome when at the political level all things seemed possible. Admittedly, part of this strategy was realized with the establishment of an internationally recognized sovereign coalition government, despite the boycott by the Khmer Rouge. However, while some semblance of centralized authority was restored to Cambodia, the UN was not able to "rebuild state legitimacy" on the scale it had been delegated under the Agreements[97] as evidenced by its inability to oversee the demobilization of the military and to fully exercise "control" over the various civil administration functions, which were critical aspects of UNTAC's mandate. Despite these problems of implementation, the Paris Agreements continue to provide a model for UN-brokered peace agreements in situations of internal conflict. The lack of success in these areas was caused by the want of positive cooperation from the Cambodian factions rather than the legal framework established by the Paris Agreements.

[97] The reasons for this are beyond the scope of this chapter and are no doubt discussed in the relevant chapters in this volume. But also see Michael W. Doyle, *UN Peacekeeping in Cambodia: UNTAC's Civil Mandate* (Boulder, Col.: Lynne Rienner, 1995) for a discussion of the successes, failures, and lessons to be learnt from the UN operation in Cambodia.

5   Holding a fragile peace: the military and civilian components of UNTAC

Cheryl M. Lee Kim and Mark Metrikas

Introduction

The destructiveness of the Cambodian conflict was directly proportional to the level of arms available to its factional armies, who had continuously used military force to intimidate the Cambodian people. Thus, the Military Component (MILCOM) of the United Nations Transitional Authority in Cambodia (UNTAC), was to play a critical role in the creation of a "neutral political environment" through its monitoring of ceasefire, disarmament, regroupment, cantonment, and demobilization of factional forces. Though UNTAC included several civilian components, it was the deployment of armed UN soldiers which distinguished UNTAC as a peacekeeping mission.

Complementing the work of MILCOM, the Civilian Police Component (CIVPOL), was tasked with stabilizing the security situation. The seed for a UN police presence in Cambodia was first sown in the "Australian plan,"[1] which suggested that the CIVPOL presence in Namibia had been "more significant than the military presence in encouraging a sense of day-to-day security and impartiality in running the country," and advocated a significant police monitoring presence in Cambodia.[2]

This chapter will review the mandates of MILCOM and CIVPOL according to the Paris Peace Agreements and examine their execution. The final section will examine lessons suggested by the UN's experience in Cambodia.

---

[1] Commonwealth of Australia, *Cambodia: An Australian Police Proposal*, Working Papers prepared for the Informal Meeting on Cambodia, Jakarta February 26–28, 1990 (also known as "The Red Book") (Canberra: R. D. Rubie, Commonwealth Government Printer, 1990).
[2] Ibid., p. 36.

The mandate

The military component

The military functions of UNTAC included: monitoring and verifying ceasefire between factions; supervising, monitoring, and verifying the withdrawal of all foreign forces; monitoring the cessation of all outside military assistance to the Cambodian factions; and most critically, the regroupment, cantonment, disarmament, and demobilization of factional forces (70 percent were to be demobilized prior to the electoral registration, the remaining 30 percent were to be demobilized before or shortly after elections; to the extent that full demobilization was not possible, the parties committed to respect the decisions of the new government as to the disposition of their armies).[3] As part of its disarmament task, MILCOM was responsible for locating and confiscating weapons caches and storing the weapons of the demobilized factional forces. MILCOM was also charged with investigating alleged non-compliance with any of the military arrangements delineated by the Paris Agreements.

In practice, MILCOM pervaded almost every aspect of UNTAC's mandate. With 15,900 personnel, it was the largest of UNTAC components and it possessed strengths other components lacked: a disciplined organizational structure, standardized operating procedures, mobility, adequate communications, and the only significant logistical capacity in Cambodia.

The civilian police component

Each of the Cambodian factions had its own "civilian" police force. More accurately, the police were extensions of the military, with the State of Cambodia (SOC) being the only faction which possessed a non-military police element. The Paris Agreements stated that local civilian police in Cambodia were to "operate under UNTAC supervision or control, in order to insure that law and order are maintained effectively and impartially, and that human rights and fundamental freedoms are fully protected."[4] The presence of UN police monitors was to neutralize

---

[3] "Regroupment" is to move troops from their deployed sites to a specified location. "Disarmament" means the giving up of weapons and armaments. "Cantonment" refers to having troops stay in a confined area, under UN supervision. "Demobilization" denotes the return of soldiers to civilian life.

[4] *Agreements on a Comprehensive Political Settlement of the Cambodia Conflict*, annex 1, section B, para. 5(b). The Agreements required the parties to furnish details on police strengths, deployment, and structure. The Agreements also required UNTAC, in

any political advantage that might be gained by factions with larger police forces and was to contribute to a stable environment conducive to free and fair elections.

It was hoped that regular patrolling and contact with locals would help engender public confidence in the peace process, while providing useful police intelligence on the situation in villages and communes. To assist CIVPOL in the execution of its mandate, the UN intended to develop codes of conduct and other operational guidelines. Cognizant of the inadequate and partisan nature of policing in Cambodia, the Secretary-General's plan displayed foresight in recommending that training courses be conducted for all levels of local police. The objective of training would be to familiarize local police with the role of UNTAC, teach basic policing skills and introduce the concepts of human rights and fundamental freedoms.

It was projected that CIVPOL would undertake secondary duties to help secure the electoral process.[5] CIVPOL was also to provide security for Cambodian refugees and displaced persons undergoing resettlement. Initially, CIVPOL escorted convoys of returnees from the Thai border to reception centers and then on to resettlement areas. MILCOM later took over responsibility for escorting returnee convoys and for security at reception centers, but CIVPOL continued to provide security for returnees by regularly accompanying SOC police on patrols to new settlements and aid distribution points.

United Nations Advance Mission in Cambodia

On October 16, 1991, through Resolution 717, the Security Council established the United Nations Advance Mission in Cambodia (UNAMIC), whose purpose was to assess the conditions under which UNTAC would operate and to determine the requisite strength and mode of deployment. A phase I ceasefire went into effect upon signature of the Paris Peace Agreements on October 23. UNAMIC was also to assist the Cambodian parties address and resolve any violations of the ceasefire. Strategically, UNAMIC functioned as a UN "placeholder" presence, serving as a reminder of the UN's commitment to Cambodia until a full-scale mission could be launched.

Operational on November 9, 1991, UNAMIC numbered 379, composed of civilian and military liaison staff, logistics and support

consultation with the Supreme National Council, to supervise other law enforcement and judicial processes.

[5] Report of the Secretary-General on Cambodia, S/23613, February 19, 1992, at para. 127.

Table 1 *UNTAC military component*

Subcomponent	Size	Tasks
Headquarters	204 officers	Main force headquarters and two sector headquarters
Infantry battalions	12 battalions, 850 soldiers each	Regroupment, cantonment, disarmament, custody of monitoring cessation of outside military assistance to troops in cantonment sites, provision of security for refugees
Military observers	485	Supervision of demobilization, investigation of non-compliance with agreements, establishment of checkpoints to monitor cessation of outside military assistance to Cambodian factions, verification of the withdrawal and non-return of all foreign forces, establishment of liaison offices with Laos, Thailand, and Vietnam
Signals unit	582	Establishment of communications net (including ground-to-air communications) and provision of communication to UNTAC civilian components
Engineer unit	2,230	Mine clearance, mine swareness, and training of Cambodians in mine clearance
Air support group	326	Support for reconnaissance tasks, troop technical support, logistics support, and overall air support to civilian components using ten fixed wing aircraft and twenty-six helicopters
Naval Unit	376	Patrol of coastal and inland water ways to monitor cessation of external military assistance, assist in regroupment, cantonment, and demobilization of naval forces
Logistics battalion	872	Provision of logistical support to MILCOM and to the civilian components, as required
Medical unit	541	Medical support to all UNTAC components
Military police	160	Military discipline

personnel, and a military mine awareness unit. In January 1992, the Security Council enlarged UNAMIC's mandate to include mine clearance, and the training of Cambodians in this task.[6] UNAMIC was to be absorbed by UNTAC once the latter was formally established by the Security Council.

Mixed Military Working Group

The Mixed Military Working Group (MMWG) was formed as part of UNAMIC, with each faction designating a representative of brigadier

[6]   Security Council Resolution 728 (1992).

rank or equivalent. The MMWG proved to be a critical conduit for diplomacy; it became Force Commander Lieutenant General John Sanderson's primary instrument for working and problem-solving with the Cambodian factions. In many ways the MMWG was more successful in maintaining dialogue between the factions than the Supreme National Council. When the National Army of Democratic Kampuchea (NADK), the armed forces of the Khmer Rouge, detained UNTAC personnel in late 1992 and early 1993, the MMWG successfully negotiated for their release. Despite its general recalcitrance and its refusal to participate in the Supreme National Council, the Khmer Rouge maintained an almost continuous representative presence in the MMWG until April 16, 1993, when all of its representatives left Phnom Penh.[7] By maintaining open communication lines, the MMWG worked to bring the Khmer Rouge back into the peace process and kept the Khmer Rouge apprised of the positions of UNTAC and the international community with respect to its non-compliance with the Paris Agreements.

The MMWG also served as a forum for discussing problems among the three cooperating factions. Beginning in January 1993, the MMWG began to focus on post-election security issues, with particular attention given to the amalgamation of factional armies into a unified Cambodian armed forces. Facilitating the transfer of factional military allegiances to the newly elected government was the MMWG's greatest achievement as it improved the likelihood of the military serving as a stabilizing force after UNTAC's departure.

Mine clearance training units

The Mine Clearance Training Unit (MCTU) was established as part of UNAMIC and began its work February 1992. Estimates of the number of mines in Cambodia varied from 6 to 10 million. Due to the scarcity of arable land, a situation further aggravated by the repatriation of refugees, hazardous areas continued to be occupied and farmed. Cambodia had the highest percentage of physically disabled citizens in the world with over 30,000 amputees, and between 300 and 700 new mine-related amputations took place each month.[8] The parties to the Agreements were to provide "detailed record of their minefields,"[9] and UNTAC was

---

[7]   The NADK absented itself from the MMWG for approximately three months between June 1992 and September 1992. It re-established its presence on September 17, 1992.

[8]   Human Rights Watch, *Landmines in Cambodia: The Coward's War* (New York: Human Rights Watch, September, 1991) p. 1; "Cambodia: The Facts," *The New Internationalist*, April 1993, p. 19.

[9]   Agreements on a Comprehensive Political Settlement of the Cambodia Conflict, annex

to assist with mine clearance, as well as establishing mine clearance training and mine awareness programs for the Cambodian populace.

By August 1993, more than 4 million square meters of land had been cleared, with the removal of some 37,000 mines and 2,330 Cambodians had been trained in mine clearance techniques – many of whom were employed by non-governmental organizations involved in demining.[10]

Pre-deployment planning

Though a substantive draft of the peace agreements was forwarded to the Secretary-General in January 1991 and it was clear by August that the factions were on the verge of signing a peace agreement, planning did not begin until after the Paris Agreements were signed on October 23, 1991. Through Resolution 717 (October 31, 1991), the Security Council requested that the Secretary-General present a draft implementation plan and an estimated cost of its execution. No substantive information which could serve as the basis for an implementation plan had been gathered prior to October 1991, assuring a significant delay between signature of the Agreements and UNTAC deployment.

Poor pre-deployment planning was dramatically compounded by the late appointment of component heads, some of whom were appointed only days before the "official" mission was to begin on March 15, 1992. Lacking familiarity with the Cambodian situation and denied the opportunity to work together in developing common objectives and procedures for UNTAC, component heads were not able to engage in operational planning until the mission had already begun.

Five months after the Paris Peace Agreements had been signed, on February 19, 1992, the Secretary-General released a plan for implementation of the UNTAC mandate.[11] The Security Council approved the report and, by Resolution 745, formally established UNTAC for a period not to exceed eighteen months.

The military component

In its planning for MILCOM, the Secretariat was heavily dependent on information gathered by UNAMIC, but UNAMIC lacked the staff to

---

2, para. 3(c). Available evidence indicates that none of the factional armies kept detailed records of the mines they laid. See *Land Mines in Cambodia*, at pp. 23 and 28.

[10] Further Report of the Secretary-General Pursuant to Paragraph 7 of Resolution 840 (1993), S/26260, August 26, 1993, at para. 25. Non-governmental organizations participating in demining included Halo Trust, Norwegian People's Aid, Mine Action Group, and Handicap International.

[11] Report of the Secretary-General on Cambodia, S/23613, February 19, 1992.

meet the demands of its investigatory functions. Cambodia's severely deteriorated infrastructure presented difficulties in gathering the detailed information needed for accurate planning and UNAMIC's investigatory efforts proved less than rigorous. Most critically, UNAMIC did not possess an independent capacity to accurately assess the size and deployment of the factional armies and relied instead on information volunteered by the factions. Hence, planning for MILCOM deployment occurred in the absence of accurate, in-depth information. In his February 19, 1992 report, the Secretary-General acknowledged that "[I]n spite of the efforts made by these missions, the information obtained cannot be regarded as complete ... "[12]

The civilian police component

Planning and preparation for CIVPOL's deployment was virtually non-existent. The UN had no professional police planning or operations capability. Little attention was paid to police matters until a technical survey in December 1991, which included assessment of civil administration, police, and human rights. Despite earlier UN police operations in the Congo, Irian Jaya, Cyprus, and Namibia, the UN had failed to capture those experiences in the form of doctrine, training manuals, model standard operating procedures (SOPs), CIVPOL codes of conduct or guidelines for police-contributing countries.

Concept of operations

MILCOM

The implementation plan called for phased deployment of MILCOM. The first phase involved deployment of engineer units which would continue and expand UNAMIC's work in mine clearance and initiate rehabilitation of the essential infrastructure. The engineers were to be followed by the logistics units which would prepare a firm logistical base for deployment of twelve infantry battalions. For UNTAC's operational purposes, Cambodia was divided into nine sectors; the force headquarters was located in the capital city of Phnom Penh. Seven of the sectors had one battalion assigned to them, along with appropriate support units. In two of the sectors, two battalions were deployed, along with separate sector headquarters.

The bulk of MILCOM – 10,200 soldiers – was to be posted at

---

[12] Ibid., at para. 3.

Table 2 *The factions*

Party name	Army	Troop strength	Police component
Cambodian People's Party (CPP) State of Cambodia (SOC)	Cambodian People's Armed Forces (CPAF)	60,000–130,000 (estimated)	47,000
Party of Democratic Kampuchea (PDK) (Khmer Rouge)	National Army of Democratic Kampuchea (NADK)	27,000–40,000 (estimates)	9,000
United National Front for an Independent, Neutral, Peaceful and Cooperative Cambodia (FUNCINPEC)	Armée Nationale Sihanoukiste (ANS) *National Army of Independent Kampuchea*	15,000	150
Khmer People's National Liberation Front (KPNLF)	Khmer People's National Liberation Armed Forces (KPNLAF)	10,000	400

regroupment and cantonment sites, providing monitoring and oversight. Despite the seemingly large number of infantry personnel, the scale of deployment was one UNTAC soldier for every fifteen Cambodian soldiers.[13] Other military personnel were to monitor border points to verify and buttress cessation of external military assistance. Once demobilization had occurred, the number of infantry personnel was to be reduced from 10,200 to approximately 5,100.

CIVPOL

The concept of operations envisaged in the implementation plan saw CIVPOL deploying down to district level with regular mobile patrols to monitor and supervise local police at sub-district (commune and village) level. It was estimated that CIVPOL would need to monitor some 50,000 local civil police deployed in some 1,500 police posts. Two CIVPOL personnel were to be assigned to each of the 1,500 posts, requiring a total of 3,000 monitors deployed in 200 district-level units. The balance of CIVPOL personnel was to be deployed at CIVPOL headquarters in Phnom Penh or in the twenty-one provincial head-quarters. This scale of deployment would give an estimated ratio of one CIVPOL monitor in the field to fifteen local civil police, or one monitor to approximately 3,000 Cambodians.[14]

[13] Based on middle of the road estimates of CPAF and NADK troop strength.
[14] Report of the Secretary-General at para. 131.

Deployment

MILCOM

By April 1992, MILCOM had still established only a minimal presence, with a total number of 3,694 troops in Cambodia.[15] MILCOM was not fully prepared for phase II of the ceasefire – cantonment and demobilization – which was due to begin on May 31, 1992 and be 70 percent complete in September. Even if full cooperation had been immediately forthcoming from all factions, it is unlikely that MILCOM would have been able to establish the necessary number of cantonment sites. Full deployment of MILCOM did not occur until August 1992, some ten months after signature of the Paris Peace Agreements.

CIVPOL Deployment

Deployment of CIVPOL observers did not begin until March 31, 1992 when eight Singaporean police arrived. By the end of April, only 193 police monitors had arrived.[16] Only 50 percent of CIVPOL's total strength had been deployed as of July. The pace of deployment accelerated during the second half of 1992, reaching 95 percent of CIVPOL's total strength by mid-November. Full deployment was not achieved, however, until February 1993 – sixteen months after signature of the Paris Peace Agreements.

Struggling to cease the fire

Despite its expressed commitment to the peace process, the Khmer Rouge never adhered to the ceasefire, and even intensified its attacks subsequent to the Paris Agreements.[17] It "delayed" UNAMIC's access to areas under its control, impeding the reconnaissance UNAMIC needed to prepare for Phase II of the ceasefire when cantonment and demobilization would begin. Prior to UNTAC's arrival, the Khmer Rouge expanded its territorial control. The SOC responded with "defensive" ceasefire violations. However, the SOC's

---

[15] First Progress Report of the Secretary-General on the United Nations Transitional Authority in Cambodia, S/23870, May 1, 1992, at para. 20.

[16] The Secretary-General warned that slow deployment of civilian staff "could impair UNTAC's ability to exercise adequate supervision and control where required," ibid. at paras. 47–8.

[17] Ben Kiernan, "The failures of the Paris Agreements on Cambodia, 1991–93," in *The Challenge of Indochina: An Examination of the US Role* (Congressional Staff Conference, April 30–May 2, 1993), p. 8.

"counter-offensive" had a clearly strategic intent. It, too, was attempting to expand territorial control. The clashes were most frequent in Kompong Thom, where all four factions had troops deployed.

On February 28, 1992, an UNTAC helicopter on a reconnaissance mission in Kompong Thom came under Khmer Rouge fire, injuring the force commander of the Australian contingent. UNTAC responded by deploying 200 troops to Kompong Thom to effect a ceasefire and supervise troop withdrawal. Ceasefire violations subsequently diminished in frequency. The Khmer Rouge began to allow UNTAC some freedom of movement in the areas under its control, but stopped short of allowing the full freedom UNTAC needed for reconnaissance.

After preparations for regroupment and cantonment had been made, General Sanderson announced on May 9, 1992 that Phase II of the ceasefire would begin on May 13. On June 10 the Khmer Rouge presented a new interpretation of its commitments under the Paris Agreements: the Khmer Rouge was not obligated to comply with UNTAC's requirements until UNTAC's obligations under the Agreements were met, namely the removal of all foreign military personnel from Cambodia.[18] Vietnamese soldiers in disguise were still in Cambodia, the Khmer Rouge claimed.[19] The Khmer Rouge further accused UNTAC of favoring the SOC rather than working with the Supreme National Council, thereby violating UNTAC's obligation under the Agreements to neutralize the SOC's control of Cambodia. The Khmer Rouge wanted a stronger Supreme National Council. In the interim, it steadfastly denied UNTAC access to any zones under its control.

At this juncture, UNTAC had established only three border checkpoints (along the Vietnamese border), manned by a a small contingent of the 193 CIVPOL monitors then present in Cambodia. While rejecting the legitimacy of the Khmer Rouge's interpretation of the Agreements, UNTAC quickly established ten additional checkpoints on the Cambodia–Vietnam border and launched strategic investigation teams to investigate any alleged violations of annex 2 of the Agreements.[20]

[18] Curiously, article VI (1) of the Paris Agreements does not specify who would be responsible for providing UNTAC with information on the withdrawal of foreign forces.

[19] When asked to provide evidence for this allegation, the Khmer Rouge refused, claiming that providing evidence was not its responsibility. Quite possibly, the Khmer Rouge were emphasizing concern over a Vietnamese presence as a political ploy, a not so subtle reminder of the SOC's affiliation with Vietnam, and an insinuation that the Khmer Rouge was the party of "true patriots."

[20] Annex 2 delineated the conditions for withdrawal of foreign forces, ceasefire, and general security measures. Strategic investigation teams were empowered to conduct investigations as to the presence of foreign forces and present their findings and recommendations to the Special Representative. In March 1993, UNTAC investiga-

Implementation of the UNTAC mandate reached a critical juncture in July 1992. Despite the continued non-cooperation of the Khmer Rouge, Phase II of the ceasefire – regroupment and cantonment – went into effect on June 13 as planned. Because some battalions had difficulty in reaching their areas of operations and others lacked mobility and communication capacity, MILCOM commenced phase II of the ceasefire with only nine of the twelve infantry battalions. Cantonment of the three other factions' troops began and efforts to coax the fractious Khmer Rouge back into the peace process continued.[21] At some cantonment sites, Khmer Rouge troops expressed a desire to participate in the regroupment and cantonment process, but stated that they could not do so without instructions from their commanders.[22]

The Security Council, through its Resolution 766, "strongly deplored" the Khmer Rouge's continued refusal to cooperate with UNTAC, reiterated the international community's commitment to the peace process, and demanded Khmer Rouge cooperation. The Council also urged the Secretary-General to accelerate the deployment of the civilian components, especially those involved in the supervision and control of administrative structures. By late August, all twelve infantry battalions had deployed and MILCOM was supervising some 33,000 cantoned soldiers.

As diplomatic efforts to elicit its compliance with the Agreements gained force, Khmer Rouge ceasefire violations increased in severity, as did the brutality of its attacks against ethnic Vietnamese. The Secretary-General urged perseverance in the process of cantonment and disarmament in order to demonstrate "that despite the lack of cooperation of one party [the Khmer Rouge], the international community remains determined to assist the Cambodian people."[23] At the same time,

---

tions identified three individuals, Vietnamese nationals, who were "foreign forces" within the terms of the Paris Agreements. The men had resided in Cambodia for some time, had been issued Cambodian identity cards, and had married Cambodian women. Two of them were serving with the SOC army. UNTAC requested that the SOC authorities discharge them from their armed forces and withdraw their identity cards.

[21] As of July 10, 1992, the Cambodian People's Armed Forces (SOC) had cantoned 9,003 troops, the National Army of Independent Kampuchea (FUNCINPEC) 3,187, and the Khmer People's National Liberation Armed Forces (KPNLF) 1,322.

[22] "Urge full deployment of UN transitional authority in Cambodia," *United Nations Chronicle*, vol. 29, no. 3, 1992, p. 20.

[23] Second Special Report of the Secretary-General on the United Nations Transitional Authority on Cambodia, S/24286, July 14, 1992, at para. 19. On August 27, a senior Khmer Rouge spokesman announced that it was prepared to enter cantonment but the Khmer Rouge did not set a date for commencement of cantonment, and the Khmer Rouge never did canton any of its troops. See Second Progress Report of the Secretary-General on the United Nations Transitional Authority in Cambodia, S/24578, September 21, 1992, at para. 21.

however, he recognized that the cantonment process could not proceed indefinitely with the cooperation of only three of the Cambodian factions. In order not to foster the vulnerability of those who continued to canton, some of the cantoned troops were permitted to retain their weapons. By September 10, 1992, UNTAC had cantoned 52,292 troops and taken custody of 50,000 weapons.[24]

In its Resolution 783 (October 13, 1992), the Security Council demanded that the Khmer Rouge immediately comply with the requirements for Phase II of the ceasefire, and allow the full deployment of UNTAC in areas under its control. The resolution also demanded that all parties refrain from any activity which would enlarge territories under their control.

In a further attempt to resolve the Khmer Rouge's continued non-compliance with the Paris Agreements, a series of meetings took place on October 22 and 29 in Beijing. In attendance were Prince Sihanouk and other members of the Supreme National Council (representing the four Cambodian factions), Special Representative of the Secretary-General Yasushi Akashi, and representatives of concerned members of the international community.[25] No resolution was reached during the consultations; the Khmer Rouge refused to comply while a "neutral political condition" was lacking.[26] Indeed, it became bolder in its non-compliance, moving into areas vacated by the cantonment of other factional forces. In the face of Khmer Rouge violence, the continued cantonment, disarmament, and demobilization of the other factions became an imprudent course of action and was suspended.

Tensions between the Khmer Rouge and SOC, the largest and most heavily militarized faction, escalated once again in the fall of 1992. Violence against UNTAC personnel and helicopters also increased. As of September 1992, CIVPOL was still far short of its full deployment strength of 3,600 but a diluted force of 2,500 had established an UNTAC presence in every province, a presence which was vital to the demonstration of UNTAC's commitment to the peace process. In November, the Secretary-General reiterated his belief that "patient diplomacy" was the "best means of getting the peace process back on

[24] Cantonment of factional troops: Cambodian People's Armed Forces (SOC), 42,368; National Army of Independent Kampuchea (ANS), 3,445; Khmer People's National Liberation Armed Forces (KPNLF), 6,479. See Second Progress Report of the Secretary-General on the United Nations Transitional Authority in Cambodia, S/24578, September 21, 1992 at para. 22.

[25] Representatives of the five permanent members of the Security Council as well as Australia, Germany, Japan, and Thailand took part in the consultations.

[26] Report of the Secretary-General on the Implementation of Security Council Resolution 783, S/24800, November 15, 1992, at para. 5.

track."[27] Boutros-Ghali raised the possibility of "a different approach" – possibly a circumspect synonym for using military force – to enjoin the PDK's cooperation, but noted that any "such measures would depend critically on the full cooperation of neighboring countries and other Member States."[28]

Changing the mandate

By November 1992 UNTAC was in a serious quandary. The scheduled date for elections was only six months away, yet the neutral political environment envisioned in the Agreements was elusive. The Secretary-General observed that the United Nations had only three alternatives: to admit the impossibility of fulfilling the Agreements as originally envisioned and simply leave Cambodia; to suspend the peace process until conditions were more conducive to rigorous implementation of the mandate; or, continue under the extant conditions.[29] Boutros-Ghali rejected the first option as a profound betrayal of the Cambodian people. He argued that given the deterioration of the Cambodian economy and the continued destabilization created by ongoing armed conflict, it was unlikely that a better environment for peace would emerge. As unsatisfactory as the third option was, it seemed the best of an array of less than ideal options.

On December 9, 1992, MILCOM adopted a new mandate whose objective was "to create a secure environment conducive to the preparations for, and later the conduct of, an election in Cambodia".[30] As a result of the Khmer Rouge's refusal to enter Phase II of the ceasefire, MILCOM's primary task became guaranteeing the security of the electoral process and its deployment shifted to mirror the deployment of the Electoral Component.

In the latter half of 1992, as the cantonment process stalled, releasing demobilized soldiers on "agricultural leave" increased rural banditry and seriously threatened the maintenance of law and order. Khmer Rouge violence once again escalated; skirmishes between standing armies attempting to improve their ground positions increased; the number of attacks on UNTAC rose; attacks on ethnic Vietnamese and politically motivated acts of violence against party officers and workers

---

[27] Ibid., at para. 24.

[28] Ibid., the Secretary-General recommends that other approaches not be implemented "at this stage."

[29] Report of the Secretary-General on the Implementation of Security Council Resolution 783 (1992), S/24800, November 15, 1992, at paras. 24, 25 and 26.

[30] Operation Order no. 2 for the Joint Military Component of UNTAC, issued December 9, 1992, p. 2.

became more numerous.[31] MILCOM and CIVPOL cooperated closely as CIVPOL increased its monitoring of local police patrols and established checkpoints in areas where banditry was prevalent.

As UNTAC shifted emphasis towards the administration of elections, however, CIVPOL's capacity to control and supervise the local police in their maintenance of routine law and order was seriously diminished. During voter registration, from October 5, 1992 to January 31, 1993, some 65 percent of CIVPOL monitors were engaged full-time in providing security to mobile registration teams and 800 registration sites. As voter registration progressed, politically motivated intimidation and attacks on anti-government party offices and staff increased sharply, seriously jeopardizing UNTAC's mandate to achieve a neutral political environment. Further, it became clear that factional police (most notably those of the SOC) were either incapable or unwilling to protect party offices and staff. In mid-December, in cooperation with MILCOM, CIVPOL conducted patrolling and static guard duty of those party offices (primarily FUNCINPEC) assessed to be more vulnerable to attack during the hours of darkness.[32]

Alarmed that spiraling politically motivated violence might derail the peace process and pressured by Prince Sihanouk, who threatened to resign unless steps were taken to curb the level of violence directed at FUNCINPEC, Akashi issued on January 6, 1993 a directive unprecedented in the history of UN peacekeeping operations. Directive 93–1 conferred on CIVPOL and MILCOM powers to arrest and detain suspects in cases involving serious human rights violations and established the Special Prosecutor's Office. To assist the Special Prosecutor, CIVPOL established a Special Task Force of forty-five police charged with investigating politically sensitive crimes and serious human rights violations, including the massacre of Vietnamese settlers. Although hundreds of investigations were conducted by CIVPOL officers, prosecution was hampered by excessive reliance on inadequate local public security structures and the absence of impartial judicial mechanisms. The absence of competent courts led

---

[31] UNTAC investigations indicated that the Khmer Rouge were primarily responsible for attacks against ethnic Vietnamese and that the SOC was behind attacks against members and offices of other political parties, particularly FUNCINPEC. See Report of the Secretary-General on the Implementation of Security Council Resolution 792 (1992), S/25289, February 13, 1993, at para. 13.

[32] More than 600 party offices were established. However, due to limited resources, attention was focused on the sixty offices considered to be most at risk. No attacks were recorded while party offices were guarded by UNTAC. CivPol remained unarmed throughout the eighteen-month transitional period.

to the prolonged detention of prisoners, in violation of international human rights conventions.[33]

As the May 23 date for elections drew nearer, violence escalated to a level unprecedented during UNTAC's presence. During the month of March, approximately a hundred people were killed, many for political reasons.[34] Hoping to stem the violence, Akashi issued another directive on March 17 prohibiting the possession of firearms and explosives by unauthorized persons.

On April 13, Khieu Samphan, president of the Party of Democratic Kampuchea (the political party of the Khmer Rouge), left Phnom Penh declaring in a letter to Prince Sihanouk that he would no longer attend meetings of the Supreme National Council because there was insufficient security in the city; the PDK was temporarily withdrawing from Phnom Penh. During the month of April, the Khmer Rouge intensified its attacks on other factions and declared that it would disrupt the elections by violent means, if necessary.[35] The SOC increased its harassment of other parties. Attacks on UNTAC personnel became more numerous. On May 3–4, the Khmer Rouge launched a large-scale attack on Siem Reap. Further attacks on May 19 caused several hundred refugees to seek shelter in Angkor Wat. A neutral, secure environment was far from being realized.

Despite strong pressure from the international community, Force Commander Lieutenant General Sanderson refused to place MILCOM in direct confrontation with the Khmer Rouge in order to force compliance with the Paris Agreements. He felt a confrontational course of action might destroy UNTAC's posture of impartiality and endanger the lives and tasks of both the UNTAC civilian and military personnel, thus placing the entire UNTAC mandate at risk. In the period leading up to the elections, a campaign of violence directed at UNTAC civilian and military staff and UN volunteers caused a crisis of confidence within UNTAC. Many UNTAC officials called for the postponement or the cancelation of elections.

Though unable to disarm the factions, MILCOM did strengthen security for the civilian components of UNTAC, including the unarmed

---

[33] Article 10 of the Universal Declaration of Human Rights, art. 9(3) of the International Covenant on Civil and Political Rights.

[34] Fourth Progress Report of the Secretary-General on the United Nations Transitional Authority in Cambodia, S/25719, May 3, 1993, at para. 109.

[35] In the month of April, UNTAC received reports of 44 separate attacks on civilians by the Khmer Rouge. These attacks resulted in 62 deaths, 137 injuries, and 31 abductions. Source: UNTAC daily press briefing of May 11, 1993.

CIVPOL monitors.[36] MILCOM sector commanders conducted daily security status reviews for every district in the country. Increased security measures included fixed guards and mobile patrols and, in high-risk areas, MILCOM personnel were stationed at polling stations, staff issued with protective gear, and medical support units deployed. In support of the six-week electoral campaign beginning April 7, 1993, CIVPOL successfully monitored over 1,500 campaign rallies, ensuring they were free from political intimidation.

In May 1993, the Secretary-General declared that initial expectations had been overly optimistic and that it was neither realistic nor fair to hold the elections to standards prevailing in stable or democratic countries. He asserted, "UNTAC will be conducting the most impartial election that is possible in conditions that are not susceptible to its full control."[37] CIVPOL's contribution to the election process culminated with the conduct of elections from May 23 to 28, 1993. Generally, CIVPOL provided a security presence at the polling sites while MILCOM secured the approaches to the sites.

Conclusion of the elections did not result in peace. The SOC initially rejected the legitimacy of the election results, and the post-election period was marked by renewed Khmer Rouge violence. On July 1, General Sanderson met with a Khmer Rouge representative to negotiate a ceasefire. By July 16, both the SOC and PDK had agreed to accept the election results.

UNTAC withdrawal

UNTAC was unusual among UN peacekeeping missions in that its mandate had an eighteen-month time limit. Successful conduct of the elections resulted in the conclusion of the CIVPOL and MILCOM mandates. The two components initiated phased withdrawals; CIVPOL began disengagement on July 16 and MILCOM on August 1. The phased withdrawals allowed UNTAC to serve as a stabilizing force until a new constitution could be drafted. Internal security remained a problem, however, as disarmament had never been successfully completed and many Cambodians retained high-power weapons. The Khmer Rouge persisted in sporadic attacks and widespread banditry continued to plague the country. On October 5, 1993, First Prime Minister Norodom Ranariddh and Second Prime Minister Hun Sen

---

[36] Report of the Secretary-General in Pursuance of Paragraph 6 of Security Council Resolution 810 (1993), S/25784, May 15, 1993, at paras. 14–9.

[37] Report of the Secretary-General in Pursuance of Paragraph 6 of Security Council Resolution 810 (1993), S/25784, May 15, 1993, at para. 22.

requested the continuation of a UN presence of twenty to thirty military observers in order to maintain confidence in the fledgling government.[38] The Security Council authorized the continued presence of twenty unarmed military liaison officers who were to remain in Cambodia for a period of six months. The team was to liaise with the Cambodian government and the Secretary-General, and to resolve residual military matters related to the Paris Agreements. CIVPOL completed its withdrawal on October 15, 1993 and MILCOM on November 15.

Evaluating the success of MILCOM and CIVPOL

MILCOM

If MILCOM is judged on the mandate originally envisioned by the Paris Peace Agreements, it failed. It neither disarmed the factional armies nor established a neutral political environment. To some extent, MILCOM's failure must be attributed to the inachievability of its mandate in the absence of factional cooperation. However, UNTAC's execution of the MILCOM mandate was also hampered by the inefficiencies of the UN bureaucracy. The most serious consequence of those inefficiencies, delayed deployment, may have contributed to Khmer Rouge recalcitrance.

MILCOM came under greatest fire for failing to disarm the Khmer Rouge, but this "failure" was largely the consequence of a political failure at the negotiation stage. Critically lacking in the text of the Agreements was a clear plan of action in the event that one of the parties would fail to comply with the Agreements's disarmament provisions. Section IX of the Final Provisions stated:

[I]n the event of a violation or threat of violation of this Agreement, [the two co-Chairmen of the Paris Peace Conference on Cambodia] will immediately undertake appropriate consultations, including with members of the Paris Conference on Cambodia, with a view to taking appropriate steps to insure respect for these commitments.

Article X of annex 2 (Withdrawal, Ceasefire and Related Measures) declared only that possible non-compliance would be investigated. The omission of enforcement provisions may have resulted from the understandable desire on the part of the negotiators to reach some kind of settlement. Those involved in the settlement and the negotiations – the members of the Security Council's Permanent Five, as well as other

---

[38] This request was supported by France, Pakistan, New Zealand, the United Kingdom, and ASEAN.

interested international parties – proceeded as if the four factions were fully and sincerely committed to the peace process when, in fact, the preceding negotiations had indicated there were a number of potential stress points. Failure to address withdrawal of cooperation during the negotiation stages left UNTAC to deal with it *in media res*.

Commentators have suggested that a greater use of force could have had a decisive impact and allowed the conduct of elections in a secure and stabilized political environment. However, such a use of force would not have been consonant with prior UN peacekeeping doctrine and the practice of maintaining neutrality. The UN's decision not to use force to disarm the Khmer Rouge was consistent with a vision of peacekeeping described by one commentator as a "temporary expedient to contain conflict and prevent further violence and to create a favorable climate conducive to peacemaking."[39] In broadest terms, UNTAC's mandate was to give Cambodia a chance to establish a peace. It could not force a peace on unwilling factions, if for no other reason than that it lacked the capacity to do so. General Sanderson repeatedly emphasized that UNTAC was a diplomatic mission with a military component, not a military mission with a diplomatic component. Disarming the Khmer Rouge would have required a military force much larger than the 15,900 UNTAC soldiers deployed.[40]

Nonetheless, delayed deployment may have contributed to the Khmer Rouge's refusal to cooperate with UNTAC. Between signing of the Agreements and full deployment of MILCOM, there was a gap of ten months, a delay which proved highly detrimental.[41] The UN ignored a critical element of the peacemaking process: signing of an armistice agreement in and of itself cannot guarantee continued stabilization. The goodwill between parties at the conclusion of a lengthy negotiation is highly contingent; ground conditions and the disposition of the parties is subject to rapid changes unless forces quickly enter to stabilize the situation. Cambodians expected that the creation of UNTAC would bring immediate peace and stabilization. The factions expected that an immediate UN presence would serve to militarily "neutralize" the other factions. Instead there was a period of power vacuum during which the

[39] K. Venkata Raman, "United Nations peacekeeping and the future of world order," in Henry Wiseman (ed.), *Peacekeeping: Appraisals and Proposals* (New York: Pergamon Press, 1983) p. 375.

[40] Lindsay Murdoch, "The Peacemaker: our diplomatic coup in Cambodia," *The Sydney Morning Herald*, October 2, 1993 at p. 3A; Masanor Kikuta, "Akashi goes Asian way on his UN peacekeeping mission," Japan Economic Newswire, September 26, 1993.

[41] Although UNTAC was formally in effect on March 15, 1992, deployment was still ongoing. "Full" deployment of MILCOM was not completed until August 1992. CIVPOL completed deployment even later, full strength was not reached until February 1993.

SOC and Khmer Rouge recommenced their battle for political and military supremacy. The delayed deployment of MILCOM contributed to an environment of instability which made all parties – particularly the skittish Khmer Rouge – reluctant to demobilize and disarm.

Fuller execution of the UNTAC mandate might have been possible through extension of its eighteen-month time frame or by deferring elections until the full cooperation of all parties had been obtained through more intensive diplomatic efforts. Common sense would seem to dictate that if a stable peace was the objective of the United Nations, greater effort should have been expended to guarantee that peace. Instead, despite the flaws in UNTAC's implementation, and in the face of valid criticisms of UNTAC's efficacy, the "peace process" kept stumbling forward. Raoul Jennar has suggested that the purpose of UNTAC was not to establish peace, but rather to "erase the Cambodian file from the [Security Council's] list of international problems" and install "a government whose recognition will not raise problems between the great powers."[42] Indeed, the Security Council seemed less concerned with establishing a durable peace in Cambodia than in establishing a legitimate, "recognizable" government.

Within the limitations placed upon it by the nature of peacekeeping and the deficiencies of the UN bureaucracy, MILCOM was relatively effective in providing the conditions necessary for the elections to take place. Its presence made it possible for the other UNTAC components to continue their work despite an atmosphere of violence, and its securing of approaches to polling sites made it feasible for the vast majority of Cambodians to vote without harassment. However, MILCOM's efficacy might have been greatly enhanced by timely deployment.

CIVPOL

At best, CIVPOL's record of achievement was mixed. In conjunction with MILCOM, CIVPOL made a valuable contribution in promoting security for the electoral process, the fulcrum of UNTAC's activities. CIVPOL, however, fell far short of fulfilling its primary mandate of supervising and controlling the local police. Challenged by an overly ambitious mandate and frustrated by poor planning, staffing, and the absence of a working justice system, CIVPOL had limited success in fostering law and order. The significant involvement of CIVPOL in the electoral process further weakened its ability to supervise and control the local police. In common with other components, CIVPOL's successes in

[42] Raoul M. Jennar, *Cambodian Chronicles (III)* (Joidoigne, Belgium: European Far Eastern Research Center, 1992), p. 2.

securing physical electoral processes involved actions that, by and large, did not require the active cooperation of the Cambodian factions. While CIVPOL conducted hundreds of criminal investigations, prosecution was frustrated by the absence of a functioning justice infrastructure. Although the human rights situation improved during the transitional period, CIVPOL made few contributions toward post-conflict peace building. Most significantly, it failed to prepare factional police for unification.

Lessons

In most cases, the observations that follow are by no means unique to UNTAC. The lessons learned generally serve to reinforce the enduring and widely supported principles governing peacekeeping missions.[43] Though the UN had mounted twenty-three previous peacekeeping missions, these missions were limited in scale and mandate due to the restrictions imposed on UN actions by deadlock among the permanent members of the Security Council. The UN was ill prepared to take on the challenges of a mission of UNTAC's mammoth dimensions, and needs to draw certain lessons from this experience.

Achievability of the MILCOM mandate

Operationally, the Paris Agreements, as clarified by the Secretary-General's implementation plan, provided a relatively clear and achievable basis on which to develop plans and mission statements. The time frame delineated by the plan, however, was unrealistic from the outset. The plan was released on February 19 and full deployment was to occur by May – a deployment span of a little over two months. The pace of deployment outlined by the Secretary-General would have been realistic only if the UN had engaged in contingency planning some six to eight months prior to signing of the Agreements.

The achievability of the mandate was rendered even more unlikely when, soon after implementation began, it became clear that two conditions necessary for a successful peacekeeping operation were lacking: the cooperation of the parties, and agreement on the mandate. The Khmer Rouge refused to cooperate because it claimed that UNTAC had failed to establish effective control over the SOC's governance

---

[43] The commonly accepted principles of traditional peacekeeping are listed in Gareth Evans's *Cooperating For Peace: The Global Agenda for the 1990s and Beyond* (St. Leonards: Allen and Unwin, 1993), p. 104. A useful discussion on the conditions for effective peacekeeping appears on pp. 109–13.

structures and because foreign forces (i.e. Vietnamese soldiers) remained in Cambodia. UNTAC did have significant problems exercising "control and supervision" over the SOC, but the Khmer Rouge's version of "control and supervision" was so extreme as to be unworkable. What the Khmer Rouge wanted was complete dismantling of the extant SOC governmental structures. Further, the Khmer Rouge's definition of "foreign forces" was inordinately broad. Ethnic Vietnamese who had long lived in Cambodia, as well as Cambodians associated with the Vietnamese-installed regime, were put in the category of "Vietnamese soldiers."[44] Given these "disagreements" over the meaning of the mandate under the Agreements, the achievability of the MILCOM mandate became more and more improbable.

With each peacekeeping mission that falls short of its stated mandate, greater doubt is cast upon the UN's credibility – its ability to do what it says it will. In defining the mandates of future peacekeeping missions, the UN must carefully balance the need to formulate politically viable mandates with a cognizance of the practical constraints which will be encountered in the course of executing those mandates. Potential barriers to implementation need to be examined, with the worst case scenario included in the realm of possibility. On an operational level, the UN should insure that it has the institutional capacity to fulfill the obligations assigned it by a specific accord before it agrees to undertake those obligations.

Planning peacekeeping missions

MILCOM deployment was slow primarily because there was lack of information on which to base a plan of deployment. Preparations for deployment should commence early in the negotiation process, as soon as it becomes apparent that a multinational peace operation may be required. Pre-emptive planning could also support the negotiation process and might insure that mandates and timetables for implementation match the realities of available resources and conditions on the ground. Planners should aim to release a detailed plan immediately after the signing of a peace agreement. The early identification of key mission staff, preferably during the negotiation phase of conflict resolution, would insure greater familiarity with mission objectives and continuity of knowledge into the deployment and operational phases of a peace operation.

While improved planning mechanisms may reduce the timing required

---

[44] Nayan Chanda, "Cambodia: in search of an elusive peace," *The American-Vietnamese Dialogue*, February 8–11, Conference Report (Queenstown, Md.: The Aspen Institute, 1993) at p. 22.

for deployment, there will inevitably be difficulties in mounting any peace operation of this scale. UN negotiators need to be cognizant of the practical difficulties of establishing peace operations and educate the parties accordingly. When drafting peace agreements, every effort must be made to factor in deployment timings. Peace agreements should set flexible timings for key events such as ceasefire monitoring or the conduct of elections. Where circumstances warrant, as in the case of non-cooperation by one party to an agreement, the occurrence of key events could be made conditional upon the full deployment of peacekeepers.

Competent planning is contingent upon reliable information. There is a demonstrated need for the UN to develop an autonomous information collection and assessment capability. While there are sensitivities within the international community regarding the provision of intelligence to the UN Secretariat, this only serves to strengthen the argument that the UN needs to develop an independent capability for information gathering and assessments. Much of the information needed could be collected from open sources, utilizing the vast network of UN agencies, non-governmental organizations and academic institutions to provide information and assessments on a targeted range of social and geopolitical issues. Aerial imagery to obtain specific infrastructure and military geographic information could also be sourced commercially. Improved information collection capacity must be accompanied by a competent assessment staff if the information is to be of any value. The UN continues to dispatch survey missions that are poorly planned and staffed. Key mission staff designates and subject experts must form part of survey teams with clear terms of reference.

The UN bureaucracy

Aside from inadequate planning, effective deployment was constrained by cumbersome and inflexible procurement and budgetary processes. Although the General Assembly had approved an advance budget of $200 million, the Secretariat's equipment procurement, staff recruitment and transport contracting procedures were unable to match a demanding timetable. As a priority, member states must press the UN to overhaul its outdated and inflexible financial rules and regulations and contracting procedures. Start-up funding must also be enlarged to accommodate the high initial costs of establishing peace operations.

Command and control

General John Sanderson, UNTAC's force commander, faced a number of command and control challenges. National restrictions seriously diminished Sanderson's ability to employ the peacekeeping force to maximum advantage. The French battalion, for example, was initially to be deployed to the remote eastern provinces because it was well equipped and had substantial logistical support. However, at the insistence of the French government, the battalion was eventually deployed to Sihanoukville and reportedly operated almost completely autonomously from UNTAC. In order to replace the French, the underequipped Uruguayan battalion was sent to the remote eastern provinces. Thai and Japanese engineers were restricted from taking any part in defending the electoral process. Out of UNTAC's force of 15,900 a mere 9,000 could be employed in a flexible manner.[45]

Another constraint on unified command and control was the inclusion of national guarantees in the concepts for operations (limitations which were demarcated by national governments), especially in the coordination of logistical support and rules of engagement in cases of self-defense. For some directives, several UNTAC contingents refused to act without their home government's approval. A uniform concept of peacekeeping operations is critically needed, given the diversity of languages, standards of training, and contingent expectations. Member states and the UN need to clarify and reduce limitations on the deployment of their troops and whatever limitations are placed on national troops should be known well in advance of deployment.

Communication between New York and Phnom Penh

In standard military practice, field commanders usually report to headquarters, but in Cambodia, the UN's Department of Peacekeeping Operations (DPKO) exercised no command function. Distracted by Bosnia and Somalia, UN headquarters functioned only as a resource coordinator. When there were ambiguities in priorities – for example, between operations and logistical matters – Sanderson was left to negotiate his own way through. New York was twelve hours ahead of Phnom Penh and the DPKO could not be contacted after working hours or on weekends. Sanderson subsequently suggested the establishment of a liaison cell in New York, with the cell to be staffed by personnel from the mission and reporting to the Force Commander.[46] This suggestion was adopted for UNPROFOR and UNOSOM II and resulted in improved field/headquarters communications. It is to be hoped that the

---

[45] Interview with a senior UNTAC military officer.
[46] Lieutenant General John M. Sanderson, "Preparation for, deployment and conduct of peacekeeping operations: a Cambodia snapshot," paper presented at UN Peacekeeping at the Crossroads, International Seminar, Canberra, March 21–24, 1993.

liaison cell will become a standard feature of peacekeeping operations, and the UN will, in future peacekeeping operations, provide improved backstopping for its commanding field officers.

CIVPOL

CIVPOL's failure to fulfill its mandate can be distilled to five key interrelated deficiencies: the unrealistic nature of its mandate, lack of adequate preparation and planning, command and control issues, the quality of its personnel, and the absence of a criminal justice infra- structure in Cambodia.

Achievability of the CIVPOL mandate

While CIVPOL's mandate to "control and supervise" was clearer than the vague "monitoring" mandate allocated to the United Nations Transition Assistance Group for Namibia (UNTAG) civilian police element, it is arguable whether the mandate was achievable or realistic given the state of policing and the law and order situation in Cambodia. As UNTAC's Civil Administration Component quickly discovered, the ability to "control and supervise" depended largely upon the willingness of the factions to cooperate. It needs to be recalled that in Cambodia, the SOC alone possessed a civilian police structure (although centralized control of provincial police was weak). Local police were poorly paid and trained, lacking investigative skills and a basic understanding of life in an open society. Although the local police continued to be responsible for law enforcement under the Paris Agreements, they possessed neither the competence nor the resources required to carry out that responsi- bility.

Though some CIVPOL officers saw training as the key means of setting standards, arguing that control and supervision could not be attained until standards had been established, CIVPOL failed to establish minimum police standards. With minimal direction and support from CIVPOL headquarters and no provision in the UNTAC budget for the training and recruitment of factional police, CIVPOL's training effort was largely ineffectual and failed to make a significant contribution toward the creation of a unified national police force.

Future UN civilian police mandates should be based on achievable goals, taking into account the status of police operations as the UN enters the host country. Further, UN CIVPOLs must be allocated the resources necessary to execute the tasks delineated by their mandates, including requisite monies for training and equipment of local police.

Planning and preparation

As previously noted, planning and preparation for CIVPOL was seriously lacking. Given the paucity of reliable information on the policing situation in Cambodia, the UN made a serious error in failing to capitalize on the advance mission UNAMIC by deploying an advance police planning unit. Until a police advisor was appointed in May 1993 to establish a Police Unit in the DPKO, the UN had no professional police planning or operations capability. Police deployments continue to be managed by military and civilian political officers, however, rather than by those with policing experience.[47]

When a peacekeeping mission is to have a police component, a police planning unit should be part of its advance mission. Planning units must be staffed by experienced police personnel who will take part both in the deployment of CIVPOL and, upon completion of deployment, in oversight of the general police operations.

Quality of personnel

Undoubtedly, the greatest obstacle CIVPOL faced in implementing its mandate was the poor quality of many CIVPOL monitors. Due to limited planning and varying national standards, many contingents arrived inadequately trained and prepared. Although the UN had set minimum standards for police monitors (specified police experience, medical standards, driving skills and the ability to communicate in French or English), these were found to be absent in far too many instances. Many contingents lacked basic community policing skills, particularly investigative skills and a knowledge of human rights. Some countries ignored the UN's experience criteria by providing military police, gendarmerie, border police, or some others "dressed in police uniform without even being a policeman."[48] Discipline and motivation were lacking in many cases, leading one senior CIVPOL officer to report that "a number admitted that they were only staying for MSA [mission subsistence allowance] purposes and did not want to be here or work."[49] Many CIVPOL monitors were reportedly unwilling or unable to conduct investigations. While some observers have called for the enforcement of more rigid selection criteria, the reality of competition for scarce

---

[47] In early 1994, a second police officer was posted to the Police Unit and plans have been submitted for a modest enlargement of the unit.

[48] Klaas Roos, *Evaluation Report: UN CIVPOL, UNTAC, Cambodia*, Phnom Penh, August 1993, p. 8.

[49] CIVPOL District Commanders' "end of mission" report (UNTAC internal). Some forty-six CIVPOL monitors were repatriated on disciplinary grounds.

personnel resources, complicated by factors of national balance and impartiality, generally reduces the UN to accepting what is offered.

Command and control

Ineffectiveness of command and control also limited CIVPOL's ability to fulfill its mandate. CIVPOL headquarters failed to set clear objectives and measurable standards appropriate to the Cambodian situation. At provincial and district levels, CIVPOL officers were left to write their own objectives based upon their interpretation of the mandate. In some cases this resulted in an overly restrictive interpretation of the mandate with CIVPOL monitoring, rather than controlling local police, as well as a reluctance to undertake independent and proactive investigations. If similar mandates are to be achieved in the future, setting clear objectives and measurable standards for civilian police will be critical.

Lack of a justice infrastructure

Finally, the absence of a comprehensive and functioning justice infrastructure "frustrated many attempts to demonstrate the effectiveness of the rule of law."[50] Although judicial and penal standards had been set, and CIVPOL monitors had been granted powers of arrest and detention, the absence of an independent, functioning court system hampered CIVPOL's criminal investigation process.[51] Where the crime involved sensitive political or ethnic considerations, Special Representative Akashi raised the issue with the Supreme National Council and the parties concerned. Investigations did not lead to prosecution, prompting Special Prosecutor Mark Plunkett to comment that "in order to effect a peaceful settlement UNTAC compromised justice for political considerations."[52]

Conclusion

MILCOM and CIVPOL were far from perfect in the execution of their original mandates; but they were successful in providing the Cambodian

[50] Commissioner Peter McAulay, "Civilian police and peacekeeping challenges in the 1990s," in Hugh Smith (ed.), *Peacekeeping: Challenges for the Future* (Canberra: Australian Defense Studies Centre, Australian Defense Force Academy, 1993), p. 37.

[51] In addition to discouraging independent investigations, this led to the embarrassing and illegal situation where UNTAC had to keep two suspects in detention for over six months.

[52] Ian Phedran, "UNTAC's success questioned," *Canberra Times*, August 20, 1993, p. 11. UNTAC's apparent unwillingness to take action against SOC officials is described by Nate Thayer in "UNTAC fails to stem political violence," *Phnom Penh Post*, February 12–25, 1993, pp. 3, 16.

people an opportunity to experience the democratic process for the first time. In this, the two components fulfilled the most fundamental task of peacekeeping: they gave Cambodia a chance to establish its own peace. The deficiencies and failures of both components reiterate many of the lessons that past peacekeeping operations should have instilled in the UN and its member states. UNTAC also served to highlight the complexities of current peacekeeping operations. Current demands on the UN's peacekeeping capacities are enormous, with each new mission adding new challenges. It is hoped that the UN will become more adept at peacekeeping through assimilation of lessons drawn from its past.

Authority and elections in Cambodia

Michael W. Doyle

Introduction

Between May 23 and May 28, 1993, the citizens of Cambodia, who had lived through more than twenty years of civil war, massacre and invasion, voted in a long-awaited election run by the United Nations. The election was the culmination of years of peace talks as well as fifteen months of peacekeeping by the United Nations Transitional Authority in Cambodia (UNTAC).

The news from Cambodia over the preceding months seemed uniformly bleak – massacres of ethnic Vietnamese, attacks on UN soldiers and civilians, harassment of opposition political parties, and incidents of renewed fighting. Journalists, following leaks from critics within UNTAC, had been drawn to the setbacks; and many had written off UNTAC as a failure. Once the election was successfully completed, an opposite pattern was set in the reporting. All the problems that plagued the conduct of the eighteen-month operation were swept aside by the glow of a successful week of elections.

UNTAC assumed an unprecedented degree of "transitional authority" over Cambodia. Not since the colonial era and the post World War II allied occupations of Germany and Japan had a foreign presence held so much formal administrative jurisdiction over the civilian functions of an independent country. In Cambodia, unlike what the UN would next be expected to achieve in Somalia, this authority was exercised with the formal consent of the four parties to Cambodia's long civil strife, a consent negotiated in painstaking detail and embodied in the Paris Agreement of 1991.

I would like to thank Jarat Chopra, Ian Johnstone, F. T. Liu, Mark Metrikas, Florence Musaffi, Robert Orr, Steve Ratner, Nishkala Suntharalingam, Ayaka Suzuki and Elisabeth Uphoff for their various contributions and suggestions. Parts of this paper draw on my *UN Peacekeeping in Cambodia: UNTAC's Civil Mandate* (Boulder, Col.: Lynne Rienner, 1995) and on Michael Doyle and Ayaka Suzuki, "Transitional Authority in Cambodia," in Tom Weiss (ed.), *The United Nations and Civil Wars* (Boulder, Col.: Lynne Rienner, 1995).

It is time to explore the significance of UNTAC's civil mandate for other complex, multidimensional peacekeeping and peacebuilding operations that the United Nations may be undertaking in the future. In this chapter, I will take a look at the central elements of UNTAC's civil mandate. I focus on the civil administration and electoral components. The election, with the vital support of all of UNTAC, became the successful centerpiece of the Cambodian peace; civil administration, by and large a failure, reveals the challenges of multidimensional peace-keeping in the midst of civil strife. After examining what worked well and what didn't, I assess the factors that produce success and failure in civil peacekeeping and peacebuilding operations.

UNTAC's civil mandate

UNTAC, in many ways, was a landmark mission that clearly symbolized a new generation of peacekeeping operations in its scope of mandate and size of deployment. The civil components of UNTAC took on very ambitious functions of state-building unprecedented in the history of UN peacekeeping. The peacekeeping mission in the Congo (now Zaire) in the 1960s was the first time an operation involved a large civil component. That situation was different, however, as the Congo was not prepared to conduct its own administration when the Belgians, then the colonial power of the Congo, abruptly departed the country amid the chaos of independence. The situation in the Congo was extremely challenging, requiring substantial technical administrative assistance. The situation in Cambodia, though, posed much more intricate political challenges.[1]

After the ravage of conflicts, the infrastructure of Cambodia was completely devastated to the extent that the deployment of civilian peacekeepers was delayed. Beyond the effects of delay lay unprecedented conceptual challenges. There simply was no prior UN equivalent of exercising control over an existing administrative structure as part of the peace settlement process. The civil control of ONUC was predomi-nantly technical (with political implications), while the civil functions of UNTAC were heavily laced with political complications as UNTAC sought a "neutral environment" conducive to free and fair elections. UNTAC had to assume control over a country which had been actually run by four bitter political rivals.

UNTAC's civil mandate included not only civil administration and the national election, but also human rights, civil police, rehabilitation,

---

[1] For a valuable reflection on the significance of the Congo operation see Alan James, "The Congo controversies," *International Peacekeeping*, vol. 1, no. 1, 1994, pp. 44–58.

and information.[2] Each component was affected by the continuing civil war and the defection of the Khmer Rouge from the peace, but their experiences in attempting to meet the mandate differed. In the two key areas of civil administrative control and the election, one overall was a failure, the other overall a success. Rehabilitation also by and large failed, while human rights came closer to achieving its mandate and information exceeded its mandate.

None of these constitutes individual failures or successes of the specific UNTAC components, per se, though some of the components operated much more effectively than others (as I will note). The mandates were too interdependent – on each of the other components and on the Cambodians and the international community – to analyze outcomes in simple bureaucratic template.

I devote most of the chapter to an assessment of the two key mandates – control of civil administration and the election. I also briefly consider two other components that shared many features with the two main civil mandates, grouping human rights with the former, while considering information/education with the latter. I then turn to some of the general factors that can serve to account for their varying outcomes.

Civil administration

The Security Council mandated UNTAC to control five areas of civil administration over each of the four factions: defense, public security, finance, information, and foreign affairs. By controlling them – so it was anticipated – UNTAC would be able to "ensure a neutral political environment conducive to free and fair general elections," the provision of article 6 of the Paris Agreement.[3] If successful, no faction (and especially not the predominant faction of the State of Cambodia) would be able to employ sovereign resources to tilt the electoral contest in its

---

[2]   Elisabeth Uphoff discusses rehabilitation issues later in this volume.

[3]   See the Secretary-General's Report of February 19, 1992, S/23613, paras. 92–111. Civil administration drew its specific framework of activities from annex 1 of the Paris Agreement as well as the Proposal for Discussion ("non-paper") drafted by participants at the Tokyo Ministerial Conference on the Rehabilitation and Reconstruction of Cambodia (S/24286, annex). Although the elections seem to limit the five areas of the control mandate, foreign affairs had little potential effect on the elections. The five areas also reflected the five areas introduced by China at the behest of the Khmer Rouge into the failed negotiations for Paris I, when the object was quadripartite sovereignty, not elections. This together with the fact that the UN mandate, the Secretary-General's Report of February 19, was never translated into Khmer occasioned some confusion.

favor. Though ambiguous in parts, UNTAC's central mandate was not to govern Cambodia, simply to "control" it.[4]

In order to achieve this, UNTAC's civil administration component (CIVADMIN), headed by Gerard Porcell, had the authority to issue "binding directives," but it was urged to rely on "codes of conduct and guidelines for management." [5] In his Second Progress Report on UNTAC, the Secretary-General stated that he envisaged UNTAC not as an "administrative bureaucracy" but rather as the monitor and supervisor of existing administrative structures at both national and provincial levels.[6] The civil administration component attempted to exercise control via three operational means: control a posteriori, control a priori, and control by appraisal. Control a posteriori involved obtaining all the documentation dealing with the activities of the existing administrative structures (EAS)[7] in areas of their decision-making, personnel policies, and *materiel* questions. Control a priori involved having CIVADMIN obtain prior knowledge of all decisions made on such matters as personnel and finance, and giving the UN the authority to change the decision if it deemed necessary. Finally, control by appraisal was exercised by proposing improvement in the activities of the EAS. CIVADMIN also attempted to exercise direct control by inserting UNTAC staff in the EASs and by holding weekly meetings with decision-makers of the EAS.

CIVADMIN was organized into several specialized sub-components. Five specialized services were to control the Phnom Penh authority's ministries (the State of Cambodia's existing administrative structure). The Complaints and Investigation Service was asssigned responsibility for handling civilian complaints against the Phnom Penh regime's existing administrative structure (EAS). Provincial offices, located in all twenty-one provinces, were to cover the EASs in the rest of Cambodia. By August 1992, a total of 818 civil administration staff members were deployed, consisting of 157 professional international staff members, 62 general service international staff, and 599 local staff members.[8]

On July 1, 1992, the component began its effort to exercise "control" of the mandated areas of the Phnom Penh administration, where

[4] For a good analysis of the CIVADMIN role see Lyndall McLean, "Civil administration in transition," ADFA Seminar, Canberra, May 1994, and UNTAC, Final Report of the Civil Administration Component, Phnom Penh, September 16, 1993, pp. 1–37.

[5] Secretary-General's Report of February 19, 1992, para. 95.

[6] UN doc. S/24578.

[7] Existing administrative structures (EAS) refer to Cambodia's de facto administrations. The main four EASs were the State of Cambodia (the Hun Sen) government, and its three major opposition groups: FUNCINPEC (the royalist party), PDK (Khmer Rouge), and BLDP (Son Sann).

[8] UNTAC doc., "Note sur le contrôle de l'administration civile," August 19, 1992, p. 5.

CIVADMIN personnel were deployed in the ministries of defense, national security, foreign affairs, consular affairs, finance, and the national bank. By July 15, 1992, UNTAC civil administration provincial offices were established in all twenty-one provinces including 95 international staff in Phnom Penh and 123 in the provinces. The typical provincial office consisted of four to six officers, the number varying because some officers such as the human rights officer or the financial controller were not present in all provincial offices. In particular, district controllers were only present in the SOC-controlled areas. The control team, established in January 1993, supplemented the regular supervision that the component exercised over the EAS outside Phnom Penh because it "otherwise would tend to be inadequate because of the relatively small number of UNTAC personnel devoted to each province."[9] Headed by an inspector, the team was composed of representatives of military and civilian police components, staff from finance and public security services of CIVADMIN, and analysts and interpreters from the Information and Education Division. This mobile team, using its authority of unrestricted access to documents, was to verify if the EAS administration at the provincial and district levels was being conducted in a politically neutral manner during the electoral process.

The Foreign Affairs Service took on three major areas of activities: overhauling the visa and passport system, streamlining immigration processes, and monitoring the distribution of foreign aid.[10] The officers from this unit joined the border control unit to collect information on border practices as well as to secure the implementation of the Supreme National Council moratoria on the illegal export of logs and petroleum.[11] The Defense Service's primary task was to "depoliticize" the SOC defense structure by eliminating political units within the armed forces. A priori control was exercised over the decisions of the Ministry of Defense with respect to issues such as the sale, lease, and exchange of land.[12] The Public Security Service trained magistrates and police officers of the EAS, drafted the penal code, and visited prisons both in Phnom Penh and the provinces. This service also organized a biweekly working group on public security attended by representatives of all four

[9] Ibid.
[10] "Notes on the control exercised by the civil administration component," UNTAC doc. Activity Reports of Civil Administration – September–October, November, December, 1992, and January 1993; "Report on UNTAC's activities: civil administration component," September 7, 1992.
[11] UNTAC doc., "Border control unit final report, " September 1993.
[12] UNTAC doc., "Activity report of civil administration, September–October, 1992," November 27, 1992, p. 4.

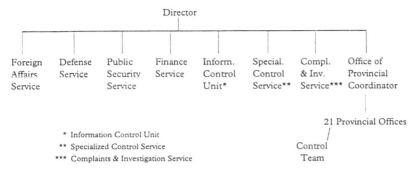

Figure 1   UNTAC CIVADMIN

parties to discuss issues such as banditry (a major security concern in Cambodia), traffic, and penal procedures.[13] From the Finance Service, financial controllers were dispatched to each of the ministries, to the National Bank of Cambodia, and to most of the provincial administrations for the purpose of controlling budgetary expenditures. In an effort to be even-handed, they audited the operating costs of the community development and health programs of the KPNLF and FUNCINPEC. The service also was directed to exercise control over taxation and customs revenues.[14] The Information Control Unit monitored more than twenty Cambodian media institutions, information activities in the provinces, and prepared the media guidelines signed by all four parties.

The Specialized Control Service had the authority to supervise the areas deemed "optional," which included public health, education, agriculture, maritime and riverine fisheries, communications and posts, energy production and distribution, navigable waters and public transport, tourism and historical monuments, mines and general administration.[15] The objectives envisaged for the Complaints and Investigations Service were twofold: its immediate function was the resolution of particular complaints, but its second and wider objective was to obtain a country-wide profile of the nature and extent of complaints. By January 1993, more than 140 complaints had been lodged, most of them concerning land and property disputes, including disputes over evictions from land.[16] The Office of Provincial Coordination was established at the headquarters of the civil administration to coordinate the operation of CIVADMIN's twenty-one provincial offices. The office dispensed information as well as provided assistance, training, logistical, and other

[13] UN doc. S/25719, p. 15.   [14] UN doc. S/24578, September 1992, p. 8.
[15] UN doc. S/24578, p. 9   [16] UN doc. S/25124, January 25, 1993, p. 16.

support to the provincial offices.[17] Exasperated by the resistance of SOC to UNTAC control and concerned about the mounting political violence, in January 1993 UNTAC established Control Teams, reporting directly to Deputy Special Representative Sadry, in order to investigate possible abuses of the Paris Agreements.

From the outset, the Civil Administration Component was plagued with various ailments shared by all the components of UNTAC: delays in staffing, the collapse of the Cambodian bureaucracy, and Cambodia's lack of infrastructure.[18] The central challenge for CIVADMIN, however, was special: the attempt by a foreign entity to exercise intrusive control over an existing set of heretofore sovereign authorities, and a fortiori a centralized, communist bureaucracy such as the SOC. The local authorities naturally resisted to the degree that they could in those areas that they judged most vital to their survival.

Accomplishments and limitations

The Civil Administration component's overall performance was far from a success; but neither was it a complete failure. Overall, there were some accomplishments together with many serious setbacks. It is therefore useful to break down the functions of the component into micro-objectives, such as controlling the country's exchange rates, to gain insight as to what worked and what did not, before assessing the overall impact of the effort to induce political neutrality through civil control.

The Finance Service, for example, succeeded in supervising and actually controlling the issuance of currency. It also controlled (legal) border trade (customs activity) and the expenditures and revenues of the state budget.[19] In February and March of 1993, it succeeded in stemming the depreciation of the riel by controlling the money supply and introducing rice supplies on the Phnom Penh market.[20] In speaking of the functions of the Civil Administration Component, an officer from the Ministry of Finance stated: "if UNTAC thought that the proposal by the State of Cambodia was not appropriate according to UNTAC's standards, they would not allow the expenditure by the national bank, city bank, or overseas banks."[21] But only a few have argued that UNTAC successfully separated the finances of the Cambodian People's

[17] UNTAC doc., "Report on UNTAC's activities: the first six months," March 15–September 15, 1992, p. 24.
[18] UNTAC doc. "Report on UNTAC activities," p. 3.
[19] Ms Elisabeth Uphoff's (IPA Research Fellow) interview with officials from the Ministry of Finance in Phnom Penh, 1993.
[20] Fourth Progress Report of the Secretary-General, S/25719, May 3, 1993, para. 71.
[21] Uphoff interview with a senior official at the Ministry of Finance, 1993.

party (CPP) from those of SOC.[22] UNTAC Control Team investigations discovered, for example, "widespread and persistent use of SOC state apparatus to conduct political campaign activities of the CPP in which state employees – police, armed forces, and civil servants – were mobilized for CPP electioneering."[23]

In the area of foreign affairs, the component was successful in overseeing the abolition of entry and exit visas as well as in ensuring that SOC recognized a Supreme National Council-endorsed passport and visa, permitting officials of the other factions to travel through the Phnom Penh airport without having to obtain the direct permission of a hostile rival. Having full access to files at SOC's "Ministry of Foreign Affairs" concerning passport applications, the controllers maintained their presence in the Passport Section of the "Ministry" six days a week.[24] Between late January and March, 1993, the Supreme National Council endorsement was obtained for over 5,000 passports.[25] The component tended to be most successful when the objectives were relatively limited and UNTAC could draw on international bargaining chips such as in endorsing passports and monitoring the distribution of foreign aid.[26] But in more demanding responsibilities, such as preventing smuggling or avoiding corruption in the issuance of passports it was not as successful.[27] A Cambodian observer noted, the border is "long and the committee walks only on paper, so they cannot see everything."[28]

Control over public security had little impact, but one of its programs

---

[22] James Schear, an UNTAC consultant, gives UNTAC credit for some success in controlling this area. But the runaway inflation of March and April, 1993, questions the significance of the currency control that was achieved and persisting charges of CPP employment of SOC resources, buildings, personnel etc., raise some doubts with respect to the degree of control achieved outside Phnom Penh. See James Schear, "The United Nations operation in Cambodia: a status report," in *The Challenge of Indochina*, Congressional Staff Conference Report, April 30–May 2, 1993 (Queenstown, Md.: The Aspen Insutute, 1993), pp. 21–6.

[23] Secretary-General's Fourth Progress Report, p. 14.

[24] The UN did not recognize the SOC Ministry of Foreign Affairs as a state ministry because legitimate authority for foreign affairs was vested in the Supreme National Council, the repository of Cambodian sovereignty established by the Paris Peace Agreement for the duration of the peace process.

[25] Control exercised over civil administration, March 9, 1993.

[26] Where UNTAC had the bargaining chips firmly in its own hands, it was able to impose its will when it came into conflict with the parties. UNTAC controlled currency because it could control access to the technically crucial prerequisite, international printing. Civil administration appears to have successfully gained control over visas and passports largely because passports gain their utility through international governmental recognition.

[27] CIVADMIN Final Report, para. 82.

[28] IPA interview with a high-level official of Ministry of Foreign Affairs in Phnom Penh, 1993.

– regular visits to prisons – did have some positive effect. In accordance with article 9 of the Transitional Penal Code, officials of the Public Security Service along with officials from the Human Rights and Civil Police components were responsible for regularly visiting prisons to verify prison conditions and to insure that the dispositions of the Code were implemented correctly. As a direct result of those visits, some prison conditions such as water and sanitation services improved. Prison conditions, nonetheless, remained poor, and the use of shackles persisted in several provincial prisons despite UNTAC's complaints.[29] UNTAC also provided training to about two hundred judges, prosecutors, and police officials in the Penal Code which the Supreme National Council adopted at UNTAC's initiative in September 1992. Still, overcoming the usual features of a police state apparatus was far from achieved. Many abuses persisted at the provincial level, despite UNTAC efforts.[30] In the spring of 1993 UNTAC had just begun a program to investigate the detention of prisoners without trial by the security forces, a program itself hampered by the lack of appellate courts.[31]

Beyond these specific accounts of accomplishments and failures, operational problems emerged in four areas: communications, coordination, logistics, and staffing. In the early stages of UNTAC's operation,[32] provincial directors complained of being uninformed about activities of other components while the Office of Provincial Coordination complained about receiving conflicting information from different components at its headquarters.[33] The problem of staffing (the lack thereof or high turnover) combined with serious logistical problems seemed to hamper the activities of all the services, although the provincial offices were hit hardest by these difficulties. In a devastated country such as

[29] UN doc. S/25719, p. 15.

[30] According to a public security official, the Control Team, designed to improve the control mechanism of provisional offices, proved to be quite effective in putting some pressure on SOC, "judging by the complaints from SOC." According to him, the control team "just went in with portable photocopiers and photocopied every document we could get our hands on ... It was an effective way to keep the pressure up" (UNTAC doc., UNTAC Report of the Fourth Civil Administration Seminar, December 10–12, 1992). In describing the standard operating procedure of the Control Team, the Civilian Administration Component stated that the team "will use the tactic of surprise in its intervention with the Cambodian provincial authorities ... No prior authorization or other form of public warning is therefore warranted." This capability of UNTAC, its unrestricted access to any information, illustrates the potential, but unfulfilled promise it was given by the Paris Agreement.

[31] Fourth Progress Report of Secretary-General, S/25719, May 3, 1993, pp. 15–16. Mark Plunkett, the former special prosecutor for UNTAC, concluded, "UNTAC could not even establish the rule of law ... ", *Canberra Times*, August 20, 1993, p. 11.

[32] As discussed in the Fourth Civil Administration Seminar, held in December 1992

[33] UNTAC doc. UNTAC Report of the Fourth Civil Administration Seminar," December 10–12, 1992.

Cambodia in 1992, the civilians depended on the logistics only a fully deployed military component could offer. With 170 UN officers assigned to control twenty-one provinces and a total SOC civil service estimated at 200,000 members, the problem of staffing stood out as one of the most serious problems faced by UNTAC. Secretary-General Boutros-Ghali acknowledged that the recruitment process for civilian peacekeepers proceeded slowly, attributing the problem to "the high degree of specialization in the functions required to be performed."[34] A shortage of Khmer speakers in CIVADMIN was an obvious difficulty in any attempt to control a Khmer-speaking bureaucracy. In addition, not enough international civil servants, whose typical background was diplomatic, had experience in customs, public finance, and public security.

While each of those operational problems was serious enough to hamper the activities of the Civil Administration Component, other issues challenged the fundamental objectives of the mission that the component pursued.

The other factions

One of the most consistent complaints from the SOC Phnom Penh administration was that UNTAC was treating it too harshly compared to its treatment of the other factions such as FUNCINPEC and the KPNLF, which had no existing administration in their zones to control, and the Khmer Rouge, which did not allow UNTAC access to its territory. Due to a shortage of staff, the Civil Administration Component had very limited functions outside of Phnom Penh. More importantly, UNTAC's complete lack of control over the Khmer Rouge – who barred UNTAC controllers at the point of a gun – undermined the impartial credibility of UNTAC's impartial control mandate. UNTAC had to try to control SOC in order to establish a neutral environment, but its complete lack of control of the other factions made this effort appear inherently biased. As the Director of CIVADMIN, Gerard Porcell, observed, UNTAC was reduced to negotiating with SOC, rather than controlling SOC, because it negotiated with the Khmer Rouge, rather than controlling the Khmer Rouge.[35]

"Cosmetic" vs. "real" control

UNTAC had the apparent authority to control the factions, including the right to insert its officials within the factional administrations and to remove factional officials who did not respond to its directive. Yet in

[34] UN doc. S/23870, May 1, 1993, p. 7.
[35] Doyle interview, Phnom Penh, March 1993.

fact, what UNTAC seemed to control, it usually did not. One provincial director in a difficult province described the control mandate in his province as a "joke from the beginning."[36] As one instance of cosmetic control, a public security service official noted the example of UNTAC's prohibiting the SOC police and army from wearing Cambodian People's Party badges in order to "depoliticize" them. They were "probably glad to yield on cosmetic issues," he added, "because they knew it wouldn't affect their real control. And the police were very involved in politics as we knew from the Control Team."[37]

Central "shells" and provincial autonomy

The breakdown of Phnom Penh's own control of the provinces and of the lower level bureaucracy made it very difficult for UNTAC to control the officials that the SOC itself could not control. The activities UNTAC seemed to control – e.g. expenditures in the "Ministry of Finance" of SOC – on closer examination were a mere "front" for decisions taken elsewhere. Much of the SOC administration had collapsed; the "Ministry of Defense" was a "shell," according to a senior UNTAC CIVADMIN official. When real salaries stopped being paid, the SOC "Ministry of Transportation" disappeared and became ad hoc private contractors, noted another senior UNTAC official.[38] Effective control had slipped to provincial governors and generals, so that "controlling" ministries that themselves did not control their nominal areas of responsibility meant very little.

Concealed parallel structures

Even in Phnom Penh, in the areas of policy making where a central administrative apparatus was still functioning, the SOC administered around UNTAC. When the factions wished to be controlled, they allowed themselves to be "controlled." But usually, the actual chain of policy bypassed UNTAC control, as the UNTAC officer was kept busy controlling an official without function and the real budgetary (or other) mechanism flowed elsewhere, diverted out of UNTAC's sight. A high-ranking SOC official in Phnom Penh instructed the ministries in October 1992 in how not to cooperate with UNTAC, reminding his subordinates that "What determines the point at which UNTAC dies is

---

[36] Doyle interview, March 1993, in Cambodia.

[37] Uphoff interview with official in UNTAC Civil Administration, Phnom Penh, 1993.

[38] Doyle interviews with senior UNTAC officials in Phnom Penh, March 1993. Corruption became endemic in these circumstances as state officials regularly sold "state" property for personal profit. See the striking accounts in Stan Sesser, "Report from Cambodia," *The New Yorker*, May 18, 1992, pp. 43–74.

whether we cooperate with it or not."[39] In these parallel structures orders were passed by word of mouth. Or, as in Sihanoukville, a SOC document of March 1993 captured by UNTAC instructed local officials in "Maintaining the initiative with regard to the storage of documents to prevent control of them by UNTAC."[40] The Cambodian People's party (the political party of the state of Cambodia) thus enjoyed the service of officials on the public payroll and access to public assets, while obtaining revenue from sales of those assets. At a meeting on January 19, 1993, UNTAC came to a full realization of the problem and decided to set up Control Teams to probe SOC:

It was agreed at the 12 January meeting that the central force behind the recent outbreak of incidents of political intimidation was not necessarily the Phnom Penh offices of the "Ministry of National Security" or "Ministry of Interior" of the SOC administrative structure, but most likely the Council of Ministers and the CPP [NB the executive and the party, two "non-controlled" entities]. This source of authority is exercised at the provincial and local level largely through familial and personal ties with the "Provincial Governors."[41]

CIVADMIN did not become idle. It attempted to train government bureaucrats in uncontroversial administrative skills. Responding, moreover, to the failure of the control mandate, Civil Administration unofficially (as the Military Component did officially) adjusted its mandate by concentrating its efforts on monitoring the electoral activities of the factions by means of control teams and by encouraging the parties to organize for legitimate campaigning.[42]

The head of the Human Rights Component, Dennis McNamara, offered an informed assessment of UNTAC's efforts in civil control:

The exercise of "control" in order to secure a neutral political environment and end human rights abuses would have been a daunting task even if the peace process had gone exactly as planned, given the time-frame involved and the resources available to UNTAC. With the refusal of the Party of Democratic Kampuchea [the Khmer Rouge] to demobilize its troops and continue to

---

[39] The official also cited as an example to avoid in the future that "the Minister of Finance was so pliant that he virtually gave into everything they (UNTAC) wanted ...," quoted in CIVADMIN Final Report, p. 16

[40] Quoted in the CIVADMIN Final Report, p. 16.

[41] "Briefing note: terms of reference of the proposed UNTAC control mechanism at the provincial level", January 19, 1993, unpublished UNTAC document.

[42] Interviews with Gerard Porcell, Phnom Penh, March 1993 and various members of the CivAdmin component. I observed a political meeting among Cambodian parties organized by the provincial director in Sissophon, Banteay Meanchey Province, in April 1993. The Control Teams had a useful effect: "judging by the complaints from SOC," stated a Public Security Service official, "we just went in with portable photocopiers and photocopied every document we could get our hands on ... It was an effective way to keep the pressure up." See Uphoff interview with official involved with Public Security, UNTAC Civil Administration, Phnom Penh, 1993.

participate in the process (which led to all factions not demobilizing) and the related resistance to close UNTAC supervision of the State of Cambodia's security apparatus, UNTAC through its control function was hard pressed to prevent mounting political crimes.[43]

Human rights

The Paris Agreements, on the one hand, and the actual planning for UNTAC, on the other, incorporated an extraordinary disjunction. Never before had a UN peacekeeping operation assumed so intrusive and authoritative a mandate to implement universal human rights. Articles 15 and 16 gave UNTAC the responsibility of "fostering an environment in which respect for human rights would be ensured" and of preventing a return to "the policies and practices of the past" (i.e. genocide). Section E of annex 1 (the UNTAC mandate) further authorized the development and implementation of a program of human rights education, a provision for general oversight of human rights, and the duty to engage in investigations and, "where appropriate, corrective action." Nonetheless, in the initial planning for UNTAC the Human Rights Component was assigned only ten officers.

It was assumed that all of UNTAC would strive to implement human rights and that the Human Rights Component thus would serve as a central coordinating agency. But the local political environment of the four factions (none of which had a record of respect for human rights), the many compromises already embodied in the Paris Agreement (especially the decision not to prosecute leaders of the Khmer Rouge for genocide),[44] and the lack of human rights awareness among the bulk of the UNTAC staff made a rapid revision necessary. Ultimately, only one human rights officer was assigned to each of Cambodia's twenty-one provinces; ten more were added in Phnom Penh.[45]

Radically understaffed, suffering from a constant shortage of vehicles in a mission notorious for its vehicular cornucopia, the Human Rights Component found the mitigation of human rights violations to be a constant challenge. Nonetheless, in its monitoring role, the component succeeded in having the Supreme National Council adopt all the major

---

[43] Dennis McNamara and Thant Myint-U, "Human rights in Cambodia: what it means?," *Phnom Penh Post*, May 21–June 3, 1993, p. 13. And for a valuable survey of these issues in the early stages of the operation see John Mackinlay, Jarat Chopra, and Larry Minear, *An Interim Report on the Cambodian Peace Process* (Oslo: Norwegian Institute of International Affairs, 1992).

[44] See Stephen Marks, "Forgetting 'the policies and practices of the past': impunity in Cambodia," *The Fletcher Forum of World Affairs*, vol. 18, no. 2, 1994, pp. 17–43.

[45] UNTAC, Human Rights Component Final Report, Phnom Penh, September, 1993, p. 8.

human rights covenants and in correcting some of the worst abuses in the prisons. In its educational role, the component oriented UNTAC's other components to the human rights mandate and, relying on the Trust Fund independently established in October 1992 and working through schools and universities, it organized an extensive information program for the Cambodians themselves, all for the purpose of raising an awareness of basic human rights. As importantly in the long run, it was instrumental in the founding of Cambodian human rights groups, which together mobilized a membership of over a 100,000. This, together with the freest press in Southeast Asia and radically new freedom of movement and association, were the key legacies of UNTAC in human rights. In addition, UNTAC Human Rights left behind an important institutional legacy, the UN Human Rights Center, headed by a special envoy with a continuing responsibility to monitor Cambodia's progress in implementing "liberal democracy."

Yet serious violations of human rights continued. Far from ensuring an "environment" respecting human rights, the corrective role of UNTAC met little success. Failure of "corrective action" arose when Vietnamese immigrants in Cambodia were attacked and political parties were targeted for violent intimidation. On December 28, 1992, twenty to twenty-four Khmer Rouge soldiers attacked the Vietnamese village of Taches on the shore of the Tonle Sap; sixteen villagers died. A Khmer Rouge soldier later confessed and was placed in custody by the UNTAC special prosecutor (see below). On March 10 an even worse attack occurred on the village of Chong Kneas on the Tonle Sap; eighteen died and again the Khmer Rouge were identified as participating in the attack.[46] Political violence directed against citizens and rival parties increased as the election approached. Party workers were murdered, as was Suern Sour, a FUNCINPEC member, allegedly by a SOC policeman and two militia men. UNTAC itself was attacked as well. Of the total of summary killings, the Khmer Rouge engaged in the vast preponderance of ethnic killings (of Vietnamese): 104 out of 111. But UNTAC assigned SOC responsibility for forty-six deaths of political opponents, the Khmer Rouge thirty-seven and (reflecting the general lawlessness of the country) seventy-six were unattributed.[47]

Responding to the mounting political violence and abuse of human rights in the fall of 1992 and the unwillingness of the SOC and other authorities to prosecute suspects, UNTAC took a revolutionary step. It appointed its own special prosecutor, an Australian barrister, Mr. Mark Plunkett. Established in January 1993, the Special Prosecutor's Office

---

[46] Ibid., pp. 32–3.   [47] Human Rights Final Report, Appendix 3.

proceeded to issue warrants against suspected violators of human rights. Difficulties immediately arose: UNTAC lacked a jail (soon remedied with the first UN Detention Facility), CIVPOL was not armed and the UNTAC military force lacked what they interpreted to be the authority to exercise force for this purpose.

The single largest cause of the failures UNTAC experienced in public security, including both Human Rights and CIVPOL,[48] lay in the absence of a judicial framework. Unable to rely on the SOC framework of courts, prisons and police for reasons of neutrality and human rights, UNTAC human rights and CIVPOL were asked to protect human rights and secure law order without a court system. CIVPOL, after the appointment of the special prosecutor, had the authority to arrest, it even acquired a UN prison, but it had no way to prosecute.[49] The inability to prosecute in either Cambodian courts or UNTAC courts established for the purpose or at an international tribunal meant that no complete system of legal order existed.[50] This produced a supreme irony: UNTAC, sent to protect human rights and secure law and order, began holding prisoners in violation of habeas corpus.

The elections

UNTAC and the ordinary Cambodian entered into a unique partnership. It is no exaggeration to say that the courage of Cambodia's voters rescued UNTAC from what appeared to be, with the mounting violence in the Spring of 1993, a looming disaster. But equally, UNTAC gave the ordinary Cambodians, for the first time in their history, an authentic voice in their future.

The elections between May 23 and May 28 represented not only Cambodia's best, but seemingly its only hope. The famous Churchillian dictum that democracy is the worst of all possible forms of government – except all the rest – was borne out almost as a laboratory test case in Cambodia's troubled history. As David Chandler has noted in his chapter, Cambodia has experienced a quasi-feudalist parliamentary yet princely reign under Prince Sihanouk; a violent military coup in 1970 under republican auspices organized by Lon Nol; the terrors of Khmer

---

[48] For a discussion of CivPol's role see the chapter by Mark Metrikas and Cheryl Kim in this volume.

[49] Mark Plunkett, the UNTAC Special Prosecutor, described the result as "lawless ... The judges here are a bunch of party hacks and flunkeys and they simply refuse to even issue warrants if the accused is of their ilk or connected to any of the dangerous politicians," in *Canberra Times*, May 25, 1993, p. 6.

[50] J. Basil Fernando, *The Inability to Prosecute: Courts and Human Rights in Cambodia and Sri Lanka* (Hong Kong: Future Asia Link, 1993).

Rouge Maoism beginning in 1975; and the oppression of the quasi-Stalinist regime installed by the Vietnamese in 1979.

The elections also represented an historic departure for the United Nations. Having monitored and supervised many elections, for the first time the UN was charged, in the Paris Agreement, to "organize and conduct" from the ground up a national election in an independent country.[51] The Electoral Component was well aware that it would be establishing a record that could determine whether the UN would ever again be entrusted with this fundamental responsibility. UNTAC as a whole realized that by December 1992 its multifunctional mandate, which included demobilization of warring factions and control of their civil administration, had been effectively reduced to the single task of holding "free and fair" elections.

Implementing the mandate

In his implementation plan, the Secretary-General specifically identified the election as the "focal point of the comprehensive settlement" – the point that would govern the entire schedule of the peace operation. The Electoral Component was given five tasks: first, to establish, in consultation with the Supreme National Council, the legal framework of electoral laws and regulations for a national election for the 120-member Constituent Assembly; second, to develop an extensive information/education campaign directed toward the general public in order to persuade them of the importance and the integrity (secrecy and hence safety) of the ballot; third, to organize and conduct a national registration of all voters on a provincial basis to determine both who is allowed to vote and how many seats should be allocated to each province; fourth, to organize and supervise the registration of political parties; and fifth, to conduct a general election in 1,400 polling stations and count the ballots – all before the beginning of the 1993 rainy season, that is before the middle of May 1993.

Although the Electoral Component bore primary responsibility for the registration and election, here, as in other aspects of the UNTAC operation, effective responsibility lay in a partnership among UNTAC units, in this case the electoral, military and information/education units.

The Electoral Component

The component was headed by Dr. Reginald Austin, who had previously supervised the UN election for UNTAG in Namibia. The Electoral

[51] Section D of annex 1, the UNTAC mandate, Paris Agreements.

Component had four branches: Operations and Computerization, Administration and Coordination, Information/Communications/ Training and Complaints/Compliance/Enforcement. Each was headed by a deputy director, with the computerization branch identified as the senior division, reflecting its crucial role. Each of Cambodia's twenty-one provinces also received a small staff headed by a provincial electoral officer. But the "arms, legs and hearts" of the election were to be found in the 460 UN Volunteers who staffed the district level operations.[52]

Advanced planning

Perhaps the most remarkable feature of the entire electoral effort was the degree of advanced planning that it incorporated. Planning for an election began with the Australian "Redbook" in February 1990 and continued with the Electoral Planning Mission in November 1991 and the team (including Austin) charged with the composition of a draft electoral law for Cambodia (which met in New York in January 1992). The planning process culminated with the Advanced Electoral Planning Unit which deployed with UNAMIC and performed valuable statistical estimates of the eligible voter population province by province, which were published in the report completed in August 1992. The Electoral Component, starting with its arrival in March 1992, nonetheless encountered the typical UNTAC delays ranging from inappropriate equipment, missing furniture and late staff (many reportedly delayed by slow medical clearance in New York).[53]

Organizing the registration and the election

The Component's first major challenge arrived with the need to register Cambodia's voters. In the fall of 1992 the logistical and political environment could not have been more trying. The country was totally unfamiliar with a national election, and it lacked the infrastructure that would have made registration straightforward. With the assistance of the Military Component, the Electoral Component was nonetheless able to reach and register 4.76 million voters, around 90 percent the estimated potential voters. The process was assisted by the obvious attraction of laminated, secure photo identity cards to Cambodians who appeared to relish the symbol of citizenship (and perhaps security) they conveyed.

Planning for the May 23–28 election involved even greater efforts. Designed to include a combination of fixed poll for three days and

---

[52] Michael Maley, "Reflections on the electoral process in Cambodia," in Hugh Smith (ed.), *Peacekeeping: Challenges for the Future* (Canberra: Australian Defense Studies Centre, 1993), pp. 88–99.
[53] Ibid., p. 90.

mobile polling for the entire six days, with a day of rest in between, the process required identifying (but keeping confidential until the election) the planned 1,800 polling sites and recruiting and training 48,000 Cambodian election workers and 1,000 international poll supervising officers (IPSOs).

The Electoral Component experienced planning and technical problems, as well as successes. Contracting out the computer system on a turnkey basis proved to be an efficient solution to achieving timely output and clear responsibility. But there were technical glitches elsewhere. Notorious were the failed plastic seals on the ballot boxes that broke in transit on Cambodia's bumpy roads. They gave rise to (unsubstantiated) SOC charges of UNTAC tampering. The greatest difficulties were in policy choices. During the registration process, they arose in connection with UNTAC's slow decision on how to determine Cambodian citizenship, a choice negotiated in detail with the Cambodian factions. The result was a ruling that, while not explicitly ethnic, excluded Cambodia's Vietnamese immigrants and permitted overseas Cambodians to return to Cambodia to register. The election itself was complicated by the controversy over whether to hold a separate and prior presidential election, designed to install Prince Sihanouk as the commanding figure of the peace process. Manifestly non-constitutional, in the sense that it was not included in the Paris Agreements, this initiative nonetheless could not be dismissed due to the support of France and the ASEAN countries, who were skeptical of the prospects (and perhaps desirability) of "pluralist democracy" in Cambodia.[54]

The Military Component

None of the electoral successes would have been possible without the active assistance of UNTAC's military. In the fall of 1992, after the failure of cantonment and demobilization became evident, the UN redefined the Military Component's role, redeploying from a zonal deployment designed to accommodate cantonment of the military forces of the factions to a provincial deployment designed to support the provincial organization of the election. Completed on December 31,

---

[54] Sihanouk himself clearly favored this enhanced role for himself, as he still does today (June 1994) when he is attempting to establish himself as a constitutional dictator ("like in ancient Rome"!) with the support of the Assembly, see Nate Thayer, "King talks of taking power," *Phnom Penh Post*, June 17–30, 1994, p. 1. Sihanouk abandoned the earlier effort at presidential democracy (said to be Gaullist in inspiration) after he realized that he would be president before presidential duties had been defined by the soon-to-be-elected constituent assembly's formulation of a constitution, scheduled for the summer of 1993.

1992, UNTAC's Military Component became an election protection and implementation force. With 16,000 soldiers distributed in 270 locations around the country it offered the most spread out organization, one capable of both protecting the electoral process and providing the transportation and logistics essential for the conduct of the election.[55]

Information/Education Division

Widely recognized as one of the stars of UNTAC, this division headed by US diplomat and old Cambodia hand Tim Carney enjoyed the sort of independence characteristic of the full fledged components. It played a central role in three of UNTAC's mandates. It supplemented the educational functions of Human Rights by producing videos, posters, leaflets and large banners that publicized the human rights adopted according to the provisions of the Paris Agreements. The division also supplemented the control function of Civil Administration, establishing media guidelines in October 1992 which were designed to meet UNTAC's mandate to offer fair media access to all Cambodia's political parties.[56] Here the division experienced "limited success" as not only the Khmer Rouge but also the SOC media refused to cooperate with UNTAC. The SOC rejected the UNTAC attempt to exercise a priori editorial control of TV Kampuchea and its newspapers.

The division achieved its real success in directly communicating the meaning and importance of the election to the Cambodian people. It was the key factor that allowed UNTAC, in the words of General Sanderson, to "bypass the propaganda of the Cambodian factions" and forge "the alliance with the Cambodian people" that became the essence of UNTAC strategy.[57] The division, working with its own audio–video studio in Phnom Penh, produced nine half-hour programs each week on UNTAC's own Radio UNTAC. These programs reached most of Cambodia, thanks to Japanese private donors who offered 143,000 radios to the Cambodian people.[58] As the electoral campaign began, it broadcast daily electoral programs and offered time for each registered political party, allowing the division candidates or

---

[55] Report of the Secretary-General November 15, 1992 S/24800 and Third Progress Report of the Secretary-General, January 25, 1993, S/25124, paras. 39–43.

[56] Third Progress Report of the Secretary-General, S/25124, January 25, 1993, para. 70–1.

[57] Unfortunately, Radio UNTAC was also very late due to UN bureaucratic obstacles and did not become operational until November 1992. See Lieutenant General John Sanderson, "UNTAC: successes and failures," International Peacekeeping Seminar, May 2, 1994, ADFC, Canberra, p. 9.

[58] Secretary-General's Third Progress Report, S/25124, para. 91.

parties to counter unfair attacks.[59] Its central accomplishment lay in persuading the people that their act of voting, despite all the threats of the factions, would at least be secret (and because district votes would not be tallied except at the provincial level; villages, too, would be secure from possible retaliation).

Though not widely recognized outside UNTAC, the division played one more role, one sensitive yet important in multidimensional peacekeeping operations. Information/Education, in the act of assessing how well its own message was being received by the Cambodians, also developed what may have been the UN's first political intelligence department. Benefiting from its recruitment of an outstanding group of Khmer-speaking scholars, the division wrote systematic political reports on the activities of the various factions in each of Cambodia's key provinces.

The election: free and fair?

Special Representative Akashi defined "free and fair" in a statement before the Supreme National Council on April 21, 1993:

A victory marred by violence and intimidation is not worth having. UNTAC and the international community will judge the freeness and fairness of the election by three criteria: the technical conduct of the poll; the extent to which the campaign is marred by violence, intimidation, and harassment; and the extent to which the incumbent party enjoys unfair advantages, whether by using the apparatus of state for its own political ends or by denying opposition parties access to public media.

The last two conditions seem to have been very much absent.[60] The State of Cambodia clearly enjoyed unfair advantages with its ownership of the Cambodian media and mobilization of public officials for CPP campaigning. A highly expert Information/Education information officer, for example, reported on March 29, 1993: "In Seam Reap, as observed elsewhere, CPP and SOC structures are inseparable, and that there seems to have been no attempt whatsoever to at least make them look even formally separate. It appears that, on the contrary, CPP's control over SOC structures has been reinforced to the point of total fusion, SOC's structures being CPP's instrument to implement its policies and achieve its objectives."[61]

---

[59] See S/25719, the Secretary-General's Fourth Progress Report. UNTAC Radio also challenged the Khmer Rouge propaganda that Cambodia occupied by Vietnam and SOC propaganda that the Khmer Rouge about to take over again.

[60] The UN, nonetheless, declared each separate stage of the elections – the polling and counting of ballots, and the campaign – free and fair. See Report of the Secretary-General, S/26090, July 16, 1993, para. 3.

[61] UNTAC information officer (not for attribution), Report on the Political Environment

In early 1993, opposition political offices were attacked, ransacked and burned, and party members beaten, kidnapped, and killed. Judy Thompson, a senior Manitoba Elections Commission official and a UN Volunteer serving as deputy chief electoral officer acknowledged, "Voter intimidation is widespread."[62] In Prey Veng, the SOC set about an orchestrated policy of violent intimidation. An internal SOC document captured by the UNTAC Control Team noted:

However, confronting all such movements with counter-attacks; the District Party Committee has conducted constant and regular activities in every locality, thereby progressively reducing the influence of these political parties. They are therefore so frightened that they no longer have the courage to engage in any political activities."[63]

Security conditions, moreover, leading right up to the eve of elections were precarious at best. The town of Stoung in the central province of Kompong Thom was shelled by Khmer Rouge artillery throughout the night before balloting began until 6.00 a.m. on the morning of May 23. Three days earlier in Stoung, the Khmer Rouge overran the town and attempted to assassinate a UN civilian electoral worker and several military observers.[64] According to a conservative report issued by UNTAC's Human Rights Component, there were over a hundred violent incidents during the campaigning period between March 1 and May 14 for which responsibility could be imputed. Casualties included 200 deaths, 338 injuries, and 114 abductions. This culminated in a large-scale attack on Siem Reap on May 3–4 by 400 Khmer Rouge. Following further attacks on May 19; hundreds took refuge in the temple complex of Angkor Wat.

UN officials in Phnom Penh and New York prepared a concerned international community for the likelihood of electoral disruptions. Secretary-General Boutros Boutros-Ghali issued on May 3 a fourth progress report on the situation in which he stated: "It may well be, in the light of the sobering experiences of the last 13 months, that the expectations originally entertained for ensuring that the election is free and fair and for the success of national reconciliation were overly optimistic." He further stated that the "freeness and fairness" of the elections would be measured according to "acceptable minimum standards" – effectively, UNTAC's ability to insure a secret ballot.[65]

in Siem Reap Province: Discussions with Political Parties (UNTAC Memorandum, March 29, 1993).

[62] Peter Goodspeed, "UN flirting with disaster," *Toronto Star*, February 28, 1993, p. 13.

[63] Quoted in CIVADMIN Final Report, p. 13.

[64] I served as an international observer in Stoung, Kompong Thom, on May 28, the last day of the poll, and interviewed the individuals involved.

[65] S/25/24, January 25, 1993.

Days before the election, dependents of UN agency officials were ordered out of the country by UN headquarters in New York. Security concerns canceled more than 300 polling sites in trouble spots, particularly in the provinces of Siem Reap and Kompong Thom. The Security Council issued a final warning to the parties that it would "respond appropriately" should they fail to honor their obligations.[66]

The UN and its member states thus faced a painful dilemma by having to hold elections in a country not yet at peace, with possible disruptions during the polling, and where the political "playing field" was far from completely "level." The elections could not be as free and fair as those in established democracies or even other states (like Nicaragua or Namibia) where the UN had overseen elections.

But the other conditions – the conduct and count of the poll by UNTAC itself – appear to have been technically free and fair. As importantly, UNTAC seemingly had succeeded in persuading the Cambodian voters that their votes mattered and would be kept secret. Despite monsoon rains, 42 percent of 4.7 million registered voters cast their ballots on the first day; by the end of the process 90 percent had voted. The Electoral Component, despite the disputes over the broken plastic seals discussed above, performed with impressive dedication as it completed a non-stop count in the full sight of electoral observers from the parties.

In the end, two key factors made the difference. First, in the face of months' long intimidation and violent threats, Cambodia's voters showed they were prepared to face the risk. Even in the areas of bitter fighting in Kompong Thom, where voters were shelled on their way to polling sites, the turnout was about 80 percent. Second, UNTAC's Electoral Component organized a nearly flawless poll and count, the Military moved the ballot boxes and protected the polling sites and Information/Education succeeded in persuading the Cambodian voter that despite all threats their vote would be kept secret.

Perhaps UNTAC's greatest achievement was enabling a population to participate in the struggles for power for the first time in Cambodia's entire history. Likely, the most lasting effect of UNTAC will be a sense in the population that it can demand accountability from those who govern.

If the success of the election was remarkable, so was the fragility of the process. Had the Khmer Rouge attacked the polling sites more effectively, they might have succeeded in stopping the election.[67] A

[66] UN doc. S/RES/826, May 20, 1993.
[67] The reasons why the Khmer Rouge, after months of intimidation against Cambodians and attacks on UNTAC, failed to disrupt the poll are speculative. General Sanderson

large-scale attack on the Cambodian populace was not the only threat, however, as focused violence directed at UN personnel almost derailed the process. On April 8, Atsuhito Nakata, a 25-year-old Japanese electoral UNV, and Lay Sok Phiep, his Cambodian interpreter, were killed in Kompong Thom.[68] In an interview with UNTAC's own media services before the election, Special Representative Yasushi Akashi said that if one more electoral worker was killed, the UN Volunteers – the principal electoral organizers in the field – would be withdrawn, raising the question of whether the elections could have been carried out. In May in Stoung this nearly happened.[69]

Sources of failure and success

Why did seemingly essential parts of the original civil mandate fail? Why, overall, did UNTAC emerge a success? Why did civil administrative control and human rights by and large fail; why did registration, election and information succeed? Within civil administration, why were Foreign Affairs and Finance relatively more successful controllers and the rest so much less so? Within human rights and civilian police, why was training more effective and "corrective action" ineffective?

Turning first to the general roots of the failures, the simplest, and seemingly the most powerful, explanation focuses on the unwillingness of the parties to cooperate and UNTAC's decision not to try to enforce the mandate. Why, if the parties were not willing to abide by mandate, did they sign it?

Incomplete reconciliation

In part, well-informed participants at the Paris negotiations speculate, the parties had no real option. Their international patrons had cut them

has suggested that in the weeks preceding the election the armies of the factions cooperating with UNTAC pushed the Khmer Rouge back from the population centers. Others have noted that the Khmer Rouge was under diplomatic pressure to cooperate, particularly from China. Did local commanders lacking the means to do so simply refuse orders from the leadership to attack? Did the Khmer Rouge leadership decide it was not in their interest to destroy the elections, since they would have a better hand to play in the new government if they did not alienate irrevocably the population or the other parties with which they would have to cooperate in a coalition? Did they strike a deal with Prince Sihanouk, favoring FUNCINPEC in return for a promise of their being invited to join a coalition government? Informed speculation and some evidence support each of these.

[68] The official account of the investigation, implicating disgruntled Cambodians turned down as electoral workers, is in *Free Choice*, Electoral Component Newsletter, April 30, 1993 p. 27.

[69] Yasushi Akashi, "The challenge of peacekeeping in Cambodia: lessons to be learned," Lecture, SIPA, November 29, 1993, p. 6.

off. Vietnam and the PRC, patrons respectively of the SOC and the Khmer Rouge, had normalized relations in 1991, ending a bitter rivalry that had provoked a war and Vietnam's invasion of Cambodia in 1978. Both communist states, now "flocking" together, may have felt somewhat isolated and threatened in the aftermath of the Cold War and the global "triumph" of democratic capitalism. Relatedly, both also sought Western contacts and trade and more normalized relations with the world market, which the strife in Cambodia only hindered. The collapse of the USSR, furthermore, removed another powerful patron of the SOC; Russia with its massive domestic challenges apparently had little interest in sustaining Southeast Asian clients.

Another interpretation suggests that perhaps the parties did want the Paris Agreement – but only to the extent that they were able to exploit it. All were exhausted by war, falling apart internally; and so each may have sought Paris as the final nail in the coffin of their rivals. The Khmer Rouge may have wanted to use the provisions of civil control over the five areas in the Paris Agreements as the means to destroy the SOC. The Khmer Rouge might have demobilized (and they did, it appears, draw up demobilization lists) if they could have been assured that the SOC would have been controlled from above and below by UNTAC and by a revival of effective quadripartite rule through an invigorated Supreme National Council.[70] Functioning administration over almost the entire country was the great advantage that the SOC possessed over the other factions. Observers argue that the Khmer Rouge probably judged that no centralized Leninist bureaucracy could sustain itself under a regime of effective even though partial outside control. (Significantly, perhaps, it had been the PRC, the Khmer Rouge's one-time patron, that had written these provisions of the Paris Agreement.) The SOC, on the other hand, may have sought the cantonment and demobilization provisions of the Paris Agreement as the vehicle through which to destroy the Khmer Rouge's single most vital asset – its disciplined army. Consequently, the Khmer Rouge was determined not to disarm, but hoped that UNTAC would succeed in controlling and thus gutting the SOC's administrative apparatus. The SOC was prepared to cooperate in cantonment and disarmament in hopes that a disarmed Khmer Rouge would dissolve, but were determined to prevent any effective control of their administrative assets.[71] FUNCINPEC and KPNLF – the two very lightly armed factions at the border – wanted the Accords, perhaps principally in order to have the elections, and this because they had no other asset apart from

---

[70] Doyle interview in Phnom Penh with a Khmer-speaking expert in UNTAC.

[71] Making different arguments, Nayan Chanda, an experienced commentator on Cambodia, is also skeptical of whether there ever existed a willingness to reconcile

their popularity with the mass of the Cambodian population. We cannot eliminate the possibility that the Paris Accords represented a true reconciliation and an acceptance of peace through pluralist democracy by the four factions; it is just that it is very difficult to find evidence in their previous or later actions to support it.[72]

Operational factors also played a role.

Timely impact

It is difficult to overemphasize the importance of rapid deployment. The temporal gap between signature of the peace agreement (October 23, 1991) and the full deployment of UNTAC was nine months, and even then some important units of the civilian police were not fully deployed. The peace agreement was not even implemented by the Secretariat (given an organized, specified mandate) until March 15, 1992, five months after its signing. A small interim advance mission (UNAMIC) was sent to Cambodia in November of 1991, but its mission was limited to liaison ("good offices") between the parties, monitoring the anticipated ceasefire, and mine clearance training. It lacked both the mandate and the wherewithal to impress the parties.[73] Late deployment loses the momentum derived from popular support, from the commitment of the parties, and from the psychological weight associated with a large operation moving rapidly toward an agreed goal.

Insufficient planning

The Civilian Police Component (CIVPOL) should, as noted, have had a crucial impact on the neutralization of factional intimidation, but the director was not appointed until March 1992 and even then there was no clear doctrine of operations.[74] Special Representative Akashi, himself, was not appointed until January 1992, more than two months after the Paris Agreement had been signed and five months after the

---

between SOC and the Khmer Rouge, in "The UN's failure in Cambodia," *Wall Street Journal*, March 11, 1993, p. A14.

[72] An internal Khmer Rouge memo of February 6, 1992 stated that: "The contents of the Paris Agreement are to our advantage ... if the Agreements are incorrectly implemented we are dead (disarmed), but if they are correctly implemented then we will win."

[73] Lieutenant General John Sanderson, "Preparation for, deployment and conduct of peacekeeping operations: a Cambodia snapshot," paper presented at the International Seminar: UN Peacekeeping at the Crossroads, Canberra, March 21–24, 1993, pp. 4–5.

[74] Mr. Nick Warner, of the Australian Mission to Cambodia, makes this argument in, "Cambodia: lessons of UNTAC for peacekeeping operations," in Kevin Clements and Christine Wilson (eds.), *UN Peacekeeping at the Crossroads* (Canberra: Peace Research Centre, School of Pacific and Asian Studies, 1994), p. 5.

substance of agreement had been achieved. Some military units did not arrive soon enough; others were not well enough equipped or trained (with enough French or English speakers, qualified drivers, etc.).

Interestingly, the elections unit did have effective advance planning – the Advance Electoral Planning Unit – that identified the challenges an election would face in Cambodia and so helped avert future crises. But then so did the Military Component, whose planning team surveyed Cambodia in December 1991 and also alerted New York to the special problems presented by effective operation in Cambodian conditions. Yet this had little impact on the Khmer Rouge's reluctance to cease fire, canton, and disarm.

Discontinuity

Lying behind both of the above was a lack of continuity between the development of the peace plan and its implementation in Cambodia. Rafeeuddin Ahmed represented the UN in the lengthy negotiations leading from informal contacts through Paris I (1989) and the Jakarta Initiatives to Paris II (the 1991 Peace Agreement). In the course of these talks he, together with an expert staff, acquired a familiarity with the players and the issues unrivaled among UN diplomats. Whatever the advantages of a fresh approach and a clean slate (and some observers think there were advantages), a great deal of institutional knowledge was lost when the Secretary-General replaced Ahmed and his team in January 1992 with Yasushi Akashi. Few disagree that both the force commander and the special representative should be appointed at the time negotiations move toward an agreement. They will know much better the meaning of what was agreed and by whom. They will, it is hoped, earn the trust of the parties, contribute to an assessment of what is feasible before the unfeasible is declared to be part of an agreed mandate, and have an interest in beginning to plan to implement the peace as soon as is possible.

Quality of staff

UNTAC displayed courage in sticking out a difficult assignment that compounded a trying climate with unanticipated levels of violence. Some also displayed extraordinary courage, dedication, and ingenuity in meeting their mandate. Nonetheless, observers have noted a number of deficiencies. Some units (CIVPOL is frequently mentioned) suffered from serious language incompatibilities, with officers occasionally unable to speak either French or English (UNTAC's two official languages). Very few could speak Khmer (partially a casualty of Cambodia's long isolation and of course its small size). The UN Volunteers, most of whom worked in the Electoral Component, engendered widespread praise, even after a few decided to withdraw in the face of extreme violence from one or two provinces. Moreover, there appear to have been considerable returns to experience: veterans of previous, comprehensive peacekeeping operations capitalized on their experience, as did those who were able to draw upon their similar experiences of pre-UNTAC employment. Others were "at sea" in the world of complex peacebuilding.[75]

Administration and coordination

Of course, there were also simple administrative problems. UNTAC, like the UN as a whole, often attempted too much, which partly reflected a long-standing commitment to ensuring strictly impartial universality. Some functions now performed by the UN staff, apolitical now in an era of Security Council unanimity, could have been contracted out to private management when the security situation permitted.

International interference

Most observers agree that the unofficial support the Khmer Rouge allegedly received from various Thai generals on the western border undermined the peace accords. There, in violation of UN embargoes, logs, gems, arms, and ammunition flowed freely, filling the Khmer Rouge's coffers and bunkers, permitting them to disdain the carrots of economic aid and ward off the sticks of an embargo that the UN had counted upon to encourage their cooperation with the peace plan.[76] On the eastern border, a similar but much less extensive trade in logs allegedly occurred and widespread (though unsubstantiated) rumors floated through Phnom Penh of continuing ties between the SOC's secret police and the Vietnamese intelligence service. Other powers, such as the United States, occasionally meddled with inappropriate publicity in the internal politics of Cambodia, such as when, in June 1993, US diplomats publicly threatened the tottering interim govern-

---

[75] Reginald Austin, for one example, had participated in the implementation of the Commonwealth-sponsored election in Rhodesia-Zimbabwe as early as 1979. UNTAC contained a number of "graduates" from UNTAG (Namibia). The CivPol were particularly disadvantaged. Effective policing is essentially a matter of local knowledge, trust, and small unit coherence. Foreign police dropped into a remote Cambodian town with no knowledge of Khmer, no common standards, and no experience of working together faced formidable hurdles.

[76] Philip Shenon, "Cambodia arms flow back to Thailand," *New York Times*, March 7, 1993. See also the account by Raoul Jennar, "Thailand's double standards must be stopped," *Phnom Penh Post*, October 8–21, 1993, p. 8. Jennar alleges not only financial but also military cooperation between the generals and the Khmer Rouge, claiming that it has continued after the May elections.

ment with a loss of US aid, if it brought leaders of the Khmer Rouge into an association with the government.[77]

UNTAC's success in the election and information and in parts of civil administrative control (such as foreign affairs) also has both general and operational sources.

A multidimensional mandate

UNTAC's overall success can in large part be credited to the multidimensional character of the mandate and, perhaps ironically, to its lack of clarity. With Security Council approved adjustments in the mandate, reconciliation and peace could have been achieved by disarmament, control, education, and then renegotiation. Reconciliation through national election was available if and when the other dimensions failed. Multidimensionality – distributing eggs across baskets – thus allowed for single failures and yet overall success.[78]

International support

International support is vital. The Extended Permanent Five in Phnom Penh and the Core Group in New York included the Permanent Five members of the Security Council and leading troop contributors. The first played a key role in advising Special Representative Akashi in Phnom Penh and the second in supporting UNTAC with additional finance, *materiel*, and diplomatic clout. UNTAC enjoyed particularly extensive support from a number of countries, including Japan, Indonesia, France, Australia, the United States, Thailand, and Malaysia – as well as the patient acquiescence of Vietnam and China in a considerable loss of regional clout. Without their support and the participation of dozens of other UN members, the Paris Agreements could never have been implemented.

Direct implementation

Each of the successes enjoyed at least the passive support of the factions. The parties were not prepared to organize an active opposition to their operation. But more strikingly they all had, it seems, one additional crucial characteristic in common – they were actions taken by or directly organized by UNTAC that did not require the positive cooperation of the four factions to be effective. The UNHCR conducted repatriation,

---

[77] The USA said it would refuse to provide aid to a goverment including the Khmer Rouge: Philip Shenon in the *New York Times*, July 14, 1993.

[78] My views on this point benefited from an interview with Miss Hisako Shimura, DPKO, October 2, 1993.

with the assistance of the International Committee of the Red Cross, the Cambodian Red Cross, and various independent non-governmental organizations. The Human Rights and Information Components conducted human rights education with the help of international and local non-governmental organizations. And, most importantly, UNTAC's Electoral Component registered Cambodia's voters (with the help of the military), recruited and trained a 50,000 person Cambodian electoral staff of poll workers, established 1,800 polling sites, and conducted the poll (again with the crucial help of UNTAC's military forces) between May 23 and 28.

UNTAC's guarantee of a secret ballot rescued the peace in Cambodia. Without UNTAC's direct role in the election, it probably would have had to declare defeat and retreat from Cambodia. The Khmer Rouge prevented the conduct of the election in the villages it controlled. The SOC was prepared to tolerate an election, expecting to win from it international legitimacy. But recalling the SOC's record of violent intimidation, what sort of election would have been conducted if the UN were merely in the capacity of a monitoring force? The UN would have had to have withdrawn from Cambodia altogether, citing SOC's intimidation during the campaign, or have tolerated the additional manipulation that would have been likely had the SOC actually conducted the poll.

There are some exceptions. Where UNTAC had the bargaining chips firmly in its own hands, there too it was able to impose its will when it came into conflict with the parties. UNTAC controlled currency because it could control access to the technically crucial prerequisite, international printing. Civil Administration, for example, appears to have successfully gained control over visas and passports (foreign affairs area) largely because passports gain their utility through international governmental recognition. The UN as the universal intergovernmental organization could rely on its members to enforce its decree against any Cambodian faction that defied its will. So the SOC accepted the Supreme National Council-endorsed passport to avoid having all its passports decertified. UNTAC did not, of course, have equivalent success in controlling Cambodia's borders or its border trade, for the simple reasons that these functions were important to the factions and some of Cambodia's international neighbors obtained great advantages through their complicity with smuggling.[79]

---

[79] One surprising case of foreign affairs "out of control" was an aviation treaty negotiated and signed by SOC with Malaysia in defiance of the Paris Agreements, which allocated sovereign rights to the Supreme National Council during the transitional period.

Lessons

The UN has not altered the historical nature of power in Cambodia, but it has empowered the people, with whom Cambodia's hopes rest for the first time.

Election results shifted the balance of bargaining chips between the factions, empowering the princely party FUNCINPEC; but it was the overall military-political balance that would determine the new authority in Cambodia and not the results of the election poll. FUNCINPEC won fifty-eight seats, the CPP (the Hun Sen – State of Cambodia party) fifty-one, and two small parties, the BLDP (associated with the KPNLF) ten and Molinaka, one. More significant than the CPP's votes, however, was that the State of Cambodia retained its control of the only effective army (apart from that of the Khmer Rouge) and the existing police force (itself organized in paramilitary fashion). The Khmer Rouge contemplated playing their well-deserved reputation for ruthlessness into a seat on a future Cambodian coalition. Therefore the summer 1993 negotiations regarding a coalition arrangement were as significant as the elections themselves. The eventual decision to create a coalition government with the prime ministership for FUNCINPEC (Prince Ranariddh) and the deputy prime ministership for CPP (Hun Sen) and to divide the ministries, while Prince (now King) Sihanouk took overall charge as head of state, well reflected Cambodian realities. So, too, did the particular logic of giving finance and foreign affairs to FUNCINPEC because they were more acceptable to foreign donors, who will be relied upon to assist the coalition coalesce with desperately needed development funding. As the government pursued its policy of interdiction against the Khmer Rouge, the political strength of the CPP (controlling owner of the army and the police) rose.[80] The post-game in Cambodia, therefore, can still erode the gains made by the UN in the opening of the political system. The UN's failures to solidify the rule of law through the "control" of the factions and to demobilize the factional armies may come back to haunt its electoral success.

The experience of civil peacekeeping and peacebuilding in Cambodia thus highlights important lessons. First, time is critical. The UN should be ready to implement the mandate as soon after the peace treaty is signed as is practicable. UNTAC suffered a large decrease in authority

---

[80] For a well-informed assessment of the negotiations during June and July 1993, see William Shawcross, "A new Cambodia," *New York Review of Books*, August 12, 1993, pp. 37–41. A useful continuation appears in William Branigin, "Cambodia means to monarchy," *Sydney Morning Herald*, August 27, 1993, p. 7.

in early 1992 as time passed and expectations of the factions and the Cambodian people were disappointed.

Second, the UN should attempt to design in as many bargaining advantages for the UN authority as the parties will tolerate. Even seemingly extraneous bargaining chips will become useful as the spirit of cooperation erodes under the pressure of misunderstandings and separating interests. The UN counted upon the financial needs of the Cambodian factions to insure their cooperation and designed an extensive Rehabilitation Component to guarantee steady rewards for cooperative behavior. But the Khmer Rouge's access to illicit trade (with the apparent connivance of elements of the Thai military along the western border) eliminated this bargaining chip. And the suspicion of SOC's rivals prevented a full implementation of rehabilitation in the 80 percent of the country controlled by the SOC. Passport and visa control succeeded simply because the UN, as a representative of the international community, had the leverage to persuade the SOC to comply.

And third, the UN should design into the mandate as much independent implementation as the parties will agree to in the peace treaty. The Electoral Component and Information/Education seem to have succeeded simply because they did not depend on the steady and continuous positive support of the four factions. Each had an independent sphere of authority and organizational capacity that allowed it to proceed against everything short of the active military opposition of the factions. Civil administrative control and human rights (not to speak of the military cantonment of the factions) failed because they relied on the continuous direct and positive cooperation of each of the factions. Each of the factions, at one time or another, had reason to expect that the balance of advantages was tilting against itself, and so refused to cooperate. And now, all Cambodians have cause to regret that the UN did not acquire a mandate for UNTAC to train a national Cambodian army and police force. These are the two institutions that could have been decisive in ensuring that the voice of the people, as represented by their elected representatives, would shape the future of Cambodia.

7   Returning home: the repatriation of Cambodian refugees

Brian Williams

The peaceful and orderly return of the Cambodian refugees is both a clear expression of the confidence that the Cambodians have in the peace process and a decisive contribution to national reconciliation.

Yasushi Akashi, Special Representative of the Secretary-General in Cambodia,
April 30, 1993.[1]

Introduction

Between March 30, 1992 and April 30, 1993 the United Nations High Commissioner for Refugees (UNHCR) facilitated the return of 361,462 refugees to their native land of Cambodia.[2] While the logistical challenges involved in this exercise were imposing enough, the Repatriation Program for Cambodian Refugees aimed to be much more than a simple transport service. It endeavored to restore refugees – approximately 75 percent of whom were women and children – to their original homes, or somewhere else if they so chose, and provide the refugees with the raw materials with which to build a productive life: tools, land, building supplies for a new house, and food during a readjustment period.

In addition to affecting profoundly the futures of these 361,462 individuals, the UNHCR's program shouldered the burden of being one of three visible symbols of the success or failure of the United Nations' general program in Cambodia. At the time of the repatriation, the cantonment/disarmament of the factions' troops was already stalled in fundamental ways, and elections were not to come until later. The need for the UN repatriation program to be perceived as a success by the international community was therefore never far from the minds of the decision-makers. Moreover, that everyone saw the repatriation as a success was not only important from a narrow public relations point of view for the UN, but also for the overall peace process. As Special Representative of the Secretary-General Yasushi Akashi noted in the

---

[1]   UNTAC Daily Press Briefing, April 30, 1993.
[2]   UNTAC Daily Press Briefing, April 30, 1993.

epigraph above, observers took the fact that refugees had returned home without apparent widespread problems as evidence of a workable peace.

The purpose of this chapter is to evaluate the repatriation program not only because of its importance for the lives of the refugees and their communities, but also because of the fact it was received as an important validation of the peace process. The analysis will be simple and in many ways tentative. It is simple because it is based mostly on reports and observations of the repatriation program and of the context in which it operated. A preferred analysis would study quantitatively the impact of the repatriation program on returnees' lives. It is tentative because sustainable peace and reintegration are the only sufficient indicators of success. Nevertheless some useful analysis can be done even before such definitive evidence is in.

First, *voluntary* repatriation has been oft repeated as the preferred durable solution.[3] Though certainly claimed as voluntary, does the Cambodian repatriation pass a rigorous examination of its "voluntariness'? How does the result of this examination affect the claim that the repatriation was a genuine success? The first section explores these questions and concludes that the success of the repatriation needs to be qualified in fundamental ways, most importantly by the fact that it was not as voluntary as perhaps apparent on the surface. Next, given that the repatriation was, in fact, a qualified success, what were the circumstances which led to its success? The second section explores the context in which the Cambodian repatriation took place, focusing on key variables such as the quasi-trusteeship role of UNTAC in Cambodia. This section also notes some drawbacks of the extensive role of the UN and some risks that the UN took in making the repatriation the logistical success that it was. Finally, with the benefit of hindsight, the final section explores ways in which the UN could learn from the Cambodian experience as it struggles with civil conflicts and displaced populations in other regions around the globe.

Was the Cambodian repatriation a success? Was it voluntary?

From the beginning the repatriation was recognized as one of the key components of the peace plan[4] and there is no question that UNHCR

---

[3]   The primary example being the 1985 *Durable Solutions* report of UNHCR.

[4]   The refugee problem was explicitly recognized in the peace agreement itself: "the signatories request the Secretary-General of the United Nations to facilitate the repatriation in safety and dignity of Cambodian refugees and displaced persons, *as an integral part of the comprehensive political settlement*" (emphasis added), Agreement on a

can claim the Cambodian repatriation as a logistical success. UNHCR was responsible for moving 360,000 refugees from Thailand to within several kilometers of their new homes in Cambodia; each refugee received a household kit and was registered to receive food for 400 days. In addition, 88 percent of the refugees were given a cash grant, 8 percent were given land and wood for building a house, and 3 percent received land to farm.[5] UNHCR managed the entire operation (contracting out specific assignments to various NGOs) and UNTAC provided security throughout. The refugees were free to choose where they wished to return and could change their minds even once in Cambodia.[6] Though there were some negative incidents, on the whole the operation proceeded smoothly. In addition to the physical return of refugees and the distribution of the returnee package and food, UNHCR in cooperation with UNDP managed to implement $9.5 million worth of quick impact projects focused on the rehabilitation of communities.[7]

Despite these logistical successes, however, there are further criteria by which a repatriation can be judged. International protocols have firmly established the principle of *non-refoulement*, that refugees must never be forcibly returned to their country of origin. Stated in another way, *non-refoulement* requires that if a refugee does return to her own country, that she must have done so voluntarily. Clearly the voluntary nature of a refugee's return, the extent of her enthusiasm and optimism for return, will have a large impact on her success during the process of "rehabilitation," the finding of a productive niche in society. In the sections below, the nature of a refugee's decision – and why the "voluntary" is so important – will first be discussed. Next, the way in which this principle is translated into acceptable behavior on the part of international institutions will be presented. Finally, given this background, the Cambodian repatriation will be evaluated.

Comprehensive Political Settlement of the Cambodia Conflict, October 30, 1991, A/46/608, S/23177, art. 20, p. 16.

[5] UNTAC Daily Press Briefing, April 30, 1993.

[6] Raoul Jennar, *Cambodian Chronicles (VII): before it comes too late. Letter to the members of the Security Council* (Jordoigne, Belgium: European Far Eastern Research Center, 1993), p. 4. Mr. Jennar also notes that 77,000 thousand refugees who had been living in Khmer Rouge camps were able, with the assistance of UNHCR to move to parts of Cambodia not controlled by the Khmer Rouge thereby "rediscover[ing] a degree of freedom."

[7] For a detailed review of the Cambodian repatriation, see *"Something Like Home Again":The Repatriation of Cambodian refugees,* by the US Committee for Refugees with primary authorship by Court Robinson, May 1994.

Making the decision to repatriate

Ultimately, the refugee herself has the right to decide whether or not to run the risk of returning as compared to staying where she is. As one commentator on the legal issues pertaining to repatriation has remarked:

> The voluntary character of repatriation can thus be seen as the necessary correlative to the subjective fear which gave rise to flight; willingness to return negates that fear. The act of will is also essential as evidence of abandonment or conscious surrender of the particular legal interest which the status of refugee . . . comprises.[8]

In a best-case scenario, the refugee makes this decision based upon the improving nature of conditions at home, usually a function of the government's behaviour: "[i]n ideal circumstances, voluntary repatriation will follow a basic change in the conditions that caused flight, the feared regime be gone, and the refugees will be welcomed home."[9]

Unfortunately, the refugee cannot make her decision solely upon the changing nature of the "feared regime." Whatever refugees can learn about the conditions in the country of origin – whether improving or worsening – must constantly be compared to the real conditions in which the refugee finds herself. The conditions in the host country depend upon the policies of the host government and the extent of international refugee assistance.

The host country has the most direct impact on the conditions in which refugees find themselves. The Thai government, for example, limited the mobility of the Cambodian refugees, prohibited relief NGOs from paying their Khmer staff in money for fear of affecting the local Thai economy, and was often suspected of physically abusing refugees.[10] The attitudes taken by host governments, however, can vary widely between countries. The Pakistani government, for example, welcomed the Afghan refugees with relatively open arms. Throughout the 1980s nearly two and a half million Afghans were living in the Northwest Frontier Province of Pakistan. Though the Afghans certainly did not inhabit prime real estate, they were free to build their own homes, look for work in the local economy and, perhaps most importantly, travel back and forth to Afghanistan at will.

[8] Guy Goodwin-Gill, "Voluntary repatriation: legal and policy issues," in Gil Loescher and Laila Monahan (eds.), *Refugees and International Relations* (Oxford: Oxford University press, 1989), pp. 255–92.

[9] F. Cuny and B. Stein, "Prospects for and promotion of spontaneous repatriation," in *Refugees in International Relations*, pp. 293–312.

[10] See William Shawcross's *Quality of Mercy: Cambodia, Holocaust and the Modern Conscience* (New York: Simon and Schuster, 1979) for an assessment of the conditions which prevailed in the refugee camps.

In addition to the government of the country of asylum, the UN and non-governmental relief agencies shape the conditions in which refugees find themselves. Particularly in cases where the UN is providing food, changes in the ration or in the definition of who is eligible can greatly influence a refugee's decision to return. Consider again the example of the Afghan refugees in Pakistan. In the spring of 1992, the fall of the Najibullah government – which the *mujahideen* had been fighting since 1979 – triggered a massive spontaneous repatriation of over one million people. The military victory, however, may not have been the only factor: "the fact that the distribution of food rations was suspended in most refugee camps for several months in early 1992" undoubtedly had an effect on refugees' decisions.[11] After all, as we have subsequently seen, the fall of the former regime in no way guaranteed peace. Though food and medical care are probably the most important relief factor, the reduction of other services which NGOs provide, such as education, may also affect the decision to return.[12]

In addition to sometimes encouraging refugees to return early, relief assistance can also have a "pull" effect, encouraging flight in the first place. The opportunities for resettlement in third countries can also attract refugees. To counter this, governments have upon occasion resorted to "humane deterrence": in Southeast Asia "the policy had three main facets: the imposition of austere camp conditions; the denial of resettlement processing to new arrivals and, at least implicitly, renewed efforts to apprehend and expel arrivals at the border."[13]

Host government policies, though perhaps less important than the size of the international "assistance package" can also heavily influence the refugees' climate. Moreover, host governments face policy dilemmas of their own – having to worry, for example, about the resources devoted to the refugees as well as the perception of how their own people are being treated as compared to refugees. These concerns can contribute to severe problems, as they did in the case of Bangladesh in 1978, when an undersized food ration for over 200,000 Burmese refugees led to a mortality rate four times higher than expected.[14] The policy leading to the undersized ration resulted not only from interagency disagreements over the appropriate ration size, but also an established Bangladeshi policy on the size of an "emergency ration" for their own disasters (and

[11] Hiram A. Ruiz, *Left out in the Cold: The Perilous Homecoming of Afghan Refugees* (Washington, DC: US Committee for Refugees, 1992), p. 7.
[12] Ibid., p. 8.
[13] Dennis McNamara, "The origins and effects of humane deterrence policies in Southeast Asia", in Loescher and Monahan, *Refugees and International Relations*, p. 127.
[14] Cato Aall, "Disastrous international relief failure: a report on Burmese refugees in Bangladesh from May to December 1978," *Disasters*, vol. 3, no. 4, 1979, pp. 429–34.

a consequent interest in maintaining an image which did not treat the refugees better than they treated "their own"), and an interest, on the part of at least some members in the Bangladeshi government, in encouraging the refugees to return home.

These types of policy decisions taken by the host government, the UN, and relief programs provide the context critical to the refugee's decision about whether or not to return. The heart of the problem, however, is that the international community – mostly manifested through UNHCR policies which, in turn, result from myriad pressures of donor governments – must factor in all these carrot-and-stick angles when making their own decisions about repatriation programs. It is particularly problematic because of the dynamic feedback element which this introduces: though UNHCR may create a policy in reaction to a condition on the ground, their policy, in turn, becomes yet another factor conditioning the environment.[15] Thus, the return of refugees after the implementation of a repatriation program does not guarantee that the program was appropriate; the refugees might be responding more to the changing equation of expected benefits/risks of staying as refugees (if possible) versus expected benefits/risks of participating in the repatriation program, rather than genuine changes in the conditions in the country of origin. Needless to say, it is difficult to disentangle this imbroglio of cause and effect and consequently the UNHCR's and refugees' desires may not always correspond. One example occurred in Africa when over 200,000 refugees returned to Tigray (Ethiopia) when UNHCR and the United States had both recommended that they not go.[16] Another case is that of refugees from El Salvador. UNHCR agreements with the government of El Salvador regarding the return of refugees were sometimes ignored by the refugees who attached their own more stringent conditions to return.[17]

Due to the complexities in determining when it is safe to return, the majority of refugees in the world repatriate voluntarily and on their own

[15] The donor pool of money for any particular "situation" is usually limited. Therefore, every dollar going to a refugee camp is a dollar not going to the other side. The Rwandan government, for example, has recently felt the sting of this situation. They have argued that while the international community continually demands that they improve in-country conditions so that refugees are encouraged to come home, that simultaneously the international community is contravening efforts in this direction by investing in non-critical refugee programs. From the government of Rwanda's point of view, international dollars should go to building permanent schools in Rwanda, not temporary ones in Zaire. It is certainly true that if the international community spent more on schools in Rwanda, and less on plastic-sheeting in Zaire, that it would change the equation which refugees face.

[16] Cuny and Stein, "Spontaneous repatriation," p. 298.

[17] Dennis Gallagher, Susan Martin, and Patricia Weiss-Fagen, "Temporary safe haven," in *Refugees and International Relations*, pp. 333–54.

rather than with internationally assisted repatriations. Ironically, the majority of dollars spent on internationally sponsored repatriations is thus spent on a minority of refugees. In the year of the Cambodian repatriation, 1992, for example, the UN spent over $90 million on the repatriation of 360,000 Cambodian refugees, while over one and a quarter million Afghans went home by themselves.[18] In any event, it is this complex situation that has raised the "voluntary" issue to such importance: only if individual refugees presented with real choice make an informed decision to return can one have confidence that the refugees are not in some sense being manipulated to return. The greater the degree of voluntariness, the more robust is any claim of success.

International guidelines for repatriations

In the end, a set of agreed conditions has evolved by which a repatriation can be judged voluntary. The Executive Committee of UNHCR has twice endorsed the following principles, among others, which apply to the voluntary nature of a repatriation. The repatriation must be voluntary with respect both to mass movements and those of the individual – this can be taken to mean that refugees have the right at any time to change their mind. Secondly, refugees should be provided with as much information as possible prior to and throughout a repatriation – this should include being able to visit their country of origin in advance of their decision to return without necessarily losing their refugee status. UNHCR must then have free access to the returnees during and after the repatriation if they have participated in assisting the refugees to return home.[19]

The Cambodian repatriation

In judging the case of the Cambodian repatriation, an analysis of the formal documents and the declarations of the relevant institutions suggest a near-ideal program. First, in writing the comprehensive agreement the UN insured that its principles regarding repatriation were explicitly encoded into the document:

[18] *UNHCR Bulletin*, no. 8, March 30, 1993, p. 3. In reality this caricature is slightly unfair to UNHCR. A food and cash package was available to Afghans going home, though by and large they were responsible for finding their own transportation and there is certainly not the degree of follow up as in Cambodia. Afghan families received approximately $130 and a one-time distribution of 300 kilograms of wheat.

[19] Both the 1980 Executive Committee (31st Session) and the 1985 Executive Committee (36th Session) reinforced these principles. See annexes II and III in Guy Goodwin-Gill's "Voluntary repatriation," pp. 288–91.

¶2 – "return to their place of choice";

¶4 – "full respect for human rights and fundamental freedoms ... freedom of movement within Cambodia, the choice of domicile and employment, and the right to property";

¶7 – "repatriation should be voluntary ... choice of destination within Cambodia should be that of the individual";

¶8 – "full access by the Office of UNHCR, ICRC and other relevant international organizations should be guaranteed to all Cambodian refugees and displaced persons";

¶11 – "adequately monitored short-term repatriation assistance should be provided ... replaced in the longer term by the reconstruction program."[20]

Second, the repatriation was voluntary if considered from an institutional point of view. The factions' leaders who comprised the Supreme National Council, who additionally represented the refugees on the grounds that the factions were all based in the camps, were all signatories to the peace agreement. The interest of these parties in repatriation was further recognized in a tripartite agreement between the Thai government, the Supreme National Council, and UNHCR.

Despite the fact that these documents suggest that the program was voluntary, however, from an individual refugee's perspective that might not have been the case. As noted above, the Cambodia repatriation was declared voluntary because of the role of the Supreme National Council and the UN in negotiating the comprehensive peace agreement which called for the repatriation. An individual refugee, however, had little choice. The tripartite agreement between UNHCR, the Royal Thai government and the Supreme National Council, for example, had the following to say regarding the "voluntary" repatriation:

The Contracting Parties shall cooperate with one another to insure that repatriation will be on a voluntary basis. *Where the Contracting Parties agree that*, with regard to the Cambodian refugees and displaced persons in the border camps in Thailand, *the circumstances that create the status of genuine refugee have ceased to exist, this principle will no longer be relevant.*[21]

Thus, the individual refugee had very little power over whether or not to return; her status as a refugee had been effectively nullified. At the grassroots level, while refugees may or may not have been aware of the legal implications of the tripartite agreement, the evidence supports the

[20] Agreement on a Comprehensive Political Settlement of the Cambodia Conflict, pp. 42–4.

[21] Tripartite Memorandum of Understanding among the Royal Thai Government, the Supreme National Council of Cambodia and the Office of the United Nations High Commissioner for Refugees relating to the Repatriation of Cambodian Refugees and Displaced Persons from Thailand (November 21, 1991), ¶1 "Voluntary character of repatriation," in *International Journal of Refugee Law*, vol. 4 no. 2, 1992, p. 277 (emphasis added).

notion that the refugees repatriated because the UN told them to. In the words of one early analysis of the repatriation: "the early arrivals neither sensed nor displayed a great deal of ownership of their repatriation. UNHCR had chosen the location, they [returnees] said, and promised them land. 'I went,' said one, 'according to the UN'."[22]

In theory this issue – that individuals had little choice about the repatriation – was not supposed to be a problem. There would be no reason why a refugee would not want to return to a peaceful, democratic Cambodia which they could leave if they wanted. At the time, however, there was in fact a significant amount of evidence which portended that perhaps everything would not turn out as planned. Indeed, from early on it was clear that the Khmer Rouge were not participating at all as they had agreed in the peace process. They did not participate in the demobilization, did not allow the UN access to their territory, pulled out of the election process and incited violence against ethnic Vietnamese, many of whom fled.[23] This problem alone would have been a good reason for an individual refugee to doubt the future peace and security within Cambodia. As the repatriation continued and the elections approached, the signals suggested further deterioration. The level of violence increased significantly and the Khmer Rouge were on the verge of making a peaceful election impossible.[24] Fortunately, on the day before the vote, the Khmer Rouge issued orders to stop interfering with the elections,[25] though since that time the Khmer Rouge have continued to disrupt the peace in Cambodia. Had not the election and post-election process run as smoothly as it did, however, would not the UN be under ethical obligation to protect those that had returned home on the UN promise of "peace?"

The Cambodian repatriation also displays the dynamic element mentioned previously. The UNHCR repatriation program had a deterministic effect on a refugee's decision about whether or not to repatriate. Refugees knew that the UNHCR would be closing down the camps and that their status as refugees had been terminated. Further-more, the various political parties all were pushing for the refugees to return quickly to their regions to help their chances in the elections.

---

[22] Court Robinson, "Still trying to get home: the repatriation of Cambodian refugees in Thailand," *Refugee Reports*, vol. 13, no. 11, 1992, p. 6.

[23] See for example the Fourth Progress Report of the Secretary-General on the United Nations Transitional Authority in Cambodia, Security Council, S/25124, May 3, 1993, ¶130.

[24] See for example the Fourth Progress Report of the Secretary-General on the United Nations Transitional Authority in Cambodia, Security Council, S/25124, May 3, 1993, ¶124–6 and ¶130. The same report also notes that PDK (Khmer Rouge) radio has repeatedly launched "vitriolic" attacks against UNTAC.

[25] For an excellent review of the election process, see the UN video on the subject.

Finally, there was a feeling among some refugees that if they wanted UNHCR assistance and/or land in Cambodia, that they had to go back quickly.[26] Thus, in reality there was never an option to stay in Thailand. In fact, 573 refugees did refuse to repatriate with the UN program. UNHCR made it clear to these refugees that support for them would be withdrawn. The Thai government's position was that they were illegal residents and they were subsequently deported to Cambodia.[27] UNHCR's role is a delicate one, as they need to respond to the very real geo-political pressures of the donors – everyone wanted the refugees to go home – while maintaining their role to protect refugees' against some of those very same pressures. In signing the tripartite agreement which effectively nullified the refugees' status, the UNHCR gambled, on behalf of the refugees, that they would be better off in Cambodia.

Given the drastic nature of this decision, the fact that the refugees returned with UNHCR's repatriation program cannot be counted as sufficient evidence that the refugees individually chose to return. Moreover, even for those who may have agreed to return, it is not clear that they made that decision based upon the appropriate information, that is, evidence of genuine, positive, and sustainable change in conditions in Cambodia. To be sure there was some evidence pointing in this direction, but the decision whether the evidence was sufficient or not, should have rested with individual refugees, not with the international community, regional governments, or faction leaders.

In sum, we can declare the Cambodian repatriation a qualified success. The UN deserves credit for integrating the refugee problem into the peace agreement and for carrying out a difficult logistical operation on the ground. Notwithstanding these laudable achievements, however, the repatriation was flawed insofar as it removed the ability of individual refugees to decide if and when to return home. This may be a dangerous precedent for other repatriations around the world.

The Cambodian repatriation: a new model or a unique solution

Despite the reservations cited above about the degree of voluntariness, the repatriation of Cambodian refugees was a success. Refugees were transported home in safety, food was provided during a critical transition

---

[26] In the end, this turned out to be for good reason. While early on agricultural land was an option for any returning refugee, the program shifted mid-way through the year and the opportunity for a returning refugee to receive agricultural land ceased to become an option. See Robinson, "Still trying to get home."

[27] Robinson, *Something Like Home Again*, p. 9.

period, and rehabilitation programs were started. One study suggests that by May 1994 perhaps a third of refugees were still in an "at-risk" category, whereas two-thirds had managed to reintegrate at least to self-sufficiency.[28]

In order to extract ideas which might be valuable for other situations, it is necessary to understand what contributed to the success of the repatriation, both in terms of policy decisions and in terms of underlying assumptions. This analysis is necessary because, resulting from the logic of the previous section regarding voluntary repatriation, the fact that the refugees were in some ways manipulated by the context to return disallows one from using the fact that the refugees *did* return home as testimony that the policy decisions were correct. In this analysis which follows, it will be seen that it was the extensive control of the UN during the time period of the repatriation that allowed it to be a logistical success, but that this same condition – the high level of UN rather than Cambodian control – meant that the refugees were brought home under a measure of false pretense, and perhaps prematurely. It is this possibility, that a policy decision was taken which led to a premature repatriation, which may carry the warning for other repatriations. In order to decide whether or not the refugees came home prematurely, however, it is necessary to understand what enabled UNHCR to bring them home.

There can be no question that the peace agreement was, if not a necessary condition for the return of the refugees, at least the major watershed which enabled the repatriation program to get underway. In this regard, Cambodia is not likely to be unique. Peace agreements were made in the case of Salvadoran refugees, for example, and it is likely that for other large refugee populations peace agreements will be a precondition for repatriation. In Afghanistan, for example, although a remarkable number of refugees went home after the fall of the Najibullah government in April of 1992, well over a million still remain.[29] A peace settlement is probably a prerequisite for a permanent solution to that refugee problem.

Unlike other peace agreements, however, the Cambodian solution yielded considerable power and access to UNTAC, approximating a "trusteeship" role during the period between the ceasefire and elections. The repatriation program was to be carried out during this interim period. Although the Supreme National Council was the legal authority – it held the seat in the UN – UNTAC had extensive powers in the country. If for example the Council could not reach an agreement to

[28] Ibid., pp. 61–2.   [29] Ruiz, *Left out in the Cold*, p. 6.

make a decision, authority was deferred to Prince Sihanouk, but if the prince "is not, for whatever reason, in a position to make such a decision, his power of decision will transfer to the Secretary-General's Special Representative"[30] who was also the head of UNTAC. Furthermore, in the area of civil administration, all administrative agencies, bodies and offices acting in the field of foreign affairs, national defense, finance, public security, and information [were to] be placed under the direct control of UNTAC.[31]

This "trusteeship" role of the UN made the Cambodia situation highly unusual. With regard to refugees, in normal cases UNHCR must negotiate a tripartite agreement which includes the host government, the government of the country of origin, and itself.[32] But in Cambodia's case, even though a tripartite agreement was signed and although the Supreme National Council was the signatory representing the Cambodian government, UNTAC had a greater level of power than is often the case. Moreover, the sheer size of the UNTAC presence in Cambodia, a result of the combination of the large role given UNTAC in the Paris accords and the considerable financial support of the international community, added to the level of logistical control that UNTAC could exercise in the field. The reception centers where the refugees were housed temporarily were run by UNHCR-contracted NGO's and the World Food Program had a network in place to provide food for the returnees for up to a year.

In contrast, in many other situations UNHCR is left lobbying a government to abide by agreements and respect human rights. In the case of the return of Guatemalan refugees from Mexico, for example, UNHCR and the CCPPs (the committees representing the refugees) negotiated with the Guatemalan government about everything from the nature of the rights to be guaranteed to returning refugees to the particular highways traveled on the repatriation route.[33] After the agreements had been made, UNHCR and the refugees still had to worry about whether or not the Guatemalan government would adhere to those agreements. In fact, the government did back down on some of its agreements. It failed to provide appropriate services on an overnight

---

[30] Agreements on a Comprehensive Political Settlement of the Cambodia Conflict, October 23, 1991, Department of Public Information DPI/1180-92077-January 1992-10M, UN Department of Information, 1992, annex 1, ¶A2c, p.17.

[31] Agreements on a Comprehensive Political Settlement of the Cambodia Conflict, October 23, 1991, annex 1, ¶B1, p.18.

[32] See for example the 1985 Executive Committee (36th Session), item no. 40: Voluntary Repatriation, in annex III in Guy Goodwin-Gill's "Voluntary repatriation," pp. 288–91.

[33] Hiram A. Ruiz, *El retorno: Guatemalans' risky repatriation begins* (Washington, DC: US Committee for Refugees, 1993.

stop, for example, and hassling of the refugees through police interference was reported.[34]

Until the Cambodia agreement, the Guatemala case exemplified the third-party status which UNHCR usually carried. In Cambodia, however, UNHCR was in a much stronger position to insure that the rights of the refugees were respected throughout the repatriation. The UN was directly responsible for all movements in Cambodia and had full rights of movement within most of the country. UNTAC controlled the roads, UNHCR contracted NGOs to build the reception centers (transit stations), and UNTAC policed them. In short, the entire logistical side of the repatriation operation was directly under UNHCR control. In addition to the ability to control the logistical movements in Cambodia, UNHCR also had direct control over parts of the reintegration package. It coordinated the first round of quick impact projects and was directly responsible for the delivery of house building materials and food for a year.

In sum, the quasi-UN trusteeship in Cambodia, manifested through UNTAC's power during the transition period, allowed UNHCR to have extensive control over the repatriation. This control enabled UNHCR to vouchsafe the repatriation process – and even part of the reintegration assistance – in a way which had never been done before. It allowed UNHCR to declare – legitimately – that the repatriation program was one of the two main successes of the UN mission in Cambodia.[35] In any future UN operation where UNHCR has as much control, similar successes may be possible.

A repatriation, however, is composed of two parts: the physical return and re-establishment of a residence, and the reintegration into workable society. As discussed above, it is the opinion that conditions have changed that should "negate" the fear which caused the flight in the first place. This fear, it is assumed, results from fundamental dysfunction in an otherwise workable society. Thus, the conditions that one would like to see changed are integrally related to the functioning of society. The changed conditions that allowed UNHCR to bring the refugees home, however, had more to do with logistical provisions (houses, food, transport) than with fundamental aspects of society. During the window of time when the refugees made their decision to go home, Cambodia was a prosperous place for returnees: land, a house, and food were promised for a year. These offers made it logical for a refugee to return home (even to be eager to return home) by participating in the UNHCR repatriation effort despite the fact that she could not reliably judge her

---

[34] Ibid., p. 19.   [35] *UNHCR Bulletin*, no. 8, March 30, 1993, p. 2.

prospects under the new regime. This throws into doubt Akashi's claim that the "peaceful and orderly return" of refugees was a "clear expression of the confidence that the Cambodians have in the peace process." Rather, the return was simply a project made possible as a result of that peace process, specifically of the power yielded to UNTAC by the Paris Accords. This opposite view of causation also calls into question the necessity of the repatriation to the peace process. Certainly a symbolic UN success was important, and the implementation of the repatriation program probably contributed to the general liberalization of the environment in terms of freedom and security to travel. It is not clear that the repatriation was fundamental to the success of the peace process, however, except insofar as the peace process had been designed that way, placing the emphasis on the fact that the refugees had to be home before elections.

Concerning implications for refugees and future repatriations

The defining circumstance of the UN "trusteeship" – and its decision to bring the refugees home prior to the elections and the establishment of a new government – has three implications. First, the nature of the "trusteeship" may have contributed not only to the non-voluntary nature of the repatriation discussed above, but also denied refugees the opportunity to see how the "new regime" behaved. A quick comparison with the repatriation of Guatemalan refugees reinforces this point. In that case, Guatemalan refugees in Mexico who did not participate in the early repatriations observed carefully the government's reaction to the first returnees. Government comments and behavior gave valuable clues about how the refugees would be treated as they reintegrated. The government's comments about the repatriation, such as the government report that the population flows resulting from the repatriation might hide movements of guerrilla soldiers,[36] suggested that the government viewed the refugees with hostility. It was a real indicator which the refugees in Mexico could use to evaluate their future prospects. In the case of Cambodia, however, the fact that the refugees made it home safely under the logistical management of UNHCR yielded far fewer clues about how they would be treated by the future government. Thus the UN "trusteeship," at least with respect to the repatriation, is something of a double-edged sword: almost single-handedly it enabled UNHCR to transport refugees home with security and insure that the reintegration package was initiated; at the same time, however, it

[36] Ruiz, *El retorno*, p. 13.

repatriated the refugees in advance of the political resolution fundamental to the refugees' future. Thus the return of the refugees prior to
the establishment of a new government was a risk – both for the refugees
and for the UN – which in hindsight appears to have paid off.

Second, although UNHCR can expect success in those aspects of
the program over which it has complete control (such as logistics), in
aspects of the program which require cooperation with the government, UNHCR will be relegated to an advisory, monitoring agency as
is traditional. The failure of the land distribution component illustrates
the difficulties of making promises, the fulfilling of which requires
relying on a separate institution. Initially, UNHCR's plan was to
distribute approximately two hectares of land to individual refugees.
The distribution of land was intended to help returnees establish a
means for earning a living as stated in annex 4 of the Comprehensive
Agreement on the Repatriation: "Adequately monitored short-term
assistance should be provided on an impartial basis to enable the
families and individuals returning to Cambodia to establish their lives
and livelihoods."[37] As at least 60 percent of the refugees were from
agricultural backgrounds, land distribution was the preferred means of
establishing livelihood. In pursuit of this objective, a study was
undertaken during the late fall of 1991 which identified 240,000
hectares of available land.[38] As has been noted, there is not great land
pressure in Cambodia.[39] It ought to have been able to absorb the
returnees. Shortly after the program began, however, UNHCR
discovered that it was not going to be able obtain the land for the
returnees as it had planned.[40] Independent observers have stated that
the problem was that the local-level authorities were not cooperating
with UNHCR in distributing the land. Furthermore, the kind of land
which the Phnom Penh government had helped to identify was
"inaccessible, mined, on the front lines, or it was simply the worst
land around."[41] Subsequently, UNHCR abandoned offering agricultural land as one of the repatriation package options to the refugees in

[37] Agreement on a Comprehensive Political Settlement of the Cambodia Conflict, annex
4, ¶11, pp. 42–4.
[38] Robinson, "Still trying to get home", p. 3.
[39] Robert J. Muscat, "Rebuilding Cambodia: problems of governance and human
resources," in Dolores A. Donovan, Sidney Jones, Dinah Pokemper and Robert
Muscat (eds.) (with introduction by Frederick Z. Brown), *Rebuilding Cambodia: Human
Resources, Human Rights and Law* (Washington, DC: SAIS Foreign Policy Institute,
1993).
[40] First Progress Report of the Secretary-General on the United Nations Transitional
Authority in Cambodia, Security Council, S/23870, May 1, 1992, ¶52.
[41] Robinson, "Still trying to get home," p. 4.

Thailand.[42] The UNTAC press briefing stated that "three percent had opted for agricultural land" but the reality is that only 3 percent had the chance.[43]

Notwithstanding the impressive logistical achievements of the repatriation program, the abandonment of the land distribution must be seen as disappointing. The returnees had food rations for 400 days (200 days in Phnom Penh), but after that their means of achieving economic security were very uncertain. Thus, the refugees' future economic security was as uncertain as their political security. This shortcoming was particularly unfortunate because, given the lack of political resolution – in the sense that the new government was not in place yet – the receipt of land could have sent a strong signal to returning refugees that their future livelihoods were secure, even if the political resolution had not yet come about.

The inability to distribute as much land as hoped resulted from the fundamental fact that neither UNHCR nor UNTAC had enough power over any level of government to insure that land could be made available. UNHCR had control over the roads and over the reception centers; it did not have control over the land. One conclusion from this story is that the UN should be very wary of making promises about processes over which they have no control. The UN made the error not in trying to have land distributed, but in *promising* it. While this may seem a self-evident conclusion, it is important because the widespread knowledge that the "UNHCR was offering two hectares of land per family" in the camps certainly contributed to the refugees' willingness to return.[44]

The third implication is that the authority which accompanies the quasi-trusteeship comes at the cost of greater responsibility. As illustrated earlier, Cambodian refugees often cited a trust of the UN as the reason for their "voluntary" return.[45] By participating in the termination of their status as refugees, taking them home, and promising them democracy, safety, and land, the UN assumed a greater ethical responsibility in a very volatile situation than if the refugees had made their own decision based upon the changed behavior of a government in power.

In conclusion, the successes of the Cambodian repatriation are replicable in other situations where the UN has direct control over logistics as it had in Cambodia. However, the UN needs to be careful

---

[42] Actually UNHCR told the refugees that those who wanted agricultural land would have to wait, but this amounted to the same thing. See ibid.

[43] UNTAC Daily Press Briefing, April 30, 1993.

[44] US Committee for Refugees, "Something like home again," p.20.

[45] As cited earlier, in response to questions about the repatriation program, one refugee said "I went according to the UN"; Robinson, "Still trying to get home," p. 6.

about making promises over which it does not have direct control. Not surprisingly, those aspects over which the UN has little control – distribution of land, the quality of government, and the commitment of the various parties to peace, for example – are precisely those which are the most significant indicators of fundamental change and therefore the most valuable to the refugee. To bring refugees home in advance of a political resolution – necessary for the refugee to see how the government behaves in these important areas – is to tempt fate. At the very least the UN needs to recognize the increased ethical burden the UN itself shoulders in so doing.

Lessons learned from the Cambodian repatriation

Accepting and setting aside for the moment the conclusion that the repatriation in Cambodia is basically replicable under a model of comprehensive, expansive UN intervention, there at least two lessons which may aid policy-makers in future peace processes involving repatriations.

Preserving individual choice: slowing the repatriation

The loss of refugees' individual choice coupled with the lack of a political resolution upon which they could base their decision to go home added risk to the UN involvement and the repatriation as a whole. Refugees could decide where to go, but not if to go. And even if they could have decided whether or not to go, they could not observe their "new" government to see what it would be like, because it had not been elected yet. One solution to this problem is to reduce the requirements that refugees go home so quickly. This would require continuing to offer some services in the country of asylum so that the incentive balance not be so one-sided. In so doing a refugee's right of individual choice would be reaffirmed. Furthermore, had the UN given refugees the choice to stay in Thailand, it would have reduced its own responsibility to the returnees future safety and security because the refugees would have exercised their own choice. This is not an argument for reduced UN responsibility, but rather realistic responsibility. Had the situation in Cambodia become destabilized around the time of elections instead of proceeding smoothly, for example, and descended into chaotic violence, what could the UN have done? Additionally, so long as the transition to peace proceeded smoothly it probably would not have slowed down the repatriation much. On the whole the refugees were eager to go home. They had been restricted to barbed wire compounds for up to twelve years, some level of peace had at last come to their country, and the UN was promising free transport and food for over a year. If the refugees were not required to return and the transition to peace in Cambodia had not gone well, one of two things would have happened. Either the refugees would have still chosen to go home, and the UN would not have been obligated to help beyond the extent to which it always tries to help those in war zones, or the refugees would have stayed in Thailand. Instead, as actually happened, the UN bears a greater responsibility because the refugees went home under UN authority.[46]

Such a slower repatriation process is not without precedent. In the cases of both El Salvador and Guatemala, refugees were able to watch earlier repatriations before deciding whether or not to follow suit. The real issue is not so much that the repatriation is in and of itself slower – though this is the result – but rather that real, sustainable changes are effected within the host country before a refugee, or even an international policy-maker, takes the decision that it is time to go home. Just as elections do not guarantee democracy and a constitution does not guarantee the rule of law, so too one cannot take the signature of a peace treaty to be a guarantee of peace. It is far better to base one's decision on actions rather than promises. This is true both for refugees, who have the right to make their decision to return based upon actions by the government, and the international agencies who should plan their interventions around whether or not the refugees want to return – not around whether or not the international community has decided that the peace process is a safe-enough bet.

The counter-argument to giving the refugees the right to delay their return is that the repatriations had to be completed before the elections. During the negotiations, the rebel factions argued particularly hard for this because they felt that they needed "their" refugees back in the country so that they could win regional seats in the national assembly. Consequently the pressure to rush the repatriation arose principally from non-trivial political pressure. While participation in the democratic

---

[46] It should be noted that the Thais were very insistent that the refugees go home and would certainly have resisted this "slowing down." Nevertheless, from a UN perspective there might be an argument suggesting that leaving the refugees with their status might have helped with later bargaining with the Thais. The UN has had trouble making the Thais pull their gem and timber operations out of western Cambodia which support the Khmer Rouge. In a sense, the Thais won on both counts; they were guaranteed that the "burden" of refugees would be gone without having to actually stop their economic operations. Leaving the refugees with their status may have allowed the UN to argue that it was in the Thais economic interest that they abide by the UN logging ban in Cambodia to support the peace process. After all, a peaceful Cambodia would be more likely to entice the refugees to go home.

process was important both for the refugees and for the consolidation of the peace process, there may have been other options which did not involve getting the refugees home in advance of a political resolution. Since the refugees had indicated the region of Cambodia to which they would like to return, for example, they could have simply voted in absentia for those regions while residing in the camps.

Assuming for the moment that this voting issue could have been resolved, the order of operations might have been first demobilization, second voter registration (and the accompanying establishment of campaign laws), third the election, and finally, repatriation. This would have allowed the refugees to glimpse the nature of the new government and its policies before having to make their final decision about returning. Furthermore, it might have had the added benefit of allowing the reconstruction of the country to start sooner. As in fact happened, although over $800 million were promised for the reconstruction in June of 1992, by the spring of 1993 only about $100 million had been allocated and their respective projects initiated.[47] Rehabilitation and development projects, enacted in cooperation with a new government, would in and of themselves have been a genuine indicator affecting a refugee's decision to return.

Finally, an earlier election might have also helped with the complaint that the one-and-a-half year run-up to the election allowed for an incumbency advantage, particularly given that all the UN organizations ended up working through the State of Cambodia's institutions. Complaints about the incumbency advantage may have in fact impeded the reconstruction process. For example, concerned about angering the Khmer Rouge any further, the World Bank and the UN were very sensitive about assertions that tie-over loans to the SOC directly supported the SOC politically.

Having elections sooner, however, is not the only solution, and in any event may be impossible in many situations. Nevertheless, through one method or another the underlying goal is to have the next "real" government in place before refugees are faced with a decision about repatriation in order that they can make some real judgments about the expected behavior of the government. While in Cambodia elections were the negotiated process by which the next government was to be chosen, this may not always be the case. In different situations legitimate governments may arise through negotiation or even the use of force which have a trial run of several years before elections are actually held.

---

[47] Fourth Progress Report, p. 21.

During this time, the government's behavior could be judged by the refugees, influencing their decision about return. In addition, the international community could put pressure on the government in question to behave responsibly. Although this reduces the role of the international community to that of an influence-peddler rather than having its representative UN agencies acting like a "trustee," any changes in behavior on the part of the government are arguably more sustainable and therefore better indicators for the uncertain refugee. The lesson for those actors involved in peace negotiations and refugee affairs is that the more information about the likely behavior of the new government a refugee has, the better. In considering the timetable for any given peace process, therefore, the emphasis should be on having a new government established and managing the day-to-day affairs of state in advance of encouraging refugees to return home in mass.

Improving economic security

Just as a refugee must ponder her potential political security if she were to return home, so too must she question her economic prospects. Particularly because many refugee families are headed by a woman when they were not before the war, the question of how she is going to earn a living becomes critical. In cases where the political future is in question, the distribution of economic assets, especially land, can help assure people of economic security. Moreover, depending upon who is identified as the beneficiary, any proposed land distribution or reform can aid the peace process itself. In El Salvador, for example, as part of the peace agreement every demobilized soldier and every internally or externally displaced person was eligible to receive land. Other programs addressing the issue of economic/food security include school lunches (in the Cambodian case 52 percent of the returnees were school age children),[48] public works projects, and subsidized adult training programs. Any of these policies need to consider how to build communities, of course, and avoid exacerbating the rift between returnees and those who never left. In El Salvador, for example, land was also provided for squatters who had been farming throughout the war.

The implementation of economic policies such as land reform, however, cannot occur without a government and so the interest in economic security also argues in some ways for the establishment of a governing polity in advance of repatriation. The Cambodian experience provides evidence of this link in an unfortunate way. Without a real

[48] World Bank, *Cambodia: Agenda for Rehabilitation and Reconstruction* (Washington, DC: World Bank, 1992), p. 8.

government in place which had effective control of the countryside, there was really no way to distribute the land to returnees despite early projections and statements by the SOC that land was available.[49]

Conclusion

Overall, the repatriation of Cambodian refugees can be called a qualified success. Given the time period in which UNHCR moved 360,000 refugees, the accomplishments were completed with remarkably few incidents. Moreover, the reintegration package was delivered and rehabilitation projects initiated. The extensive UN role in Cambodia – delegated by the comprehensive peace settlement – was probably the most important factor.

Two qualifications, however, must be noted. First, the lack of real choice about whether or not to return on the part of individual refugees could have backfired had the elections failed. A return to violence would have created problems not only for the refugees, but also for the UN who would have had to shoulder greater responsibility for the refugees. Second, although early on UNHCR promised two hectares of land to each returning family, in the end only 3 percent of the returning families received land. The inability to find land for the returnees highlights several difficulties for future repatriations. Regardless of the extent of authority which the UN has in any given situation, it should be wary of making commitments in those areas over which it has little control. In the case of Cambodia, it could not control the local governments' power over distributing land. Rather than suggesting that the UN should not have tried to facilitate the distribution of land, this argues again for establishing a more permanent government able to take policy decisions in advance of encouraging repatriation.

Notwithstanding these qualifications, the UN would do well were it able to undertake a repatriation such as that in Cambodia for all the world's refugees.

[49] See the discussion of land issues in US Committee for Refugees, "Something like home again," especially pp. 19 and 24–9.

8 Quick impacts, slow rehabilitation in Cambodia

Elisabeth Uphoff Kato

> There will be no peace without development, and no development without peace.
>
> Sergio Viera de Mello, UNHCR Special Envoy and Director of the UNTAC Repatriation Component

Introduction

Although the participants of the Paris peace conference considered rehabilitation important enough to include a separate Declaration on the Rehabilitation and Reconstruction of Cambodia as one of the three parts of the Paris Agreements, UNTAC itself did very little in terms of rehabilitation during the eighteen months it was in Cambodia. Like several other UNTAC components, the Rehabilitation Component was slow to become operational, lacked a clear mandate, suffered from staffing and leadership problems, and was given neither the resources nor authority to carry out its primary responsibility of aid coordination. Donor hesitancy to commit money to an unstable political situation and to a disliked government slowed and skewed the flow of aid, and the myth of four equal factions enshrined in the Paris Peace Agreement (when in fact one faction controlled and bore the responsibility for administering 75–80 percent of the country) allowed the other factions to block desperately needed public sector assistance for political reasons.

In fact, it can be argued that some aspects of the economy deteriorated further under UNTAC. Urban booms, generated in larger part by UNTAC spending, increased the rural–urban gap, promoted shallow "consumer" economic activity and corruption, and encouraged an influx of Vietnamese laborers and prostitutes, which exacerbated anti-Vietnamese tensions. While not directly caused by UNTAC, inflation and lack of revenue eroded public services and infrastructure and the looting of Cambodia's natural resources by neighboring countries and the Cambodian factions themselves, although eventually slowed, continued long into the mission.

At the same time, the UNTAC rehabilitation component did have many positive accomplishments late in the mission, such as controlling inflation and facilitating a ban on logging, as did other UN agencies and NGOs concerned with rehabilitation. Because so many different actors were involved in rehabilitation, this chapter looks first at the activities of the UNTAC rehabilitation component, then at actual rehabilitation efforts by UN agencies, NGOs, and UNTAC military units, and finally at the positive and negative effects of the UNTAC mission itself on the Cambodian economy. Finally broader lessons are drawn about managing rehabilitation within the context of a peace-keeping operation.

The challenge

When UNTAC arrived in the spring of 1992, Cambodia was one of the poorest countries in the world. Simply to note that Cambodia's annual per capita income was less than $200 does not begin to describe the problem. Cambodia's physical infrastructure had been largely destroyed by more than two decades of war and isolation, and agriculture – the major economic activity – was disrupted by fighting and land mines. Although the People's Republic of Kampuchea (PRK, renamed the State of Cambodia, or SOC, after 1989) deserves full credit for rebuilding basic economic and social institutions from the devastation caused by the Khmer Rouge, continued war and an international embargo helped prevent full-scale reconstruction. When UNTAC arrived, agricultural and industrial production, exports, and many social indicators had still not recovered to pre-war (1960s) levels. Major roads and bridges had not been repaired for decades; there was virtually no telecommunications system; only 12 percent of the individuals in rural areas had access to drinking water; and preventable diseases, such as malaria and tuberculosis, were widespread. Average life expectancy was less than fifty years.

The destruction was not only physical, but social as well – an entire generation of educated persons had been killed or forced to flee by the Khmer Rouge, and the governments had lacked the resources to establish more than a very basic educational system. By 1992, still less than 1 percent of primary school teachers had completed high school, and only 0.5 percent of primary school students studied beyond high school. As a result of the Khmer Rouge period and the war, 60–65 percent of the adult population were women, and 1 out of 236 Cambodians was an amputee. Altogether, 20 percent of the population fell into the category of "vulnerable" – widows with children, orphans, handicapped, or elderly living alone.[1]

To complicate matters further, when UNTAC arrived, the SOC government (which was responsible for administering most of Cambodia) was in the middle of a fiscal crisis. First, the Socialist bloc aid, on which the SOC had depended for most of its budget, stopped in 1990; and the SOC did not have the administrative capacity to cover the shortfall through tax collection. By 1992, the budget gap was 4.5 percent of GDP. As the SOC tried to finance the gap by printing money, inflation rose from under 10 percent before 1988 to between 100 and 150 percent in 1991.[2] The government's other method of dealing with the deficit – not raising civil servant salaries to match inflation or simply not paying salaries at all – steadily eroded government morale and effectiveness. Meanwhile, public sector capital investment sank to almost nothing.

The fiscal crisis was exacerbated by the SOC's decision in 1989 to accelerate the transition to a market economy. The negative effects of liberalization were felt immediately, as revenues from state-owned enterprises dropped 95 percent; but the economic benefits did not materialize as quickly. Foreign investment did not increase as rapidly as expected because of the unstable political situation, and the government did not have the administrative capacity to control the investment that did occur. What developed was a "jungle economy," where Cambodian businessmen and government officials and foreign investors scrambled to grab what they could by whatever means necessary before the political situation stabilized – or collapsed.[3]

UNTAC's rehabilitation mandate

The fragility of Cambodia's economy called into question whether it would be able to withstand the demands that the peace process would place on it. The Paris Agreements required the reintegration of 300,000 returnees from the border camps, 150,000 internally displaced, and thousands of demobilized soldiers – as well as sufficient stability to bolster the political aspects of the peace plan. Since the SOC did not have enough money to pay its civil servants, let alone invest in rehabilitation projects, the Paris Agreements assumed that Cambodia

---

[1] See Donovan, Dolores A., Sidney Jones, Dinah Pokemper and Robert Muscat (eds.) (with introduction by Frederick Z. Brown), *Rebuilding Cambodia: Human Resources, Human*, Foreign Policy Institute, SAIS, Washington DC, 1993, for additional data.

[2] The World Bank, *Cambodia: Agenda for Rehabilitation and Reconstruction*, June 1992, p. 40.

[3] The term "jungle economy" was coined by the former finance minister and current head of the opposition, Sam Rainsy.

would need massive amounts of foreign aid both for the transitional period itself and in order to give the new government a solid base from which to build.

Therefore, the Declaration gave UNTAC a clear mandate to coordinate rehabilitation aid (as opposed to reconstruction aid which would be the responsibility of the new government) through a rehabilitation coordinator chosen by the UN Secretary-General. The rehabilitation phase was to address the immediate needs and to lay the groundwork for the preparation for medium- and long-term reconstruction plans. Aid was supposed to be coordinated, as much as possible, to be neutral and to be directed to all areas of the country, especially to the most disadvantaged. During the rehabilitation period, particular attention was to be given to food, security, health, housing, training, education, the transportation network, and the restoration of Cambodia's existing infrastructure and public utilities. This mandate was reiterated in the Secretary-General's February 19, 1992, report; and a comprehensive rehabilitation plan – complete with recommended projects, rationales, and dollar amounts – was put forward in the Secretary-General's May 1992 consolidated appeal to the international community for the rehabilitation of Cambodia.

The Rehabilitation Component

The function and structure of the rehabilitation component was spelled out in the Secretary-General's Report of February 19, 1992, where rehabilitation was established as a separate component, with a Rehabilitation Coordinator responsible for making ongoing assessments of needs, ensuring efficient and effective coordination, and raising resources. Like most of the other UNTAC components, the Rehabilitation Component was slow to become operational, a problem complicated by personnel problems. The first two coordinators were dismissed/resigned within months, and what was left of the unit was finally combined with the Office of Economic Affairs under the direction of the Economic Advisor in the fall of 1992. Even then, not all the staff had arrived, and the component was not fully operational until January 1993.

The Component's main activities were coordinating international aid and providing technical assistance for public administration issues related to the economy. In addition, the Component prepared reports, chaired donor meetings, and was instrumental in mobilizing information and funds for several emergency intervention. UNTAC did no rehabilitation work itself until the very end of the mission, because there was no budget. Although other UN agencies and most NGOs working on rehabilitation were aware of the existence of an UNTAC Rehabilitation Component, most interviewed were uncertain as to what the component's function actually was. When the Component closed down in September 1993, there seemed to have been little planning for the handing over of information or projects, either to Cambodian or international partners; and the unit vanished without a trace.

Aid coordination

Although aid coordination was one of the Rehabilitation Component's primary responsibilities, it had neither the staff nor the means to enforce cooperation from donors or projects. International aid was channeled through a Technical Advisory Committee, made up of delegates from all four factions and chaired by the rehabilitation component, which was supposed to review and coordinate aid proposals before passing them to the Supreme National Council for final approval.

By the time the Technical Advisory Committee was set up, considerable aid had already been pledged at the June 1992 Tokyo Conference in response to the Secretary-General's consolidated appeal, which called for $595 million for the rehabilitation phase that was to restore a sustainable degree of economic and social stability and establish the base for the broader long-term reconstruction effort by 1994. This included $116 million for repatriation, $82.8 million for resettlement, $44.8 million for food security and agriculture, $40 million for health and sanitation, $33.6 million for education and training, $150.3 million for public infrastructure restoration, and $111.8 million for program support.

Donor response was far greater than anticipated, and a total of $880 million was pledged at the Tokyo Conference. However, by February 1993, when the first donor review meeting was held, the Component's database indicated that the pledged funds were not materializing as expected. Less than $100 million had actually been disbursed by February; and most of that came from programs that were already established, particularly from repatriation and resettlement activities.[4]

This was partly due to technical delays – it was probably unrealistic to think that $880 million could be mobilized and spent within eighteen months, especially in Cambodia. And as the world economy slowed down, and other peacekeeping missions were launched, many donors found themselves unable to meet their pledges in Cambodia as easily as

[4]   UNTAC, Rehabilitation and Development in Cambodia: Achievements and Strategies, February 25, 1993, table 1.

they had expected. Prior to the May 1993 election, donors and agencies also pointed to the problem of limited absorption capacity, especially the lack of a national development plan or of government officials with the technical skills to function as counterparts, as reasons for the delay.

However, the slowness of aid disbursement also had to do with political factors and donor choice. The speed of disbursement was partly determined by the kind of aid donors chose to provide. Donors ignored the priorities set out in the appeal (small grassroots projects and program aid) and focused instead on traditional large-scale rehabilitation projects, which are slower in disbursing and which demand more counterpart time.[5] While Cambodia needed virtually everything, the choice of projects affected when and where the money was spent. Aid workers, especially those in the provinces, were emphatic that, if Cambodia did have a "limited absorption capacity," it applied only to large projects that required the involvement of the central government. No limit ever came close to being reached for much needed small grassroots or infrastructure projects.

In particular, program aid was almost completely absent, despite the UN's repeated pleas. The 1992 Appeal stated, "Initially, quick dispersing program aid should make up the bulk of external assistance so as to arrest the deterioration of the public service and protect the national currency"; but only $17.7 million of program support out of the $111.8 million requested arrived by the end of the transition period – and most of this arrived after the elections.[6]

Part of the blame lies with FUNCINPEC, which vetoed a $75 million emergency rehabilitation loan for essential imports and services from the World Bank in March 1993, on the grounds that it would favor the SOC – even though the money would not arrive until after the election. However, donors were also reluctant to give money for budget or balance of payments support. Part of this may have been for the traditional reasons that donors prefer project aid (program aid is difficult to account for and has no concrete product to hang a sign on), but part of it may have been political – Western donors were not comfortable giving budgetary support to a former enemy government and preferred to wait until after the election. The Paris Agreement's emphasis on four "equal" factions legitimized this reluctance, since the SOC was the only faction with a national administration.

In addition to the virtual absence of program aid, certain sectors were favored over others. Of the international aid spent, as of the February 1993 meeting, 68 percent was for repatriation, resettlement, and food

[5] Ibid., p. 3.
[6] UNTAC, The Secretary-General's Consolidated Appeal, May 1992, p. 2.

security, compared to 8.6 percent for community development, 6.6 percent for health and sanitation, 5.8 percent for education and training, 3.7 percent for public administration, and 5 percent for public utilities and infrastructure.[7] The flow of aid also had a geographical and sectoral bias. Though the Declaration called for special attention to the rural areas and stipulated that aid not be disproportionately directed to returnees, in practice, aid was biased towards urban populations and to the four northwest provinces where most of the returnees were.[8] Although 80 percent of Cambodia's population lived in the rural areas, 22 percent of all aid was spent in Phnom Penh alone (which represents less than 10 percent of the population) while 42 percent of rehabilitation was spent in the northwest.[9]

In all these cases, the Rehabilitation Component had no power to control donor bias and no ability to compensate.[10] Although the component was able to point out priorities and funding gaps, donors generally did not respond. Therefore, the Component's role was therefore largely limited to keeping count of what aid came in, and much of the Component's time was spent on developing a computer database of all international aid received. While very useful in theory, the database had many flaws, in part because donors had no standard definition for "pledge," "commitment," and "disbursement." This led to an embarrassing situation, where a Component report claimed that, as of July 1993, only half the aid pledged had been committed – to which the donors retorted that actually $714 million had been committed, over 80 percent. The database was released to other development agencies only after the end of the mission; and United Nations Development Program (UNDP) began building a new one, using the UNTAC database only as a reference.[11]

The second type of coordination was that of ongoing rehabilitation efforts within the country. Although this role was implied, the Secretary-General's February 1992 Report, which emphasized that aid needed to

---

[7]   UNTAC, Rehabilitation and Development in Cambodia, table II.
[8]   UNTAC, The Secretary-General's Consolidated Appeal, p. 5.
[9]   UNTAC, Rehabilitation and Development in Cambodia, table Va.
[10] In the fall of 1992, the component had planned a network of provincial rehabilitation officers to ensure a balanced distribution of rehabilitation funds, on the assumption that money would be available from the Cambodia Trust Fund. However, the money was not forthcoming, nor was there any donor response to their February 1993 request for $10 million for projects outside the northwest. In August 1993, in the process of finishing up paperwork, the Component discovered $300,000 of the trust fund marked for use in Cambodia. With this money plus an additional $100,000 solicited from donors, one staff person with two Cambodian assistants completed thirty-one small-scale rehabilitation projects in fifteen provinces by October 31.
[11] Interviews with UNDP officials.

be coordinated as much as possible and which said that the Rehabilitation Coordinator would establish the necessary coordinating bodies, the component never seriously attempted to do so. The first director did hold a few meetings with other UN agencies and NGOs, but these stopped after he left. Much later in the mission, the UNDP resident representative was invited to meetings with Special Representative Akashi and the economic advisor, but these do not seem to have had any impact at all on any other agencies involved in rehabilitation. If anything, the existence of a Rehabilitation Component may have been a hindrance to coordination, since most UN agencies (particularly UNDP) and international NGOs assumed that the UNTAC Component would take a lead, which it never did.

This hands-off policy seems to have come from a decision at the top that "coordinate" meant only to monitor aid flows into the country; but it was also the practical consequence of the Rehabilitation Component having activities of its own. With no budget for projects and no field presence, the component had no practical way to influence other rehabilitation projects on the ground. What coordination took place, did so in an *ad hoc* manner at the province level or among international NGOs through "sectoral meetings" which pre-dated UNTAC. In the northwest provinces, UNHCR and CARERE/UNDP-OPS took a lead in facilitating communication and cooperation and, in at least one province, local government officials were also active in initiating regular provincial sectoral meetings where international NGOs, the government, and UN agencies could exchange information about what was being done, what was needed, and how they could best work together to accomplish it.[12]

In both the approval of international aid and in the actual coordination of rehabilitation projects, Cambodian participation was not utilized as fully as it could have been. The Technical Advisory Committee served primarily as a rubber stamp, since in most cases the details of the project proposal had already been worked out before it reached the committee. In general, the factions were willing to accept any offer of assistance, but little effort was made to solicit their input. Documents were often not available in Khmer, the Cambodian parties were not informed in advance of important international meetings, and at least one of the Cambodian members of the committee felt that UNTAC discouraged Cambodian input for fear of politicization.

This was even more true at the local level. Although the Secretary-General's report stated, "Rehabilitation and Reconstruction represent a

---

[12] Interviews with provincial officials in Battambang.

continuum ... This means working with and through the existing structures such as provincial and local authorities, public works departments, schools and health clinics, local community organizations throughout the entire territory of Cambodia, as well as helping to train counterparts," in practice, most donors tried to avoid working with the SOC administration wherever possible.[13] "Working with" seems to have been widely interpreted as "occasionally tell them what you are doing"; and UN agencies and many international NGOs working in the provinces admitted that they tried to avoid contact with local officials as much as possible. While the corrupt nature of many local governments may have made this necessary in some areas, as a general policy it undoubtedly detracted from the long-term effectiveness of rehabilitation work and missed an opportunity to expand and improve local administrative capacity.[14]

Public policy and administration

Although the Declaration does not specifically mention public policy and administration, the Rehabilitation Component worked with the Supreme National Council and UNTAC Civil Administration on several economic issues involving policy and administration which had a major impact on Cambodia's rehabilitation – perhaps even more impact than the Component's efforts to coordinate aid and rehabilitation activities. The two most important areas were control of national resources (natural resources and public property) and macroeconomic and fiscal management. In addition, members of the Component were involved in two emergency interventions in order to maintain economic stability during two critical periods: the elections and the transition to the new government.

In July, the Supreme National Council set up a second Technical Advisory Committee on the Management and Sustainable Exploitation of Natural Resources (TAC2) to review and examine different contractual arrangements related to the exploitation of natural resources. Throughout the transitional period, the committee proposed a number of important laws to halt what had been, up until then, a fire sale of Cambodia's national assets. For several years (especially since the Paris Agreements), all of the political factions had been allowing Thai and other Asian logging companies to clear the Cambodian forests for personal profit and to pay for the continued war. By early 1993,

---

[13] UNTAC, *The Secretary-General's Consolidated Appeal*, p. 6.
[14] Aid workers, who did work with local governments, insisted that every administration had some good individuals who needed encouragement and support.

deforestation had reached a peak of 1 million cubic meters a day, a rate that would destroy Cambodia's forests in five to ten years.[15] In addition to robbing future generations of one of Cambodia's few economic assets, this deforestation also threatened the complex ecology of the Tonle Sap, from which comes the fish that provides much of the protein in the Cambodian diet. At the same time, the Khmer Rouge made an estimated $1 million a day by allowing Thai miners in the Pailin gem mines, while SOC officials sold public buildings and land to foreign businessmen.

The first recommendation of the second Technical Advisory Committee was a moratorium on the export of logs, which was announced by the Supreme National Council in September 1992 and went into effect at the end of the year. The committee then worked out the legislation for a moratorium on the commercial extraction and export of mineral resources (adopted in February 1993) and a moratorium on the sale, transfer, and leasing of public assets (June 10, 1993). The Committee was also charged with developing regulations to guide industry which would balance environmental and sustainability concerns.

Although this might not traditionally be considered rehabilitation, it was considerably more efficient, since it prevented the need for more extensive rehabilitation later and since it gave the new government a jump-start (in terms of legislation, information, and organization) in efforts to control natural resources. It is also worth noting that the Committee's success has been credited to active Cambodian participation and that several of the most active members of the committee, now ministers in the current government, have continued meeting together to discuss natural resource issues.

The second area, where UNTAC Rehabilitation in conjunction with the Civil Administration Component, had an impact was in macroeconomic and fiscal management. As noted earlier, the budget deficit – and the SOC's practice of printing money to cover it – had resulted in severe inflation by the summer of 1992; and some observers predicted hyperinflation by the end of the year. To prevent this, the SOC reached an agreement with the International Monetary Fund (IMF) to stop printing money and place cash limits on wages and salaries, under UNTAC supervision. Despite pressure to resume printing money, especially after the promised budgetary support did not materialize, the SOC kept to the agreement; and inflation indeed slowed in 1993, the exchange rate stabilized, and consumer prices rose more slowly. The trade-off was that by early 1993, in the absence of budget support, average civil service salaries had fallen to less than 25 percent of their

[15] *The New York Times*, February 7, 1993, sec. 4, p. 4.

value in early 1992 and were paid less and less regularly. This encouraged corruption and absenteeism and weakened the control of the central government over the provinces.

Recognizing the desperate need for increased revenue in order to stabilize the fiscal situation, Rehabilitation (with UNTAC Civil Administration) also worked with the SOC to introduce new taxes and improve collection of existing ones. In the final quarter of 1992, the government introduced a tax on hotel services and vehicle licensing and implemented a new dollar-based tariff system to bring customs valuation in line with the value of imports. Although tax revenue declined with the general economic downturn surrounding the elections, revenue improved dramatically after July 1993; and, by the late fall of 1993, the new government was able to pay government salaries (albeit low ones) out of revenue for the first time in decades.

In order to monitor these new policy measures, UNTAC created in February 1993 a Border Control Unit (BCU) within the Foreign Affairs Service of the Civil Administration Component, to be responsible for coordinating and directing border control functions related to the civilian part of the border control operation. Considering its size and short duration, the BCU was one of the most efficient and effective parts of UNTAC. BCU officers, a total of twenty-one officers for nineteen checkpoints, were first deployed in March 1993 although, due to lack of personnel, some were not posted until August. Under isolated and dangerous conditions with little support, they made an assessment of existing border checkpoints, worked with each faction to supervise customs and immigration, established immigration and customs records and began training local officials, and reported incidents of corruption or violations of the moratorium. In most cases, custom officials were cooperative and willing to learn the new methods and skills.[16] At the end of the mission, the BCU handed over to the new government a working system of customs and immigration record collection, a somewhat better trained customs personnel, increased customs revenue (an average increase of 45 percent between March and August for those checkpoints monitored), and a report assessing the state of border control, with detailed recommendations for reforming each of the different aspects of control and individual checkpoints.

The one area where the BCU was not very effective was in terms of stopping violations of the moratorium. This was partly because of their late deployment and partly because they were not given the authority and resources to stop violations. Again, this was a decision at the top –

---

[16]   UNTAC, *Border Control Unit Final Report*, September 1993, p. 7.

that the BCU's role should be restricted to observation only – although one person who worked with them felt that with a little more money and authorization, they could have done more to discourage violations without overstepping the UN's mandate or risking violent confrontation.

The final area of the Component's involvement with public administration was in the form of emergency interventions. In March 1993, when the riel dropped almost 70 percent against the dollar overnight, UNTAC (with the help of the World Food Program (WFP) and the Dutch government) intervened in the market to bring down the price of rice. A second intervention took place after the election, when the interim coalition government found itself with no money for government salaries – most of which hadn't been paid or months anyhow. This had serious implications for government stability, given FUNCINPEC's lack of control over the civil service, Hun Sen's strained relations with the hardliners in the CPP, and the accelerating decentralization of power ("warlordism") in the provinces. Despite the fact that this problem had been identified and discussed for more than two years, nothing had been prepared; and the Rehabilitation Component, along with the Civil Administration and the Military Component, had to scramble to raise the $30 million necessary to pay salaries for the three months of the transition government.

Rehabilitation activities by other agencies

While the Rehabilitation Component focused on keeping track of aid contributions and providing tactical assistance, the actual work of rehabilitation was carried out by UN agencies, UNTAC battalions, and NGOs. The strengths and weaknesses of different organizations and their approaches are worth examining, since they are the channels through which aid flows, and their effectiveness determines the ultimate effectiveness of rehabilitation aid.

Of the UN agencies, UNHCR's QIPs program and UNDP/OPS-CARERE are the most interesting since they provided the only coordinated and widespread village-level rehabilitation activity. QIPs were first discussed during the planning stage of repatriation as a way of helping impoverished communities absorb returning refugees. Modeled on an earlier program in Nicaragua, they were supposed to be short (less than three months) projects in the villages with an immediate impact, such as roads, schools, clinics, small credit schemes, field preparation, wells, and latrines, to improve local infrastructure and to jump-start development.

Although UNHCR provided the money and supervision, QIPs were actually implemented by a range of sixty other partners – UN agencies, NGOs, and local communities. This gave UNHCR added flexibility, and they were able to match QIPs to the actual returnee population, province by province, with reasonable accuracy.[17] In total, eighty projects were completed, at a cost of $9.5 million. In addition to expanding the resources in areas receiving returnees (and a subtle bribe to encourage village leaders to accept more returnees), several UN staff cited their symbolic importance – physical proof in the villages that the war was over and things were changing.

The program was not without its problems, however. In particular, the projects lacked adequate guidelines and monitoring; not enough attention was given to issues of community participation and long-term development.[18] On the one hand, there is an inherent tension between "quick" projects and development; but several UNHCR staff felt that they could have done a much better job with better planning. In particular, the program needed more staff, especially staff with experience in community development. The entire program was run by only two individuals who, because of the tight schedule, were under pressure to accept partners and projects without sufficient consideration or monitoring. Finally, although most UN and NGO staff interviewed were satisfied with the QIPs, it would have required a follow-up field survey six months to a year after the conclusion of the UNTAC mission to determine whether the projects really had any impact at all.

CARERE, a UNDP program, also focused on QIPs (in part with UNHCR funds), but it was also intended to provide a more coordinated and long-term development approach. Projects were carried out by Provincial Support Units (PSUs), which gave CARERE a strong field presence and high visibility. CARERE ended up coordinating rehabilitation activities and security in the four northwest provinces. CARERE had an advantage in that many officers were former UNBRO staff and were familiar with the UN, the border area, and the people and that several spoke Khmer. They brought with them a "can-do" attitude, which helped CARERE get set up and have projects off the ground quickly.

CARERE's problems were similar to UNHCR – inadequate guidelines, especially regarding community participation and sustainability, and officers more experienced with relief than with development. By focusing surveys on the district rather than the village level, projects

---

[17] UNHCR, *Cambodia Repatriation Operation*, August 31, 1993, Table 2.

[18] Although some argue that "quick" infrastructure projects do not require community participation, the northwest has enough broken wells, roads in the wrong places, and houses "improved" in areas which are not economically viable, to argue otherwise.

occasionally responded to the needs of political leaders rather than the villagers.[19] Other problems had to do with UNDP's bureaucracy. CARERE was set up in July 1992, but its budget was not approved by UNDP headquarters until December, and at times UNHCR had to advance funds to CARERE in order to get projects done. Unlike UNHCR, CARERE was unable to adapt projects to the fact that only 75 percent of the returnees went to the northwest, rather the 80–90 percent originally predicted, and it was slow to expand to the rest of the country. Another concern was that, despite public statements of support, donors had not funded CARERE fully for the post-UNTAC period. If more funds did not emerge, refugee reintegration and the expansion of the QIPs into development (for which CARERE was supposed to assume responsibility) would be interrupted.

Two other programs which deserve mention are the World Food Program's Food for Work program and the International Labor Organization's Labor-Based Roads program, both of which were successful in getting resources into the hands of villagers quickly. The former, in the case of projects negotiated directly with villages, encouraged villagers to organize themselves, while the latter had a rapid multiplier effect, as villagers used their salaries from road-building to start small-business activities or repair their houses.

Another source of UN rehabilitation work was the UN soldiers themselves. Although there was no plan to use the UN soldiers for rehabilitation work, several battalions stationed in remote areas felt compelled to respond to the poverty around them. On their own initiative and often with their own or their government's money, UN battalions built schools, cleaned temples, and taught villagers how to construct energy-efficient stoves. Although the battalions would have needed more guidance to make a long-term impact, these projects improved soldiers' morale and relations with the local people, as well as making use of the (expensive) skilled labour and equipment sitting idle out in the provinces.[20]

In addition to UN agencies, international NGOs played an unusually large role in Cambodian rehabilitation and development. As virtually the only non-socialist source of development assistance prior to the Paris Agreement, the handful of NGOs that braved the international embargo developed an unusually strong relationship with the administration and an exceptionally deep knowledge of the country. They were also relatively organized, with an apolitical umbrella organization, a political

[19] Interviews with NGO staff in Battambang.
[20] In March 1993, the Military Component formed a Civic Action Cell to coordinate these activities, although it is not clear how much impact it had.

forum, and sectoral groups for health and agriculture, among others. Although the UN gave a great deal of lipservice to the knowledge and experience of NGOs, UNTAC officials generally seem to have viewed NGOs as implementing agencies at best (and a way of bypassing government structures) and whining gadflies at worst. There was little real communication between the two groups and many missed opportunities for greater exchange of information and cooperation.

A final category of rehabilitation efforts, the full impact of which remains to be seen, is that of Cambodian NGOs and associations. Between the signing of the Paris Agreements in October 1991 and the final withdrawal of UNTAC troops in November 1993, the number of Cambodian NGOs and associations climbed from only one to over eighty. Many of these groups received money and training from the UNTAC Human Rights Component, and all were encouraged by a provision allowing Cambodian associations to register with UNTAC. During the transitional period, Cambodian NGOs were active and effective in promoting human rights and voter education and in monitoring the elections, and they played an important role in the writing of the new constitution.[21] Although it is too soon to tell, given Cambodia's history of abusive and corrupt governments and the precarious nature of the current political alliance, an active community of civic organizations may be crucial to keeping Cambodia on the path to democracy, respect for human rights, and equitable economic development.

The impact of UNTAC

In addition to explicit rehabilitation activities, several other aspects of the mission affected the Cambodian economy and influenced – both positively and negatively – Cambodia's prospects for rehabilitation. One such aspect was public security. To the extent that UN troops and police were able to discourage fighting and bandits (an ability which varied considerably by province and which decreased over time), they increased the opportunity for economic activity, especially in the rural areas. However, the situation has deteriorated rapidly since the elections, and widespread banditry has emerged as one of the major obstacles to economic development, especially in rural areas. Guns and ex-soldiers

---

[21] Ponleu Khmer, an umbrella group for more than a dozen Cambodian human rights and development associations, was the only national or international group to protest attempts to push the first draft through in one day and successfully pushed for provisions to protect human rights, women and children's rights, and social security, and for a clearer separation of powers.

are common, jobs and land are scarce, and the Cambodian police have virtually no training or equipment. Three months after taking office, the new government announced that it would begin to tackle the crime problem; but it has few resources and many other problems competing for its attention. In retrospect, one of the most effective "rehabilitation activities" UNTAC could have undertaken would have been a program to train (and pay) the national police, so that the new government could have inherited a competent, organized, and disciplined police force.[22]

Another area, which is crucial to Cambodia's reconstruction and development, is demining. Cambodia has 6-10 million mines, strewn throughout forest and paddy land, most virtually undetectable. In an agricultural country, they render over 700,000 hectares of fertile land unusable; and the social and economic cost from loss of life and productivity, due to land-mine casualties, has yet to be calculated.[23] Despite the magnitude of the problem and the publicity that has been focused on it, demining has been slow. This is to some extent unavoidable – there is no way to demine quickly, especially when a state of war still exists and new mines continue to be laid – but demining activities have also been seriously underfunded. Only $744,000 had been pledged for demining by the end of the mandate, whereas the institution responsible for mine awareness and demining, the Cambodian Mine and Awareness Center (CMAC), required an estimated $15 million for 1994 – plus $3.5 million more if the UNTAC demining equipment were withdrawn.[24]

A third issue is the distortionary effects of UNTAC spending. In 1992, UNTAC spent over $200 million in Cambodia – equivalent to four times total Cambodian exports for that year, or 10 percent of GDP – and over $403 million for the entire mission.[25] Although this spending was not the primary cause of inflation, it caused sharp price increases in some areas (skilled labor and housing), corruption, and shallow and imbalanced economic growth. While price increases were inevitable, there was no attempt to keep prices within limits or prevent brain drain.

[22] Several senior members of UNTAC Civilian Police advocated such a program from the start but were overruled on the grounds that it was not CIVPOL's responsibility.

[23] Estimates are that Cambodia has between 18,000 and 41,000 amputees and that mine accidents have now fallen from a peak of 400–500 a month to "only" 100–200 a month. See Susan Atkin, *Getting the Message about Mines*, CMAC/UNESCO, September 1993, for various estimates.

[24] In fact, CMAC was almost forced to close in November because no arrangements had been made to replace UNTAC demining experts and equipment. So far, UNDP and severalNGOs have cobbled together temporary funding to keep the center going.

[25] UNTAC, Rehabilitation and Development in Cambodia, p. 10, and *Phnom Penh Post*, October 22–November 4, 1993, p. 16.

Similarly there seems to have been no concerted effort to discourage corruption.[26]

UNTAC spending did stimulate the local economy, but primarily in the form of an urban boom in construction activity, trade, and services for foreign consumption (notably beer and prostitutes). This alone is not necessarily bad; but, in the absence of security and reconstruction in the rural area, it may have set Cambodia up for the urban migration and income disparities that plague other developing countries. Although some Cambodians became very rich (there was soon a Mercedes-Benz dealership in Phnom Penh), many more saw their standard of living drop due to inflation and growing insecurity.

Another consequence of the cash injection was a rise in ethnic tension as thousands of Vietnamese construction workers and prostitutes poured across the border to take advantage of economic opportunities, rekindling Khmer fears of Vietnamese imperialism and triggering massacres among some segments of the population.[27] A more subtle issue is the psychological impact of thousands of UNTAC staff throwing around huge sums of money on a population suffering from inflation and unemployment, and on their perception of the UN's motivations and legitimacy.[28]

A final issue is AIDS. Although the entry of AIDS into Cambodia cannot be blamed on UNTAC, UN troops contributed to its spread both directly and by encouraging the growth of the sex industry wherever they were stationed. Given the current state of knowledge about AIDS and the existence of an AIDS epidemic in Thailand (where UNTAC troops stopped for transit and R&R), the open condonement of promiscuity by top UNTAC officials was staggeringly irresponsible. Doctors now estimate at least 150 UNTAC staff will die of AIDS (compared to 58 killed through hostile fire, accidents, or illness during the mission); and Cambodian deaths could, if the epidemic follows the same path as in Thailand, reach as high as 1 million.

Conclusion

The post-UNTAC economic situation in Cambodia, like the political transition, has been better than many observers predicted. The end of UNTAC expenditures did not cause a deflationary shock and refugees

[26] The one exception was for visa and passport fees, where the Foreign Affairs Division posted the correct scale of government fees, and which proved very effective.

[27] UNTAC Information/Education Division Report, September 18, 1992.

[28] Compare UN per diems of $140 a day to the per capita income of $200 a year. This disparity caused the greatest resentment and loss of respect in 1992 when UNTAC appeared to be inactive or incapable, but diminished after the successful elections.

have not flooded the cities following the end of UNHCR rice rations. As the political situation stabilized and the UNTAC-generated flow of dollars dried up, the riel has strengthened and consumer prices have stabilized. Increased customs and tax collections have allowed the finance ministry to raise civil servant salaries (although not yet to adequate levels). Contrary to fears that the government would permanently lose control over the development process and become dependent on donors and foreign advisors, the new government has played an active and assertive role in ICORC meetings and in reshaping its relationship with local and international NGOs.

At the same time, a staggering amount of work remains to be done. The majority of Cambodians remain desperately poor, including between 30 to 40 percent of returnees who are living hand to mouth. Only a fraction of the millions of mines littering the country have been cleared, and more have been laid in the meantime. Major roads and bridges have been repaired, but security problems limit their use.

Was the UNTAC rehabilitation effort a success? To the extent that many positive things happened (aid did flow into the country and was kept track of; several important financial and administrative reforms were put into place) and several major disasters were averted (hyperinflation, rice shortages, government bankruptcy), it succeeded. If judged according to the original mandate, the picture is less bright. Aid did not "benefit all areas of Cambodia, especially the more disadvantaged, and reach all levels of society," as the Declaration called for and, in fact, showed a strong urban/returnee/relief bias in contrast to the appeal's emphasis on rural areas/development/local capacity building. The trends established under UNTAC, such as urban concentration, a greatly expanded service sector (including prostitution), high rates of consumer imports, and growing inequality have continued. Nor did significant coordination (as opposed to enumeration) take place at the national or provincial level. In many sectors, particularly, demining, agriculture and rural development, tuberculosis and malaria control, and infrastructure rehabilitation outside the northwest, the new government faces the same problems that existed before UNTAC arrived. Meanwhile, in the absence of budgetary support, the national administrative structures have eroded, leaving the national government less capable of handling the problems than before.

These shortcomings need to be seen in context: the UNTAC mission was the first of its kind, charged with a herculean task and given inadequate resources. Nevertheless, several lessons can be learned.

First, rehabilitation is political. This fact needs to be taken more seriously during the planning phase. In particular, it may be worthwhile to take time during negotiations to work out a clearer definition of what "neutral" means in the context of rehabilitation aid and to get agreement from the different parties on the outlines of rehabilitation for key areas such as macroeconomic stabilization, fiscal management, public administration, etc., before the political stakes are raised.

Second, coordination is essential. Donors have their own agendas and priorities, and certain kinds of aid are always likely to be unpopular. Therefore, if it is felt that a particular kind of aid is necessary, the UN needs to have independent means of getting it done. In the case of program aid and geographical distribution, the kind of rehabilitation trust fund that was original planned for UNTAC might work if donors could be persuaded to fund it. Since it takes a long time to set up individual projects in the rural areas, decentralized programs like CARERE, UNHCR's QIPs, or even battalions which are already on location, may need to be given extra support to counter the inherent urban bias of most aid – although all of them need more development expertise, better criteria, and better follow-up. For other issues, such as demining and public security, either the costs may need to be folded into the peacekeeping budget or creative efforts be made to make sure they are financed.

Since the actual work of rehabilitation is carried out by a wide range of actors with very different capacities and goals, the coordination of all rehabilitation projects with each other and with existing administrative structures is also very important, to make sure that scarce resources are put to their best use. Information exchanges and cooperation require active coordination at both the national and local level. It may be that UNDP or another agency is more appropriate than the UN peace-keeping mission to take on this role – but part of the job of UN rehabilitation should be to make sure that someone does.

A third lesson arising from UNTAC is that public policy and administration is an important part of rehabilitation. Competent admin-istration is also one of the first things to break down under the conditions of civil war and anarchy that necessitate peacekeeping operations. Therefore, rehabilitation planning should anticipate these kinds of problems and try to identify area of concern from the beginning. In Cambodia's case, these were public finance (especially revenue), macroeconomic management, regulation of national property and natural resources, and border control – all areas that are likely to be neglected or turned for private profit in other troubled countries as the political situation becomes more uncertain, even as they are critical for the new government. Assistance may need to be in the form of financial support, advice, training, or enforcement. Of these, training can most easily be merged with other aspects of peacekeeping, since it complements and enhances the task of control.[29]

The importance of public administration in rehabilitation also highlights the value of greater local participation in rehabilitation decision-making from the national to the village level. It is the local population, after all, who assumes responsibility after the UN leaves. This would require the UN to translate more documents into the local language to give considerably more access to, and show more respect for, local counterparts.

A fourth lesson is that large peacekeeping operations can have a significant impact on weak, war-torn economies. Therefore, steps should be taken to minimize the negative effects (such as price distortion, increasing geographic and income disparities, corruption, alienation, sexual harassment, prostitution, the increased spread of AIDS) through monitoring, coordination, realistic per diems, and a code of conduct. Also, consideration should be given to the possible effects of mission spending on ethnic tensions and border flows.

All of these recommendations can be folded into the concept of "hand over" – the idea that peacekeeping operations should look beyond simply getting to the elections and getting out, but should also consider what they will hand over to the new government and how it will enhance or detract from future stability. Examples from UNTAC of "hand over" include the work of the border control unit, UNTAC advice on tax reforms and revenue enhancement, the work of the Technical Advisory Committee, and the encouragement of local human rights associations. Examples of where this mentality was lacking include the decision not to train the police, the confusion that attended the disposal or withdrawal of UNTAC data and equipment, and the low level of Cambodian participation throughout the mission.

Although this perspective blurs the neat lines between "rehabilitation" and "reconstruction" and between "development" and "peacekeeping," in the long run, it should prove more efficient by preventing later duplication of effort, giving the peacekeepers themselves positive rather than negative objectives, and contributing to the sustainability of the mission's efforts after the UN has declared victory and gone home.

[29] Interviews with Cambodian officials indicated that those, who had received training from UNTAC, had more respect and identification with their "controllers."

El Salvador

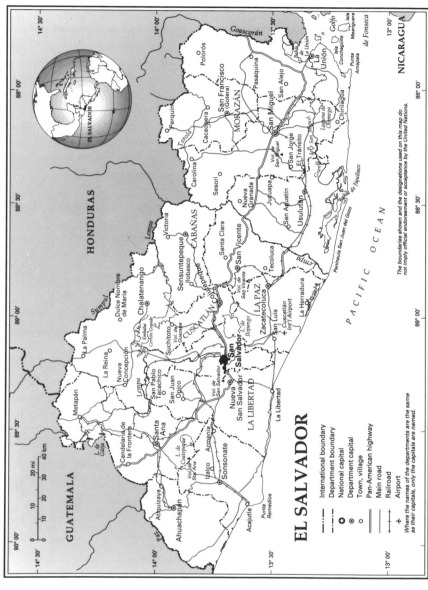

EL SALVADOR

	International boundary
	Department boundary
⊛	National capital
⊙	Department capital
○	Town, village
	Pan-American highway
	Main road
	Railroad
✈	Airport

Where the names of the departments are the same as their capitals, only the capitals are named.

The boundaries shown and the designations used on this map do not imply official endorsement or acceptance by the United Nations.

Map No. 3903 UNITED NATIONS
August 1995

Department of Public Information
Cartographic Section

9   Insurrection and civil war in El Salvador

Edelberto Torres-Rivas

Introduction

During the 1970s El Salvador experienced the final phase of a historical cycle characterized by the accumulation of many problems to which the sole answer for many was violence. The events of this decade help explain the advent of popular insurrection, which did not take on the abrupt form of a social explosion but rather that of a gradual and foreseeable outcome driven by socio-economic and political-ideological polarization, constantly exacerbated by governmental repression and the shortsightedness of those in power. The history of the origins of El Salvador's civil war consists of three periods: a long period of intractable social and economic development problems rooted in the agricultural structure, labor relations, and authoritarian government from 1932 to the dictatorship of General Martinez ending in 1944; a pre-revolutionary period of popular pressure, failed reform, and subverted democracy from the fall of the Martinez dictatorship in 1944, to the dramatic election fraud of 1972; and, finally, the transformation of the political crisis into a revolutionary crisis, and the outbreak of civil war in the 1980s. This last period, from the general offensive of 1980 to the signing of the peace agreements in 1991, will be the principal focus of this chapter, though each period will be analyzed in turn.

The origins of the crisis which led to the war

The origins of the political crisis grew out of an incomplete and exogenous modernization process in a society which systematically generated exclusion at all levels. The term systematic exclusion, from the Salvadoran perspective, refers to a long historical process of economic marginality, social segregation, and politic repression. In a modern society, political and social rights benefit the majority, who comprise the heart of the system. In societies like El Salvador, the poor majority has been systematically marginalized. The people lack regular income and do not enjoy social or political rights. The policies of marginalizing the population by force can be explained in the case of El Salvador by the nature of its oligarchic culture.

The systematic exclusion of broad social sectors became increasingly incompatible with the economic/social development already achieved as well as with the demands for political democracy, which important social sectors of an already diversified society beganto make. The country had in fact changed in the post-war period, made more dynamic by the role of the government as promoter of economic growth, modernization, and diversification of agriculture for export as well as the introduction of an industrial park encouraged by the Central American Common Market (MERCOMUN). There was economic progress and, at the same time, extreme poverty.

Backward societies are more stable than those experiencing forms of incomplete modernization because the latter begin to change in an uneven fashion. Driven by forces exerted from outside the country, the result is often a breakdown of traditional structures. Incomplete modernization causes many peasants to lose land, becoming instead seasonal salaried workers. This process of proletarianization of the peasantry produces great stresses on the existing structures, because it causes greater poverty among these agricultural workers at the same time as it increases their expectations. The product of this process is instability as well as social and political violence. In El Salvador, this process began when the agrarian/exporter society was formed at the end of the nineteenth century.

Economic modernization makes social exclusion more visible and transforms it into an explosive situation. As various North American authors have argued,[1] when the modernization process is incomplete, it produces an incomplete social incorporation even as it creates expectations and makes social injustice more visible. At the same time, it leads to decomposition in the backward areas of society. This is what took place in El Salvador.

El Salvador's democratic struggles – over the establishment of the rule of law, political parties and competitive elections, free association of people and civic rights, especially after 1944 – were the most expressive demonstrations of the various methods of fighting and overcoming social and political exclusion. Another aspect of the fight against social exclusion was land reform, a problem in El Salvador for a good part of

---

[1]   Classic authors on social change such as S. Huntington, D. Lerner, L. Pye, D. Apter, and W. Kornhauser, have analyzed the passage from traditional to modern societies through Asian, African, and Latin American experiences, finding that incomplete reforms and truncated social changes generate high levels of violence.

the twentieth century. In 1932 the coffee-growing bourgeoisie and the military founded an alliance due to the threat of a peasant uprising. Through tacit accord, the coffee-growing bourgeoisie (which expressly rejected the option of running the government in order to keep its social power intact) was able to safeguard the oligarchic style characterized by the patronage of the ruling elite, disrespect for majority rule, the use of social privileges, which became confused with political rights, and the discrimination and exclusion of non-elites in order to insure their social and cultural subordination. The alliance arose as a tacit accord due to the threat of the 1932 peasant uprising and the corresponding massacre, or *Matanza*. The oligarchic landowners, constantly afraid of another peasant insurrection, allowed the military to retain the reins of the government while they maintained their economic and social power.

After the 1932 massacre, the policy of social exclusion was applied more violently by the government and the landowners, supported by the legitimizing force of tradition, the backwardness of the peasant population, the conservative educational system, and the impossibility of organization and protest. The ability to control the Salvadoran population rested in the passiveness of the people, who were frightened and carefully watched. The obsession for order, encouraged by the land-owning class, superseded the possibilities of modernization.

This traditional order experienced its first crisis in 1944–5, with the downfall of General Martinez's dictatorship. However, since the forces that defeated him restricted themselves to calling for generic "freedom and democracy" without bringing with them the concrete mechanisms of democratic governance, social exclusion was perpetuated through an environment of ever growing political violence. Only the popular struggles of the 1970s, fed by the instrument of repressive violence, made it possible, finally, for the populace to engage in a participatory process.

The crisis, which built up over time within the country, grew out of the explosive combination of a weak civil society based on the social exclusion of the majority through violent means, and a government that lacked any legitimacy in the eyes of the majority. Popular struggles to attain political democracy were denied by ongoing exclusion of large segments of the population from meaningful political participation. Exclusion was practiced in the economic and social domains, as well by impeding access to the market, education, health care, housing, and culture.

Socio-economic polarization was extreme, based on the concentration of land in the hands of a very few, beginning in the nineteenth century with the creation of a primary-export economy. A small group of landowners monopolized land, water, and financial resources, to the constant exclusion of four-fifths of the population. A mere 0.1 percent of the population controlled 26.5 percent of the land, while 87 percent of the parcels of land consisted of less than one hectare (2.47 acres) and together made up only 18.6 percent of the land available.[2]

It is important to note that in El Salvador all forms of capital have traditionally been concentrated among approximately thirty family groups which have monopolized the most important productive activities. Their coffee-growing/landowner base is combined with the output of industrial activities, and investments in foreign trade with majority interests in financial capital. In 1971, thirty-six large groups controlled 66 percent of the capital of the 1,429 largest productive firms. In the mid 1960s, the bottom 50 percent of the population received 16 percent of all income earned, while the top 5 percent received 27 percent.[3]

Political modernization began slowly and reluctantly. The model of the political regime from 1960 onwards consisted of military control of the government with preeminence over the executive branch; a corporate relationship in which the oligarchic bourgeoisie dictated economic policy; limited electoral opportunity for opposition in the legislative branch and municipal government; mass media intimately connected with the politics of the executive branch and big business; and social demobilization through blatant and constant repression of the people.

The power of the military, buttressed by increasing political control, began to grow in 1932 with the high degree of autonomy it was accorded from the social forces of society. The Salvadoran army was not merely another institution of the government, but the government itself. From 1961 on, the armed forces respected the formality of the electoral calendar and the prohibition against re-election. The formula of a civilian-based political party under its control was established with the creation in 1948 of the Revolutionary Democratic Unification party (PRUD), and continued after 1961 with the National Conciliation party (PCN). The PCN, the political party of the military, monopolized all the deputies. However, to provide some evidence of democracy, they allowed small victories for the Christian Democrats. In 1964 the Christian Democrat party was allowed to seat only fourteen deputies of a total sixty deputies in the legislature, despite the fact that it had enough popular support to elect more than fourteen deputies. This number was

[2]   Edelberto Torres-Rivas (ed.), *Centroamerica la crisis en cifras* (San José: FLACSO-UCA, 1989).
[3]   E. Colindres, *Fundamentos economicos de la burguesia salvadorena* (San Salvador: Universidad de Centroamerica, 1977), p. 51 and following section.

allowed to increase to fifteen in 1966 and to nineteen in 1968. In 1966, the Christian Democrat party won a third of all the mayoralties in the country, including San Salvador. Nevertheless, the PCN always maintained control of the legislative branch and won all the presidential elections until the military coup in 1979.

The creation of a pre-revolutionary situation

The events of the 1970s appear as an excellent lesson in the errors and the weaknesses of the ruling political forces, which resulted from the political backwardness they repeatedly manifested when faced with a crisis. This shortcoming was due perhaps to the memory of the Indian Rebellion in 1932, which encouraged an age-old fear of revenge on the part of the dominated. Among the peasantry, there was also the memory of the most widespread genocide to have previously taken place in the region.[4]

In the political arena ruling political forces demonstrated glaring weakness in 1972 when they perpetuated overt electoral fraud. Not only did they lack popular support, as evidenced by the election returns, but their overt resort to fraud transformed popular discontent into demands for free association and free participation, as well as an end to the tradition of political activity based on social status. The electoral fraud of 1972 opened up the biggest crack in the government's legitimacy.

For this election, the PDC had formed an alliance with the Social Democratic National Revolutionary (MNR) and the Nationalist Democratic Union (UDN) forming a front called the National Opposition Union (UNO). Led by José Napoleon Duarte and an unusually broad electoral alliance, the Christian Democratic party won the election against the incumbent PCN's candidate, Colonel Arturo Armando Molina. The military, however, fraudulently snatched victory from UNO and installed its own candidate.

The folly of this decision seriously undermined the internal mechanisms of representation of the dominant class, stretching the legitimizing mechanisms of the military regime, inaugurated in 1932, to its limits. With this departure from institutional legality, the restraints on social order began to give way. As the government attacked and closed the National University, and later acted against workers' strikes, as well as student and peasant demonstrations, the crisis worsened.

An urgent and long overdue governmental initiative, the restructuring of rural property, to the benefit of poor peasants, failed halfway through

---

[4] This was later surpassed in scope by the massacres in Guatemala at the hands of the army between 1980 and 1982.

1976 due to a struggle between military reformists and the agrarian sector's upper echelons of power. These military reformists, referred to as such because of their favorable views on agrarian reform, would later be responsible for the coup against General Romero in September 1979. The defeat of the reform project at the hands of the dominant class, under the conditions of its illegitimate mandate, discredited the political regime even further.

Another electoral struggle in 1977, also tainted by the fraudulent appointment of General Carlos Humberto Romero as president, once again manifested the inability of El Salvador's ruling classes to succeed legitimately in the forum of public liberties and electoral freedom. After 1977, any centrist, legal, reformist, or peaceful illusion of progress was crushed. The violence which accompanied and followed this last opportunity to resolve the legitimacy of political rule paved the road to war.

The war had multiple causes. The political disillusionment, paralleled in the rest of Central America, continued to convince people that their only alternative was direct action. The electoral fraud of 1972 was obvious and clumsy; while it demoralized some, it convinced others to begin to organize themselves in insurrectional groups.

Deep general discontent began to take concrete form with a rapidity equaled by the government's bloody response. No traditional organization remained the same, and popular organizations, which arose or evolved in the heat of the struggle and repression, adopted forms of internal organization, programs, strategies, methods, and objectives designed to mitigate the age-old problem of the relationship between the vanguard and the masses. Their formation and growth polarized the spectrum further and lent a violent rhythm to the process, which, in its turn, increased governmental repression.

In March of 1970, Salvador Cayetano Carpio resigned from the communist party and founded the Farabundo Mart Popular Forces for National Liberation (FPL) with the aim of making military and political action compatible. In 1971, another splinter group from the communist party, together with radicalized groups from the Christian Democrat party, founded the People's Revolutionary Army (ERP), hoping to become the military vanguard. In 1975, the FPL put together a popular front, the most important of its kind in the country, called the People's Revolutionary Bloc. The ERP did likewise later in 1977, with the formation of the February 28th Memorial Leagues of the People.

The People's United Front for Action (FAPU) emerged in 1974 as a splinter group of the ERP, a mass movement created by Christian and labor union leaders, which, in 1975, formed the Armed Forces for

National Resistance (RN), with openly militaristic aims. Finally, the Workers' Revolutionary Party of Central America (PRTC), founded in 1976, formed its own military organization, the People's Liberation Movement. Prior to its formation as a legal, political front in 1970 called the Democratic National Union, from the time it was created in 1930, the communist party, due to its clandestine nature, was dedicated to military struggle. The leaders of the Farabundo Mart National Liberation Front (FMLN), who founded and directed political-military organizations in the 1970s, were beset by a host of problems during the years of struggle. Some of them were murdered (Roca and others) or died; Salvador Cayetano Carpio committed suicide. Military leadership during the years of armed struggle gave those who remained prominence.

Revolutionary organizations in El Salvador were created by men and women who rebelled against the same institutions they were a part of, such as the Church, the Christian Democrat party, the communist party, and the university. They fought for social changes hitherto unheard of in El Salvador. They became more and more violent in their protests, convinced from the outset that no agreement with the government or centrist forces was possible. Consequently, they were convinced there was no alternative whatsoever to preparing for war.

Although the increasing virulence of social conflicts in the latter part of the 1970s radicalized the left and polarized its strategies, it also had a unifying effect which was important in that it enabled leftist forces to overcome their traditional disunity for the first time ever.

The creation of the popular fronts described above was followed immediately by the creation of military organizations. This political-social-military construction directly reflected the nature of the Salvadoran conflict, which led to the longest civil war in Latin America during the twentieth century.[5]

What stands out most in this process was the speed of the revolutionary learning process among the masses, which is never spontaneous nor the result of isolated academic efforts. Rather, it is the awakening of the consciousness of the subordinate and the exploited, the humiliated and the excluded. It is the awakening of those who, having become militant and faced and practiced violence, make their presence known to their government, boss, or landowner. A leap was made from focusing on the personal to emphasizing the collective. The identity of the combatant was acquired in battle, which broke the cultural and psychological ties of subordination. Nevertheless, the crisis

---

[5] While Colombia has experienced the longest periods of violence and civil strife, the Salvadoran conflict was the longest formal, high-intensity civil war.

produced only class consciousness among the governing elite, who experienced the process as an immense disorder, a total threat induced from outside the country.

In its stimulation of violence among the peasantry, the effects of the government's approach in punishing the Catholic Church, its leaders, and its adjunct secular institutions, made a previously unheard of contribution to the process. As in Nicaragua, religious elements were especially committed to poor peasants in a new pastoral form, a practice which took its inspiration from Liberation Theology's defense of the poor. In order to organize the rural population, preachers of the word had established base communities, cooperatives, and other social-religious group arrangements as far back as the 1960s. In so doing, they unwittingly created the rural organizations whose vast majority would join in the armed struggle.

From insurrection to war

The departure from the social relationships of domination and sub-ordination throughout the 1970s brought the economic and political fronts into the realm of military struggle. The social crisis unveiled the repressive face of the government, which inevitably brought on the dual movement of a breakdown in society's upper echelons and a rebuilding of its base. A crisis in the age-old alliance between the oligarchy and the army occurred within the army – government as well as among landowner groups. The tacit alliance fell apart as a result of the political crisis. The civil war divided the opinions of the oligarchy. The breakup did not occur on a specific date, but evolved over time. Democratic processes have the virtue of breaking apart old arrangements. The revolutionary storm brought with it the classic inability to govern among the upper echelons of the hierarchy. At the base of society, the decision not to tolerate the status quo any further explained the decision to form the FMLN as well as the call for insurrection and war.

The symptoms of the insurrectional situation were many. The workers' movement, which was traditionally a minority opposition movement that had been repressed for decades, began to grow and the number of work stoppages began to increase. Between 1974 and 1976 there were only ten, while in 1977 alone there were eleven, all involving the takeover of factories, and during just the first three months of 1979 there were forty![6] Beginning in 1977, labor protest went beyond pure economic issues, attracting the solidarity and support of other sectors

---

[6]   Sara Gordon, *Crisis política y guerra en El Salvador* (Mexico City: Siglo XXI, 1989), pp. 236 ff.

which moved along distinctly political ground. The traditional profile of the labor movement began to vanish in the maelstrom of struggle, as evidenced by the events of November 10 and 12, 1977, when, in an act of political disobedience, the unions occupied the Labor Ministry. At this time three labor union organizations merged into the United Workers' Confederation (CUTS), which was closely linked with political-military organizations.

Rural organization and mobilization became the greatest challenge to the established order, which was already in a state of crisis. Agrarian exporters perceived the armed peasantry as disobedience in its purest form. The social struggles began in the city and reached their climax there, but the rural areas did not escape violence on both sides. The assassination of community leaders and parish priests began, as did the kidnapping of several landowners.

In May of 1977, the charismatic rural priest Rutilio Grande was assassinated. Monsignor Romero, Archbishop of San Salvador, cele-brated his Sunday burial mass, which was attended by more than 100,000 people. Later on, in the maelstrom of the 1970s – before the war – eleven priests and hundreds of peasants were assassinated by clandestine paramilitary squads, by the National Guard, by the legal paramilitary organization ORDEN, by the police and by the national army. In January of 1979, one of these clandestine groups, the Fighting White Union (UGB), sentenced to death all Jesuits who refused to leave the country. Churches became one of the new bases of protest.

As social agitation shifted to rural areas, the dynamics of the crisis deepened. In April of 1977, FECCAS and the UTC, the largest of all peasant organizations, called for the invasion of rural estate properties and the burning of sugar plantations and harvested produce in San Vicente, San Salvador, La Paz, and Cabanas. The demand for land was less important than the struggle for political participation. The execu-tions of landowners and the kidnapping of important coffee growers by the political-military organizations in order to demand ransom, the destruction of cotton plantations and harvests, and assaults on property began to indicate a state of insurrection. It should be pointed out that the deepening of the crisis (1977–9) dovetailed with a brief boom in export trade and favorable prices on the international market, which perhaps had a hypnotic effect on the landowners.

The government responded with a bloody escalation, which brought the disorder and violence to a fever pitch. In the first nine months of 1979 alone, the legal office of the archdiocese accounted for the assassination of 800 community leaders and militant members of people's organizations. During a demonstration to protest the electoral fraud of 1977, on February 28 in the Plaza Libertad square, soldiers opened fire on the crowd for four straight hours, killing more than 100 demonstrators. Events like this occurred time and again. Day by day, the political-military organizations confirmed the discrediting of reformism and electoral activity, and advocated direct military confrontation.

In January and April of 1977, Roberto Poma was kidnapped and Mauricio Borgonovo was killed. Both of these men were important figures in the upper echelon of the bourgeoisie, the latter being the chancellor of the republic. Crimes of state were being answered with executions, kidnappings, acts of financial "recuperation," bombings, and mass action. New places for protest appeared. To resist the acts of repression in February 1978 and to publicize them to the world, demonstrators took over the El Calvario cathedral and the Costa Rican, Panamanian, Venezuelan, and Swiss embassies. The Mexican embassy and OAS headquarters were taken over several times in order to demand freedom for prisoners and other concessions. Many were also assassinated by the political-military organizations: General Osmín Aguirre, the president of the National University, Carlos Alfaro Castillo, and the industrialist, Molina Cañas. In retaliation for the assassination of labor union leader Guillermo Rivas, the former president of the legislative assembly, Alfonso Rodríguez Porth was executed. On May 13, 1979, the Minister of Education, Carlos H. Rebolledo, was murdered. The list goes on and on, reflecting the atmosphere of imminent insurrection.

The political initiative set forth during General Romero's regime in 1978, which called for a National Forum, failed. Business organizations and rightist political groups began to complain about blatant Soviet and Cuban Communist intervention. They requested and were granted, mainly from 1977 on, help from the United States, which became a central player as it assumed the role of military provider.

The fall of Somoza in July of 1979 exacerbated the confrontations, which by then had brought society to a state of anarchy. To government sectors, the victory of the Sandinista Liberation Front in Nicaragua confirmed the onset of an international communist offensive. The army prepared itself for a strategy of total annihilation, and revolutionary forces, instigated preparations for battle, convinced that armed struggle was the only road to acquiring power. By the end of July, two more priests had been assassinated and an opposition newspaper and the Catholic radio station YSAX had been burned down. Dozens of businessmen fled the country and, on October 12, the first coup attempt directed at the heart of the army, was initiated by its most recalcitrant groups. On the 15th of the same month, junior officers led by Colonel

Majano deposed President Romero, thus beginning a new cycle in the crisis. The pre-revolutionary situation had come to an end.

The outbreak of war

Fully escalated military actions on both sides had already shaped this period into a state of war. Since these events happened in close correspondence with political events, many wondered if they were part of a revolution. Then on October 15, 1979, the first civil/military junta was established, putting an end to nearly fifty years of direct military predominance. The junta was presided over by Guillermo Manuel Ungo, president of the MNR (Social-Democrat), Romón Mayorga, president of the University of Central America (UCA), Mario Antonio Andino, a businessman, and Jaime Abdul Gutierrez and Adolfo Majano, both from the military. Six of the thirteen ministers in the new government were from democratic institutions or parties. However, this brief experience in reformism failed to limit the repressive actions of the army and the guerrilla activity of the political-military organizations, who, with the exception of the communist party, denounced the pact as a shady reformist deal.

After the collapse of the first civil-military junta, a second one was created on January 9, 1980, by means of a pact between the armed forces and the Christian Democratic party. The tormentors and some of the tormented joined together to build what President Carter wanted, a political middle of the road. This faced immediate challenges, however, when on January 22 over 200,000 Salvadorans gathered as part of the recently founded Revolutionary Coordinator of the Masses and were savagely attacked by machine gun fire from the armed forces who already considered themselves to be in a civil war. As repression continued, the government junta offered an ambitious government program on February 13. On March 5, the Land Reform Law was issued, calling for the expropriation of 376 large rural estates (greater than 500 hectares, or 1,235 acres). Its application cost the lives of 135 peasants in the first five days. Days later, banks and foreign trade companies were nationalized.

The breakdown of the armed forces and the Christian Democratic party forced the creation of a third government junta on March 29, 1981, with a new shift to the right, spearheaded by the Christian Democratic leader José Napoleon Duarte. On March 24, Monsignor Oscar Arnulfo Romero, who days earlier had asked soldiers to disobey, in the name of God, orders to kill, was assassinated by a man under orders by Major D'Aubuisson, the founder of the ARENA party. His burial attracted over 100,000 people, who were fired upon, leaving 600 wounded and 50 dead, thus inciting the repudiation of the international community. On April 18 the Democratic Revolutionary Front (FDR) was founded and on May 22 the Unified Revolutionary Directorate came into existence. Between May 14 and 15, the criminal slaughter of 600 peasant women, elderly people, and children, took place at the Sumpul River, revealing the army's capacity for brutality. The armed forces had already planned their strategy of annihilation. In 1981 alone, 9,825 civilians were assassinated, illustrating the magnitude of the war. Between June 24 and 25 and later between August 13 and 14, two different general strikes were held, paralyzing the nation. Finally, on October 10, the FMLN was created as a result of the extraordinary surge of the masses after the death of Archbishop Romero. It was a tacit union of the five major revolutionary organizations the FPL, RN, PC, ERP and the FRTCA. They did not form a singular organization, but rather a front with a collective leadership. By January 1981, the FMLN was calling for a military offensive against the regime. From that moment on, the struggle was transformed into a civil war.

Rightist sectors coopted the reformist Social Democrat program, waging war alongside the social democrats, while maintaining their repressive orientation. In the FMLN's revolutionary program, several documents reiterated that "the revolutionary transformation of our society, (which) to date (has been) subjected to injustice, (as well as) the pillaging and selling out of our country, is today a possible reality close at hand. Only through this transformation will our people prevail and ensure the democratic freedoms and rights that they have been denied."[7]

The escalation in violence and the political events experienced by the Salvadoran society in 1980, turned social struggles into military confrontations. On January 10, 1981, the FMLN began its general offensive, simultaneously attacking the main Air Force base and eight military barracks. In the process it captured four departmental capitals, twenty lesser towns, several areas of San Salvador and, with several radio transmitters that were captured, it called for a general strike. However, the rebel insurrectional strategy failed, probably due to an underestimation of the enemy as well as overconfidence in their own forces.

It is also possible that the bloody, repressive response, including the lethal efficiency of the death squads, which failed to diminish with the incorporation of the Social Democrats into the government, led Salvadoran revolutionaries to clearly militaristic definition of the

[7]   Proclamation of the Direccion Unificada Revolucionaria (DRU).

struggle. The programs of the political-military organizations and the FMLN-FDR did point toward maximalist objectives which could only be reached through the military defeat of the enemy.

The civil war, which lasted twelve years, took place in a very small country with an area of 22,000 square kilometers (8,580 square miles) and a population density of 230 inhabitants per square kilometer (590 per square mile). Without mountains, jungles or natural barriers, it offered guerrillas no refuge whatsoever. The struggle was located mainly in the north and northwestern region of the country, which was greatly under-populated, less productive, and less urban than the southern section of the country, where sixteen of the seventeen most populated cities and the agricultural areas which grow export produce are located. The physical size of the country made all military objectives close at hand, thus making it impossible to maintain liberated areas or a duality of power. For troops mobilized by air, any point in the country could be reached within thirty minutes.

It is difficult to indicate precisely when the war started. Guerrilla warfare, especially urban guerrilla warfare, began at least two years before the general offensive in January 1981. In terms of Clausewitz's guidelines, for a state of war to exist, there must be a balanced relationship between the forces in conflict, which only happened during 1981. One should take special note of the initial virulence of the conflict. From 1972 to 1977 there were 37,342 casualties from the revolutionary front and the popular sectors, and 10,073 from the government, while between 1979 and 1980 alone there were 12,708 on the guerrilla side and 5,859 on the government side.[8]

The best explanation for the long duration of the war lies in the balance between revolutionary forces with broad popular support and the best armed military forces in the region which were aided by a geographical environment hostile to guerrilla activity. It was not a civil war against a single, particular dictatorship, but rather a revolution against a political system and, as such, it had much in common with class wars, which history indicates is the bloodiest type of conflict. The "low-intensity conflict" campaigns characterized by the US strategy of avoiding direct combat, accentuated these results.

The armed forces had been preparing a counter-insurgency strategy since the 1960s with the complete support of the USA, but their training turned out to be outmoded and insufficient, as indicated by their track record up until 1983. The army's offensives were tactical and no more

---

[8]   *El Salvador Proceso*, Informativo Semanal del Centro Universitario de Documentacion e Informacion, San Salvador, University of Central America, various of the weekly editions.

than 20 percent of their entire forces were committed in any single operation. Up to 1979, 2,097 officers had been trained in US schools, and later, US advisors of the so-called "special forces" created a parallel staff. The amount of military equipment donated by the USA has been well documented, especially the helicopters and other aircraft previously used in Vietnam.

In August of 1981, before the final offensive, there were fifty-six high-level US officers in El Salvador and financial aid jumped from $9.4 million in 1979 to $897.8 million in 1986. Intervention was practiced in a systematic fashion during the Reagan administration as part of its Central American foreign policy. The US commitment to the armed forces and the government was both deeply rooted and multifaceted. By the end of 1980, the armed forces numbered 9,850 men, including 750 air force personnel, as well as 7,000 paramilitary and intelligence agents. At the beginning of 1985, the total was 39,000, and at the end of the war, there were 62,000 men. On the other hand, the FMLN began the general offensive phase with approximately 2,000 men with no combat experience whatsoever. By 1984 it had 12,000 armed men in its ranks, a number which reached close to 15,000 near the end of the conflict.

As a result of the general offensive in October 1981, the FMLN built up four battle fronts. The armed forces carried out several quick operations, especially in San Salvador, which paralyzed worker support for a general strike that had been organized by the DRU. The country split militarily and geopolitically. The first year of the war was clearly unfavorable to the army, which employed surround-and-destroy tactics with poor results. During this initial phase, both armed camps continued to consolidate, creating over time a favorable balance for the armed forces, which formed special battalions trained by US Green Berets and possessed sophisticated arms as well as technical support.

Political aspects of the war were repeatedly more important than its military dimension, clearly proving the dictum that "war is but a continuation of politics by other means." Due to direct US pressure, which was not always well received, the armed forces and those in power accepted the strategy of legalizing political power to undermine the legitimacy of the insurgent forces. The United States convinced the armed forces to accept the challenge of free elections as a condition for foreign aid. In March of 1982, during the first year of the war, elections were held to form a constitutional assembly. Although the Christian Democrats won, the assembly was controlled by the extreme right (ARENA-PCN). ARENA had allied with the PCN, securing two more votes, thus allowing them to impose on the Christian Democrats, who had relative majority. In January 1981, sectors of the armed forces led by Major Roberto D'Aubuisson and several businessmen formed the Nationalist Republican Alliance (ARENA), which won its first important victory by capturing second place. Henceforth, the country was deeply split by the existence of a constitutional, civilian-based government surrounded by a society deeply changed by war.

Between 1981 and 1983, the military progress of the FMLN convinced the army of the impossibility of short-term victory. The dual strategy of striking the armed forces while causing damage to economic assets (e.g. destroying harvested produce, bridges, electric lines, telephone lines, buildings and other public works) produced favorable results and served to keep the FMLN on the offensive for long periods until 1983. The notion of low-intensity conflict as a form of all-out war began to take on relevance. In 1982 serious crises occurred within both the armed forces and the FMLN (FPL), culminating in the expulsion of several generals in the former, and in the death of Mélida Anaya and the suicide of Cayetano Carpio in the latter.

A new constitution, approved in December of 1983, was followed by the election of a banker by the name of Alvaro Magaña as provisional president. Presidential elections, scheduled for March 25, 1984 were won by the Christian Democratic party whose leader, José Napoleón Duarte, was elected president. These elections were the first open, non-fraudulent elections in over fifty years. From that point on, as the following four elections were boycotted by the FMLN, an ambiguous process of electoral democratization began, helping to consolidate ARENA as the leading party on the right, particularly in the last three elections after 1986. In the 1990 elections, Alfredo Cristiani was elected president. The FMLN made a risky six-month peace proposal, offering to disarm and participate in the elections if they were postponed until September, allowing time to arrange security guarantees and register supporters. In the words of FMLN representative Ana Guadalupe Martinez,

We made an analysis just before making the proposal public about what the conduct of the parties would be. Obviously we knew ARENA would at first say no, since the polls virtually guaranteed them victory. We thought the PDC would speak of unconstitutionality, but search for a formula that would make them appear favorable to the idea ... and this is what happened. Arena said no, but the PDC though not agreeing, did not dismiss the idea, thus facilitating the political game for other parties, while creating an environment for us to make other procedural proposals to keep the debate alive.[9]

---

[9] "The FMLN: new thinking," in CINAS, *El Salvador. Guerra, politica y paz* (San Salvador: CINAS-CRIES, 1988), p. 56.

There were many shifts back and forth during the war. It is important to point out that due to the Sandinista victory in Nicaragua and the crisis in Guatemala, US foreign policy made El Salvador the definitive test of its foreign security in the Americas and provided extraordinary support to the army and the government, with all kinds of resources. Without US aid, the armed forces would have lost the war within the first eighteen months. The Salvadoran military were not prepared for war. When comparing the flow of US aid to Nicaragua and Guatemala with deliveries to El Salvador, their desperation becomes evident.

The armed forces made substantial improvements in their offensive capacity, quadrupling the number of men and beginning a new phase with the Christian Democrat government. However, the FMLN adapted, reinforcing its mobility with small units and dispersing them. Consequently, it broadened the battleground area and concentrated its efforts on acts of sabotage and political activity, in order to create an infrastructure of support, even in San Salvador itself. Between 1985 and 1986, with overwhelming air power, the army undertook military actions against areas under guerrilla domination, in an effort to weaken their social support. This campaign culminated in Operation Phoenix in January of 1986, the aim of which was to dislodge the FMLN from Guazapa volcano, in close proximity to San Salvador. The armed forces succeeded only partially, as the FMLN held the position until the end of the war. Relentlessly harassed, mainly by the business-based right, unable to fulfill its promises to the people, corrupt and, above all, unable to put an end to human rights violations, Duarte's government ended up severely discredited.

Damages to infrastructure between 1979 and 1984 have been estimated at $146 million, and damages to economic production itself at $537 million. According to UN estimates, the war left a sum total in damages of between $1.8 billion and $2 billion. US aid up to 1986 amounted to $2.586 billion, including economic aid.[10] In October 1986, an earthquake partially destroyed the capital city, accentuating the hardships of the Salvadoran people.

After 1987, the armed forces reached a saturation point. They kept up the offensive, but at a tremendous cost in lives. Ultimately, they were unable to oust the FMLN from those regions where they traditionally drew their support, in the north and northwest part of the country. After mid-1987, the FMLN undertook several initiatives: it called for a transportation strike, made surprise attacks on armed forces barracks and, most importantly, carried out actions in San Salvador which lent

---

[10]   J. Dunkerly, *Power in the Isthmus: A Political History of Modern Central America* (London: Verso, 1988), p. 370.

the guerrillas added social support and prestige. The army, acting on the advice of foreign advisors, responded with an ambitious plan called "United for Reconstruction." Actions on both sides became more substantial, but the new presence of the FMLN in San Salvador knocked the armed forces' tactics off balance. The FMLN became undefeatable, while being simultaneously incapable of triumph. Its offensive in November of 1989, in which it entered San Salvador twice and withdrew, illustrated its extraordinary tactical mobility and technical skill. By this point it wanted a political rather than military victory. This was only partially accomplished, due to the extent of casualties and the impression that it was an instigation of conflict leading to more bloodshed. The situation became an unstable balance between two experienced armed camps.

At the same time, the FMLN discovered that its support had dwindled among a civilian population tired of receiving the war's cruelest blows of violence. Sensing this, the FMLN voiced the need for negotiation and dialogue to put an end to the fratricidal war. Moreover, the international situation after 1989 militated against further conflict. The end of the Cold War affected military strategies and facilitated negotiation on both sides. Alfredo Cristiani's electoral victory in 1989 convinced all sides that a new atmosphere had been created for achieving peace. It was now the responsiblity of the political right to finally accept the incessantly repeated proposals of the FMLN. In Cristiani's election platform he was presented as the only candidate who could obtain peace, with the support of the military and the entrepreneurs. The end of the war seemed attractive. After twelve years of conflict, victory for either side did not seem close at hand. Economically, all were losing.

Some statistics say a great deal about the character of this war. In 1981 alone, the armed forces suffered 5,133 casualties, including deaths, woundings and desertions, while the FMLN suffered only 200.[11] Between 1982 and 1984, the armed forces suffered 9,923 casualties, a third of which were deaths. All together, the armed forces suffered at least 21,000 casualties between January of 1981 and December of 1985. The FMLN experienced fewer casualties; but not so with the civilian population. In later years, the annual casualty counts were lower, but they indicate the bloody nature of the conflict. Between 1985 and 1990, the armed forces suffered 32,066 casualties and the FMLN suffered 13,985; but these figures do not mention the civilian death toll of at least

[11] This and all subsequent casualty figures are drawn from *El Salvador Proceso, Informativo Semanal de la UCA*, San Salvador, various editions.

100,000.[12] It has been calculated that each of the two sides reached the sum of 25,000 wounded. Approximately 467,000 persons were displaced by the conflict and over a million Salvadorans immigrated to the United States. The material damage caused by the war is incalculable, but the amount necessary to recover productive potential has been estimated at one billion dollars.

Peace was finally achieved, after three years of negotiation, through the New York agreements in December 1991 and the January 1992 signing of the final agreement in Chapultepec. The process, succeeded for many reasons but mainly because of the US decision to force negotiations by threatening either to withdraw aid or contribute to reconstruction if progress was achieved. The strong intervention of the United Nations and of numerous countries helped as well. After twelve years of war, political and military forces had changed. Many of the circumstances which had fomented war, especially at the economic level, remain unresolved. Electoral democracy is making progress, and the will of the Salvadoran people is the best guarantee that the country will peacefully resolve the serious challenges which pushed it toward this terrible conflict.

[12] While other observers have estimated the total number of casualties at approximately 75,000, this author believes that the higher numbers indicated by the Central American University's *El Salvador Proceso* are more likely.

10 Peacemaking in El Salvador

Mark LeVine

Introduction

The Salvadoran peace process has been hailed by diplomats as a "negotiated revolution,"[1] a "jewel in a crown of thorns."[2] Secretary-General Boutros Boutros-Ghali further labeled it a "definitive moment in the history of El Salvador,"[3] as well as a "pioneering effort in peacekeeping."[4] Only the coming months and years will tell whether these accolades were premature or if in fact, after one hundred years of internal struggle and bloody conflict, the peace process will prove irreversible. Whatever the final outcome, the complex negotiations, which culminated in the formal cessation of hostilities on December 16, 1992, witnessed the creation of many new mechanisms that will prove essential to future UN peacekeeping, peacemaking and peacebuilding activities.[5]

The purpose of this chapter is to review the diplomatic history of the Salvadoran peace process with the aim of revealing the many unique and unprecedented features of this process. The discussion will begin with an overview of the diplomatic efforts and negotiations during the 1980s which gradually paved the way for the peace process that began officially in Geneva on April 4, 1990. It will end with the signing of the Chapultepec Accords on January 16, 1992, after which I will highlight several of the important innovations of the United Nations role in the Salvadoran negotiations.

---

[1] Alvaro de Soto, quoted in George Vickers and Jack Spence, *End Game: A Progress Report on the Implementation of the Salvadoran Peace Accords* (Cambridge, Mass.: Hemisphere Initiatives, 1992), p. 1.

[2] Interview with a senior UN diplomat, New York, April, 1993.

[3] Quoted in UN Peace-keeping Operations Information Notes, 1993: Update no. 1, p. 28.

[4] S/25521, para. 13.

[5] According to one senior UN official, the organization's role in El Salvador was, comparatively, perhaps more important than any previous operation because it was so involved in both the peacemaking and peacebuilding phases (interview, New York, April, 1993).

In contrast to the Cambodian peace process, where four years of negotiations culminated in one all-encompassing agreement, the negotiating process in El Salvador was piecemeal and more spontaneous. Seven separate agreements were negotiated in a two-year period; each one forging a link in the chain that increased trust between the warring sides, while laying the legal and political framework for the termination of the armed conflict. At the same time, the process was relatively spontaneous in that the pace and direction of the negotiations, which produced those agreements, was scripted neither by the belligerents nor the mediators. Indeed, the adaptability of the process was one its hallmarks.

Each agreement, far from being part of some overall negotiating strategy or theme, simply reflected what could and could not be agreed upon at a given time. This is not to say that the parties and mediators had no broader vision of the final settlement; all realized that the war had toend and national reconciliation begin. As we shall see, it took a decade of labor to give birth to this new, shared vision of El Salvador's future.

Peacemaking efforts in Central America in the 1980s

During the 1980s peacemaking in Central America had little chance of success, most notably because of the international polarization resulting from the renewed Cold War and the Reagan administration's determination to "roll back" communism from the region. Within this extremely unfavorable environment, however, the UN began to play an increasingly active role. By the end of the decade the UN had helped to facilitate resolution of two out of three of the Western hemisphere's major conflicts.

Both the UN and Latin American countries, specifically the members of the Contadora Group (Colombia, Mexico, Panama, and Venezuela), were involved in regional peace efforts since 1983. Beginning that year a series of agreements were drafted by the Group and subsequently by the Central Americans themselves,[6] culminating

---

[6]   The UN began with Security Council Resolutions 530(1983) and 562(1985). The Contadora Group began with their Cancun Declaration on Peace in Central America of July 17, 1983 (S/15877). This was followed by the Contadora Act (S/16041) and several amendments to it one year later (A/39/630) which marked the first time the Central Americans participated in drafting an agreement. In 1986 the Latin American governments signed the Esquipulas I Agreement (S/18106), which was the first time the Central Americans themselves drafted an agreement. This agreement is especially important because it represented the first formal acceptance by all the governments that "peace in Central America can be achieved only through an authentic democratic process ... which entails the promotion of social justice and respect for human rights."

in August 1987 with the signing of the Esquipulas II Agreement[7] by the presidents of five of the six Central American countries (El Salvador, Nicaragua, Costa Rica, Honduras, and Guatemala). This agreement, which is credited as marking the "official" birth of the Central American peace process, led to a process of consultation between the Central American countries, the Contadora Group (later to be known as the Four Friends of the Secretary-General with the addition of Spain and the deletion of Panama) and the UN/Secretary-General that proved vital to the eventual peace agreements in both Nicaragua and El Salvador.[8]

With the Esquipulas Agreement in mind, the Contadora countries urged the FMLN to negotiate with the government and sent a message to the Secretary-General that they would welcome a more direct involvement of the UN, as opposed to the USA and OAS, in the region. Attempts at restarting direct negotiations between the government and the FMLN failed during the next two years,[9] but three important developments did occur. First, in 1989 Salvadorans elected a new president, Alfredo Cristiani of the right-wing ARENA party. The choice of Cristiani, a US-educated member of the landed aristocracy and successful businessman,[10] as ARENA's candidate, signaled the ascendancy of a wing that, though remaining staunchly anti-communist, wanted to fight the FMLN with the economy as opposed to the army. Peace – a major campaign theme for Cristiani – was seen as the sine qua non for rebuilding and liberalizing the "broken" Salvadoran economy,

---

[7] S/19085. It was also known as the Guatemala Procedure. Aside from promoting an "authentic" democratic process, human rights, and elections it called for the termination of aid to irregular forces of other countries and for the prohibition by countries on the use of their territory by rebel groups to attack neighboring countries. The Agreement set out in some detail the measures the five governments were willing to take to end the inter-state conflicts as well as the civil wars within Nicaragua, El Salvador, and Guatemala.

[8] During the mid-1980s, a lack of political will within El Salvador coupled with unfavorable international conditions left the Contadora countries, the Central American governments and their respective rebel movements unable to negotiate seriously. It was not until 1986, with US interest in the region decreasing, that the Contadora group could take the diplomatic initiative, pressing the opposing sides in the region's internecine conflicts to begin serious negotiations.

[9] One FMLN negotiator described this period as one of "dialogs" between the two parties, but no substantive "negotiations" (interview conducted by Ian Johnstone, San Salvador, August, 1993).

[10] Cristiani was the personification of what party leaders billed as the new, non-violent ARENA, symbolic of a two year effort to transform the party from its paramilitary roots to a sophisticated political party accepted by Washington. Rather than being one of the old-time latifundia owners, he was also part of a new breed of businessmen, who realized that a well-trained, educated workforce was more important for raising profits than a crushed, obedient peasantry.

in line with the emerging regional and world trade order, a much higher priority than achieving an increasingly impossible military victory over the FMLN. This economically motivated "pragmatism" and lack of ideological commitment to continuing the conflict was instrumental in shepherding the government side through the successful negotiating process.

The second development was the signing by the five presidents of two important agreements – the Costa del Sol Agreement and the Tela Declaration – which, though concerned with the Nicaraguan and not Salvadoran civil war, brought the UN for the first time directly into the Central American negotiating process, thus helping open the way to direct negotiations between the government and FMLN under the sponsorship of the Secretary-General.[11] The third development was the winding down of the Cold War, which meant that the United States and Soviet Union were no longer as ideologically committed to continuing their proxy wars in Central America, and were willing to put significant pressure on the two sides to negotiate, including cutting off arms supplies and reducing funding.

In the wake of the Costa del Sol and Tela agreements, the two sides in El Salvador met face to face in September and again in mid-October 1989.[12] The government pressed the FMLN to agree to an immediate ceasefire while the FMLN, understanding that the government was waiting for changes in the communist world to undermine the movement, countered that reforms to the constitution, judicial system, and the military had to be made first.

These competing demands became the core issues on whose resolution the final peace agreement would depend. Unfortunately, the impetus for compromise at this early stage was not strong enough to overcome either the wide gap in the two sides' negotiating positions or the advantages of continued fighting.

The FMLN did subsequently agree not to boycott the next local and National Assembly elections, but the bombing of a trade union office on October 31 led to their launching the largest offensive of the war on November 11.[13] Though it did not have the desired effect of fomenting

[11] In the Costa del Sol Agreement of February, 1989 (S/20491) Nicaraguan president Daniel Ortega agreed to call early elections, while in the Tela Declaration of August of the same year (S/20778) the presidents asked the UN to monitor the elections and the subsequent demobilization of the Contras.

[12] During this same month the General Assembly, in Resolution 44/10, requested the Secretary-General to continue to lend full support to regional peace efforts, and he in turn appointed Alvaro de Soto as his special mediator for the Central American Peace Process.

[13] The FDR, one of the five groups that make up the FMLN, actually planned to field candidates, but the bombing of the local trade union headquarters (FENESTRAS,

a national revolt, the offensive proved to be the turning point of the war.[14] On the government side, it shook the army by demonstrating conclusively that it would not be able to defeat the rebels in the near future,[15] while from a political standpoint the government realized that victory against an enemy that targeted its legitimacy through subversion and guerrilla tactics would be exceedingly difficult, if not impossible.[16] Additional impetus to begin serious negotiations came from the infamous murder of the six Jesuit priests, their housekeeper and her daughter on November 16, which resulted in growing pressure on the government to take action to curb human rights abuses and death squad activity by the military.

On the rebel side, the winding down of the superpower conflict meant that a continued military stalemate was the best long-term outcome the rebels could hope for, as Soviet military aid to Nicaragua, which along with Cuba was the FMLN's chief provider of arms and logistical support, was cut off in 1989. Moreover, the end of the Cold War and the increasingly evident failure of communism in the Soviet Union made it difficult to sustain the ideological and emotional motivations for continuing the war.[17] Thus convinced that their strategy of "prolonged war" was no longer possible, the FMLN leadership realized that negotiation was "the only rational solution."[18] During the same period – at the annual summit of Central American presidents in Costa Rica –

Federacion Nacional Sindical de Trabajadores, killing ten people) caused them to pull out. The bombing was most likely carried out or at least sponsored by the government. The rebels had bombarded the military's headquarters only days earlier.

[14] Terry Lynn Karl, "El Salvador's negotiated revolution," in *Foreign Affairs*, vol. 71, no. 2, 1992, p. 151. One senior FMLN negotiator explained that by October 1989 the leadership felt that the government was clearly looking for the FMLN to surrender and lay down its arms; the November offensive was thus designed either to win the war outright or force the government to negotiate. If the latter occurred the rebels had planned from the start to bring the UN into the process as a counter-weight to the USA (interview conducted by Ian Johnstone, San Salvador, September, 1993).

[15] Soon after the offensive the High Command "voiced support" for peace talks, (FBIS, March 23, 1990, p. 20).

[16] George Vickers, "The political reality after eleven years of war," in Joseph S. Tulchin and Gary Bland (eds.), *Is There a Transition to Democracy in El Salvador?* (Boulder, Col.: Lynne Rienner, 1992), p. 36.

[17] As one leader described it, the rebels realized that the unity of effort and consistency of support – two keys for any rebels movement – were also waning on their side; thus, despite the success of their offensive they knew that they "were in a period of weakness, no longer on the offensive" (rebel leader Miguel Castellenos).

[18] Ruben Zamora, quoted in FBIS, January 31, 1990, pp. 18–19. Coleman also points out the effect of the "economic nightmare" being presided over by the FMLN's close ally, the Sandinista government in Nicaragua, and the desire of Cuba to "extract themselves from El Salvador," if the FMLN could receive political access commensurate with its military power; Christopher C. Coleman, *The Salvadoran Peace Process: A Preliminary Inquiry* (Oslo: Norwegian Institute of International Affairs, Research Report no. 173, 1993), p. 15.

President Oscar Arias, until then the motivating force behind the Esquipulas peace process, realized that he alone could not bring the parties together. Thus he publicly called on the Secretary-General to become more involved and help "facilitate" the process.[19] The five presidents also requested the Secretary-General to expand the UN's Nicaraguan observer mission's (ONUCA) mandate to include the verification of any future demobilization and ceasefires in the region.

The events of late 1989 brought about a fundamental re-examination of strategies and tactics by the FMLN and the government. The United States, the government's patron, also saw its policy consensus shattered by the November offensive, giving the arguments of those favoring negotiations with the FMLN more credence.[20] Thus as a new decade approached, both the parties and their sponsors all concluded that negotiations were now the only viable option. The FMLN consequently approached the Secretary-General in late 1989 and asked him to intervene to get the talks back on track, while President Cristiani went to New York on January 31, 1990 where he gave the Secretary-General his blessing to talk with the FMLN.[21] Sensing the opportunity to use his good offices without the previous high risk of failure (and consequent loss of credibility for the UN), Pérez de Cuéllar decided the time was ripe to become personally involved in the talks. This paved the way for the Geneva Agreement, the first bilateral agreement of the UN-sponsored peace process.

The Geneva Agreement

While it took the better part of a decade for the Contadora Process to come to fruition, it established a framework for the inter-regional negotiations on a political (as opposed to military) level and minimized US intervention.[22] This does not mean that the wider international community played no role during this period. During the 1980s,

[19] According to senior UN officials, the outgoing and incoming Mexican administrations also pushed the Secretary-General to get more involved in the peace process. The new US administration, in contrast to its predecessor, also signaled its support of stepped up UN and regional efforts to end the war.

[20] Stephen Baranyi and Liisa North, *The United Nations Role in El Salvador: The Promises and Dilemmas of an Integrated Approach to Peace* (Toronto: York University Press, 1993) p. 7.

[21] As recounted by Alvaro de Soto in "The Negotiations Following the New York Agreement," in Tulchin and Bland, 1992, p. 139. He had broached the general idea about increased UN involvement in his first meeting with the Secretary-General in the fall of 1989 at the General Assembly debate.

[22] Francisco Villagràn Kramer, "Understanding the crisis in Central America, essential facts," in Jack Child (ed.), *Conflict in Central America: Approaches to Peace and Security* (London: Hurst, 1986), p. 4.

peacemaking efforts were in fact important, but "unsynchronized."[23] The cumulative effect was not strong enough to push the two sides to begin serious negotiations.

The gradual coordination of cooperative efforts, spearheaded by the leadership of the Secretary-General and helped by the changing attitude of the US toward the peace process, finally brought the two sides to the negotiating table in earnest; beginning an "irreversible process," as one FMLN official described it. The immediate result was the Geneva Agreement of April 4, 1990,[24] which became the cornerstone upon which the negotiating process developed. The Agreement created a framework which led to the end of the armed conflict under the auspices of the Secretary-General;[25] and furthering the pledge of the Esquipulas II Agreement, it provided that the UN would verify all subsequent agreements. This marked a new high in UN involvement in the region over the course of seven years.

Immediately after Geneva, UN Secretary-General Pérez de Cuéllar sought and elicited the support for the peace process from the now receptive patrons of the warring sides – the USA, the Soviet Union, and Cuba. After a meeting in May in which a negotiating agenda – the Caracas Agenda[26] – was agreed upon, substantive negotiations began in June. The army was the first topic of discussion, as stipulated by the Agenda, but it was immediately apparent that military reform was going to be the most difficult topic of the negotiations. The FMLN initially took a hard line, as they viewed the military through the prism of sixty years of army domination of the country's politics, ten years of civil war, and innumerable human rights abuses. Hence, in line with their pre-Geneva position they pushed for the ultimate abolishment of the armed

---

[23] Interview with senior Salvadoran diplomat, Washington, DC, April, 1993.

[24] S/23128. The purpose of the peace process was to end the armed conflict by political means as quickly as possible, promote democratization of the country, guarantee unrestricted respect for human rights and reunify Salvadoran society through reintegrating the FMLN back into civilian life.

[25] S/23402.

[26] S/23129. The Agenda was divided into two parts. The first encompassed political agreements on seven crucial issues which would create the conditions for a ceasefire (the army, human rights, the judicial and electoral systems, constitutional reform, economic and social issues and UN verification of the agreements). Once a ceasefire was achieved the second phase would begin, in which the same issues would be addressed once again with the goal of establishing the necessary guarantees and conditions for "reintegrating the members of the FMLN, within a framework of full legality, into the civil, institutional and political life of the country." This two stage process represented a major concession on the government's part, as until then it had insisted on achieving a ceasefire before it would negotiate on political issues such as reforming the armed forces and the judicial system. The Agenda involved the UN in all aspects of the potential agreements and committed the two sides to achieve a ceasefire by mid-September, 1990.

forces. For its part, the military saw peace as a threat to its position as the most powerful institution in Salvadoran society, if not to its very existence.

Fortunately, a note within the Caracas Agenda specifically pointed out that the order of items on the agenda could change "depend[ing] on the dynamic of the negotiations." Thus after four days of fruitless negotiations, the UN mediators, realizing that the army was too difficult an issue to deal with first, held a two-day brainstorming session in Geneva with twenty or so human rights and El Salvador experts (but without the parties) to discuss the feasibility of moving to the second item on the Agenda, human rights.[27]

The San José Agreement on human rights

When they reconvened the two sides in San José on July 26, the UN team put the draft of a human rights agreement on the table, and after eleven hours of negotiations the two sides signed the agreement without any serious modification. Called the San José Agreement on Human Rights,[28] it was the first substantive agreement of the negotiating process.

The Agreement was "unprecedented in UN history,"[29] as it was the first to detail specific actions the two sides of a conflict would take to insure respect for human rights. It was also a confidence-building measure, a tangible success early on in the negotiations which helped solidify the peace process.[30] It demonstrated that the two sides could reach agreement on divisive issues and that they felt they could trust the

[27] The minutes of the meetings show that a primary concern of those present was to put the UN in a position to "exercise political pressure" in order to "shed full light on the violence," with the hope of significantly reducing human rights abuses. Human rights was also seen by participants as a means to accomplish the ultimate goal of achieving a ceasefire and holding free and fair elections. Baranyi and North add that "contradictory signals emanating from Washington" on military and political reforms also led to human rights being brought to the front burner, as it was the one item "everyone could agree upon" (*United Nations Role in El Salvador*, p. 13).

[28] S/21541. The Agreement laid out in detail the modalities for respecting and guaranteeing human rights on the part of both sides – who agreed to stop practices which contravene international human rights laws, punish any one who continued to violate them, and create a monitoring mission which both sides agreed to cooperate with fully.

[29] A/47/596, para. 260. Cf. DPI-1149A, 1991, p. 5. De Soto's active involvement is two months earlier than the August session which was described by Terry Lynn Karl as "changing de Soto from merely a facilitator of the dialogue to a mediator and permitted the UN team to put forward proposals to either side" ("El Salvador's negotiated revolution," p. 156). A senior Salvadoran diplomat pushed the date for active involvement by de Soto back even farther, noting that while de Soto was present only as a "witness" in the talks of October 1989, from the Geneva Agreement onwards he was a major player in the negotiations.

[30] Interview with senior UN official, NY, April, 1993.

UN to verify and implement the controversial agreement.[31] Moreover, the presence of human rights monitors would "make it difficult for the two sides to intensify the fighting or to walk away from the negotiating table,"[32] fulfilling exactly the function assigned to it by the UN negotiators. The dynamics of the negotiations which led to the San José Agreement – the willingness of the UN, the Friends, and the parties themselves to adapt to changing conditions and "recalendarize" the negotiating agenda – proved to be a hallmark of the negotiating process and crucial to the eventual securing of the peace agreements.

Secretary-General Pérez de Cuéllar was instrumental in securing an agreement on human rights. When he realized that the Caracas Agenda was untenable as originally constituted, he supported replacing military issues with human rights issues at the top of the agenda and convinced President Cristiani to accept human rights monitors. He did so by offering to create a mission that would verify the Agreement (ONUSAL), train a police force, and take other steps to demonstrate both his and the UN's long-term commitment to the peace process.

There was, as one might expect, criticism of the agreement from quarters on both sides. On the government side, many hardliners were upset that the government even conceded that there had been human rights violations and that "subversives" currently in jail would henceforth be considered political prisoners. Yet for his part, President Cristiani understood that he had to sign a human rights agreement in order to prove he was negotiating in good faith. He also realized that in accepting most of the blame on the human rights issue he would gain considerable negotiating power, taking pressure off the government for the near future while forcing the FMLN to make the next major concession. Human rights proved to be "a good concession," and by using it to his advantage in the overall negotiations Cristiani was able to face his constituents in the army and the business elite, whose interests would be damaged by it.[33]

On the rebel side, many argued that without real reforms to the army and judicial system a human rights agreement would be worthless, while others felt that the negotiators had given up too much in not pushing military issues.[34] Hence, though talks were held in August and

---

[31] This was especially important for the UN mediators because they realized they could not wait for the parties to moderate in other areas, as agreements had to be reached while public opinion was ripe for the peace process.

[32] In the words of one ONUSAL official (cited in David Holiday and William Stanley, "Building the peace: the role of the United Nations in El Salvador," *Journal of International Affairs*, 1992-3, p. 4, note 17).

[33] Interview with a senior Four Friends diplomat, Washington, DC, April, 1993.

[34] Recounted in the Economic Intelligence Unit, 1990, no. 4, p. 20.

September, they also foundered on the issue of the armed forces' future role and structure and the question of military impunity for human rights abuses.[35] These serious problems in the months after the San José Agreement revealed that while human rights could anchor the negotiations, it could not move them forward.[36] Until the myriad of issues surrounding the armed forced were addressed, peace would prove elusive.

However, in the midst of the stormy and stalemated talks, the UN mediators were gathering elements that would help future efforts to reach a possible agreement.[37] First, they persuaded the rebels to drop their insistence on being part of a coalition or transitional government and instead focus on reforming existing political structures. Secondly, the two parties agreed in late October to expand the role of the UN mediators in order to help unlock the stalemated talks. Aided by a determined increase in the role of the Friends, the mediators quickly helped secure compromises which laid the groundwork for eventual agreement on purging the armed forces.[38] As a result of their efforts, a partial blueprint for compromise on the armed forces issue began to emerge the end of 1990.[39]

Around the same time, Under Secretary-General Marrack Goulding

---

[35] The rebels presented an eighteen-point plan which called for, among other things, the *demilitarization* of the armed forces (as opposed to the disbandment, although the gradual elimination of both armies was their ultimate goal), the dissolution of various bodies accused of the most serious abuses (e.g. the Atlacatl Battalion and the National Intelliegence Directorate), and trials to punish those responsible for the most heinous crimes (such as the murder of Archbishop Romero and the FENESTRAS bombing). The argument over when a ceasefire should occur – before or after substantive agreements had been reached – continued, with the rebels feeling that it would be "irresponsible to agree to a ceasefire without first putting a full stop to the impunity enjoyed by the military" (FMLN chief delegate Shafik Handal, quoted in FBIS, July 27, 1990, p. 32).

[36] While most FMLN officials interviewed felt that the San José Agreement was important in its own right because it "alleviated the conditions of war on the civilian population" (interview, September, 1993), others felt, as one senior FMLN negotiator remarked, that while the agreement could keep the negotiations alive, it had no "transcendental meaning" (interview, San Salvador, August, 1993). This fact, coupled with the lack of a similar role for human rights monitoring in current conflicts, would tend to downplay the ultimate significance of the San José Accords as a model for future UN peacemaking operations (as opposed to the view of, for example Coleman, who felt that the accord held great significance for the emerging UN role of peacebuilding (Coleman, *The Salvadoran Peace Process*, p. 19)).

[37] FBIS, September 9, 1990, p. 11.

[38] Specifically, de Soto made a proposal to review the records of army officers and to retire those found to have committed serious abuses, as well as to abolish the Treasury Police, National Guard and National Intelligence Directorate. Yet the talks were still deadlocked on substantive issues and the rebels launched an offensive in at least seven of the country's fourteen departments in order to push the negotiations forward.

[39] Karl, "El Salvador's negotiated revolution," p. 156.

was sent to El Salvador to give the parties a "101 lesson in ceasefires," after which two missions were sent to study the feasibility of early deployment of the human rights monitors mandated by the San José Agreement.[40] The key objective of the study was to examine the potential danger to UN personnel of operating in conflict areas and to determine the necessary logistics for setting up such a mission. With their positive recommendation the Secretary-General requested Security Council approval for the deployment of ONUSAL before a ceasefire, feeling that ONUSAL's early deployment would improve the human rights situation and help the negotiations move forward.

A temporary setback in the negotiations occurred at the end of the year when the rebels downed a US helicopter and killed the two surviving pilots, an act which removed some of the pressure on the government by weakening a United States threat to cut United States military assistance by 50 percent. The opening of a Preparatory Office for ONUSAL in January 1991 and the resumption of negotiations in Mexico the next month,[41] however, rekindled pressure on the government, which on March 10 lost its majority in the National Assembly in an election that the FMLN, for the first time, did not attempt to disrupt.[42] The lack of broad and conclusive support for the ruling party heartened the rebels, and on March 19 they proposed an accelerated agenda which would combine the political and military issues, constitutional reform, and a ceasefire.[43] The UN and the Friends also applied significant pressure to move the negotiations forward.[44] The FMLN

---

[40] During this period the army also accepted consultative as opposed to participatory status on a proposed commission which would review the human rights records of army officers. Another positive step was President Cristiani's decision in December to retire almost all of a list of thirty army officers the FMLN singled out as having egregious human rights records, thus indicating the military's willingness to make concessions and restructure. This was furthered by its agreement in early January 1991 to de Soto's proposition for the abolishment of the National Guard and Treasury Police.

[41] The basis for which was a "working document" presented by de Soto in 1990 as their point of reference, and which dealt with the "most difficult issues of the negotiations, reform and purging of the armed forces" (Baranyi and North, *United Nations Role in El Salvador*, p. 14, note 24). This document gave the to sides a "mechanism" to identify their differences in a systematic way.

[42] Although it did not allow voting in the areas it controlled, supporters were encouraged to vote for opposition party candidates in the rest of the country.

[43] In another sign of the gradual moderation on the armed forces issue, the rebels now discussed "achieving the highest degree of demilitarization *possible*" (my emphasis, FBIS, March 19, 1991, p. 10).

[44] After a year of only indirect contacts, the US during this period played its most important role yet, beginning its first direct contacts with the FMLN. The US pressured both sides to negotiate, as Joint Chiefs Chairman Colin Powell was sent to El Salvador on April 8, and Assistant Secretary of State Aronson on the twelfth. For a

proposal was accepted, and new talks were held virtually non-stop in Mexico from April 4–28.

Perhaps the greatest pressure to speed negotiations was the need to come to an agreement that the Legislative Assembly could ratify before the end of its term. Due to a clause in the country's constitution that stipulated that changes to the constitution would have to be ratified by two consecutive legislative assemblies, missing the current assembly's ratification would necessitate a minimum two-plus year wait. After eight months of fruitless talks the two sides were ready to negotiate seriously, and the pressure of the legislative deadline created an auspicious opportunity for compromise. As rebel leader Manuel Melgar commented, "during this historic time the idea is not to cause any of the negotiating sides to cave in, but to find a face-saving political settlement in which neither side appears defeated."[45] Thus, on the rebel side, the leadership formally agreed to accept a ceasefire before all substantive issues were decided, while the government finally gave in to the idea that the armed forces would have to undergo a comprehensive restructuring, including the purging of its worst human rights violators.

The Mexico Agreement

On April 27, after two weeks of "frenzied negotiations," the parties signed the Mexico Agreement,[46] the second substantive accord of the peace process. This agreement dealt with six central issues: reforming the armed forces (among other things it called for the creation of a new national civil police force which, unlike the old public security bodies, would be completely independent of the armed forces);[47] the judicial system; human rights; the electoral system; the forming of a Truth Commission which would investigate the most heinous crimes committed by both sides during the civil war; and, in a separate addendum, reforms to the country's constitution.[48]

detailed description of the negotiations during this period, see Vickers, "The political reality after eleven years of war," pp. 44–7.

[45] Quoted in FBIS, March 15, 1991, p. 15. The negotiations were facilitated by the fact that there were two tables, one political – headed by de Soto, and one dealing with the ceasefire – headed by Marrack Goulding. The government liked this arrangement because it wanted a ceasefire as soon as possible, while for the rebels it allowed political issues to be described before the signing of a ceasefire.

[46] April 27, 1991, S/23130.

[47] The successful training and deployment of the National Civil Police is, in the view of both commentators and senior UN officials, "key" to the success of the accords.

[48] In addition to the reforms cited above, the Agreement called for the creation of a human rights ombudsman, the assigning of at least 6 percent of the government's revenue to the justice system, and the restructuring of the Supreme Court and its control over the national judiciary.

By dealing specifically with several of the most difficult substantive issues of the negotiations, the Mexico Agreement created momentum which opened the way for a larger settlement. At the same time, the agreement reflected each side's opinion that root causes of the conflict had yet to be dealt with. The FMLN insisted that a passage be inserted stating that the description of the armed forces as a "permanent" institution was incompatible with its position, and that it considered there to be certain constitutional reforms still awaiting negotiations, including land ownership and reforming the Constitution. This insertion was especially significant from the FMLN's perspective as it "mark[ed] the insurgents' determination that the armed forces be placed under civilian control and that military impunity is ended."[49] On the government side, Cristiani had to scramble to reassure the military that dissolution of the armed forces was not on the table.

Despite the decision by the Security Council on May 20 to authorize the early deployment of ONUSAL to monitor the implementation of the San José Agreement,[50] the negotiations soured once again soon after the Mexico Agreement and remained deadlocked for the next three months. In general, the army refused to continue discussing political issues until a ceasefire was signed, and the rebels refused to agree to a ceasefire until they had final agreement on military reforms and guarantees on their reintegration into society.[51] The two sides also fought over the implementation of the Mexico Agreement as well as some important issues it did not deal with such as the purging of the army, land reform, and the logistics of a ceasefire.[52]

Thus while the deployment of ONUSAL (which occurred on July 26,

[49] Economic Intelligence Unit, 1991, no. 3, p. 20.

[50] In fact, the FMLN had insisted on early deployment from the signing of the San José Agreement, but the government took longer to warm to the idea of early deployment. Specifically, human rights acted as a buffer, preventing the two sides from allowing their natural inclinations to let them slide back into all out war. Most importantly, the presence of ONUSAL reassured the FMLN that it could safely enter the political arena, thus "mak[ing] the process irreversible" (in the words of one senior UN official close to the negotiations).

[51] They felt it was impossible to join the political process until sufficient guarantees were given and consequently continued fighting was the only leverage they felt they had to push talks along from their side, though they realized that the process was irreversible.

[52] The FMLN was still most concerned with defining the status of the forces during a ceasefire, that is, whether they could keep their arms after a ceasefire, where they would be cached, etc. They were also concerned about guaranteeing their political freedom. Yet they also continued to moderate their position toward the army. Thus, rebel spokesmen declared that Salvadoran society must be reunified "under new conditions, namely, liberty, justice, democracy, with a purged [as opposed to a "demilitarized" or "disbanded"] army" (quoted in FBIS, May 13, 1991, p. 13). Thus, we see that the rebels demand for disbanding the army, which had already been modified to "demilitarization," was now within the more realistic realm of "purging."

one year to the day after the signing of the San José Agreement) improved the climate for human rights, on the battle field violence persisted as each side sought to gain greater leverage at the negotiating table through military victories. The military stalemate meant neither side wanted to make further concessions at the negotiating table, and the ensuing stalemate in the negotiations led the mediators to realize that the whole Caracas Agenda would have to be restructured by "simplifying" the original two-phase process into a one-phase process in which negotiations on a ceasefire and political issues would take place simultaneously. Realizing this, Pérez de Cuéllar "courageously convened a meeting in New York, a very risky step because the mood of the parties and their supporters in the country were at one of its lowest levels."[53]

Ten days of sometimes around the clock sessions, personally directed by the Secretary-General (in which US Representative Thomas Pickering, played a key role),[54] were necessary to achieve an agreement restructuring the Caracas Agenda.[55] Ultimately, pressure from the UN and the Four Friends helped push the negotiations forward. The rebels, fully "coming of age" as negotiators,[56] gave up their long-standing demand to merge with or disband the army, and also agreed that no new issues would be added to the ceasefire talks. The government agreed to protect the right of rebel families to hold onto land they had occupied during the war.

A series of proposals put forward by the outside mediators assuaged the FMLN's fears on military reform. Among them was the creation of an ad hoc commission which would evaluate the records of the officer corps and recommend purges for those found to have unsatisfactory professional or human rights records.[57] Further, in a key compromise, the rebels were persuaded to drop their demand to integrate with the armed forces in exchange for the right to participate in the new National Civil Police force called for in the Mexico Agreement.[58] With this

[53] Interview with senior Four Friends diplomat, NY, February, 1993.

[54] Baranyi and North, *United Nations Role in El Salvador*, pp. 19, 23.

[55] Even days before the New York talks the rebels had retreated to their former positions on the armed forces, asserting that the army had to be dissolved even if there was a UN verification mechanism. The judicial system, the electoral system and the ratification of the constitutional reforms were also still on the agenda.

[56] According to several diplomats close to the talks.

[57] The negotiations which led to the creation of the Ad Hoc Commission were described by one senior UN official involved in the talks as "the most carefully negotiated part of the peace agreement." The UN suggested two independent processes as precedents: the independent jurist who assisted in identifying political and common criminals held by South Africa in Namibia, and the Chilean Truth and Reconciliation Commission.

[58] As Holiday and Stanley described this aspect of the negotiations, "the UN was able to secure an agreement between the two sides by presenting the issues as a matter of

important step – the civilian police was the cornerstone of the attempt to
end the public security functions of the armed forces – the FMLN was
assured that "impunity was over, henceforth human rights violations will
be punished."[59]

The New York Agreement

Finally, on September 25, 1991 the two sides signed the New York
Agreement,[60] which was immediately hailed as a definitive moment in
the peace process and a "new victory for democracy in El Salvador."[61]
The agreement's goal was to "give final impetus to the process of
negotiations," which would henceforth be conducted according to a
"compressed" timetable.

The New York Agreement laid down basic directives intended to
guarantee a purge and reduction of the armed forces, establish a new
doctrine and training system, and insure the guerrillas' incorporation
into Salvadoran society.[62] It also called for disbanding of the National
Guard and the Treasury Police, and replacing the National Police with a
civilian police force. Further, for the first time, the issue of land
redistribution and economic and social reforms were directly addressed.[63]

The agreement also created a new national body, known by its
Spanish acronym COPAZ (Comisión Nacional para la Consolidación
de la Paz), which was composed not just of the government and FMLN,
but of representatives from all major political parties, with the UN and
the church acting as mediators. COPAZ was designed to act in a
supervisory and implementing role for all political agreements and peace
negotiations, and was the first link for the FMLN to the legislative and

---

guarantees for the FMLN rather than as a device for power sharing, and by proposing
that COPAZ be responsible for overseeing the process of admitting FMLN combatants
into the PNC" ("Building the peace," p. 4).

59 Interview with senior UN official close to the talks, New York, April, 1993.
60 S/23082.   61 *New York Times*, September 26, 1991, p. A16.
62 The new doctrine set out its functions as defending the sovereignty of the state and the
integrity of its territory, and stipulated that its activities would be based on the rule of
law and respect for human rights. While the New York Accords originally provided for
a reduction of 50.2 percent, the army subsequently sped up its force reduction and
increased it to 54.4 percent according to official figures (see S/25812, paras. 16–8).
Though as McCormick has pointed out in another chapter in this volume, this was
likely accomplished by padding the original numbers of soldiers.
63 State or private land holdings that exceed 245 hectares and land that was not destined
for ecological preservation would be subject to redistribution. This plan was never
implemented, and in May 1993 the Secretary-General offered a "no-refusal"
compromise which they accepted (S/25812). The Agreement also called for the
establishment of a "forum for economic and social accommodation," in which the
government, labor, and business sectors would participate.

political processes in the country. As such it was hailed by FMLN leaders, who called it the "most outstanding point in the New York Agreement."

After the New York Agreement, the two sides moved to amplify their new understanding, forming "an unlikely tacit alliance to overcome widespread skepticism about the prospects for peace and the opposition of hard-liners."[64] The FMLN announced a unilateral ceasefire to which the government responded favorably, and President Cristiani declared that there could be a ceasefire without the rebels turning over their weapons. Each side professed its willingness to sign a ceasefire as soon as possible (while accusing the other of being obstructionist).

It was clear at this point, as a US–Soviet joint statement noted, that "a UN monitored ceasefire [was] urgently required to consolidate the progress that has been made and put a definite end to the conflict."[65] Thus on December 17 negotiations resumed in New York to resolve the four major areas which still needed to be partially or completely negotiated: the National Civil Police; the specifics of the reduction of the army and land redistribution; and the guarantees for the FMLN to re-enter civilian life as a political force. Both land and police issues were deferred to COPAZ to be taken up after the signing of a peace agreement (demonstrating its essential role in the peace process even before it was established), thus allowing the two sides to reach agreement on the less contentious remaining issues.[66]

Despite the removal of these difficult issues from the negotiations, the lack of trust between the two sides prevented agreement on the remaining issues.[67] As was the case with the previous round in New York, only the presence of President Cristiani could push the talks forward and give the agreements reached the necessary credibility. The Secretary-General, helped by the Venezuelan and Mexican presidents,

---

[64] Karl, "El Salvador's negotiated revolution," p. 159. The second ONUSAL report describes the close working relationship which was developing between the highest echelons of the FMLN and the government. As Karl points out, however, even some formally hardline military officers had realized by this point that "the military must subordinate itself to the executive branch. A coup would be insane" (p. 160).

[65] Quoted in the Economic Intelligence Unit, 1992, no. 1, p. 24.

[66] For example, the rebels softened their demand for a handful of command positions in the new National Civil Police by letting COPAZ decide the matter. These successes aside, it must be pointed out that most observers, in and out of the UN, feel that COPAZ has failed to live up to expectations in its dealing with the contentious issues it was created to tackle. The number of parties with competing interests on the Commission has inevitably meant that consensus is rare, and thus progress on the legislation it was supposed to design for consideration by the legislature is minimal.

[67] According to Four Friends and UN mediators. See *The New York Times*, December 31, 1991, p. A1.

persuaded Cristiani to come to New York and assume control of the government delegation.[68]

With Cristiani in attendance all the players and pieces were in place. Everyone understood that Pérez de Cuéllar's retirement would be a major set back if an agreement was not reached by December 31, his last day in office. The Secretary-General used this to his advantage in the last days and even hours of the negotiations by postponing his retirement hour after hour to prod negotiations along. The US and Four Friends also stepped up pressure, with Assistant Secretary of State Aronson constantly present at the UN during the final days and the Four Friends continuously shuttling back and forth between the parties' hotels and the UN. As an incentive to both sides, the Friends promised to back up the UN's overseeing of the peace agreements and to work to secure international funds for reconstruction.

At 6 p.m. on December 31 the agreement remained elusive on issues relating to the army, land redistribution, and the National Civil Police. Pérez de Cuéllar threatened to leave the UN – or at least that is what the parties were led to believe – but the Friends prevailed upon him to give them one more hour, then another hour, while they went to each side and pressed them to compromise, especially on the land issue which earlier in the day had threatened to unravel the negotiations. This process went on until ten minutes before midnight, when the outgoing Secretary-General was literally heading for the elevator. The parties went upstairs and signed the agreement at one minute before midnight.

The New York Acts I and II

The New York Acts I and II,[69] were, as their joint preamble states, "definitive agreements which, combined with those previously signed at San José, Mexico City and New York, complete the negotiations on all substantive items of the Caracas Agenda and the New York compressed Negotiations." The parties had agreed to the mechanisms for a ceasefire, which would take effect on February 1, 1992 and conclude on October 31, 1992. The agreements led to the signing of the formal peace agreement in Mexico City on January 16, 1992,[70] which set up a three-stage process whereby the two armies would be concentrated in special

---

[68] Cristiani explained that his presence in NY signaled "flexibility" on the government side, a signal that could not be conveyed without him, as his representatives in NY did not have a mandate, to decide issues not previously discussed or agreed upon by the whole government negotiating team (interview with Ian Johnstone and Michael Doyle, San Salvador, January, 1994).

[69] S/23504, 12/31/91, annexes I and II.

[70] Mexico was perhaps the key country in the process because of its relationships with

zones, followed by the FMLN's surrendering its weapons and demobilization, and finally their return to civilian life.

On January 10, in the midst of crucial and difficult post-Agreement negotiations to resolve the many "bracketed" issues temporarily laid aside to reach an Agreement by December 31,[71] the new Secretary-General requested that the Security Council expand the mandate of ONUSAL to enable it to supervise the peace agreements, which the Council did with Security Council Resolution 729 on January 14. The signing ceremony was held on January 16 in Mexico City, and was attended by the new Secretary-General, the US Secretary of State, and the Heads of State of the Four Friends and the Central American governments. After ten years of war, 75,000 deaths, and almost two years of difficult negotiations, the possibility of peace was finally at hand.

Lessons of the UN-sponsored negotiations in El Salvador

The UN-sponsored negotiations in El Salvador involved a type of activist diplomacy which will likely prove indispensable in future UN-sponsored mediation efforts. To understand how remarkable the UN's role was, we need only to consider Alvaro de Soto's view that "the UN role in the peace process would probably have been unthinkable even a few years ago."[72]

During the early and mid-1980s, when the organization was incapable of playing a constructive and unbiased mediating role, the Contadora/Esquipulas process helped push the peace process forward, acting as a conduit between the UN and the Central American countries. One thing that this government sponsored process could not do, however, was find a satisfactory means of bringing the various insurgency movements to the negotiating table and convince them to lay down their arms for the vague and uncertain promise of political freedom. Only the UN could do that. Thus, the Secretary-General and his senior advisors "decided that we had to get directly involved" to push the process to the next level.[73]

UN sponsorship of the Salvadoran negotiations heralded a new era of multidisciplinary peacekeeping operations. Never before had the organi-

both sides and the fact that hundreds of thousands of Salvadorans had either transited through, or remained in Mexico during the war.
[71] At least one observer to these post-New Year's Eve negotiations called them "the most difficult moments of the negotiations" (cited in Baranyi and North, *United Nations Role in El Salvador*, p. 22).
[72] Alvaro de Soto, "Case study: the peace process in Central America," *Singapore Symposium*, p. 42.
[73] Interview with senior UN official, April, 1993.

zation become so involved in negotiating an end to a civil, as opposed to inter-state, war.[74] Nor, with the possible exception of the Congo,[75] had the UN and the Secretary-General played such a central role in the negotiating (as opposed to the implementation) phase of a peace process. As a senior UN official involved in the Central American peace process since the mid-1980s described it, "we weren't going to sort out the conflict with just a ceasefire. We needed to alter the face of El Salvador by alleviating as many of the root causes of the war as possible in the agreements while leaving a mechanism to deal with the rest afterwards."[76]

The UN's role in the Salvadoran peace process was pivotal, but the real key to the success of the negotiations was the "will" of both parties to finally end the war.[77] By almost all accounts conditions were ripe in El Salvador for a solution to the military conflict. First of all, the conflict in El Salvador was essentially ideological, not ethnic or religious.[78] This

---

[74] Yet the parties approached the UN as if they were engaged in an inter-state conflict, which probably helped the UN adjust to the new post-Cold War situation (see de Soto, *Singapore Symposium*, p. 49).

[75] Yet even here the differences outweigh the similarities. In the Congo the UN was brought into an immediately post-colonial situation to help restore law and order, and end foreign intervention in the newly independent country as Belgian troops withdrew. It was a situation more reminiscent of Somalia in the period before the US/UN intervened, and perhaps the Congo could have been used as an example for early and deep UN involvement in that country before the situation became so dire. Similar to El Salvador, however, was the fact that the Secretary-General used a regional "reconciliation council" composed of neighboring countries to help reconcile the opposing sides and eliminate foreign interference, which was the original aim of the Contadora countries; cf. *The Blue Helmets: A Review of United Nations Peace-keeping* (New York: United Nations Department of Public Information, second edn., 1990), pp. 374–6. *Blue Helmets*, p. 238.

[76] This attempt to alleviate the root causes of the conflict went beyond the goals of the previous UN missions, from those like UNTSO, UNEF and UNFICYP which were purely traditional peacekeeping operations, to ONUC which set up a civil administration without dealing with the root causes of the country's problems, to the election monitoring of UNAVEM and UNTAG, to organizing a national referendum as might happen with MINURSO. Only ONUSOM and UNTAC have come close, if not surpassed El Salvador in their complexity and extensiveness. The UN's involvement in Namibia was similar to El Salvador in tone, as both were "extremely political operations in which the tasks of each elements – civilian, military and police – were bonded together" (*Blue Helmets*, p. 342), and both had the political task of ensuring that a major change in the political atmosphere took place. Yet the UN's role in El Salvador differed from Namibia in that the entire peace process was UN sponsored and mediated, as opposed to the former country, as well as Angola and Cambodia, where the UN became directly involved only in the implementation phase. In contrast, in Central America the UN had to improvise and create the conditions for its successful entrance into the peace process (cf. De Soto, *The Tokyo Symposium on the Evolution of UN Peace-keeping: Recent Experiences and Future Prospects*, 3-4 September, 1991, p. 15).

[77] Interview with senior ONUSAL official, NY, April, 1993.

[78] They shared not only the same religion, ethnicity, and culture, but even more, some of the top leaders of both the FMLN and the army were schooled by the same Jesuit

made it the kind of conflict whose resolution was made easier with the end of the Cold War, as the combination of "sheer exhaustion" among the belligerents[79] and the end of superpower sponsorship left the warring parties with little option other than a negotiated settlement.[80]

The specific personalities of the major players in the peace process were also important. For his part, Secretary-General Pérez de Cuéllar (and his staff) was "remarkably able and innovative, with an active and energetic understanding of his responsibilities."[81] In fact, the involvement of Pérez de Cuéllar in El Salvador will not be "a precedent easily repeated,"[82] both because of his intimate knowledge of the region and the window of opportunity for diplomatic initiative that the immediate post-Cold War environment engendered. The present Secretary-General, Boutros Boutros-Ghali, coming in at the successful conclusion of the peace process, witnessed first hand the importance of the combination of peacekeeping, peacemaking and peacebuilding which were to be the bywords of his *Agenda for Peace*.

President Cristiani was another pivotal figure, though his role is not as universally acclaimed. Many diplomats credit Cristiani personally with being committed to human rights and reform and allowing the human rights observers in early, originally an FMLN idea. Further, once the diplomatic process began, he achieved and maintained close coordination between the military and diplomatic arms of the government. Indeed, most diplomats from the UN and Four Friends had high regard for his statesmanship and courage in leading a recalcitrant military down the path of peace, which was in many ways against its institutional

---

priests. This was, as one Jesuit close to the negotiations put it, an upper middle class conflict at the leadership level of both sides.

[79] Ambler Moss Jr., "Peace in Central America?" in *Survival*, nos. 9–10, 1990, p. 421. Similarly, in Liberia, a more constructive political atmosphere was only possible because of "exhaustion rather than [because of] any real entente" (*New York Times*, February 8, 1993, p. A2). One only has to contrast the events in El Salvador with the situation and Somalia, Angola or the former Yugoslavia to understand how peace will remain elusive as long as one party thinks it can achieve its aims on the battlefield.

[80] This echoes the situation in Southern Africa where, according to one principal participant, willingness to negotiate depended on the "collapse of the existing status quo, the elimination of the parties' unilateral options, greater balance of power in the equation, and the identification of a formula for resolution of the conflict." See Chester Crocker, *High Noon in Southern Africa: Making Peace in a Rough Neighborhood* (New York: W. W. Norton, 1992), p. 469.

[81] Thomas Boudreau, in his extensive study of the UN's Secretaries-General (*Sheathing the Sword: The UN Secretary-General and the Prevention of International Conflicts*, New York: Greenwood Press, 1991), describes how, in comparison to his predecessor Kurt Waldheim, who was reluctant to assert his office, Pérez de Cuéllar strove to make the Secretary-General's role more assertive and forthright, despite opposition from the superpowers (p. 88).

[82] De Soto, in the *Singapore Symposium*, p. 49.

interests. Many in the human rights community, however, felt he did not pursue the process in good faith and only did the bare minimum to fulfill the agreements. In addition, if the new Bush administration had not changed US policy from opposition to support of a negotiated settlement, and moreover actively pressured the Salvadoran military to accept the reforms mandated by the proposed agreements, Cristiani would never have had the political space to negotiate seriously with the rebels.

Looking at the process, it is evident that the innovations contained in the various agreements, particularly those pertaining to human rights, judicial and military reforms, were not just ends in and of themselves but also the means to reach the final ceasefire and peace agreement. It is clear, for example, how the San José Agreement on human rights served not just to improve the human rights situation in the country, but more importantly, gradually built the trust necessary to allow the FMLN to end its ten-year war against the government without obtaining the dissolution of the armed forces and power sharing with the government in return, its major historic demands. On the government side, while its priority was to end the war, not improve human rights, once it became clear that human rights could serve as a means to secure FMLN concessions and achieve a ceasefire, it supported both the San José Agreement and the early deployment of human rights monitors.

The manipulation of substantive issues of the conflict as means to achieving a settlement had its drawbacks, especially from the opposition's perspective. From the beginning of the negotiations, the government was adamant (though not publicly) that economic issues would not be substantively addressed in the peace process.[83] Thus, by most accounts the issues surrounding the armed forces received a disproportionate share of the attention during the negotiations, while land and other economic issues were put on the back burner as long as possible to placate the government.[84]

As these issues were of vital and immediate concern to the rebels, the FMLN pressed for and ultimately secured a commitment to deal with economic and social issues in the New York and final peace agreements. They were addressed hastily, however, and in hindsight it is clear that the government's concessions on these issues were more tactical than

[83] Interview with senior government negotiator, conducted by Ian Johnstone, San Salvador, January, 1994.

[84] Interview with senior UN official, NY, December, 1993. Since purging and reducing the armed forces actually strengthened the power of the president *vis-à-vis* the military, Cristiani was much more willing to negotiate these issues than risk having to make concessions on economic issues which ran counter to the emerging neo-liberal consensus among the country's business elite.

substantive, and that its view of peace was much narrower than the broad framework outlined in the agreements.[85] Unfortunately, this has meant that the very breakthroughs which convinced the FMLN to lay down its arms have been inadequately addressed in the post-conflict peacebuilding phase, thus threatening the consolidation of the peace.[86]

The UN, the Four Friends and the United States: a model for future mediation

The relationship between the United Nations, the Four Friends, and the United States and the dynamic engendered by that relationship was singularly important to the successful outcome of the peace process.[87] The UN has long worked with regional and sub-regional organizations, yet in El Salvador the UN leadership decided to avoid working with the traditional regional organization, the OAS, instead using the less official Friends format. The UN avoided bringing the OAS directly into the negotiating process not only because of the Latin American states' traditional wariness of the OAS, but also because, in the words of one senior official, working with the OAS would have been "like playing piano with four hands." That is, the all important ability for all mediators to speak with one voice would not have been possible unless

[85] Interview with opposition member of the legislative assembly, conducted by Ian Johnstone, San Salvador, February, 1994.

[86] Many FMLN and opposition figures interviewed believed that the problems encountered in the peacebuilding phase make the prospects for long-term peace and national reconciliation gloomy. An additional problem associated with implementing the economic aspects of the accords is that the hasty manner of their inclusion in the peace process meant that there was very little coordination between the UN and the IMF and World Bank during the peace process. As a result, the accords called for an ambitious reconstruction and development program on which most donor nations have not followed through (Alvaro de Soto and Graciana del Castillo, "Obstacles to peacebuilding," *Foreign Policy*, vol. 94, 1994, pp. 69–83).

[87] Olara Otunnu points out how "the external friends of the parties to a conflict play a crucial role in making it known to them that the option of reneging on an agreement is not available" (*Singapore Symposium*, p. 38). In general, the importance of the role of third parties in a negotiating process is illustrated by Benkata Raman, who points out that they help force the parties to justify rejecting peace proposals, internationalize the conflict, give legitimacy to the weaker party and facilitate a comprehensive agreement, all of which occurred in the Salvadoran case (see *The Ways of a Peacemaker*, New York: UNITAR, 1975). Further, the combination of mediators in the UN/Friends dynamic helped insure a successful conclusion to the negotiations because it combined both principal mediators – the USA and to some extent the Four Friends – who were interested parties to the dispute and who had the power and leverage to both coerce the parties and arrange worthwhile payoffs, and the neutral mediators – the UN and the Four Friends – who were not directly involved in the conflict but who could offer a low risk environment for negotiating (Tom Princen, *Intermediaries in International Conflict*, Princeton: Princeton University Press, 1992, pp. 8–25).

the UN was clearly the ultimate authority, which was unmistakably the case in its relationship with the Friends.

The informality of the Friends process allowed the mediators to expand or diminish their role as called for by the dynamics of a particular period in the negotiations. This was made necessary by the history of interventionism in Latin America, which made the "character" of UN involvement especially important.[88] The government's interpretation of the UN's role in the negotiations evidences this wariness, as from the beginning it insisted that the UN act only as an "intermediary" in the negotiations, not as a "mediator." According to government negotiators, this meant that the UN would not "lead" the negotiations, meaning it would not be in a position unilaterally to put forward proposals or act as an arbitrator. Rather, the government wanted the UN to refrain from active involvement in the negotiations unless the parties requested it to become directly involved. The FMLN, for its part, wanted the UN to play the more active role of "mediator." While originally the government accepted only the UN's "good offices," the least intensive form of involvement in the negotiations, the compromise language of "intermediary" was agreed upon because it was ambiguous enough to allow the parties, the UN and the Friends to interpret the UN's role as they wished.

The key to the success of the UN-sponsored process was that the Friends understood that the UN was the apex of this triangle. As the Secretary-General gradually took over the reins from the Contadora countries and Costa Rican President Arias in the late 1980s, he christened the reformed Four Friends as *his* Friends in order to leave no doubt as to his control of the process, and they understood this right up to the highest levels of their governments. Almost every Four Friends diplomat interviewed stressed the fact that the UN took the lead role, and that they generally followed the UN mediators' lead in formulating negotiating strategy. Only rarely did they take the initiative, doing so only at especially sensitive times when the UN needed the weight of friendly governments to push one side or the other to accept a specific compromise.

UN stewardship of the peace process paid off in several ways. While each Friend helped to balance the others' perspectives and relationships with the two parties, it was the UN and Mexico[89] which were the most unbiased mediators. They, for example, reminded the other Friends as well as the Salvadoran government of the necessity of a detailed verification mechanism if the FMLN was going to feel safe enough to lay

[88] Interview with senior UN diplomat, April, 1993.
[89] Interviews with several senior UN diplomats.

down its arms and enter the political arena. Further, the UN mediators sometimes had to fend off one or more of the Friends who wanted immediate and concrete results when some of the most difficult issues were being negotiated. Finally, only the UN mediators had the patience to remain engaged and relatively unbiased through all the ups and downs of the process.[90]

UN leadership in no way diminished the importance of the role of the Four Friends, which was as critical as it was innovative. Because of Latin America's colonial past and historic US intervention in the region, sovereignty was always a principal concern among Latin American countries. Particularly during the 1980s, the notion of a United States dominated OAS or UN monitoring or even participating in a Central American peace process was not realistic. In acting as a counter-weight to the lopsided influence of the United States in both the OAS and the UN, the Contadora countries were able to demonstrate that the Latin Americans were the ones who could "best work out their own problems without allowing outside actors to insert their own agendas."[91] Thus it was the countries of the region that succeeded in setting the terms and agenda for future mediation (the Esquipulas process) which the United States eventually accepted and adhered to.

Given the successes of these countries, the Secretary-General created an official Friends mechanism to address the concerns of the FMLN that the United States, then its enemy, had too much power (both on its own and within the OAS and UN) to interfere in the negotiations on the side of the government. The particular make up of the Friends[92] and their genuine willingness to work in unison under UN direction provided a relatively unbiased forum of peers who not only related to the Salvadorans culturally, but who also could mollify the government's concerns (being governments themselves they understood the constraints of diplomacy), even as they exerted tremendous pressure on the government (as democratic countries) to make the tough compromises at key moments in the negotiations.[93] Further, they played an important

---

[90] Further, as one senior UN diplomat remarked, it is only because the mediators, especially de Soto and Goulding, have remained so involved in watching over the implementation phase of the process that it has remained relatively on track. They have constantly pushed the Security Council to remain "seized" of the Salvadoran situation in a time when the reforms of the police hardly rank as important as the problems in Somalia, Cambodia or Bosnia.

[91] Moss, "Peace in Central America," p. 433.

[92] Spain and especially Mexico had close ties with the FMLN while Columbia and Venezuela were, because of their own history of insurrection, slightly more understanding of the government's positions.

[93] One Ambassador (interview, Washington, DC, April, 1993) described how Cristiani called him up one Thanksgiving because he needed to hear again that he had no choice

role as communicators and lobbyists, helping to convince each side that compromises suggested by the UN were fair. Equally as important, they helped push the negotiating process forward when it became bogged down in minutiae and when the UN wasn't "telling the parties what they wanted to hear" during the most sensitive moments of the negotiations.[94]

The United States played a pivotal role in the Friends process, especially in pushing the government to negotiate in good faith and the military to accept unprecedented reforms and purges. As noted above, the United States originally opposed the Central American peace process. It did so for several reasons. First, since the elaboration of the Monroe Doctrine the United States always saw Central and Latin America as its backyard, looking unkindly toward any "foreign" meddling which might interfere with its economic, political, and strategic vision for the region. Second, during the renewed Cold War period of the early 1980s it would not support any UN-based effort because it did not trust the organization to deliver a favorable settlement. Finally, it did not support the pre-UN Esquipulas process because it required no change in the Nicaraguan government while mandating required force reductions in El Salvador's military, which would both limit El Salvador's capacity to wage war on the FMLN and limit United States presence in the region in general. This was, of course, one of the principal aims of the Contadora process.

With the advent of the Bush administration, however, the United States' view of the UN and regionally based peace efforts grew more positive, especially in light of the increased cooperation between the superpowers. At first the USA was content just to "monitor" the Salvadoran negotiations and learn more about the FMLN's views, while putting pressure on the government when asked to by the Friends or the UN. According to one US official, Secretary of State James Baker in fact clearly understood that the United States' formal participation in the Friends process would hinder its effectiveness. Consequently, he was willing to keep the United States, at least officially, in the background until the dynamics of the process made a more open and direct role possible – something that occurred during the last quarter of 1991.

While some critics in the human rights community feel that the USA could have put more pressure on the government to fulfill its obligations

but to agree to certain compromises on military and judicial reform. It was the constant contact that reinforced the sense of inevitability in the difficult compromises Cristiani was forced to make.

[94] Interview with senior government negotiator, conducted by Ian Johnstone, San Salvador, September, 1993.

under the peace agreement, the FMLN grew to appreciate the critical and ultimately positive role played by the USA in the peace process, feeling that its training of the Salvadoran military has in the end helped professionalize the armed forces and reduce abuses.[95] Considering its recent antipathy toward the UN, the United States' close participation in the Friends framework and its concerted effort not to upstage the UN or force its agenda onto the other mediators was one of the harbingers of the post-Cold War UN–USA relationship. The United States was the UN's ultimate stick, and it was content to act within that framework.[96]

Together, the Friends served as an important tool for UN mediators in their delicate task of cajoling and pressuring the two sides to make the necessary compromises to achieve peace. The informal Friends process will surely prove its worth again in future negotiations as the Organization could easily encounter the same problem dealing with other official regional organizations such as the Arab League or OAU.[97]

In the wake of successful Salvadoran negotiations, Secretary-General Boutros Boutros-Ghali set up a similar arrangement for the negotiations to resolve the crisis in Haiti,[98] while the talks in Guatemala also show the influence of the Salvadoran experience, as the United States and Four Friends played a pivotal though behind the scenes role in the peace negotiations. Specifically, the importance of their being the Secretary-General's friends was demonstrated by the fact that former president Serrano, according to one Guatemalan diplomat, asked the same four to be *his* friends and not the Secretary-General's in order to retain more control over the direction of the negotiations.

More proof stems from the situation in Liberia, where the warring factions finally began searching for a comprehensive solution to their civil war only after the UN became directly involved in formerly regional negotiations. As Kenneth Noble points out regarding the renewed negotiations, "the key difference this time came from pressure from the OAU and an agreement by the UN to play a far greater role in forging a

---

[95] Interviews with several FMLN representatives.

[96] For example, it took the USA's freezing of $11 million in military aid to force Cristiani to finally remove his defense minister, as required by the Ad Hoc and Truth Commission reports and reorganize the high command of the armed forces. In line with Princen's description of the importance of a "principal mediator," both sides in El Salvador saw the US involvement as giving the negotiations a higher profile and assuring them that the other side would abide by the final outcome.

[97] The Friends process was looked at with keen interest by African governments at a 1993 Conference in Addis Ababa co-sponsored by the OAU and the International Peace Academy.

[98] In this situation the Four Friends were the United States, Canada, France and Venezuela.

settlement."[99] Here again the combination of UN and regional diplomacy succeeded where purely regional diplomacy had failed.

Conclusion

As the sixth ONUSAL report pointed out, what distinguished peace-keeping and peacemaking in El Salvador from other UN missions was that the peace agreement provided for "an interrelated series of tasks to be carried out by internal actors, and verified by the UN, with a view to generating within the State and society the necessary institutional and political conditions for the effective functioning of democracy in accordance with the rule of law while, at the same time, promoting changes in the relationship between the State and society with the ultimate goal of achieving national reconciliation and reunification."[100] That the agenda was so far-reaching reflects the farsightedness of the UN mediators and is one of the main reasons for the success of the peace process. Nothing less than a comprehensive plan which addressed the root causes of the war would have allowed the FMLN to take the risks involved in permanently forswearing their armed struggle.

Yet as the ensuing difficulties in the implementation process demonstrate, securing a peace agreement was only the beginning. The atrocities that defined life in El Salvador before and during the war went on because, as Truth Commission member Thomas Buergenthal pointed out, "no one expected to pay."[101] Thus the fundamental causes of the war must truly be addressed during the peacebuilding phase, otherwise the prospects for peace in the long term will be clouded.[102] What this means, as the UN's troubles in Angola, Nicaragua, and Mozambique illustrate, is that the same care and attention must be devoted to the implementation period – peacebuilding – as was devoted to achieving peace agreements. Moreover, the continuing inability of the international community to contribute to the process of reconciliation in such disparate crises as Bosnia, Haiti, and Rwanda attests both to the uniqueness of opportune factors in El Salvador (and perhaps also Cambodia), and the slim chance that such luck can be counted on in the

---

[99] *New York Times*, August 2, 1993, p. A2.
[100] S/25521, para. 14.
[101] Interview in *Washington Post*, March 18, 93, p. A26.
[102] Interview by Ian Johnstone with senior ONUSAL official, San Salvador, August, 1993. One feared possibility, according to Legislative Assembly Vice President Ruben Zamora, would be that the country "relapses again into a military society" (quoted in the *Christian Science Monitor*, April 2, 1993, p. 7). As of summer 1994, the major institutional changes called for in the Accords have not occurred to the degree envisioned by the UN negotiators who designed them (cf. Holiday and Stanley, "Building the peace," p. 22).

future, as the peculiar spirit of cooperation and international optimism which characterized the immediate post-Cold War period recedes further from view.

Thus the overall success of the implementation process monitored by ONUSAL will depend primarily not on the will of the international community to remain vigilant in ensuring the fulfillment of the agreements, but rather on whether the elites – especially the military and business interests – are truly desirous of peace. Only then will the "negotiated revolution" envisioned by the United Nations and the Salvadoran people truly be completed.

11 The El Salvador Peace Accords: using international and domestic law norms to build peace

Timothy A. Wilkins

Introduction

The El Salvador Peace Agreements (the Accords) represent an important step in carving out the new peacekeeping terrain between forcible intervention and respect for national sovereignty. The Accords mark the first time the government of a member state ceded to the international community a substantial role in reshaping its legal and institutional capacities. Unlike Cambodia, where the decades of civil war created a headless state,[1] the El Salvador government, identifiable and in control, granted the United Nations an extensive mandate to assist in the reformation of its military, police, judiciary, and economy. This comprehensive mandate presents a potentially powerful model for how the international community can assist in bringing democracy, human rights, and peace to a member state before the ravages of war leave it ungovernable.

Under the UN Charter, the international community can only intervene in a narrow set of circumstances. Article 2(7) prohibits the UN from intervening on matters "essentially within the domestic jurisdiction" of a member state.[2] The only exceptions are when there is a "threat to international peace and security" (chapter VII) or if the member state grants its "consent" (chapter VI). Historically, chapter VII has been invoked to halt armed attacks across borders and, most recently in Somalia and Rwanda, to alleviate humanitarian crises.[3] Chapter VI, on the other hand, has been broadly interpreted to provide the legal mandate for peacekeeping missions (sometimes referred to as chapter VI 1/2), where two disputing parties consent to a UN presence

---

[1] See Michael W. Doyle and Nishkala Suntharalingam, "The UN in Cambodia: lessons for complex peacekeeping," in *International Peacekeeping*, vol. 1, no. 2, 1994.

[2] See also General Assembly Resolution on the Declaration of Principles on Friendly Relations. "Every State has an inalienable right to choose its political, economic, social and cultural systems, without interference in any form by another State" (GA Res. 2625 (XXV), October 24, 1970).

[3] See UN doc. S/RES/794 (1992) on Somalia and S/RES/1994/935 (1994) on Rwanda.

in monitoring a ceasefire. The comprehensive settlement agreements in El Salvador expand this concept of consent even further to include monitoring human rights, supervising military restructuring, and instigating judicial reform. The duties of the international community are not specifically enumerated; rather, they are broadly defined to permit active monitoring whereby the UN has the flexibility to adopt and expand its verification responsibilities to promote compliance with the letter and spirit of the agreements.

At the heart of this comprehensive mandate lies the tension between respect for state sovereignty and the "revolutionizing"[4] of national capacities. Although handicapped by vague language and sizable omissions, the Accords effectively confront this challenge along three fronts. First, they present a unique bifurcated legal structure in which international law and Salvadoran law combine to legitimize and reinforce the parties' obligations. References to human rights conventions, customary international law and the UN Charter sit as a lattice work over a core of Salvadoran constitutional and statutory law. Second, new institutions are created to investigate human rights violations, purge the military, train civilian police, and monitor judicial conduct. These institutions promote reform where legal obligations alone are unlikely to bring about compliance. Third, the accords provide for an expanded role for the UN in verifying and monitoring the agreements. Comprehensive peace accords require time to implement and the UN's involvement as a continuous peacemaker serves to insure implementation as circumstances change and unforeseen gaps materialize.

This chapter explores each of these fronts in the five primary areas embraced by the accords: human rights, armed forces, judicial reform, civilian police, and social and economic questions. The accords can be summarized as a bargain in which the FMLN agrees to lay down its arms and join the political process in exchange for the government's agreement to end the armed conflict and make substantial political, legal, and institutional reforms. The precise legal nature of this bargain is difficult to characterize. Unlike the Paris Agreement in Cambodia, the Accords do not qualify as an international treaty since only the El Salvador state is a signatory to the agreement.[5] However, the agreements clearly have an international character stretching beyond domestic contract laws in so far as they draw heavily upon international law and

---

4   Alvaro de Soto, Special Representative to the Secretary-General, described the El Salvador peace process as a "negotiated revolution." Quoted in George Vickers and Jack Spence, *End Game: A Progress Report on the Implementation of the Salvadoran Peace Accords* (Cambridge, Mass.: Hemisphere Initiatives, 1992), p. 1.

5   See Nishkala Suntharalingam's discussion in chapter 4 on the Cambodian Agreements in this volume.

provide for an extensive role for the United Nations. The extent this international character strengthens or weakens the obligations of the parties will be explored in detail throughout this chapter.

Structure of the Peace Accords

Before embarking on an analysis of the specific provisions, it is helpful to outline briefly the legal structure of the Accords.[6] The accords were developed through a series of six principal agreements. First, the parties established a framework for the negotiation under the auspices of the Secretary-General in the Geneva Agreement (adopted in April 1990).[7] The negotiation framework had four objectives: to end the armed conflict by political means; to promote the democratization of the country; to guarantee unrestricted respect for human rights; and to reunite Salvadoran society.[8]

The second agreement, the Caracas Agreement (May 1990),[9] created a general agenda and timetable for the negotiating process. The Caracas Agreement established two phases for the process: a political phase, which sought agreement on issues such as the armed forces, the judicial system and human rights, and a reunification phase, which discussed the necessary guarantees and conditions for reintegrating the FMLN into civil, institutional and political life.

The third agreement, the San José Agreement (July 1990),[10] marked the first substantive agreement reached by the parties. The San José Agreement outlined the parties' obligations to assure unrestricted respect for human rights. The parties agreed to guarantee the security of the person, due process of law, personal liberty, and freedom of expression, association, and movement.[11]

---

[6] For a complete discussion on the negotiations leading up to each of the agreements, see Mark Levine's discussion in chapter 10 in this volume.

[7] Geneva Agreement of 4 April 1990 (UN doc. A/45/706-S/231931, annex I) (hereinafter Geneva Agreement). Texts of all peace agreements are available as official documents of the Security Council. With the exception of the subsequent lands agreement of October 13, 1992 (UN doc. S/25812/add.2) and the Agreement on a Timetable for the Implementation of the Most Important Agreements Pending of May 19, 1994 (UN doc. S/1994/612), they have been published by the United Nations in book form under the title *El Salvador Agreements: The Path to Peace* (July 1992) (hereinafter *Path to Peace*).

[8] Geneva Agreement, para. 1, *Path to Peace*, p. 1.

[9] Caracas Agreement of 21 May 1990 (UN doc. A/45/706 – S/21931, annex II) (hereinafter, Caracas Agreement).

[10] San José Agreement of 26 July 1990 (UN doc. A/44/971 – S/21541) (hereinafter San José Agreement), *Path to Peace*, p. 4.

[11] See Security Council Resolution 693 (1991) establishing ONUSAL, an integrated operation, to monitor all agreements concluded between the government of El Salvador and FMLN.

The fourth agreement, the Mexico Agreements (April 1991),[12] comprised the constitutional reforms to clarify the subordination of the armed forces to civilian authority, improve the judicial system's response to human rights, and insure the neutrality of the electoral board.[13] In addition, the Mexico Agreement established the Commission on the Truth, a neutral independent body, to investigate serious acts of violence that had occurred since 1980 in the hopes that exposing the truth would promote national reconciliation.

The fifth agreement, the New York Agreement (September 1991),[14] created an inter-party mechanism, the National Commission for the Consolidation of Peace (COPAZ), to take responsibility for monitoring the agreements and drafting secondary legislation. The New York Agreement also set forth agreements in principle on the reduction and restructuring of the armed forces, establishment of the National Civil Police, and reforms in land ownership.

The sixth and final agreement, the Chapultepec Agreement (January 1992),[15] served as the comprehensive peace accord between the two parties. It detailed agreements on the armed forces, the establishment of the National Civil Police (PNC), judicial reform, the electoral system, economic and social questions, political participation by the FMLN, and the mechanics of the cessation of the armed conflict. In addition, the agreement set forth a timetable that coordinated the stages of the ceasefire with the implementation of the political agreements.

Human rights

The promotion of human rights is at the core of the agreements to bring peace to El Salvador. The agreements rely upon an innovative mix of

---

[12] Mexico Agreements of 27 April 1991, UN doc. A/46/533 – S/23130 (hereinafter Mexico Agreements), *Path to Peace*, p. 13.

[13] The Mexico Agreement was born out of the conundrum of how to amend the constitution in order to bring about fundamental changes to state institutions. The difficulty lay in overcoming article 248 of the Salvadoran Constitution which required that constitutional amendments be approved by one legislative assembly and ratified by its successor. The parties could either amend this article or try to push through proposed reforms by April 29, 1991, the date that assembly left office. The government strongly resisted the former option, leading to a marathon negotiating session in Mexico to draft all proposed constitutional reforms by the end of the month. On April 29, 1991, the National Assembly voted to modify 35 of the 274 articles of the 1983 El Salvador constitution, marking the first time a Salvadoran constitution had ever been amended. See Mark Levine's chapter in this volume for further details related to the negotiation process.

[14] New York Agreement of 25 September 1991 (UN doc. A/46/502 – S/23802) (hereinafter New York Agreement), *Path to Peace*, p. 32.

[15] Chapultepec Agreement (Peace Agreement) of 16 January 1992 (UN doc. A/46/863 – S/23504) (hereinafter Chapultepec Agreement), *Path to Peace*, p. 46.

legal instruments, the creation of new institutions, and the establishment of UN monitoring to embolden domestic laws and institutions to protect human rights. These provisions permit the international community to play an activist role in reshaping a member state without undermining national sovereignty.

The theoretical framework for the advancement of human rights is set forth in the San José Agreement. Referring to regional and international norms, human rights is defined as "those rights recognized by the Salvadoran legal system, including treaties to which El Salvador is a party, and by the declarations and principles on human rights and humanitarian law adopted by the United Nations and the Organization of American States [OAS]."[16] This definition places the laws of the state into a broader legal context. The norms of the region, through the OAS, and of the international community, through the UN, expand the legal bases upon which the government and other parties may be found guilty of violating human rights. By appealing to international norms, the UN's mandate is expanded beyond verifying compliance to the defined rights under the agreements to the broader lexicon of international human rights law. For example, ONUSAL in its reports cites both the International Covenant on Civil and Political Rights and the Inter-American Court of Human Rights to define El Salvador's state duties to provide safeguards to promote human rights.[17]

The human rights guaranteed in the San José Agreement closely parallel many of the standard provisions of human rights conventions. The Agreement, for example, protects the freedom and integrity of the person. These provisions include prohibiting arrests of individuals exercising political rights; requiring arrests to be made by an identified, competent authority; informing arrestees of the charges against them; and the cessation of torture and incommunicado detention.[18] The Agreement also establishes a timetable for the release of political prisoners and provides for due process for detainees. Finally, the Agreement protects freedom of association, expression, and movement, including "ideological, religious, political, economic, labor, social,

---

[16] San José Agreement, preamble, *Path to Peace*, p. 7.

[17] The Covenant on Civil and Political Rights states that state responsibility can arise not only from a lack of vigilance with regard to the prevention of harmful acts but also from a lack of diligence in prosecuting perpetrators and in applying the necessary civil penalties (see UN doc. A/46/876, S/23580, para. 29 and International Covenant on Civil and Political Rights, art. 2, paras. 1–2). Similarly, the Inter-American Court of Human Rights states that state responsibility entails the duty "to organize the governmental apparatus so that they are capable of judicially ensuring the free and full enjoyment of human rights" (see *Annual Report of the Inter-American Court of Human Rights*, 1988. OAS/Ser. L/V/III. 19, doc. 13, August 31, 1988).

[18] San José Agreement, para. 2, *Path to Peace*, p. 8.

cultural, sporting" and other affiliations.[19] Trade union freedom is also specifically protected within this right.

The right to political affiliation provided the first challenge to the UN in reconciling the Peace Accords with Salvadoran state law. Article 7 of the Salvadoran Constitution bans armed organizations from participating in the political process. Since a ceasefire had not been established at the time of the negotiations, a special legal status for the FMLN had to be created to enable its participation in the political process. The Accords call for a legislative decree to legalize the FMLN as a political party with all the requisite rights, including freedom to canvas for new members, the right of assembly, and the right to join COPAZ. This legislative decree does not violate the constitution because the disarmament of the FMLN is interpreted to be "in progress" and under ONUSAL supervision. Thus, an international presence enables the parties to expand domestic legal interpretations so that they are more compatible with the peace process.[20]

The Accords further bolster human rights by creating a new post, the National Counsel for the Defense of Human Rights. The National Counsel's duties include promoting respect for human rights through public fora and advocating judicial reform; monitoring the situation of persons deprived of their liberty; investigating complaints of violations; commenting on proposed legislation; and drawing conclusions about the efficacy of state organs in protecting human rights.[21] This mandate empowers the National Counsel to press human rights cases through the dense maze of the debilitated Salvadoran criminal justice system.

Despite the National Counsel's sweeping constitutional mandate, its real authority is quite limited. First, it does not have direct jurisdiction over any matters. It can only work through other state organs. Second, the Counsel does not have political muscle to bring to bear upon state organs, relying only upon moral persuasion through "issuing reports".[22] Finally, it is beholden to the executive branch to receive funding to create the necessary human network crucial to perform its duties.

The more effective institution provided for in the Accords to monitor human rights is the UN. The UN is mandated to monitor in both the traditional sense of reporting on violations and also by taking a more proactive role in the supervision of administrative authorities. ONUSAL's traditional mandate includes the power to receive communica-

---

[19] San José Agreement, para. 5, *Path to Peace*, p. 9.
[20] See David McCormick's discussion in chapter 12 for a detailed discussion of the tenuous nature of the UN position with respect to the arms caches.
[21] Mexico Agreement, art. 16, *Path to Peace*, pp. 23–4.
[22] See Mexico Agreement, art. 16, para. 12, *Path to Peace*, p. 24.

tions from individuals or groups; visit any place freely with or without prior notice; interview any individual, group, or institution; and collect, by any means, relevant information on possible violations.[23] These traditional activities are complemented with broader powers to "offer its support" to judicial authorities, "consult" the Attorney General, and "make recommendations" to the parties.[24] These broad terms give the Mission a legal mandate to become involved in much of the day-to-day operations of the police and judicial system. Such verification builds a partnership role for the international community allowing the UN to comment and pressure for immediate responses to problems as they occur, rather than waiting for institutions to respond to secondary reports. The UN's authority, however, does not extend so far as to be immediately legally binding. The parties are required only to give their "earliest consideration"[25] to ONUSAL recommendations.

The UN's role also serves to strengthen the Agreements by promoting the cause of human rights at the normative level. The parties agree to expanding the interaction of the UN with non-government institutions and directly with individuals. The Accords state that "The Director [of the Human Rights Division] shall work in close co-operation with existing human rights organizations and bodies in El Salvador."[26] Thus, the definition of cooperation with the state is expanded beyond the traditional government-centered view of international law[27] to one that embraces other institutions. Such a mandate, therefore, breathes life into the individual-centered norm of international law commenced with the Universal Declaration of Human Rights.[28] The Mission's mandate to conduct "educational and information campaign on human rights"[29] enables the international community to address individuals not through their government but directly about their rights under the state.

Overall, the human rights provisions of the Accords provide a unique opportunity to increase the likelihood of gaining compliance to international norms. Whereas international conventions on human rights are

[23] San José Agreement, art. 14, *Path to Peace*, p. 10.
[24] Ibid.
[25] San José Agreement, para. 12, *Path to Peace*, p. 10.
[26] Ibid.
[27] For insightful discussions of the growth of international law with respect to human rights see Louis Henkin, "The internationalization of human rights," *Proceedings of the General Education Seminar*, vol. 6, no. 1, 1977; David P. Forsythe, *The Internationalization of Human Rights* (Lexington, Mass.: Lexington Books, 1991); Antonio Cassese, *Human Rights in a Changing World* (Cambridge, UK: Polity Press, 1990); Jack Donnelly, *Universal Human Rights in Theory and Practice* (Ithaca, NY: Cornell University Press, 1989).
[28] Universal Declaration of Human Rights 1948, GA Resolution 217A(III), GAOR, 3rd Ses., Part I, Resolutions, p. 71.
[29] San José Agreement, para. 14(j), *Path to Peace*, p. 11.

designed to "initiate a process, that over time, perhaps a long time, [bring] behavior into greater congruence with those ideals,"[30] a peace agreement is an urgent means to achieve an immediate result – namely, the cessation of armed conflict. The human rights mandate in the peace accord is not a vague goal, but a product of political bargaining, binding on specific parties as a necessary pre-condition to laying down arms. Moreover, the peace agreement provides a framework for the direct monitoring of human rights by the international community. Under international conventions, the UN's persuasion mechanisms are limited to jaw-boning and publication, while under the Accords, the UN has the consent of the government to directly interact with people and institutions to encourage compliance.

Armed forces

Restructuring the armed forces was a primary prerequisite to the FMLN entering into the agreements. The Truth Commission wrote, "Not one of the three branches of public power – the judicial, legislative or executive – was capable of controlling the overwhelming military domination of society."[31] Many commentators accuse the armed forces of being behind many of the most atrocious human rights violations.[32] Drafters of the Accords faced the delicate challenge of trying to reform the military while leaving it intact as a central symbol of state sovereignty. In Cambodia, this challenge was averted by the parties agreeing to a neutral role for the state, making it easier to scale back the domestic influence of the army by reducing its international role as the "defender of the state."[33] However, the El Salvador government dismissed this option, asserting that a strong military was indicative of a strong state. The FMLN, on the other hand, argued that given the

---

[30] See Abram Chayes and Antonia Chandler Chayes, "On compliance," *International Organizations*, vol. 47, no. 2, pp. 175, 197.

[31] UN doc. S/2500 Truth Commission report, at p. 190.

[32] See e.g. Human Rights Watch/Americas, *El Salvador: The Massacre at El Mozote: The Need to Remember* (New York: 1986); Lawyers' Committee for Human Rights, *El Salvador: Human Rights Dismissed: A Report on 17 Unresolved Cases* (New York: 1990).

[33] See Steven R. Ratner, "The Cambodia settlement agreements," *American Journal of International Law*, vol. 1, no. 87, 1993, pp. 32–5. ("Cambodia agrees to refrain from entering into military alliances, without prejudice to its right to acquire military equipment for self-defense and law and order; to refrain from interfering in the internal affairs of other states; to terminate treaties incompatible with its neutral status; to refrain from using its own and other states' territory to impair the sovereignty, independence, territorial integrity or inviolability of other states; and to refrain from allowing foreign forces and bases on its soil, except as approved by the United Nations to implement the settlement." Guarantees Agreement, arts. 1(2)(a)–(d), (g)–(h).) For further discussion see Nishkala Suntharalingam's chapter in this volume.

widespread corruption, a new democratic order could not emerge unless the armed forces were completely dismantled. The Accords balance these positions by recognizing the armed forces as a permanent institution but commit the forces to a radical transformation in accordance with democratic values.[34] This transformation is accomplished by placing the army firmly under civilian control and the rule of law and also purging it of known human rights violators through an Ad Hoc Commission.

The first set of reforms, designed to place the armed forces under civilian authority, are accomplished by the creation of a civilian bureaucracy to oversee the military. Although the Accords are decorated with many high-principled phrases about subordinating the army to the "will of the people,"[35] there are only two concrete mechanisms by which civilian control is likely to become operational. First, the Accords place the military under the command of the president. The president is made commander and chief and the functioning of the military is guided by legislative authority and the president. Second, the jurisdiction of military courts is limited to "purely military offenses and misdemeanors, understood to be those affecting only a strictly military legal interest."[36] Previously, under a so-called "state of exception," the army could suspend free speech, free association, and extend the period of administrative detention from seventy-two hours to fifteen days. The amended constitution forbids military courts from trying civilians accused of political crimes and having jurisdiction when the victim of a crime is a civilian.

The second area of military reforms aim to limit the army's influence in domestic affairs. In addition to an absolute reduction in the force, the army's new mission is limited "to [defending] the sovereignty of the State and the integrity of its territory."[37] The Accords differentiate carefully the terms "defense" and "security":

National defense, the responsibility of the armed forces, is intended to safeguard sovereignty and territorial integrity against outside military threat. Security, even when it includes this notion, is a broader concept based on unrestricted respect for the individual and social rights of the person. It includes, in addition to

---

[34] Chapultepec Agreement, chapter I (1A), *Path to Peace*, p. 47.

[35] See Chapultepec Agreement, chapter I (1C), *Path to Peace*, p. 47 ("The armed forces owe respect to the political order determined by the sovereign will of the people and all political or social changes generated by that will ..." Similar language is also used to describe training programs for the armed forces. They shall "emphasize the preeminence of human dignity and democratic values, respect for human rights." Chapultepec Agreement, chapter I (2), *Path to Peace*, p. 48.

[36] Mexico Agreement, art. 23, *Path to Peace*, p. 25.

[37] Mexico Agreement, II, art. 212, *Path to Peace*, p. 25.

national defense, economic, political and social aspects which go beyond the constitutional sphere of competence of the armed forces and are the responsibility of other sectors of society and of the State.[38]

This definition demonstrates both the institutional and normative shift required to reform the armed forces. Educating the army about their new status in a democratic order is part of the comprehensive agenda to diminish the military's pervasive influence in domestic affairs. The president may only deploy the army to quell domestic disorder in extreme circumstances under consultation with the legislature and after "normal means for the maintenance of domestic peace and public tranquillity and safety have been exhausted."[39] This provision transforms Salvadoran law to be more consistent with other democratic regimes.[40]

Ad Hoc Commission

The third area of reform of the armed forces focuses on the issue of military impunity. Two new institutions are created under the Accords to address this issue: the Ad Hoc Commission and the Truth Commission.[41] The Ad Hoc Commission was born after months of intense political bargaining. The FMLN claimed that the most elaborate reforms to the structure, training and operational code of the armed forces would have little effect if the current leadership remained unchanged. The government conceded that a purge of certain officers was required but advocated a self-purge mechanism whereby the military would conduct its own internal investigation and prosecution.

Under a UN-brokered compromise, the parties agreed to create a separate commission composed of three Salvadoran civilians (chosen by the UN Secretary-General) and two military observers (chosen by President Cristiani).[42] The Commission was granted full legal authority

---

[38] Chapultepec Agreement, chapter 1 (1E), *Path to Peace*, p. 47–8.

[39] Mexico Agreement, II, art. 6, para. 12, *Path to Peace*, p. 20.

[40] For example, under United States law, the president may declare martial law as part of his civil powers to enforce federal laws. Moreover, the United States president does not have any legislative check for exercising military power to command the army to combat a "domestic enemy" in a civil war. See the United States Constitution, USCA Constitution, art. 2, section 2, clause 1 and related case law.

[41] The Truth Commission's mandate reaches beyond reformation of the armed forces, as discussed below.

[42] Chapultepec Agreement chapter I (3B), *Path to Peace*, p. 50. The Secretary-General, after consulting with the parties named Abraham Rodríguez, a founder of the Christian Democratic party, who is a corporate lawyer and close associate of the late President Duarte; Eduardo Molina, formerly associated with the Christian Democratic party; and Reynaldo Galindo Pohl, an international lawyer and UN Special Rapporteur on Iran.

to investigate and make conclusions about which officers should be transferred or discharged but did not have authority to bring formal judicial prosecutions. Evaluations of the officers were to be based on three broad criteria: record of observance of the legal order, with particular emphasis on respect for human rights; professional competence; and capacity to function in the new situation of peace within the context of a democratic society.[43]

Although the Ad Hoc Commission was established to assure expediency and impartiality, its mandate rested on fragile legal ground. First, the Accords required the Commission to complete an enormous task in a very limited time frame. The Commission was given only three months to evaluate 2,293 active duty officers.[44] Second, the findings of the Commission were to be kept secret. Neither the parties nor human rights organizations would have access to the report, making it impossible to verify the fairness of the process. Third, in conducting its investigations, the Commission was not required to follow any particular guidelines for standards of evidence. The Accords simply state: "[T]he ad hoc Commission may avail itself of information from *any source* which it considers reliable."[45] This wide reach had the advantage of drawing upon non-traditional sources, like non-governmental organizations, but it left the Commission susceptible to charges of basing findings on unsubstantiated claims. The Accords required the Commission to grant a hearing to the parties before adopting its conclusions,[46] but the Commission was still not required to justify the evidence on which the conclusions were eventually based. The entire investigation remained secret with only the bare list of transfers and dismissals published. Finally, the Accords did not provide for any appeals process for accused officers. The conclusions of the Commission were final and had to be implemented within sixty days.

Although, as a matter of law, this mandate is suspect, the political realities may demand such a mandate. A separate investigative commission enables the parties to take a long, detailed process off the bargaining table and distance themselves from direct responsibility of individual personnel decisions. The government, for example, retains political

President Cristiani named two former defense ministers, General Eugenio Vides Casanova and General Rafael Humberto Larios.

[43] Chapultepec Agreement, chapter I (3A), *Path to Peace*, p. 49–50.
[44] Hampered by a lack of documentation from the defense ministry and incomplete documentation available from human rights groups, the Commission found it impossible to meet the deadline. The Commission eventually chose to evaluate only the most senior officers (232 officers) and needed an additional thirty days to file its report.
[45] Chapultepec Agreement, chapter I (3E), *Path to Peace*, p. 51 (emphasis added).
[46] Chapultepec Agreement, chapter I (3G), *Path to Peace*, p. 51.

leverage with the military by not directly signing the demise of individual officers' careers. Moreover, an ad hoc commission allows parties to skirt the entrenched prejudices of the current judicial system. However, a lack of procedural safeguards may outweigh these political advantages. The signatories to a peace accord must still convince other parties to comply. It is easier for the military to harden its resistance to the Salvadoran government when it cannot justify its actions with sound legal principles. Although one of the main tenets of the Accords is to place the military firmly under civilian control, as a practical matter, this task is more difficult without the legal high ground of a participatory and transparent process.

The Truth Commission

The second mechanism established to end impunity of the armed forces is the Truth Commission. Organized as an independent body, the Truth Commission was created to investigate past human rights abuses during the war and document who was responsible. The legal mandate of the Truth Commission differs from the Ad Hoc Commission in two important respects – the Commission is comprised of foreign members[47] and is empowered to make recommendations on institutional reform. This mandate raises troubling questions about the enhanced role of the international community in internal affairs and the legal authority of the Commission. In several areas, the Commission's findings clash directly with Salvadoran law and other provisions of the Accords.

There are only two indirect legal precedents for such a Commission. In Argentina and Chile, commissions were created to investigate human rights abuses with a view to establishing the facts or "truth" of human rights violations during the civil wars. These commissions were organized after the transition from military to civilian power had already occurred and the names of offenders were not published. They also were not established as part of a multidimensional peace accord.[48] By contrast, the El Salvador Truth Commission affords the international community a direct role in investigating past abuses of human rights as an integrated part of the UN brokered peace process.

The Truth Commission's mandate is far reaching. Its powers include

[47] The Secretary-General named Belisario Betancur, former Colombian president, Reinaldo Figeredo, former Venezuelan foreign minister; and Thomas Buergenthal, US law professor and Inter-american Human Rights Court president.

[48] For a more detailed discussion on the Argentinean and Chilean Commissions see Human Rights Watch/Americas, *El Salvador*, pp. 4–7.

full investigative authority (e.g. the ability to obtain information, conduct interviews, and visit any location without prior notice) and the "making of recommendations about the legal, political and administrative measures which can be inferred from the investigations."[49] No specific guidelines for forms of evidence are stated, rather the Truth Commission is "completely free to use whatever sources of information it deems useful and reliable."[50] Although there is not a specific deadline for implementation of the Truth Commission's recommendations, as in the case of the Ad Hoc Commission, the parties agree to "undertake to carry out the Commission's recommendations."[51] Thus, the recommendations are binding while allowing for some flexibility on the timing of implementation.

Probably nowhere else in the Accords are the tensions raised more acutely between state sovereignty and international intervention. As noted above, the Commission's powers reach beyond evaluating single individuals to proposing reorganizations of the entire state structure – military, legal, and judicial. In this manner, the Commission's task is as encompassing as the peace accords, themselves. This broad power has the potential to place the Commission and the international community in conflict with previously agreed provisions of the Accords and the delicately struck balance struck between adherence and reformation of Salvadoran law.

The most controversial element of the Truth Commission is its power to recommend institutional changes to the judicial system. Whereas other provisions of the Accords cite Salvadoran law as authoritative, the Truth Commission makes several contrary recommendations. For example:

- The Truth Commission recommended that the entire Supreme Court should resign. Under the Salvadoran Constitution, even as amended by the Accords, the justices cannot be forced to resign by another body, including the legislative and executive branches.[52]
- The Truth Commission recommended that certain individuals named in its report not be permitted to hold office for ten years. Such a prohibition violates the San José Agreement, the Salvadoran Constitution and other international human rights instruments to

---

[49] Mexico Agreement, Commission on the Truth, para. 3, *Path to Peace*, p. 30.
[50] Mexico Agreement, Commission on the Truth, para. 8(a), *Path to Peace*, p. 30.
[51] Mexico Agreement, Commission on the Truth, para. 10, *Path to Peace*, p. 31.
[52] See UN doc. 2/25812/add. 3, para. I(4), remarks. The language of the Truth Commission report does not clearly indicate that this recommendation should be binding on the parties but strongly suggests the Supreme Court should voluntarily resign.

which El Salvador is a signatory, which guarantee freedom of political association.[53]

- The Truth Commission recommended dismissal of several members of the judiciary. Under the El Salvador Constitution, only the Supreme Court has the authority to dismiss a member of the judiciary.[54]

Based on these conflicts, President Cristiani claimed that the Truth Commission acted beyond its legal authority. In a television address, he stated, "[the] Truth Commission exceeded its mandate ... the international community should understand that our country is sovereign and we have our own laws."[55] Specifically, he argued that the executive branch did not have authority to enforce actions against the judicial branch.[56] The president of the Supreme Court, Mauricio Gutierrez Castro, agreed with Cristiani and blasted the recommendations, stating flatly that "only God" could remove him from his post before his term ends in 1994.[57]

Under a strict reading of the Accords, Cristiani's and Gutierrez Castro's arguments are not wholly persuasive. The Commission's careful documentation of the failings of the judiciary with respect to the investigation and prosecution of blatant human rights violations makes it clearly within its mandate to recommend the dismissal of individual members, as an "inference from the investigation," and their bar from future public office, as a means of preventing "repetition of such acts."[58] This would include the conduct of the president of the Supreme Court which "interfered unduly and prejudicially, for biased political reasons, in the ongoing judicial proceedings."[59]

However, the Truth Commissions' recommendations do raise important article 2(7) of the UN Charter questions about interference with national sovereignty. The spirit of the consent granted the international community by the El Salvador government requires that state law and institutions be utilized to the extent that they comport with international justice. Freedom to run for political office and a system of checks and balances between the judiciary and the executive are certainly within the

[53] See UN doc. S/25812/add. 3, para. I(3) remarks.
[54] See UN doc. S/25812/add. 3, para. I(5) remarks.
[55] Channel 2 television, March 19, 1993, as quoted in *El Rescate: Report from El Salvador*, vol. 4, no. 11.
[56] Channel 2 Television, as quoted in *El Rescate: Report from El Salvador*, vol. 4, no. 11.
[57] Tracy Wilkinson, "A matter of justices," *Los Angeles Times*, March 23, 1993. See also Resolution of the Supreme Court of Justice, March 22, 1993, signed by all fourteen members of the Court denouncing the Truth Commission report as "harmful to the dignity of the administration of justice in El Salvador."
[58] Mexico Agreement, Commission on the Truth, para. 3, *Path to Peace*, p. 30.
[59] See Truth Commission report, UN doc. S/25500, annex (1 April 1993), p. 121.

realm of acceptable international norms. For the Truth Commission to make recommendations to the contrary diminishes its legal and moral authority, despite the fact that the ends sought are noble.

Moreover, although the Truth Commission did not act *ultra vires* under the Accords, its extensive powers may undermine the efficiency of this type of comprehensive peace agreement. A durable peace requires there to be negotiations and consensus on a continual basis in order to create the necessary changes to state institutions. Although using a Commission relieves the signatories from direct political fallout, it also prohibits constructive dialogue required to encourage compliance. The relatively smooth passage of constitutional amendments and secondary legislation, in contrast, can be attributed to the parties' active consultations with politicians to gain support for the peace process. The same efforts should be made with the other governmental branches.

The judiciary

The challenge of reforming the judiciary was as daunting as the restructuring of the military. The Truth Commission report described it as follows:

The judicial system was so debilitated that it became imprisoned by intimidation and vulnerable to corruption. Given that the justice system has never enjoyed true institutional independence from the legislative and executive branches, its inefficiency only increased until it became, either because of inaction or an unfortunate attitude of subservience, a contributing factor to the tragedy that the country has suffered.[60]

Without a "complete overhaul" of the judiciary, in the words of a UN report, improvements to the civilian police and human rights monitoring would have little effect.[61] Tragically, the provisions hammered out in the Accords fall short of providing the necessary mandate. One Salvadoran commentator called the efforts at judicial reform, "without a doubt the weakest link in the institutional transformation of the country."[62] Although the Accords deserve high marks for provisions on judicial independence and UN monitoring, they fail to address the systemic problem of the Salvadoran legal system that concentrates the power of judicial administration in the hands of the Supreme Court.

---

[60] Truth Commission report, UN doc. S/25500, annex, p. 62.
[61] See UN doc. A/46/935, S/24066 (June 5, 1992) (ONUSAL Fourth Report), paras. 44–5.
[62] CESPAD, "El derecho en la vila real," *El Mundo*, September 30, 1992. See also, David Holiday and William Stanley, "Building the peace: preliminary lessons from El Salvador," *Journal of International Affairs*, 1992–3, p. 423.

The Accords promote judicial independence through constitutional amendments on the election of judges, a mandatory judicial budget, and the establishment of a "career judicial system." In the past, the appointment of judges had been widely criticized as being based on political affiliation and family ties, rather than professional capabilities.[63] The Mexico Agreement seeks to establish the impartiality of the Supreme Court judges through several specific reforms. First, election of judges requires a two-thirds majority vote in the Legislative Assembly to minimize the dominance of the majority party in the process. Second, elections are staggered every three years, with one third of the judges subject to re-election each time for their respective nine-year terms. Such staggering prevents one party control of the court as political dynamics shift in local elections. However, judges' tenures are to be renewed as a matter of right unless dismissed for cause.[64] Dismissals require an affirmative vote of two-thirds of the legislature. Finally, to promote professional competence over political ties, judges shall be elected from a list of candidates representing the main schools of legal thought, drawn up by the National Council of the Judiciary, with half of the names proposed by El Salvador lawyer associations. The Attorney-General of the Republic, Chief State Counsel and National Counsel of the Defense of Human Rights are also to be elected by a two-thirds majority of the legislature. Their terms are to be three years and they must be re-elected in order to serve another term.[65]

Further, the Accords empower the judiciary by requiring that an absolute percentage of the state budget be committed to judicial institutions. The state must allocate no less than 6 percent of current income to the judiciary.[66] Under this amendment, the judiciary is no longer at the mercy of state budgetary cuts used to censure judicial conduct. Moreover, the increased budget will enable a more stable institution through higher salaries, improvements to court houses, and additions to administrative support.

A broader and more effective approach to judicial independence can be found in the mechanisms established under the Accords to create a career judicial system. The career system will afford special privileges to its members in terms of compensation, job tenure, and promotions. These guarantees will "offer judges protection so that they can carry out their duties in complete freedom, impartially and free of any influence

---

[63] See e.g. US Department of State, *Country Reports on Human Rights Practices for 1991* (Washington, DC: USGPO, 1992), p. 598.

[64] The elements of what constitutes "cause" are to be decided under later secondary legislation.

[65] Mexico Agreement, art. 14, *Path to Peace*, p. 22.

[66] Mexico Agreement, art. 7, *Path to Peace*, p. 20.

on the cases that come before them."[67] Assuring fair remuneration is also guaranteed under the career system since under the amended constitution, judges will no longer be able to take other employment.[68] This amendment ends the common practice of judges supplementing their incomes in potentially conflicting roles as counselors, state officials or notaries on matters that come before their courts. Another means of raising professional standards is the inclusion of "justices of the peace" in the career system. Justices of the peace assume a broad role in the Salvadoran legal system, which includes taking direct responsibility in the initial phases of gathering and preserving evidence in homicide investigations. In the past, most justices of the peace were not lawyers and usually were chosen based on political party loyalty.[69] Under the Accords, the Supreme Court must select justices of the peace from a list of three nominees proposed by the National Council on the Judiciary and the candidate must be a lawyer.[70] Exceptions to the lawyer rule will only be permitted in rare cases for rural areas and in such cases the term of office will be limited to one year.

The Accords also seek to overhaul the judicial system through institutional reform. The primary institution overseeing the judiciary is the National Council on the Judiciary. The National Council presides over the nomination of judges and appellate magistrates. In a political agreement elaborating the constitutional reforms, the parties agree to reshape the National Council to "guarantee its independence from the organs of State and from political parties."[71] Under prior law, the Supreme Court retained a controlling power over the Council, with Supreme Court magistrates guaranteed five out of the ten seats, one of which was empowered to cast the deciding vote. The agreement requires the Council to be representative of a broader constituency, including both judges and "representatives of sectors of society not directly connected with the administration of justice."[72] The mandate of the Council is also broadened to include the nomination of Supreme Court magistrates, intermediate court judgeships, justices of the peace and the organization and operation of the Judicial Training School.

However, because these provisions required secondary legislation to be enacted, many of the agreed upon changes to the National Council

---

[67] Mexico Agreement, art. 11, *Path to Peace*, p. 22.
[68] Mexico Agreement, art. 12, *Path to Peace*, p. 22. "No person serving as a magistrate or judge may practice as a lawyer or notary or serve as an employee of the other organs of State, except as a teacher or a diplomat on temporary assignment."
[69] See Lawyers' Committee, *El Salvador's Negotiated Revolution*, p. 8.
[70] Mexico Agreement, art. 9, *Path to Peace*, p. 21.
[71] Mexico Agreement (A)(b)(1), *Path to Peace*, p. 27.
[72] Mexico Agreement (A)(b)(1), *Path to Peace*, p. 27.

were lost. The vague language of the Accords requiring the National Council to be independent was interpreted by the legislature, through the encouragement of the Supreme Court, in ways that disabled the spirit of the agreement.[73] The General Assembly passed legislation requiring the National Council to be elected by a two-thirds majority of the Assembly, exposing the Council to the partisanship of the controlling political parties. In addition, National Council members are still vulnerable to dismissal by the Supreme Court of Justice for just cause, keeping them underneath their authority. This authority influences the behavior of those who know that the same powers that review their judgments are also responsible for their advancement. In addition, no specific provision is included to assure the presence of non-judicial members on the Council, eliminating the possibility of a civilian check on the power of the Supreme Court.

Unfortunately, the Accords only provide for a limited UN role in judicial reform. ONUSAL's mandate is "to offer its support to the judicial authorities of El Salvador in order to help improve the judicial procedures for the protection of human rights and increase respect for the rules of due process of law."[74] However, the Accords do not provide the Mission a direct hand in the actual administration of the judicial system. ONUSAL is limited to: commenting on legislation; using good offices to solve problems at the local level; and advising authorities on judicial procedure and investigative techniques. Despite its obvious limitations, this mandate still provided ONUSAL with an important role in pointing out violations of the Accords and state law.[75] For example, ONUSAL cooperated with the Prosecutor's Office on improving evidentiary techniques, intervened on behalf of prisoners denied counsel, and even taught classes on basic criminal law. In this manner, the UN served as a continuous peacemaker, publicizing new legal requirements and negotiating case by case reforms. Yet, despite these efforts, the UN's impact was minimal due to the lack of a mandate for institutional reform.

---

[73] See UN doc. A/47/596, (the Nikken Report) para. 169. This report was prepared by Professor Pedro Nikken, the independent expert appointed by the United Nations Commission on Human Rights. The report provides a complete analysis of secondary legislation for judicial reform.

[74] San José Agreement, para. 14(h), *Path to Peace*, p. 11.

[75] As the Human Rights Division noted in its Fourth Report, "Many justices of the peace and even judges of courts of first instance act with gross negligence in securing the scene of the crime, obtaining evidence, taking fingerprints, issuing arrest warrants, interrogating witnesses, having the bodies examined by experts or conducting autopsies." See UN doc. A/46/935, S/24066, para. 17.

The civil police

The creation of the National Civil Police (PNC) is designed to counter the influence of the army in domestic affairs, political persecution, and to enable the reintegration of FMLN ex-combatants back into society. The Accords meet this challenge by separating the police from the military, placing the PNC firmly under civilian command and providing for a role for the international community in training and supervising the new force.

The PNC replaces the three existing public security forces. The National Guard and the Treasury Police are to be abolished and their members incorporated into the army. The National Police will operate during a transitional period and then subsequently be abolished when the new force is fully trained and operational. The National Intelligence Directorate (DNI) will also be abolished and replaced by a new state Intelligence Agency that will be under civilian control and trained in respecting the privacy rights of Salvadoran citizens.

To assure commitment to the rule of law, the Accords set forth guidelines for training new PNC recruits. The Accords require basic qualifying standards for officers, which include the attainment of a certain education level and the pledge of commitment to democratic norms. They also provide for a means of reintegrating former FMLN fighters into the PNC to assure a neutral force. Further, a new police academy is established, the National Public Security Academy, to conduct training. The academy's mandate is unique in the specific role afforded the international community. The academy "shall be supported by experts and advisers, under a program of close international cooperation and supervision, coordinated by the United Nations."[76]

The UN is also given an extensive mandate in monitoring the National Police during the transition period. The purpose of the monitoring is to promote a feeling of security that enables the Salvadoran people to exercise their democratic rights freely. To achieve this goal, the role of UN monitor/specialist is expanded beyond mere verification responsibilities. "The tasks of those specialists shall include, in addition to cooperating in ensuring a smooth transition and assisting police authorities, that of accompanying officers and members of the National Police (PN) in the performance of their duties."[77] This mandate surpasses mere verification by supporting the rule of law through advising on proper procedures and directly supervising

[76] Chapultepec Agreement, chapter II (7)(B)(d), *Path to Peace*, p. 70.
[77] Chapultepec Accords, chapter II (7)(B)(f), *Path to Peace*, p. 71.

implementation.[78] UN monitoring, thereby, will serve to deter intimidation while promoting impartial and non-discriminatory enforcement by local authorities.

The chapter on civil police in the Accords suffers from only two significant omissions. First, the agreements do not outline the process of how the National Police is to be phased out or who may serve in the force until it is completely replaced by the PNC. Similar to the issue of the purification of the armed forces, the timing of the implementation of the civil police was critical. The government exploited this loophole by redeploying National Police forces beyond the deadline and also by transferring officers from the Treasury Police and the National Guard to the National Police.[79] Although these transfers did not legally breach the letter of the Accords, ONUSAL made it clear that this activity clearly violated the spirit of the agreements. Second, the Accords do not address the role of the Municipal Police under the civilian police chapter. The Municipal Police are reportedly responsible for numerous human rights abuses.[80] Since many citizens may come in closer contact with these forces than the National Police, this oversight in reform may undermine the goal of providing a true sense of security to the Salvadoran people.

Despite these difficulties, the role of the UN, through a flexible mandate, appears to be an excellent model for the international community in assuring peace through activist police monitoring. UN actions moving from the policy centers of an operation down to the level of the patrol car give it the widest impact on promoting lasting peace.

Economic and social questions

The civil war left a half million persons displaced, created approximately 45,000 refugees, and engaged thousands as combatants. Despite these jarring statistics, economic issues were focused on late in the peace process and largely overlooked in the Accords. De Soto and del Castillo wrote, "the chapter on economic and social issues, of which the transfer of land is a crucial part, was a jerry-built, last minute compromise that

---

[78] See UN doc. S/23402, para. 5.

[79] See UN doc. S/25812, paras. 40–1 and UN doc. S/23999, para. 30. A separate agreement accompanying the New York Agreement provided that 60 percent of the PNC force would be non-combatants and 20 percent each could be ex-FMLN and ex-National Police.

[80] ONUSAL reported that the municipal police systematically made arrests that rarely met the minimal legal requirements. "[The Municipal Police's] repression has extended to large sectors of the population ... through procedures that flagrantly violate due process of law." UN doc. A/46/955, S/24375, para. 57.

left many loose ends."[81] Although the Accords were later supplemented by a land reform proposal offered by the Secretary-General (the October Program),[82] they are still hampered by convoluted language and sizable omissions.

The Accords call for land transfers to former FMLN and army combatants as well as to squatters who occupied land in the conflict areas during the war. The land transfer program was considered to be the principle mechanism for reintegrating ex-combatants into civilian society.[83] The Agreements set forth the following vague procedures for land exchanges:

- private land to be transferred shall be voluntarily offered for sale by their owners;
- transfer shall take place at market prices;
- beneficiaries shall repay the government loans following the agrarian reform terms of payments;[84]
- preference shall be given to ex-combatants of both sides;
- landholders shall not be evicted from the land they presently occupy until a satisfactory legal solution for the land tenure is determined and they shall be given financial support to increase production.

The responsibility for the administration of this ill-defined process is delegated to a special commission appointed by COPAZ. The commission is to verify the inventory of land and buildings within the conflict zones, use good offices to settle disputes, and "take any decisions and measures it deems necessary and proper for the prompt and effective fulfillment of the agreements."[85]

This broad mandate, in practice, is unworkable. The Accords are silent about the total number of beneficiaries, the size of the plots to which they are entitled, the amount of government credit available to beneficiaries and the practical arrangements under which the land is to be transferred. In addition, the term "conflict zone" is never defined, making it unclear which parcels of land qualify. Only some of these issues are resolved in the October Program.[86] Under the October Program, the total number of beneficiaries is set at 47,500 people (broken down as approximately 7,500 former FMLN combatants

---

[81] Alvaro de Soto and Graciana del Castillo, "Post-conflict peace-building in El Salvador: strains on the United Nations system," May 1993, unpublished, p. 11.

[82] See UN doc. S/25812/add.2.

[83] For a complete description on the land transfer program and other economic reforms see Graciana del Castillo's discussion in chapter 14 of this volume.

[84] The terms are for over thirty years, with a four-year grace period for principal and interest, and a fixed annual interest rate of 6 percent.

[85] Chapultepec Accords, chapter V (3)(D), *Path to Peace*, p. 80.

[86] See UN doc. S/25812/add.2, para. 4.

including the war disabled; 15,000 former combatants of the Salvadorian armed forces; and 25,000 landholders).[87] However, the October Program still does not define conflict zones and does not address many of the practical arrangements of the transfer process.

The COPAZ special commission proved completely ineffective at mediating disputes. ONUSAL eventually stepped in to mediate. ONUSAL reported, "Notwithstanding the role assigned to COPAZ by the agreements, which COPAZ has not been able to discharge in full, ONUSAL has, at the request of the parties, used its good offices to help the two sides to tackle the land issue in a constructive spirit at the highest level."[88] This intervention exemplifies one of the most successful attributes of the broad responsibilities afforded the UN. Even without a specific mandate, by making itself available to the parties, the UN was able to fill an important gap left by the Accords.

The Accords provide clearer direction in the area of economic reform but still are riddled with important omissions. The economic proposals are general and designed more to generate goodwill rather than practical consequences. Given the detail of the other agreements and the importance of this area, such an omission is troubling and may present the greatest threat to maintaining a durable peace. There are four broad economic measures set forth in the Chapultepec Agreement.

First, there are measures to alleviate the social cost of structural adjustment programs. These measures include a consumer protection bill, privatization of certain industries to afford workers access to ownership, and social welfare programs to alleviate extreme poverty.[89] The mechanics of these programs are not detailed in the Accords but require secondary legislation to be fleshed out.

Second, the government is to provide legal and institutional facilities to aid former combatants access to external aid, including non-government organizations, communities and social organizations.[90] This provision provides a window of access for the international community to provide care if the national welfare structure proves inadequate.

Third, the Accords call for a Forum for Economic and Social Consultation.[91] The Forum is to be comprised of representatives of the government, labor, and business community who will consult on a regular basis "for the purpose of working out a set of broad agreements on the economic and social development of the country for the benefit of

---

[87] UN doc. S/25812/add.2, para. 4.   [88] UN doc. S/23999, para. 56.
[89] Chapultepec Agreement, chapter V, para. 6, *Path to Peace*, p. 82–3.
[90] Chapultepec Agreement, chapter V, para. 7, *Path to Peace*, p. 83.
[91] Chapultepec Agreement, chapter V, para. 8, *Path to Peace*, p. 83–85.

all its inhabitants."[92] This platform sounds ideal in theory, but in practice, may offer nothing more than a debating society to air views without having to commit to any substantive steps. There is nothing in the Forum's mandate, other than the vague hope of certain "proposals" the government will make with respect to labor relations and disadvantaged areas,[93] that suggests the government is legally bound to make any concessions that will guarantee a new economic order.

The fourth economic provision, also substantially without legal teeth, is the requirement to formulate a National Reconstruction Plan to be prepared by the government in consultation with the FMLN. The Accords require the Plan to meet four broad objectives: to facilitate the reintegration of ex-combatants into the country's civil, institutional, and political life, through agriculture and other activities; to address economic, social, and environmental problems resulting from the war; to rebuild the damaged infrastructure network; and to promote solidarity among the productive sectors of the country.[94] These broad idealistic goals are not supported in the Accords by any concrete mechanisms to set them in motion. The FMLN can only make "recommendations and suggestions" and the plan will still be dependent on securing international aid. However, there are no specific provisions stipulating promises by the donor community to support any particular projects.[95]

Therefore, of the four economic reforms, only the measures to alleviate social costs of the structural adjustment programs offer anything very concrete. Ironically, these programs are only designed to tie the El Salvador people over until economic prosperity ensues. However, without a macroeconomic plan, there is good reason to believe such prosperity is still quite a ways off – raising the very real question about how long ex-combatants, with no land or economic opportunity, can be expected to wait peacefully.

Lessons

The next peacekeeping challenges for the UN may well come not from military aggression across national borders but from internal situations

---

[92] Chapultepec Agreement, chapter V, para. 8, *Path to Peace*, p. 83.

[93] For example the government shall propose that "existing labor legislation be revised in order to promote and maintain a climate of harmonious labor relations" and "the situation of disadvantaged urban and outlying urban communities be analyzed with a view to proposing solutions to problems resulting from the armed conflict." See Chapultepec Agreement, chapter V, para. 8, *Path to Peace*, p. 84.

[94] See Chapultepec Agreement, chapter V, para. 9, *Path to Peace*, p. 85.

[95] See Alvaro de Soto and Graciana del Castillo, "Obstacles to peacebuilding," *Foreign Policy*, vol. 94, 1994, p. 69 for a detailed analysis of the problems of coordinating UN peacemaking activities with international development organizations.

of member states. The parties to these conflicts are likely to seek an extensive international presence in the reshaping of state institutions while insisting that sovereignty rights not be compromised. The El Salvador Accords offer several important lessons, pro and con, on drafting solutions to this inherent paradox.

First, peace agreements to civil conflicts should draw upon both international and national legal instruments to reinforce the parties' obligations. The human rights provisions in the San José Agreement are particularly strong because they re-emphasize the parties' prior obligations under state and international law. Underscoring obligations under El Salvador law reverses a customary trend of disregarding the rule of law. Moreover, appealing to regional norms in the OAS and obligations in the UN Charter expand the normative base of the rule of law beyond state boundaries. With the consent of the parties, the international community can now directly monitor and promote compliance with international norms while simultaneously preserving the peace. In this manner, the El Salvador Accords contribute to the customary law trend establishing the protection of human rights as a prerequisite to peace.[96]

Second, the international legal status of peace agreements can be further strengthened by encouraging "friend" states to become signatories to the accords. In the Cambodian agreements, neighboring countries and permanent members of the Security Council became signatories to the agreement, binding them to various obligations to support the peace process. Their signatures changed the character of the agreement from being a contract between several domestic parties to a treaty between international states.[97] In El Salvador, the Four Friends of the Secretary-General played a crucial role in the peacemaking negotiations but ultimately did not sign the agreements. Besides the two parties, only the Secretary-General and his Special Representative signed as witnesses. Having the "Friends" sign the Accords would have created two benefits. First, it would have raised the Friends' commitments to further the peace process, in terms of technical training and development assistance, to the level of legally binding obligations. Second, the agreements would then fall under the definition of a treaty – an agreement between states governed by international law.[98] As a treaty, the Accords would benefit from the rich public international law lexicon

---

[96] For a well documented discussion of the "symbiotic linkage among democracy, human rights and peace" in international law see Thomas M. Franck, "The emerging right to democratic governance," *American Journal of International Law*, vol. 46, 1992, quote on p. 89.

[97] See Nishkala Suntharalingam's chapter in this volume.

[98] See Vienna Convention on the Law of Treaties, UKTS, no. 58, 1980, Cmnd 7964; 1155 UNTS 331; 8 ILM 679 (1969); art. 2.

related to treaty interpretation and enforcement, including taking disputes before the International Court of Justice.[99]

Third, fundamental changes to state institutions are best accomplished through constitutional amendments. The constitutional reforms advanced in the Mexico Agreements may be the most long-lasting developments of the peace process. The reforms to subordinate the armed forces to civilian authority, establish a national civil police and empower the independence of the judiciary are less susceptible to later reversal.[100] The reach of the Peace Accords, alone, is more ambiguous. As a legal document, it only binds the signatories. The president of the El Salvador Supreme Court has argued that the Accords are not binding on the judiciary since only the executive branch of the government is a signatory. (The same argument could apply to the legislature.) In the same vein, it is not clear who will advocate the FMLN's rights under the Accords if it later fragments or disappears as a coherent party. Although both of these issues are debatable under international law, their potential for controversy demonstrates the difficulty of assuring compliance to peace accords solely by their own terms. It is better to secure fundamental changes at a constitutional level where all traditional state mechanisms are securely in place to promote compliance. The El Salvador Accords can only be faulted for not going far enough – in particular, constitutional reforms to the judiciary focused too narrowly on promoting judicial independence from other branches of government and not on creating *internal* checks to diminish the domination of the Supreme Court.

Fourth, accords should rely sparingly on secondary legislation to accomplish future reform. Certainly, secondary legislation has many advantages. It frees negotiators from hammering out minute details at the bargaining table, raises the legal authority of agreements to statutory obligations, and broadens legislative support for final agreements. In this manner, the political reform effort is strengthened by a more democratic process. However, the experience in El Salvador points to the many pitfalls of this approach. Of primary concern is the fact that legislation is slow. In a timed accord where actions on political agreements are synchronized to disarmament, delays in passing legislation risk unraveling the peace process. Postponements, for example, in passing legislation to create the rules and regulations of the police academy and

---

[99] See generally O. Schachter, *International Law in Theory and Practice* (Boston, Mass.: Martinus Nijhoff, 1985), chapter V; and Ian Johnstone, *Michigan Journal of International Law*, vol. 12, no. 2, 1991, p. 371–419.

[100] This idea was also expressed by President Cristiani in a recent interview by Ian Johnstone, January 25, 1994.

for deploying the civil police substantially raised tensions between the parties.[101] In addition, legislation is subject to the volatility of electoral politics and, as passed, may not reflect the parties' original intentions. Such was the case with the establishment of the National Council for the Judiciary, which did not receive the necessary legislative mandate to overcome the vertical nature of the judicial system. Finally, the legitimacy of the enacted laws depends on free and fair elections leading to broad representation in the legislature. Since the FMLN had a poor showing in the March 1994 elections, it is less likely that new laws related to judicial and economic reform will adequately incorporate their views or get passed at all. Bargaining power, therefore, may become weaker post-elections than it was at the time of the negotiations.

Fifth, the mandate for ad hoc institutions created by accords should include clear procedures to guarantee due process and be limited to well defined and manageable tasks. The Ad Hoc Commission and the Truth Commission both served critical roles in the peace process but could have had a broader impact if their mandate had been more carefully crafted. What the Ad Hoc commission gained in expediency through bypassing the judicial system, it lost in legitimacy by not employing clear standards of evidence, not justifying its conclusions and not having a fair procedure for appeals. Similarly, the Truth Commission's fundamental purpose of achieving national reconciliation may have been undermined by its mandate. Although its recommendations were within the broad language of the Accords, they were contrary to the spirit of the bargaining process. It prohibited the parties, themselves, from building broader support through consultation with non-signatories to the agreements. This difficulty may be overcome in future commissions by either limiting such commissions to fact finding – turning the evidence over to state institutions to implement – or by making them participatory – where representatives of the parties jointly discover the truth under a flexible deadline. However, the realities of the negotiation table must govern, on a case by case basis, as to whether short-cut procedures are necessary to reach a political agreement to end the conflict.

Sixth, inter-party mechanisms designed to draft secondary legislation and monitor agreements only serve useful facilitating roles when given clear mandates and backed by the political will of the parties. COPAZ was most successful at hammering out details to agreements the basic premises of which had already achieved broad support, such as the guidelines for human rights monitoring and demobilization of the FMLN. COPAZ, however, was ill equipped to engage in ongoing

---

[101] See UN doc. S/5812, paras. 40–3.

negotiations to bring about consensus on issues to which the parties were still far apart. For example, COPAZ failed to establish a successful land reform policy because the parties, themselves, had not reached agreement on the most fundamental questions, including land designation and tenant eligibility. The role of arbiter is best delegated to the UN, a neutral party, which can draw upon its experience in negotiating the initial agreement and in peacemaking generally.

Seventh, a broad mandate should be afforded the UN, as was given to ONUSAL, in monitoring and supervising the agreements. The El Salvador Accords do not precisely enumerate the specific duties of the UN. In such circumstances, the UN should interpret its mandate broadly and actively assume the role of advisor, instructor, promoter and supervisor. This position allows the UN much greater flexibility to respond to crises as gaps and contradictions in the Accords materialize. A synchronized agreement, in particular, requires an active UN to evaluate the severity of breaches and play the role of peacemaker to forge new commitments.

Finally, the cost of implementation of a peace program should be written into the agreement. There are no references in the Accords to how costly programs such as the establishment of the civilian police, land distribution, and economic reconciliation will be funded. The clear obligations mandated to the international community in monitoring the peace also should be spelled out for institutions assisting in the area of financing and long-term economic development.[102] A peace accord without a well defined mechanism for financial support will not endure no matter how fervent the commitment of the parties and the international community.

[102] See de Soto and del Castillo, "Obstacles to peacebuilding," p. 64.

12 From peacekeeping to peacebuilding: restructuring military and police institutions in El Salvador

David H. McCormick

Introduction

On January 16, 1992, in a solemn ceremony in Mexico City's Castle of Chapultepec, representatives of the Salvadoran government and the Farabundo Mart National Liberation Front (FMLN) signed a comprehensive peace agreement ending twelve years of bloody civil war that left approximately 75,000 dead. So began a healing process designed to help Salvadoran society achieve an era of enduring peace. This momentous occasion also marked a transition of a different sort, as the role of the United Nations in El Salvador broadened from mediation efforts to an involvement in peacekeeping and post-conflict peacebuilding unprecedented in UN history. This chapter focuses on this second transition and the role played by UN military and police observers in post-conflict operations in El Salvador.

UN post-conflict efforts may be viewed as lying on a continuum of interdependent and sequential activities. At one end of the continuum is traditional peacekeeping – confidence-building measures such as verifying ceasefires and demobilizations, and more recently, monitoring public security forces. At the other end is peacebuilding – assistance and support for the reform or creation of national institutions and social and economic development. Somewhere in the middle, with the transition from peacekeeping to peacebuilding, the UN's focus necessarily shifts from reducing tensions and building confidence to creating conditions that facilitate lasting changes in a society.

A thicket of controversy surrounds the question of how far the UN should travel along this continuum, particularly in the direction of institutional reform. In the absence of functional governmental structures, for example, the UN could become involved in efforts aimed at creating new national institutions by temporarily assuming civil

The author wishes to thank the Princeton Center of International Studies for its generous support for this research. In addition, Ian Johnstone, Amy Richardson, and William Stanley offered valuable comments on earlier drafts.

responsibilities and helping to build national institutions from the ground up. Alternatively, the UN may be less ambitious in peace-building by simply expanding peacekeeping responsibilities to include monitoring, verifying, and, perhaps, assisting reform within existing national institutions, as in El Salvador.

The case of El Salvador demonstrates that overseeing reform within existing institutions raises different, but no less daunting, challenges than building them from scratch. Monitoring, verifying, and assisting reforms within a society rife with corrupt or deficient governmental structures – reforms that wrest power and influence from those required to implement them – is no small undertaking. The effectiveness of the United Nations Observer Mission in El Salvador (ONUSAL), therefore, is important not only for the Salvadoran peace process, but also as a test case that will sharpen the debate over the appropriate design and objectives of future UN post-conflict operations.

This chapter touches on a number of inextricably linked issues concerning not only the composition and effectiveness of ONUSAL, but also the nature and viability of UN post-conflict efforts more generally. It sheds light on three important questions: First, in what specific ways can the UN contribute to enduring peace in post-conflict situations? Second, how should the UN define its post-conflict responsibilities? And, third, how can the UN most effectively carry out the responsibilities of this mandate?

An objective analysis of the UN's contribution to the Salvadoran peace process informs the first question. To address the second, it is essential to consider whether ONUSAL's mandate was cost-effective, whether it recognized the inherent limitations of UN action, and whether it was consistent with role stipulated for the United Nations by the Peace Agreement. Finally, an answer to the third question requires evaluation of ONUSAL's methodology – how it interpreted and carried out the provisions of this mandate. It also requires consideration of operational issues such as ONUSAL's organizational structure, composition, and logistical capabilities. And, because the USA and other nations provided bilateral assistance for institutional reform to El Salvador, it is important also to evaluate what role the UN played in integrating this assistance into the overall peace process.

This chapter focuses on the third question – how the UN interpreted and carried out its mandate in El Salvador – by examining the activities of ONUSAL's military and police divisions. By concentrating on this third question, valuable insight into the first two is also gained. The following pages trace events beginning with the cessation of conflict in February 1992 and continuing through December 1995. The analysis is in three sections. The first two sections examine five specific post-conflict UN activities. The first evaluates the traditional peacekeeping missions executed by ONUSAL, and the second assesses UN peace-building efforts. The concluding section is a compilation of policy-relevant observations and recommendations.

Building confidence: peacekeeping

Peacekeeping activities are confidence-building measures which assist nations or factions that are weary of war, but wary of one another, to live in relative peace and eventual comity. By observing and reporting on the behavior of both sides, UN peacekeepers reassure the parties that they will not be caught unaware, and this helps to consolidate peace. Previous observer missions have fulfilled this critical role by monitoring ceasefires and the separation of forces, disarming, and demobilizing armed forces, and monitoring public security functions in the aftermath of conflict.[1] While the UN has enjoyed some success with the first two of these endeavors, its experience with monitoring public security functions is less extensive and certain.[2]

El Salvador is unique because the nature of the UN's involvement in all three of these activities is unprecedented. The UN's active participa-tion in the cessation of armed conflict, consisting of the ceasefire and separation of forces, was in the words of one seasoned military observer, "remarkably smooth compared to [previous] operations."[3] In addition, ONUSAL was only the second UN mission to assist with the demobilization of a guerrilla army and the first to be so deeply involved in the reinsertion of guerrillas into civilian life.[4] Finally, the ONUSAL police division was more actively engaged in the monitoring of public security and the promotion of human rights than UN missions in Cambodia, Namibia, or elsewhere. An analysis of these three activities in El Salvador is useful for considering the nature and viability of future peacekeeping practices elsewhere.

---

[1] W. Durch and B. Blechman, *The Evolution of UN Peacekeeping* (New York: St. Martin's Press, 1993), p. 3.

[2] The frustrations suffered by UN civilian police observers while monitoring public security in Namibia and Cambodia highlight the difficulties inherent to such operations. For an overview of UN involvement in Namibia see *The Blue Helmets: A Review of United Nations Peace-keeping* (New York: United Nations Department of Public Information, second edn., 1990), pp. 374–6.

[3] Interview with ONUSAL military observer, August 1993.

[4] The first case was Nicaragua. See Durch and Blechman, *The Evolution of UN Peacekeeping*, p. 453.

The cessation of armed conflict

ONUSAL's activities during the cessation of armed conflict were, perhaps, the most successful aspect of the UN's involvement in the peace process. The ceasefire agreement required that both the Salvadoran armed forces (FAES) and the FMLN concentrate their forces into specified locations by March 2, 1992, and that the FMLN begin demobilizing soon thereafter.[5] In preparation for carrying out the UN responsibilities enumerated in the Peace Agreement, the Security Council passed Resolution 729 on January 14, 1992. More than one hundred military observers were transferred almost immediately from the UN's Mission in Nicaragua (ONUCA) to help verify El Salvador's ceasefire. Military observers supervised the concentration of roughly 63,000 members of the Salvadoran armed forces and 8,000 FMLN guerrillas into their respective assembly areas over a 30-day period. In support of this process, UN observers reported and verified troop movements, reassuring both sides of the sustainability of the ceasefire. Following the separation of forces, observers were attached to FAES and FMLN units and responsible for monitoring them for the next eleven months.[6]

In mid-March, controversy flared as the Salvadoran government charged that the UN was partisan in its dealings with the FMLN and that the guerrillas had failed to consolidate their forces, submitted grossly inaccurate weapons inventories, and regularly violated the consolidation zones.[7] The FMLN, in turn, argued that the government had failed to dissolve the Treasury Police and National Guard as required by the Accords. To a certain extent, the complaints of both sides were well founded: the dissolution of the security forces was behind schedule and logistical shortcomings had precluded the immediate concentration of FMLN forces.[8]

Efforts by ONUSAL to defuse this explosive situation surpassed the

[5]   The timetable was designed by negotiators to insure that the FMLN's demobilization was synchronized with the institutional reforms of the government in hope of building mutual trust between the two parties during the process.

[6]   The military division deployed the majority of its 268 personnel throughout the country beginning in late January and continuing through mid-December 1992. Once the forces were consolidated, UN observers ensured that neither individuals nor units left the zones without authorization. Briefing from ONUSAL military division, August 1993.

[7]   Interview with US military official, US Embassy, San Salvador, August 1993. In this case, and a number which follow, the names of the individuals responsible for the citation are withheld upon their request.

[8]   The situation was fueled by genuine mistrust on both sides, as well as political posturing in which both parties sought to stretch the provisions of the agreement as much as possible. Interviews with ONUSAL officials, August 1993.

expectations of its mandate and are an example of the activist approach to verification that characterized UN efforts during this phase of the peace process.[9] Under-Secretary-General Marrack Goulding immediately flew to El Salvador on March 18 and pressured both parties to give assurances that they remained committed to the peace process.[10] ONUSAL served as mediator by providing a forum in which the government and the FMLN voiced their grievances and negotiated adjustments to the timetable (FAES accusations regarding FMLN weapons inventories are addressed shortly). Finally, in order to overcome critical logistical shortages in FMLN consolidation zones, ONUSAL's military division, in concert with representatives from the United Nations Development Programme (UNDP), the United Nations High Commission for Refugees (UNHCR), and other non-governmental organizations, transported and distributed potable water and provided sanitary facilities and temporary shelter.[11] By late March, these efforts proved successful as the majority of the FMLN was concentrated in the designated areas, and the peace process advanced in accordance with a revised timetable.[12]

Demobilization of the FMLN

During the same period, the military division also verified the dissolution of the military structure of the FMLN and assisted with the reinsertion of FMLN ex-combatants into civil society. As with similar operations in Nicaragua, military observers aided the transition by issuing formal identification certificates and small sums of money to ex-combatants.[13] The UN also was charged with the difficult responsibility of verifying the destruction of all FMLN weapons. Throughout the demobilization period, the FAES and ONUSAL charged that the FMLN had not turned in large quantities of its most sophisticated weaponry and urged it to be more forthright with future inventories. On December 14, 1992, however, despite government protests, ONUSAL accepted the FMLN's

[9] The Human Rights Division coined the term "active verification" to describe its approach to verification responsibilities. See Ian Johnstone's, *Rights and Reconciliation: Un Strategies in El Salvador*, International Peace Academy Occasional Paper (Boulder, Col. and London: Lynne Rienner, 1995), p. 17.

[10] See Stephen Baranyi and Liisa North, *Stretching the Limits of the Possible: UN Peacekeeping in Central America*, The Aurora Papers (Ottawa: The Canadian Center for Global Security, 1992), p. 30.

[11] For a more detailed discussion of the UNDP's role see Margaret Popkin's *Human Rights, Development and Democracy: Experience of the UN in Post-Conflict El Salvador*, UNDP working paper, April 15, 1993.

[12] Briefing from the ONUSAL military division, August 1993.

[13] Interview with ONUSAL official, August 1993.

assurances and officially verified its final weapons inventories, thereby opening the way for its legalization as a political party. Six months later, on May 23, 1993, an undisclosed FMLN weapons cache exploded in Managua; soon after, numerous other caches were discovered.

This series of events raises questions concerning the accuracy of UN verification efforts and highlights their inherent limitations. In a letter to Shafik Handal, Coordinator-General of the FMLN, Secretary-General Boutros-Ghali expressed his distress and disappointment in learning that the final FMLN inventories presented to the UN were grossly inaccurate.[14] In reality, however, an objective observer must question whether "secret" FMLN weapons caches were really a secret at all to the UN or other observers in El Salvador. ONUSAL military personnel acknowledged privately that many suspected that the FMLN had maintained significant weapons stockpiles.[15] If such suspicions did exist among senior UN officials, subsequent events proved them accurate. Following the explosion, and at the urging of the Secretary-General, the FMLN leadership disclosed the locations of over one hundred remaining weapons caches (later cataloged and destroyed by the UN) and publicly announced that the FMLN would not assume responsibility for future weapons discoveries. Fortunately, the long-term effects of this incident on the peace process were minimal. The FMLN suffered politically for its duplicity. The UN endured momentary embarrassment.[16] But, the peace process continued, albeit slowly, in the months that followed.

In contrast to the UN's successful verification activities during the cessation period, the discovery of the weapons caches highlights the inevitable limitations of such efforts. When the FMLN failed to yield to political pressure, the UN presumably took a gamble: ONUSAL verified what clearly were questionable weapons inventories in order to facilitate the certification of the FMLN as a political party, thereby advancing the peace process. In retrospect this decision appears justified. It is not clear that alternative actions would have had more desirable outcomes. From a practical standpoint, the UN was incapable of verifying, with any degree of certainty, that all of the FMLN weapons had been collected.

[14] UN doc. S/26005, p. 1.

[15] As one observer noted, "It was obvious that the weapons and equipment inventoried were not consistent with the types of military operations that the FMLN had been waging, nor the numbers of ex-combatants that were demobilizing." Interview with ONUSAL military observers, August 1993.

[16] As one senior government official remarked, "We were surprised and disappointed when ONUSAL verified the FMLN inventories, but now it is the UN and the Secretary-General who have had to pay the price." Interview with General Mauricio Vargas, Deputy Chief of Staff, Office of the President, August 1993.

Nor was it possible to conduct the type of investigation necessary to confirm or deny such allegations. More forceful political pressure from the UN might have compelled the FMLN to comply, but it might have had no effect at all. Though it seems unlikely, it might even have induced the FMLN to withdraw from the peace process altogether. If the UN did indeed harbor suspicions concerning the inventories it could, perhaps, have hedged its bets by voicing doubts more openly prior to verification, but in general, UN actions should be viewed as a politically sophisticated response to a complex and difficult situation. In this case the gamble paid off. Obviously, however, such "high stakes games" should be avoided, when possible, in the future.

Monitoring public security

A third ONUSAL peacekeeping responsibility was the monitoring of public security during the transition period. The ONUSAL police division was established in the beginning of February, and eventually placed under the command of Uruguayan General Homero Vaz Bresque.[17] Due in large part to the notorious human rights record of the Salvadoran public security forces during the 1980s, the Peace Accords were designed to separate national defense and internal public security functions.[18] They required that the National Guard and Treasury Police be abolished, and the approximately 7,000-man National Police (PN) force be incrementally eliminated during a twenty-four-month transition period to a new National Civil Police (PNC).[19] UN police observers were assigned responsibility for accompanying National Police patrols and monitoring their performance.[20]

ONUSAL enjoyed only marginal success in this endeavor. The

---

[17] By the end of March, only 285 of the promised 631 international police observers had arrived in El Salvador. As a result, the projected strength was reduced to 362, two-thirds of which were provided by Mexico and Spain. ONUSAL personnel report, March 1992.

[18] Public Security functions during this period were carried out by three forces: the National Police, the Treasury Police and the National Guard. The public security forces were under the control of the military with military officers rotated regularly to commands in all three. "El Salvador update: counterterrorism in action," *El Rescate*, 1987.

[19] Recently released CIA and State Department Documents confirm what many Salvadorans and human rights groups had known all along: the three primary public security forces during the 1980s – the National Police, National Guard, and Treasury police – were frequently involved in violent killings, torture, and kidnappings, and death squads. UN doc. S/1994/989, p. 19.

[20] ONUSAL was also assigned responsibility for overseeing the Auxiliary Transitory Police (PAT), a temporary force created to quell violence in former FMLN-controlled conflict zones during the transition. Composed of PNC cadets who had received only fifteen days of basic training prior to deployment, the PAT was woefully unprepared

assignment was complicated by the fact that the PN was composed of soldiers, not professional policemen, who lacked enthusiasm for a job that they would soon lose, and harbored resentment for the UN observers whom they blamed for their predicament.[21] Though the PN was eventually disbanded on January 12, 1995, it was a continual source of tension and contention in the twenty-four months leading up to its termination.[22] ONUSAL found that as the PN was incrementally reduced, the number of illegal acts – arbitrary executions, torture, excessive use of force, threats, and arbitrary detentions – for which it was responsible, increased.[23] The ambitious timetable established by the Mexico City Agreement, and deeply entrenched corruption within the PN, account for much of the UN's ineffectiveness, but the composition and organization of the police division were also partially to blame. Police observers, unlike most of the military observers who served with ONUCA, arrived in El Salvador unfamiliar with the customs, history, and political climate, as well as the content of the UN's mandate. Furthermore, the police division's reported insensitivity to human rights issues, and the transient nature of its observers (some were rotated as often as every six months) aggravated its strained relationship with the human rights division.[24]

A second source of tension resulted from ONUSAL's organizational structure. Soon after its creation, the police division established four regional offices and two subregional offices. Organizationally, these offices operated independently of the human rights division, although police observers were encouraged by ONUSAL headquarters to coordinate with the human rights observers in their respective regions under the supervision of the regional coordinator. In practice, the amount of cooperation varied greatly depending on the working relationships developed between the two. For this reason, although regional coordinators were responsible for integrating the activities of the various UN

and underequipped to perform this mission. UN doc. S/23402, p. 2 and interviews with ONUSAL Officials, August 1993.

[21] UN police observers suffered similar problems while monitoring public security forces in Namibia. For a discussion of the role played by police observers see Lieutenant General D. Prem Chand's "The role of military and civilian police," in Heribert Weiland and Matthew Braham (eds.), *The Namibian Peace Process: Implications and Lessons for the Future.* (This book is based on an international conference, the Freiburg Symposium, July 1–4, 1992, sponsored by the International Peace Academy and the Arnold Bergstraesser Institute.)

[22] UN doc. A/49/888, p. 10.

[23] The period of June to October 1993 was marked by a progressive worsening of the human rights situation and the re-emergence of "death squads." See UN docs. S/1994/ 385 p. 6; S/1994/47, pp. 30–3; S/1994/561, p. 2; S/1994/989; and *NotiSur,* January 6, 1995.

[24] Interviews with ONUSAL observers, August 1993.

elements within their regions, they were often ineffective, particularly with regard to overseeing the National Police.[25]

The tenuous relationship between the police and human rights divisions was exacerbated by a perceived overlap in their responsibilities. Like police observers, human rights observers also visited PN facilities, oversaw PN investigations, and conducted independent human rights investigations. Police observers asserted that "it was their job to get the cases to the criminal justice system and the responsibility of the human rights people to take it from there."[26] Human rights observers countered that cross-referrals and information-sharing occurred on an ad hoc basis at the discretion of individual officers, an oversight they attributed to the police division's lack of operational guidelines for classifying, recording, and following up on abuses. For this reason, they argued, human rights observers should have been included in all investigations with a human rights component.[27]

On closer inspection, the second set of charges appears valid. The police division provided only minimal guidance to police observers on how they were to act, report, or coordinate when faced with particular crimes or human rights violations; and there was no system for processing and cataloging reports of violations committed by the PN.[28] The absence of data, and minimal contact between senior PN and ONUSAL officials, made it difficult to determine to what extent these violations were systemic problems best addressed through the National Police chain of command. Thus, while the PN patrols consistently committed human rights violations, and UN police observers regularly reported them, ONUSAL was unable to address the underlying organizational antecedents within the PN.[29]

In the field, both police and human rights observers did their best to overcome organizational shortcomings and attempted to make the faltering judicial and law enforcement systems function. Citizens naturally gravitated to UN observers to report criminal activities because of their mistrust of the existing public security forces and their lack of confidence in the judicial system. Whether it was UN police observers encouraging, or pressuring, National Police officers to adhere more

---

[25] As one regional coordinator recalls, "police division personnel at regional offices are reluctant to accept direction from civilians, human rights personnel, and women." Interview conducted by Ian Johnstone, January 1994.

[26] Interview with ONUSAL police observer, Central Region, August 1993.

[27] Interviews with human rights and police observers, Central Regional Office, August 1993.

[28] See Gino Costa, "Naciones Unidas y la creacion de una policia Civil en El Salvador." *Analisis Internacional: revista del Internationales*, no. 11 (1995).

[29] See Costa, "Naciones Unidas."

closely to the rules of due process when making an arrest, or human rights observers cajoling a local magistrate into reviewing a case in a more timely manner, ONUSAL made a valiant effort to nudge these systems into action.[30] Ultimate success in this area, of course, depends on wide-ranging reforms in the justice system, an area where much bilateral US assistance has been concentrated, but limited progress made.

Sometimes these individual efforts were successful, but often they were not. Despite only marginal effectiveness in monitoring public security, there is little doubt that overall these and other peacekeeping activities were essential to the peace process. The presence of ONUSAL police observers alongside National Police patrols, combined with their regular visits to PN posts and local jails, undoubtedly improved human rights conditions. ONUSAL's role in engineering the separation of forces and the demobilization of the FMLN was critical in the early phases of the ceasefire. The difficulties encountered along the way do raise specific questions of how the UN might better organize similar operations in the future. Because some of these same issues arise in the analysis of institutional reforms, they are discussed in the final section.

Institutional reform: peacebuilding

The UN's effectiveness in verifying and assisting institutional reform was mixed and more difficult to evaluate. In the case of armed forces reform, ONUSAL took a less assertive approach to its verification responsibilities due, at least in part, to ambiguity in, and its passive interpretation of, UN verification responsibilities.[31] The UN mandate made no specific reference to institutional reform efforts and simply stated that the UN "shall verify and monitor the implementation" of the Accords.[32] The January 1992 Peace Agreement, on the other hand, was more specific, requiring unprecedented institutional changes in the Salvadoran armed forces and the public security forces.[33] Therefore, depending on how broadly the mandate was interpreted, ONUSAL's role in institutional reform was potentially an expansive one.

---

[30] Interviews with ONUSAL observers, August 1993.
[31] A notable exception to this charge is the UN's active involvement with the Ad Hoc Commission.
[32] SC/RES/729 and UN Press Release SC/5345, January 14, 1992.
[33] Chapter VIII of the Mexico City Agreement is relatively clear on UN responsibilities, stating that the UN "shall verify compliance with the agreement ... with the cooperation of the parties and of the authorities whose duty it is to enforce them." *El Salvador Agreements: The Path to Peace,* United Nations Department of Public Information, July 1992, chapter VIII, para. 1, p. 113.

In practice, the military division played a relatively insignificant role in peacebuilding, simply verifying that the FAES had developed, or initiated, plans for complying with the Accords, rather than verifying the implementation of the provisions themselves. In the case of public security reform, ONUSAL's responsibilities were less ambiguous, and the UN more active. The Peace Agreement clearly specified a role for the UN in assisting with the creation of a new police force, as did the UN mandate.[34] Thus, the police division supervised and assisted in the deployment of newly created National Civilian Police (PNC) and coordinated bilateral assistance provided by Spain, the United States, and other countries for the creation of a National Public Security Academy. Both endeavors have enjoyed some success to date, though they have demonstrated that verifying and assisting institutional reform is expensive and difficult.

Reform of the armed forces

At the root of more than a decade of violence and human rights violations in El Salvador was the omnipresent and repressive role played by the armed forces. An imbalance in civil–military relations existed throughout the 1980s, and by 1991 the "big class" or *tandona* (graduates from the Salvadoran Military Academy class of 1966) had ruthlessly consolidated power and dominated nearly every major command in the armed forces and public security forces, as well as directorships in numerous agencies throughout the government.[35] As part of the reform of the armed forces, the Peace Agreement required ONUSAL to verify the purge of military officers implicated in human rights abuses by the Ad Hoc Commission and to oversee dramatic downsizing and restructuring within the Salvadoran armed forces.

The establishment of an ad hoc commission was a unique and surprisingly successful aspect of the peace process. In keeping with the Accords, it was comprised of three prominent Salvadorans appointed by the Secretary-General and approved by President Alfredo Cristiani.[36]

---

[34] Chapter II, section 7 of the Mexico Agreement clearly outlines UN responsibilities during the transition period. S/23402, a UN report dated 10 January 1992, prior to the approval of the UN's expanded mandate under Resolution 729, enumerates a range of responsibilities for the ONUSAL police division.

[35] For insight into the role of the armed forces in Salvadoran society see Martin C. Needler "El Salvador: the military and politics," *Armed Forces and Society*, vol. 17, (1991), pp. 569–98 and José Z. Garcia, "The *Tanda* system and institutional autonomy of the military," in Joseph S. Tulchin and Gary Brand (eds.), *Is There a Transition to Democracy in El Salvador?* (Boulder, Col.: Lynne Rienner, 1992).

[36] A list of candidates was created by ONUSAL and distributed to the FMLN and the government for their approval. After much negotiation, both sides finally agreed on

The Commission was assigned the onerous task of reviewing the human rights records, professional competence, and suitability of all military officers for continued service in the armed forces. The findings of the Commission were to remain secret and to result in the discharges, but not the prosecution, of the active-duty officers implicated. Due to the magnitude of the task, and the limited availability of performance records – and in recognition of the symbolic importance of its efforts – the Commission chose to review only 232 records of mostly senior officers, approximately 10 percent of the officer corps.[37] The Commission submitted its report recommending discharges for 102 senior officers and reassignment for 40 others to President Cristiani and the UN on September 23, 1992.[38]

In the following months, President Cristiani refused to comply with the Commission's recommendations, instead requesting the Secretary-General's approval for an alternative plan that allowed the most powerful officers to remain in their posts until August 1993. The Secretary-General rejected the proposal and in an atmosphere of escalating tension dispatched Under-Secretary-General Goulding and Assistant Secretary-General Alvaro de Soto to El Salvador to negotiate a new timetable for adherence with the Commission's findings. In October 1992, President Cristiani agreed to incorporate the dismissal of the remaining officers into the 1992 year-end retirements, but bowed again to pressure in December, further delaying the retirement of fifteen generals and colonels, including Defense Minister General Rene Emilio Ponce.[39] Cristiani and senior military officers justified their resistance on the grounds that the Ad Hoc Commission had not respected the legal rights of the officers implicated as it failed to give reasons for their dismissals or transfers and provided no means for challenging the actions in court.[40] After a second set of negotiations, President Cristiani complied fully with the recommendations of the Commission on July 1, 1993 by replacing Minister of Defense General Emilio Ponce with Colonel Humberto Corado Figueroa.[41]

Even those critical of the pace and the nature of reform within the

Reynaldo Galindo Pohl, Abraham Rodriguez and Eduardo Molina Olivares. Interview with Abraham Rodriguez, August 1993.

[37] The Commission was given a three-month period to evaluate 2,293 active duty officers, but the documentation provided by the Defense Ministry, namely performance files, was incomplete. The information gathered by human rights groups during the war, while sometimes identifying specific units, usually failed to identify individuals. Interviews with human rights workers, San Salvador, August 1993.

[38] UN doc. A/47/596, p. 48.   [39] *The Washington Post*, January 5, 1993,

[40] *The New York Times*, January 6 and 7, 1993.

[41] S/25812, p. 2 and David Clark Scott, "Purge of Salvador's army brass dismantles military clique," *Christian Science Monitor*, July 6, 1993.

armed forces generally agreed that the Ad Hoc Commission was remarkably effective. At least part of this success may be attributed to the efforts of the United Nations. Exerting tremendous political pressure, the UN firmly refused to compromise on this aspect of the Accords which it viewed as essential to the legitimacy and sustainability of the peace process. Equally important were the Secretary-General's efforts to maintain open channels of communication. This combination led eventually to the successful mediation efforts of Marrack Goulding and Alvaro de Soto.[42] The contribution of the international community also was crucial. The Four Friends, and the USA particularly, facilitated progress by remaining uniformly committed to the position of the Secretary-General and providing reassurances to the Cristiani government.[43]

At first blush, it appeared that the Salvadoran government also implemented the majority of the other required structural and doctrinal changes within the armed forces. The government announced that the National Guard and Treasury police were abolished on March 2, 1992; civil defense units were disbanded on June 30; and a new Military Service and Reserves Act was promulgated in response to problems with illegal recruitment. ONUSAL "verified" that the FAES had reduced its forces by more than 50 percent and that all five rapid-reaction battalions were dismantled as of March 31, 1993, ten months ahead of schedule.[44]

The military division's role in facilitating these structural and doctrinal changes, however, was negligible. The military division's observer to the Salvadoran Military High Command is the mechanism through which the UN purported to verify implementation of institutional reforms. Senior UN military observers acknowledged, however, that the division simply verified that the FAES developed and initiated appropriate plans to comply with the Accords, rather than confirming that the plans were actually implemented. This approach was defended on the grounds that the military division was not sufficiently staffed to perform this mission and that the difficulties inherent in verifying implementation at the unit level made it untenable.[45] The human rights division, on the other hand, played a more active role by assisting the FAES in designing and

[42] Interview with Abraham Rodriguez, August 1993.
[43] On November 15, 1992, General Colin Powell visited El Salvador to urge the president and the High Command to find a workable solution to the impasse. Interview with senior US Military Officer, US Embassy, El Salvador, August 1993. In February 1993, the Clinton administration applied additional pressure by freezing $11 million in military aid until the ad hoc recommendations were met. See *El Salvador's Negotiated Revolution: Prospects for Legal Reform*, The Lawyer's Committee for Human Rights, June 1993.
[44] Briefing from ONUSAL Military Division, August 1993.
[45] Interviews with ONUSAL military observers, July–August 1993.

implementing the new military doctrine, delivering lectures to senior commanders, and helping to design human rights courses for the military education system.[46]

While considerable progress was made in reforming the armed forces, there is evidence that the changes were not as sweeping as hoped. Reports in July 1994, for example, suggested that a number of active duty members of the military were engaged in organized criminal activity. Likewise, October 1994 reports charged that military intelligence units still existed and were active (this issue will be expanded upon shortly). In addition, the Peace Agreement required that the "Treasury Police and National Guard ... be abolished as public security forces and their members ... be incorporated into the army."[47] However, as ONUSAL has acknowledged, both units were incorporated structurally intact into the army and simply renamed the National Border Guard and the Military Police.[48] The reduction of the armed forces also might not have been as dramatic as it first appeared. Though the FAES claimed a total of 63,175 soldiers at the time of the ceasefire, the fact that its reduction was completed almost a year ahead of time suggests that these numbers may have been padded.[49]

The large amount of unregistered military weapons held by private citizens (many of them former members of the FAES) also stands out as an unfulfilled provision of the Accords. Though the government took steps to recover these weapons through an information campaign, a buy-back program, and by passing legislation controlling weapons, munitions, and explosives, progress was extremely slow with the minister of defense acknowledging in February 1995 that approximately 300,000 weapons, "intended for military use," had found their way into civilian hands.[50] Finally, since 1993, President Cristiani has disregarded

---

[46] UN doc. S/26790, p. 9.   [47] *El Salvador Agreements: The Path to Peace*, p. 53.

[48] UN doc. S/25812, p. 9. The armed forces were predictably resistant to giving up the power and influence associated with public security functions. See William Stanley, *Protectors or Perpetrators? The Institutional Crisis of the Salvadoran Civilian Police* (Cambridge, Mass.: Hemisphere Initiatives, January 1996), p. 11.

[49] When the former Bracamonte Battalion barracks and headquarters were vacated to make room for the National Public Security Academy, it was discovered that the facilities were inadequate for a battalion-sized unit. The 29,000 active-duty force remaining is still large by Central American standards, particularly in the absence of external threats. See Jack Spence and George Vickers, *A Negotiated Revolution: A Two Year Progress Report on the Salvadoran Peace Accords* (Cambridge, Mass.: Hemisphere Initiatives, 1994), p. 17.

[50] UN doc. S/1994/561, pp. 3–4. Also, See Jack Spence, George Vickers and David Dye, *The Salvadoran Peace Accords and Democratization: A Three Year Progress Report and Recommendations* (Cambridge, Mass.: Hemisphere Initiatives, 1995), p. 8 and I. Castro, "El Salvador: crime replaces war with a murder every hour," *Inter Press Service*, February 23, 1995.

ONUSAL protests and deployed military units on major thoroughfares throughout the country to address the dramatic increase in highway banditry, protect the coffee harvest, and quell demonstrations against the government.[51] Though limited in scope, these actions set a dangerous precedent by once again legitimizing the military's involvement in public security functions.[52]

Disturbing questions also have arisen concerning the disposition of the National Intelligence Directorate (DNI).[53] This was officially abolished on June 15, 1992 and replaced by the State Intelligence Agency. Yet, there were numerous accusations that it continued to function secretly in subsequent months. Although no hard evidence exists to support these charges, it is apparent that the government was less than enthusiastic about fulfilling this aspect of the Accords. President Cristiani did not appoint a director for the State Intelligence Agency until June 12, three months after the deadline stipulated in the Accords, and there were reports that all of the Intelligence Directorate's files were not moved to the offices of the new intelligence service.[54] In November 1992, the Secretary-General's special rapporteur for human rights, Professor Pedro Nikken, suggested that the abolition of the Intelligence Directorate may "have been nothing more than a mere formality ... and that the former body continues to operate in secret while the new one does not in reality exist."[55] In November 1993, the UN expressed uncertainty over the disposition of DNI files and whether the intelligence activities of the armed forces were carried out in a manner consistent with doctrinal changes imposed by the Peace Accords.[56] In May 1994 it appeared that the situation was under control as the UN reported that it had verified that the intelligence activities of the armed forces were in compliance with mandated changes and that the DNI files were open for ONUSAL's review.[57] In August 1994, however, serious questions reemerged as a UN report acknowledged that "there are indications that certain members of the armed forces on

---

[51] See William Stanley, *Risking Failure: The Problems and Promise of the New Civilian Police in El Salvador* (Cambridge, Mass.: Hemisphere Initiatives, 1993) and Spence et al., *The Salvadoran Peace Accords*, p. 9.

[52] Admittedly, one of the greatest challenges is to find practical solutions to the dramatic increase in crime, while at the same time remaining committed to true public security reform. See UN doc. A/49/888, p. 9; UN doc. A/49/888, p. 11.

[53] DNI's historic role as the nerve center for state surveillance and repression makes this particularly sensitive.

[54] Jack Spence and George Vickers, *End Game: A Progress Report on Implications of the Salvadoran Peace Accords* (Cambridge, Mass.: Hemisphere Initiatives, 1992), p. 13.

[55] UN doc. A/47/596, p. 51.   [56] UN doc. S/26689, p. 4.

[57] UN doc. S/1994/561, p. 5.

active duty continue to carry out internal intelligence activities, contrary to the new mandate of the armed forces."[58]

The uncertain status of the DNI reveals the potential dangers of a passive approach to verification. As one senior ONUSAL military observer admitted, "It was outside our capability to determine whether DNI was truly abolished, or merely hidden beneath levels of bureaucracy."[59] Admittedly, intelligence activities are the most sensitive and secretive of all governmental functions; thus, it should come as no surprise that the reform of the intelligence service has been elusive and verification difficult. It should be recognized, however, that the UN's relatively narrow interpretation of its verification responsibilities in this and other aspects of armed forces reform are in striking contrast to its approach on other issues. The uncertainty of the outcomes in this area suggest that ONUSAL should have played a more active role in verifying military reform.[60]

While the UN was not particularly active in the reform of the Salvadoran armed forces, the US military group (MILGROUP) in El Salvador, operating independent of the UN, was more deeply involved. As of August 1993, approximately forty US military trainers, under the supervision of the MILGROUP commander, were deployed in four- to five-person teams throughout the FAES. Their responsibilities included training, advising, and assisting with the restructuring of the armed forces. US military advisors aided with the development of a new training and doctrine command (CODEM) and provided technical advice on the reorganization of the Military College.[61] In addition, MILGROUP assisted with the creation of the School of High Strategic Studies to educate senior civilian and military leaders, which opened in September 1993.[62] This is not to suggest that MILGROUP's independent involvement in armed forces reform was always favorable, or even desirable.[63] However, the deployment of US advisors at the unit level gave them greater access to reform efforts and allowed for more accurate verification.[64] This approach should be considered as a potential prototype for UN involvement in armed forces reform in the future.

---

[58] UN doc. S/1994/1000, p. 2.
[59] Interview with senior ONUSAL military observer, July 1993.
[60] UN doc. S/1994/886, p. 20.
[61] Interview with US MILGROUP Commander, August 1993.
[62] See Spence and Vickers, *End Game*, pp. 15–16.
[63] This favorable appraisal applies only to US post-conflict efforts and begs the question why US bilateral "nation building" efforts at a cost of over $5 billion were an abysmal failure in the 1980s. For a critical review of US involvement during this period see Benjamin Schwarz, *American Counterinsurgency Doctrine and El Salvador: The Frustrations of Reform and the Illusions of Nation Building* (Santa Monica, Cal.: Rand, 1991).
[64] The US military trainers assigned to FAES units completed their duties in December

Creating a national civil police

While the United Nations was tentative in its involvement in armed forces reform, it was far more active in the creation of a National Civilian Police force. The creation of a National Civilian Police (PNC) and National Public Security Academy have emerged as two of the most publicized aspects of Accords, praised by some as "the most exportable ideas" of the Salvadoran peace process.[65] Although both efforts have been plagued with numerous difficulties, they are useful examples of the instrumental role the UN can play in institutional reform.

Throughout the peace negotiations the FMLN and the UN maintained that the creation of a legitimate National Civilian Police force, with the primary function of safeguarding individual rights and freedoms, was crucial to sustainable peace.[66] The plan for the creation of the PNC was conceived during the negotiating process with the assistance of an international technical team headed by Dr Jesús Rodés of Spain.[67] The most distinctive feature of the new force was that it was to be composed of civilian, not military, personnel and was to be isolated from the influence of the armed forces.[68] The creation of the civilian force was contingent on the development of a National Public Security Academy where its members would be trained. The original timetable envisioned that the Academy would begin operating just ten weeks after the signing of the Agreement.[69]

A second team of technical experts, comprised of five representatives each from Spain and the US and a seven-person team from El Salvador,

---

1994. Telephone interview with El Salvador desk officer, US Department of State, November 1994

[65] Interview with the Spanish Political Affairs Officer conducted by Ian Johnstone, Spanish Embassy in El Salvador, January 1994.

[66] Interview with FMLN negotiator Ana Guadalupe Martínez, August 1993. This recounting of events may overstate the FMLN's role in public security force reform in the early stages of the peace process. Others suggest that it was the UN that provided much of the vision and energy behind the creation of a nationwide National Civil Police. See Stanley, *Protectors or Perpetrators?*, p. 5.

[67] Dr. Rodes is Director of the Escuela de Policía in Cataluña. The Rodes group consisted of Canadian, Venezuelan, Spanish, Swedish, and French representatives. Representatives from ICITAP, the US Justice Department's International Criminal Investigative Training Assistance Program, were also sent to El Salvador to consult with the Rodes group. Costa, "Naciones Unidas," p. 3.

[68] A 5,700 member force with 240 officers was projected for the first 24 months while a 10,000 member force with 500 officers was projected by 1998. The Peace Accords dictated that less than half of each incoming class could be composed of equal numbers of former National Police officers and FMLN ex-combatants, thereby ensuring that the majority of the new PNC would be civilian non-combatants (chapter II, 7(d) para. a); *El Salvador Agreement: The Path to Peace*, p. 70.

[69] UN doc. S/25521, p. 53.

assisted with the creation of the Academy. The three teams joined forces in May 1992 to develop and implement a detailed plan for the Academy's lesson plans, disciplinary codes, infrastructure, and budget.[70] Initially, the technical team worked under the coordination of UNDP's resident Representative, but after the FMLN objected that it had not been properly consulted, UNDP turned over responsibility for coordinating the creation of the academy to ONUSAL. Though UNDP continued to oversee the financial assistance provided by outside sources, it was, at least in this case, incapable of effectively coordinating non-state actors like the FMLN.[71]

In accordance with the Accords, ONUSAL was responsible for monitoring admissions procedures as well as coordinating bilateral assistance. In addition, a subcommission of the National Commission to Consolidate Peace (COPAZ) established by the Peace Agreement was responsible for monitoring the progress of the PNC and the Academy.[72] A third player, the US Justice Department's International Criminal Investigative Training Assistance Program (ICITAP), played a prominent, and independent, role in police reform; the United States provided the bulk of the technical instructors for the Academy and regularly advised the Directors of the Academy and PNC.[73]

The Academy was established in semi-permanent facilities and within months of its creation had over 2,200 cadets in residence. In general, both parties have viewed the Academy as one of the more successful aspects of the peace process – in the words of former ONUSAL Chief Dr. Ramirez Ocampo, "a potential role model for all of Latin America."[74] These laudatory remarks notwithstanding, the UN has discovered through its involvement in this process that assisting dramatic institutional reforms in the face of subtle, as well as overt, political

[70] Interview with Robert Loosle conducted by Ian Johnstone, January 1994. American and Chilean instructors were financed and administered through the US Department of Justice; Spanish, Swedish, and Norwegian contingents were financed by UNDP. UN doc. S/1994/561, p. 7.

[71] See Popkin, *Human Rights, Development and Democracy*, p. 7. For more on coordination among UN agencies, see also Alvaro de Soto and Graciana del Castillo, "Obstacles to peacebuilding," *Foreign Policy*, vol. 94, 1994.

[72] To involve civil society in the implementation of the Accords, the negotiators established COPAZ. Composed of representatives from each of the political parties represented in the Legislative Assembly, as well as the government and the FMLN, COPAZ oversaw various aspects of the Accords. For a more detailed discussions see Johnstone, *Rights and Reconciliation*.

[73] The US gave $13 million in assistance to Salvadoran public security forces during the 1980s, but by the time the peace process began, the US vehicles, communications equipment, and arms provided had been appropriated by the military, were missing, or were in bad condition. Spence et al., *The Salvadoran Peace Accords*, p. 6.

[74] Interview with Dr. Ramirez Ocampo, August 1993.

opposition and overseeing independent bilateral assistance efforts are difficult undertakings. In the first instance, the plan to organize and establish the Academy within ten weeks was extremely ambitious, and the difficulty of the situation was exacerbated by the fact that the project was grossly underfunded. After incessant government foot-dragging, the first classes began three months behind schedule, with delays stemming from a variety of obstacles ranging from inadequate infrastructure to insufficient financing.[75] The government asserted that the international community failed to follow through on informal commitments made during the negotiations; UN officials contended that international support was less than expected, but that the government's own lack of support raised questions concerning its commitment to real security force reform.[76]

Controversy also arose over admission procedures, the curriculum, and the appropriate role for both ONUSAL and foreign technical advisors. Human rights groups reported, and ONUSAL concurred, that large numbers of recruits from disbanded public security forces or the armed forces concealed their affiliations and entered the Academy in violation of the Accords.[77] In addition, while attempting to meet the quotas established by the Accords, the Academy had a difficult time attracting sufficient numbers of FMLN and civilian recruits to match the oversupply of former members of the PN and ex-soldiers who were overtly, and covertly, applying for admission. A UN report in May 1994 noted that, "In the long-run, this trend could result in a dangerous imbalance in the civilian composition of the PNC."[78] Based on ONUSAL's recommendations, the government complemented its recruitment campaign with field visits to areas with particularly low turnout and increased the salaries, pensions, and benefits of PNC members. The Academy was also slow to incorporate specialized training for functions such as customs, environmental protection, arms and explosives, and drug enforcement into its curriculum.[79]

[75] Because the FAES refused to turn over the former Public Security Academy, the PNC Academy was established in the refurbished facilities of the former Bracamonte Battalion in Comalapa, an hour outside of San Salvador. Spence and Vickers, *End Game*, p. 10.

[76] Only 9 percent of the project's costs were financed by the international community (primarily the USA) in 1993 and 1994. The remainder was financed by the Salvadoran government. Stanley, *Protectors or Perpetrators?*, p. 7.

[77] UN doc. A/47/596, p. 38. The government was determined to establish a power base in the with former PN and ex-soldiers, Costa argues, because of its fear that the PNC would come under FMLN control. Costa, "Naciones Unidas," p. 14.

[78] UN doc. S/1994/561, p. 8. There is some question over the extent to which the armed forces were behind the efforts to subvert the PNC. Ibid., p. 13.

[79] Stanley, *Protectors or Perpetrators?*, p. 9.

The content and quality of the Academy's instruction has also been questioned. In the first twenty-four months, the curriculum was administered by a core staff of international experts and instructors who taught the technical subjects and national instructors who assisted with non-technical coursework.[80] Reportedly, there has been some disagreement among the various international contingents about the emphasis that should be placed on human rights and "community policing."[81] In addition, the Academy has suffered disciplinary problems with some students complaining of arbitrary enforcement of internal regulations without due process.[82]

This situation suggests several shortcomings in the UN's approach to public security reform. First, UNDP was incapable of fulfilling the technical, political, and financial roles that it was first assigned. Thus, ONUSAL perhaps should have been more directly involved in the creation of the Academy from the very beginning in order to facilitate agreement between the parties and oversee the overall progress of the initiative. Second, controversy over the Academy's curriculum and the role of foreign instructors accents the absence of a sufficiently detailed plan for the Academy prior to the deployment of advisors and resources and a coordinating mechanism for ironing out differences once reform efforts began.[83]

The UN, in concert with ICITAP, made a more substantive contribution to institutional reform by advising, supervising, and assisting the newly deployed PNC forces. The Academy produced its first graduating class on February 5, 1993. The newly graduated recruits were assigned immediately to PNC posts throughout El Salvador.[84] Prior to September 1993, ONUSAL observers also assisted with the creation of police posts and standardized operating procedures, provided logistical support, and accompanied and advised rookie PNC patrols. Also, though the roles of members of the police division and Academy instructors were distinct, ONUSAL fulfilled a critical function by

[80] As of September 1993, there were forty international instructors and fifty-eight national instructors at the Academy. Ibid., p. 7.
[81] For more on the lack of coordination within the international technical team, see Costa, "Naciones Unidas," p. 25.
[82] Spence and Vickers, *End Game*, p. 11. These shortcomings notwithstanding, one of the most remarkable aspects of the Academy is that the relations between FMLN and PN cadets have been excellent. Interview with US technical advisor, August 1993.
[83] Initially, ONUSAL had difficulty performing its supervisory responsibilities because it lacked information about decisions made by the Director and Academic Council. In January 1993, a UN advisor was appointed as an observer on the Academic Council, thereby partially, but not completely, ameliorating the problem. Interview with ONUSAL official, August 1993.
[84] As of January 1996, there are 8,725 graduates of the Academy. Stanley, *Protectors or Perpetrators?*, p. 13.

providing valuable feedback concerning shortcomings that they identified in PNC training to the Academy, ultimately resulting in changes in
the curriculum.[85] In the year following its initial deployment, the PNC
was mostly lauded by observers for its professionalism and for lower
crime rates that followed in the regions in which it was deployed, despite
its inadequate equipment and facilities.[86]

By mid-1993, however, the early successes of the PNC appeared in
danger of being reversed for at least four reasons. First, the appointment
of the US-backed former head of the anti-narcotics division (UEA),
Captain Oscar Peña Durán, as Sub-director of PNC operations,
unfavorably affected the UN's ability to oversee and assist the deployment of the new civilian police force. Peña placed former UEA
colleagues in key positions and minimized the PNC's cooperation with
ONUSAL.[87] In September 1993, as a consequence of Peña's maneu-
vering, the government chose not to extend ONUSAL's technical and
logistical support for the PNC, a decision that, to the surprise of many,
was passively accepted by the United States.[88] Second, in January 1994
the human rights division reported a notable increase in reports of
human rights abuses by the PNC, an unfavorable trend that continues as
this book goes to publication.[89] Third, in the same month the
government announced the suspension of its demobilization of the PN,
defending this decision as necessary to combat soaring violent crime
rates.[90]

Finally, the 1992 transfer of the former Special Narcotics Unit (UEA)
and the Criminal Investigation Commission (SIU) into the Anti-
narcotics and Criminal Investigation Divisions of the PNC has been a
continual source of dispute.[91] In response to resistance to this wholesale

[85] ICITAP, the US Drug Enforcement Agency (DEA), and the US Agency for
International Development (AID) were all involved in the police reform effort. The US
was viewed by the international community as the leader in this effort because of its
long-standing ties to the Salvadoran public security forces. Costa, "Naciones Unidas,"
pp. 18–25.

[86] Interviews with government officials, FMLN representatives, and ONUSAL observers,
August 1993.

[87] The predominance of subcommissioners that served in the former security forces
(thirty versus seven FMLN and seventeen civilians) is an example of his influence. UN
doc. S/1994/561, p. 9. As of December 1995, ten of twelve senior officers in the PNC
previously served in the armed forces. Stanley, *Protectors or Perpetrators?*, p. 16.

[88] UN doc. S/1994/561, p. 11 and Costa, "Naciones Unidas," p. 25.

[89] Between March 1 and June 30, 1994, the human rights division reported 147 (58 were
confirmed by further investigation) cases of human rights abuses perpetrated by
members of the PNC. UN doc. S/48/281, p. 21; UN doc. A/49/888, pp. 13–4; *NotiSur*,
June 10, 1994.

[90] "El Salvador: crime replaces war with a murder every hour," *Inter Press Service*,
February 23, 1995.

[91] The USA, which had previously give millions of dollars worth of support to these units,

transfer, a review committee was established to address UN and FMLN concerns in December 1992.[92] Though members of the UEA and SIU were required by the committee to pass a specialized resident course on the new civilian police doctrine at the Academy and forbidden from accepting assignments outside of the divisions to which they were transferred in the PNC, neither stipulation was fully satisfied.[93] The UEA and SIU continued to operate with excessive autonomy and occupy key positions within the National Civilian Police.[94] As Stanley notes, "They brought with them a culture of impunity and brutality that was totally at odds with the spirit and the doctrine of the PNC."[95] Moreover, there is also evidence that the wholesale transfer of the UEA and SIU contributed to the increase in human rights violations by the PNC.[96] These developments cast a somber shadow over this much-touted "UN success story."

Despite these setbacks, notable progress was made in the months following the election of Armando Calderón Sol as president in March 1994. Under intense pressure from ONUSAL and the USA, Peña Durán resigned in May, and the new president publicly voiced his unequivocal support for the PNC and took steps to demobilize the PN by December 31, 1994.[97] In addition, by July 1994, the PNC was deployed in all fourteen departments in El Salvador, and all nine functional divisions (anti-narcotics division, border division, arms and explosives division, etc.) within the PNC were operational.[98] Also significant was a technical agreement with ONUSAL, made soon after the appointment of Mr. Hugo Barrera as vice-minister for public security, that renewed UN assistance to the PNC in certain functional areas and called for the development of standardized operating procedures for the PNC.[99]

supported this decision, arguing that the SIU and UEA would provide robust investigative capacity within the PNC. Stanley, *Protectors or Perpetyrators?*, p. 15.

[92] In Namibia the UN faced similar frustrations as the South African authorities subverted the South West African Police Forces (SWAPOL) by incorporating members of a disbanded, notorious paramilitary police unit known as *Koevoet* (crowbar). See *Peacekeeping and Human Rights* (New York: Amnesty International USA, 1994).

[93] UN doc. S/1994/561, pp. 7–12. In addition, the government submitted the relevant legislation regarding the transfer of the UEA and SIU directly to the Legislative Assembly, bypassing COPAZ. UN doc. S/26790, p. 8.

[94] UN doc. S/1994/1000, p. 4; Costa, "NAciones Unidas," p. 13; Spence et al., *The Salvadoran Peace Accords*, p. 7.

[95] Stanley, *Protectors or Perpetrators*, p. 15.   [96] UN doc. S/1994/886, p. 21.

[97] Spence et al., *The Salvadoran Peace Accords*, p. 7. The president's decision to speed up the demobilization of the PN was inspired at least in part by the involvement of a PN lieutenant in a daylight bank robbery in downtown San Salvador on June 22, 1994. UN doc. S/1994/886, pp. 3 and 21, and *NotiSur*, January 6, 1995.

[98] UN docs. S/1994/886, p. 20; S/1994/1212, p. 2; and S/1994/1000, p. 3.

[99] UN doc. S/1994/1000, p. 10. ONUSAL's involvement was far less extensive than the

But optimism was ephemeral. By the end of 1995, the progress of police reform was again hotly contested. The PNC's harsh responses to organized riots in November, and its worsening human rights record, left many in El Salvador and the international community questioning how much of an improvement the new police force was over the repressive public security forces of the past.[100] At the end of 1995, the inability to investigate and prosecute prominent suspects, continued infiltration of people opposed to its doctrine and mission, and eroding discipline remained chronic problems within the PNC.[101] And, not surprisingly, the PNC's image had been steadily tarnished with the Salvadoran public.[102]

Proposals made in late 1995 by the Salvadoran government to increase the size of the PNC may worsen this situation, rather than improve it. El Salvador's 1996 budget calls for the creation of 8,300 new police positions (to a final strength of 20,000), but this decision is likely to unduly bias the composition of the PNC.[103] The absence of a mechanism for verifying the backgrounds and impeding the entrance of former PN and ex-soldiers into the Academy has justifiably raised fears that the PNC will, over time, become increasingly militarized. Moreover, rapid growth in the PNC is likely to accelerate the erosion in competence, performance, discipline, and accountability already evident.[104] In light of these difficulties, the General Assembly extended the UN's mission in El Salvador (named MINUSAL after April 1995) until April 30, 1996 to continue oversight of public security reforms.[105] And, in January 1996, based on UN recommendations, Calderón Sol announced the creation of a Security Council of the PNC to oversee its functioning.[106] With these developments in mind, it is clear that the PNC is at a crossroads. While the UN and the international community will continue to make a limited contribution in the coming months, ultimately it will be Salvadorans who decide whether the rule of law, or the repression and impunity of the past, are El Salvador's future.

period prior to September 1993, though UN did make periodic inspections to PNC posts. Also, periodic meetings between members of the Human Rights Division and senior officers in the National Civil Police had resulted in the publication of a *Guide to Rules and Procedures of the National Civil Police* by July 1994. UN doc. S/1994/886, p. 25.

[100] Stanley, *Protectors or Perpetrators?*, p. 2. *Rocky Mountain News*, November 27, 1995, p. 20.

[101] UN doc. A/49/888, pp. 14–7.   [102] Stanley, *Protectors or Perpetrators*, p. ii.

[103] *Flor de Izote*, vol. 1, no. 7, December 1995.

[104] Stanley, *Protectors or Perpetrators*, p. 25.   [105] UN doc. A/50/499, p. 11.

[106] Federal News Service, November 1, 1995; The Council consists of Public Safety Minister, Hugo Barrera, Salvador Samayoa, David Escobar Galindo, Luis Cardenal, and Mario Velasco. *Flor de Izote*, vol. 7, no. 1, January 10, 1996.

The emergence of these serious problems has not yet erased the achievements of the PNC: it remains one of the most ambitious reform efforts, and progressive public security forces, in Latin America. At the same time, it would be premature to label ONUSAL's role in assisting this effort as an unqualified success. Based on the experience to date, however, several tentative conclusions are warranted. First, ONUSAL's assistance was essential in the initial stages of the PNC's deployment. By supervising, advising, and when necessary, assisting recently deployed forces, ONUSAL facilitated the creation of what will, it is hoped, be a sustainable and independent professional police force. Second, the ONUSAL police division provided valuable feedback on the PNC's performance to the Academy. When possible, future institutional reform efforts should be similarly comprehensive with the UN assisting not only with the creation of the plan, but also with its implementation.[107] Third, when problems did arise, it often was because the Peace Agreement, or subsequent agreements, were not specific enough, or because there was not an established verification mechanism. The UN has closely monitored the development of the PNC and used its political leverage when possible. The government, however, has been able to subvert the PNC with ex-soldiers and former PN and to delay the elimination of the PN because of ambiguity in the Peace Accords and the absence of a robust means for verifying compliance.

Lessons learned

What are the lessons to be learned from the El Salvador experience? Three broad sets of issues identified in the preceding discussion are the focus of the final section. A first set of issues is concerned with operational considerations – how a post-conflict mission should be organized, staffed, and operated. The second set of issues focuses on the unique challenges that arise for the UN when bilateral assistance efforts are included in the overall peace process. The third set of issues considers the various ways in which the UN might interpret and execute a post-conflict mandate, as well as the successes and failures in El Salvador associated with these choices. While recognizing that the problems highlighted in these three areas are, in some respects, unique to the Salvadoran peace process, a closer look at their causes and potential solutions reveals numerous lessons relevant to future UN operations.

---

[107] By fulfilling this role, however, ONUSAL created a level of dependency on the UN, forestalling the creation of a mechanism for self-evaluation and self-correction by Salvadoran authorities.

Organizational issues

The shortcomings that existed in ONUSAL's organizational structure may be attributed, at least partially, to the two-phased manner in which it was created. The initial ONUSAL human rights division was conceived in July 1991 for the express purpose of monitoring compliance by both sides to the 1990 San José Agreement.[108] The early deployment of ONUSAL's human rights division provided a framework around which the remainder of the Mission was organized when its mandate was expanded in January 1992.

Both the deployment of UN personnel to verify a human rights agreement prior to a ceasefire, and the inclusion of military and police observers in such an undertaking, were unprecedented. Notably, UN police and military observers made a unique contribution as they were better equipped than human right observers to communicate with their Salvadoran counterparts.[109] Human rights observers, however, feared that the inclusion of military and police personnel would jeopardize the credibility of the human rights mission and recommended to the Chief of Mission that independent police and military divisions be created.[110] In keeping with this request, the Secretary-General proposed expanding ONUSAL's mandate by creating military and police divisions to verify the implementation of the Accords.[111]

The unwieldy three-pronged organizational structure that emerged as a result of this decision should be reconsidered. As noted earlier, at the regional level – where problems develop and are best addressed – this organization proved ineffectual. Regional coordinators were unable to integrate and coordinate the efforts of independent police and human rights observers. Incompatible reporting procedures and quarrelsome working relationships made cooperation difficult, and in some cases, non-existent. In light of this, a more decentralized organization capable of better integrating the varied activities within each region may be more appropriate.[112] As one regional coordinator suggests, "Perhaps it would be better to reproduce in each region the kind of UN organization that exists at the national level."[113] If such changes were implemented, the

---

[108] Security Council Resolution 693, passed on May 20, 1991, authorized the deployment of forces to verify compliance to the San José Agreement.
[109] Even human rights observers acknowledge that advice from uniformed observers was more easily accepted by members of the armed forces and national police. Interviews with ONUSAL observers, August 1993.
[110] Interviews with ONUSAL observers, August 1993.
[111] See UN doc. S/23402.
[112] See Costa, "Naciones Unidas," p. 23 for a similar set of recommendations.
[113] Interview with ONUSAL Regional Coordinator, August 1993.

regional coordinators would be better able to supervise and integrate the activities of the various contingents within their regions.

A second area for improvement is the selection and preparation of ONUSAL personnel. The quality and preparedness of UN personnel are obvious concerns in any UN mission. The case of El Salvador, however, raises several specific points regarding the selection and preparation of police observers. As in Cambodia and Namibia, ONUSAL police observers tasked with overseeing public security were entrusted with substantially more responsibility, and had more interaction with the local populace, than other UN personnel. Consequently, it is essential that police observers are trained adequately to insure high levels of professionalism and performance. In El Salvador, this was not always the case. Police observers were often insensitive to political and cultural dynamics, received minimal preparation before arriving in country, and sometimes refused to cooperate among themselves because of very different concepts of "community policing."[114]

This problem could be ameliorated by instituting several organizational changes. First, the UN could improve future performance by encouraging donor countries to make commitments to maintain the same police personnel within a mission for extended periods to insure the necessary continuity. Also, UN planners should display greater sensitivity for both the advantages and disadvantages of having police and military observers selected from donor countries within the region in which they are deployed.[115] And, there must be widespread recognition that effective monitoring and public security reform is not simply a question of redeploying UN police forces from one country to another: UN police observers must understand the political context in which they are working and exemplify UN standards in their respect for human rights and conduct of enforcement responsibilities. These issues could be addressed through the development of a mandatory police observer training program that not only standardizes police procedures and provides human rights instruction, but also equips observers with the political and cultural background they need, prior to deployment. This is not a new idea. A UN observer training program has been proposed

[114] Interview with ONUSAL officials, UN human rights observers, and human rights workers, August 1993.
[115] The advantages are that similarities in language and culture are less disruptive for observers and the local populace; such a policy maintains a South–South, rather than a North–South, dialogue between the parties and the UN observers. At the same time, because so few Latin American countries have a tradition of democratic governance, respect for human rights, and civilian control of the military, a contingent comprised solely of regional peacekeepers could have been potentially destructive in the case of El Salvador.

by numerous studies in the past.[116] The El Salvador experience demonstrates how important it is that this issue be addressed, particularly for police observers.

The UN and bilateral efforts

A second issue deserving consideration is the relationship between bilateral assistance efforts and the multilateral efforts of the UN. In this respect, El Salvador is unique because of special contributions made by the Four Friends, and its long-standing relationship with the United States. This experience inspires two questions. First, is institutional reform best assisted through multilateral or bilateral efforts? The US military's involvement in armed forces reform suggests that bilateral efforts, if provided sufficient resources, may facilitate modest institutional reform.[117] Unity of effort in such cases favors efficient and less contentious operations.

It is also apparent that bilateral efforts run a greater risk of partiality, particularly when a special relationship already exists between the patron and one of the disputants. Because of its long-standing relationship with the Salvadoran government, for example, ICITAP offered its misguided support for Peña Durán, advocated the transfer of the SIU and UEA into the PNC, and passively responded to the government's decision to discontinue ONUSAL's support. Conversely, multilateral UN operations may be desirable for different reasons. Because of its multilateral composition, its deep involvement in other interdependent aspects of the peace process, and perhaps most importantly because of its purported impartiality, the UN is better suited, perhaps, to oversee and assist institutional reform.[118] For example, had the UN played a more influential role in the creation of the PNC, it may have been more resistant than the US to the appointment of Peña Durán and the transfer of the UEA. As it was, the UN lacked leverage because of the long-standing relationship between El Salvador and the USA, and because major donor countries, particularly the USA, distributed technical and logistical support directly to the Salvadoran government. It is conceivable that a more robust multilateral approach to all aspects

---

[116] See The Clinton Administration's Policy on Reform of Multilateral Operations, Executive Summary, 1994.

[117] This favorable assessment should not be seen as a wholesale endorsement of US involvement in armed forces reform. See note 63.

[118] In addition, the tensions between various international contingents evident in the case of the Academy may in fact be healthy, exposing the reforming institution to a variety of approaches and ensuring that it does not become a prototype of any one country.

of institution-building, particularly armed forces and public security force reform, would have been more effective.

Regardless of whether bilateral or multilateral efforts are more efficient, political realities, the dearth of willing donors, and the bureaucratic and financial constraints of the UN are likely to dictate that in many cases a small number of independent donors provide the bulk of post-conflict assistance directly to the recipients. Thus, a second, equally pressing question is how bilateral efforts are best integrated into the overall peace process. The most notable lesson from El Salvador is the need to clarify the content and scope of the responsibilities of the UN and the other actors involved, and to establish means for coordinating bilateral efforts. For example, the UN's contribution to institutional reform was, in some cases, negligible because of the ambiguity in, and its passive interpretation of, the peacebuilding mandate. As a consequence, while the United States remained deeply involved in certain aspects of armed forces reform, the UN struggled to determine if the implementation of reforms, such as the dissolution of the DNI, actually took place. Likewise, in the case of the Academy, the UN was only peripherally involved from the very beginning. And, despite the fact that it was explicitly assigned responsibility by the Peace Agreement, it had a difficult time coordinating the efforts of the various contingents. The result, some argue, is an ad hoc curriculum composed of a collection of lesson plans submitted by the various contingents, which none of the foreign advisors find completely satisfactory.[119]

Future UN efforts should focus on better integrating the initiatives "sub-contracted" to bilateral actors into the overall peace process. The creation or dramatic reform of state institutions requires detailed coordination between those who develop the plan and those who implement it. In El Salvador, the UN should have been more directly involved in developing a plan for the Academy and remained engaged throughout its implementation. Second, though the political situation may necessitate ambiguity on particularly contentious issues, the UN should make every effort to iron out the specific details of institutional reform efforts prior to the deployment of UN resources. If the responsibilities of various contingents had been determined during the negotiations, or in the early months of the deployment, some of the problems surrounding the creation of the Academy might have been averted.[120] Finally, the El Salvador experience suggests that in order for the UN to be successful in coordinating or supervising bilateral

---

[119] Interview with US Justice Department Official, San Salvador, August 1993.

[120] Though the political situation may require that detailed agreements on seemingly intractable issues be delayed, a certain amount of consensus on specific aspects of

efforts, its mandate must clearly specify the scope of its oversight responsibilities.

Defining verification

The most complex and controversial issue to be considered is how ambitiously the UN should define its post-conflict responsibilities. In El Salvador, Resolution 729 authorized ONUSAL to verify the implementation of all the provisions of the Accords.[121] At a minimum, this implied that the UN, serving as a neutral body, had responsibility for reporting to all parties on the status of implementation. The preceding pages, however, provide several contrasting examples of ways in which ONUSAL interpreted its mandate.

In the first case – verifying the cessation of armed conflict – the UN applied a very liberal interpretation of its mandate and engaged in a wide range of activities to insure compliance by both parties; in this instance, such an approach was hugely successful. In the second case – verifying the demobilization of the FMLN – ONUSAL did all that it could by pressuring for legitimate weapons inventories and by verifying, in good faith, the final FMLN weapon inventories. However, this action failed to deter FMLN violations and could have been disastrous to the peace process when weapon caches were discovered. In the third case – verifying armed forces reform – the UN did less than it should have by simply verifying the development of plans for institutional reform, rather than taking the more intrusive steps necessary to verify their implementation.

The lesson to be drawn from these examples is that even within a particular UN operation, verification efforts must be crafted on a case by case basis depending on the situation and the issues at stake. Because verification may entail more than simply reporting on the state of compliance, the UN should be prepared to apply political pressure, mediate controversies, provide logistical support, and deploy UN observers to overcome the inevitable obstacles that arise during implementation. Obviously, the UN should be most active in situations which threaten to undermine the peace process and in which it is well positioned to apply effective pressure. The verification of the cessation of armed conflict is an example of the successful application of an activist approach. The verification of armed forces reform was less successful because ONUSAL narrowly interpreted its responsibilities and was passive in its oversight of implementation. As the experiences of the

---

institutional reform is necessary if they are to avoid becoming mired in controversy. Admittedly, this is a difficult balancing act.

[121] Security Council Resolution 729, January 14, 1992.

police division illustrate, verification may require that UN observers be deployed at the unit level where they can effectively monitor and assist with the implementation of reforms. At the same, after exhausting all available means, the UN may be incapable of verifying certain aspects of an agreement. Such was the case with the FMLN weapons inventories. When faced with such circumstances, the UN must strike an appropriate balance between advancing the peace process by overlooking potentially incomplete compliance, and maintaining credibility as an unbiased partner. Finding this balance will never be easy; recognizing that such tradeoffs exist is a first step toward dealing with them appropriately.

Conclusion

In summary, it is useful to reflect on the three questions posed at the beginning of this discussion. First, have UN efforts contributed to lasting peace? Second, how should the UN define its post-conflict responsibilities? And, third, how effectively has ONUSAL executed its mandate? In answer to the third question, ONUSAL's engagement in the five activities discussed in this chapter was a qualified, but undeniably successful, first step toward effective post-conflict UN operations. Through the activities of military and police observers, the UN helped build confidence among the parties and lay the groundwork for lasting institutional reform.

In answer to the second question, the El Salvador experience demonstrates that in traveling along the continuum from peacekeeping to peacebuilding, the UN may be required to administer a wide range of verification efforts, that such efforts are costly in both material and human resources, and that a clearly defined UN mandate is instrumental to success. It also shows that regardless of UN efforts, the willingness of conflicting parties to adhere to agreements and to strive actively and sincerely to resolve their differences is the most crucial ingredient of success.

In answer to the first question of whether the UN has contributed to "lasting peace," it is important to acknowledge that in El Salvador the UN faced severe challenges, many of which are likely to exist in other post-conflict situations. The many setbacks suffered along the way are reminders that the path to peace will often be an arduous one. As of this writing, it remains to be seen whether Salvadoran society will be capable of consolidating and perpetuating lasting peace. It is fair to say, however, that the remarkable progress achieved thus far would not have been possible without the comprehensive post-conflict efforts of the United Nations.

13 Rights and reconciliation in El Salvador

Ian Johnstone

Introduction

The centrality of human rights to the El Salvador peace process is not surprising given the history of that country's conflict.[1] The San José Agreement on Human Rights was the first substantive agreement reached by the parties. ONUSAL was initially deployed as a human rights verification mission, and three commissions were established to investigate past abuses and make recommendations on how to overcome the culture of impunity that plagued the country. Participatory opportunities were expanded, first and foremost by legitimizing the FMLN as a political party, but also through electoral reforms and the establishment of the National Commission for the Consolidation of Peace (COPAZ) so "civilian society" could participate "in the process of the changes resulting from the negotiations."[2] Perhaps most importantly, a serious attempt was made to overhaul the justice system by renovating and reforming historically corrupt institutions.

Neither of the parties nor the UN expected to deal with human rights monitoring first in the negotiations; the armed forces headed the list of items set out in the Caracas Agenda. However, when early agreement on the armed forces (and most other items on the agenda) proved to be

---

This chapter is an adapted and condensed version of *Rights and Reconciliation: UN Strategies in El Salvador*, Boulder, Col.: Lynne Rienner, 1995. The views here are entirely those of the author and should not be attributed in any manner to the United Nations.

[1] For an authoritative account of the human rights situation during the war years, see *From Madness to Hope: The 12-year War in El Salvador*, Report of the Commission on Truth for El Salvador, S/25500 (April 1, 1993) (hereinafter cited as the Truth Commission report).

[2] The New York Agreement, September 25, 1991, art. I(1). For a compilation of the Peace Accords, see *El Salvador Agreements: The Path to Peace* (hereinafter, *Path to Peace*), published by the United Nations Department of Public Information in cooperation with ONUSAL, May 1992. For a good summary of the electoral reforms, see Jack Spence and George Vickers, *Toward a Level Playing Field? A Report on the Post-War Salvadoran Electoral Process* (Cambridge, Mass.: Hemisphere Initiatives, 1994), p. 9.

impossible, in July 1990, the UN intermediary Alvaro de Soto put the issue of human rights on the table and, after a day of intense negotiations, the San José Agreement was signed. It set out a number of basic rights the parties were obliged to respect and it called for UN verification of both individual cases and "situations which appear to reveal the systematic practice of human rights violations." It also empowered the UN to make recommendations to the parties on remedial measures and to "offer its support to judicial authorities" in order to strengthen the administration of justice.

According to the Agreement, human rights verification was meant to begin *after* a ceasefire was achieved. However, when the negotiations on subsequent issues bogged down, the parties requested the deployment of the verification mission in mid-1991, before the ceasefire was in place. The decision to deploy was unprecedented and difficult for the UN, because of concerns about the safety of the observers and whether they could fulfill their mission while fighting was continuing.[3] Nevertheless, a preliminary mission headed by Mr. Iqbal Riza sent to El Salvador in early 1991 concluded that the security risks were bearable and that "there was a widespread desire in all sectors of opinion ... that the United Nations should commence verification of the agreement ... without awaiting a cease-fire".[4]

A more fundamental concern was whether the UN could function as an honest broker in the negotiations while simultaneously investigating and publicizing human rights abuses. No matter how impartial the UN sought to be, could it criticize the human rights practices of one side or the other without its objectivity being questioned?[5] Fortunately, the risk was judged worth taking and a mission of some hundred observers was deployed in July 1991, composed of human rights officers and military and police advisors. Its mandate, defined by ONUSAL, was "to actively monitor the human rights situation; investigate specific cases of alleged human rights violations; make recommendations; and lastly report to the Secretary-General and through him to the United Nations Security Council and General Assembly."[6] The result was a decrease in the level of human rights abuses, mainly because the UN's presence and authority to "visit any place freely and without prior notice" had a dissuasive

---

[3] Interview with Mr. Iqbal Riza, New York, April 12, 1993. See also S/23037 (September 16, 1991), appendix, paras. 12–14.2

[4] S/23037 and annex (16 September 1991), para. 3. The concerns about safety were not unfounded – military clashes often occurred while ONUSAL personnel were performing their verification functions in the field – though no one was injured. S/23222 (November 15, 1991), para. 5

[5] S/23037 (September 16, 1991), appendix, para. 15

[6] A/45/1055 and S/23037 (September 16, 1991), annex, para. 1.

effect. The level of violence decreased and was concentrated away from urban centers, primarily because the parties did not want to risk UN casualties and incur the wrath of the international community.[7] The early deployment of ONUSAL also contributed to the broader peace process as a confidence building measure, by signifying that both sides had given up on seeking a military victory. Moreover, the presence of ONUSAL significantly raised the political costs to either party of breaking the talks, making the process seem irreversible.[8]

My purpose in this chapter is not to analyze the human rights-related aspects of the peace process per se, but rather to examine the role of ONUSAL with a view to drawing lessons for future multidimensional peace operations. Two themes run through the analysis. The first concerns the symbiotic relationship between human rights and the peace process: on the one hand, the San José Agreement (and the early deployment of ONUSAL) paved the way to the broader political settlement; on the other hand, the demands of the peace process opened the door to deeper human rights accountability than either of the parties anticipated or may even have desired. In other words, the success of the peace process was partly attributable to the emphasis on human rights, and progress on human rights was dependent on the broader peace-making, peacekeeping and peacebuilding efforts.

The second theme concerns the complex relationship between human rights and national reconciliation. Is it possible in the aftermath of these brutal conflicts to achieve social peace *and* justice? El Salvador illustrates that these goals are not mutually exclusive and may even be mutually reinforcing. The human rights abuses that characterized the conflict were a manifestation of the militarization of society, one of the root causes of the struggle.[9] Addressing this root cause entailed

---

[7] Interview with Salvador Sanchez-Ceren, San Salvador, August 18, 1993. Despite the dangers to which UN personnel were subjected, ONUSAL reported in November 1991 that the chiefs of the armed forces of El Salvador and of FMLN combatants were honoring their pledge to guarantee the safety of mission personnel. S/23222 (November 15, 1991), annex, para. 6.

[8] This point was emphasized by a negotiator of the Accords on the government side. Interview with General Mauricio Ernesto Vargas, El Salvador, August 17, 1993.

[9] Although the root causes of the conflict are both economic and political, the Accords themselves are more directly focused on the latter. In addition to ending the war, the Accords are designed to diminish the power of military and open "political space" for disaffected sectors of the population. Interview with Abraham Rodríguez, El Salvador, 17 August 1993. See also "Impunidad y falta de administración de justicia: obstculos al proceso de paz," published interview with Abraham Rodríguez, *Tendencias*, no. 26, December 1993–January 1994), p. 15. Militarization, it should be noted, happened on both sides. When the violent conflict erupted in 1979 and throughout the war years, the power of the military establishment over civilian authorities was so complete that, in the words of the Truth Commission, "none of the three branches of Government – judicial, legislative or executive – was capable of restraining the military's overwhelming

subordinating the military to civilian control and creating a more participatory system of governance. Tackling the human rights problem, therefore, was the wedge that opened the door to the broader political, social, and institutional transformation that the Accords were designed to bring about, which, in turn, drove the process of reconciliation – throughout Salvadoran society, as well as between the signatories of the Accords.

This chapter focuses on two human-rights related aspects of the peace process: the investigation of and accountability for past abuses, and institutional reform measures to prevent future abuses. Although the UN's mandate was limited to "verifying" implementation of all elements of the Accords, its role was more complex than that term would seem to imply. In addition to monitoring, the UN engaged in "good offices," applied direct pressure when the parties were intransigent and, when that failed, employed less direct means of securing compliance. The following analysis assesses the various strategies employed to protect and promote human rights and concludes with a set of observations and lessons for future UN efforts to help build the foundations for a just and stable peace.[10]

Investigative commissions

The aspect of the El Salvador peace process that received the widest international attention concerned three commissions established to investigate past human rights abuses. Two were agreed to in the Accords – the Ad Hoc Commission and the Truth Commission – and the third, called the Joint Group for the Investigation of Politically Motivated Illegal Armed Groups, was the product of a recommendation by the Truth Commission. Combined, these groups bring into sharp relief the delicate balance between the cause of peace and the demands of justice, providing lessons for other conflicts characterized by serious human rights violations.

control of society ... The sad fact is that they were transformed, in practice, into mere facades with marginal governmental authority." Truth Commission report, pp. 172 and 173. Meanwhile, the opposition in El Salvador became more militant during the 1970s and 1980s, progressively abandoning political tactics in favor of military ones.

[10] For a good overview of past and present UN action in the field of human rights, see Tom Farer and Felice Gaer, "The UN and human rights: at the end of the beginning," in Adam Roberts and Benedict Kingsbury (eds.), United Nations, Divided World, (Oxford: Clarendon Press, 1993), pp. 240–96. See also Peter R. Baehr and Leon Gordenker, The United Nations in the 1990s (London: Macmillan, second edn., 1994), chapter 5.

The Ad Hoc Commission

Overview

After months of some of the most difficult negotiations in the entire process, the parties agreed in the New York Agreement to the establishment of an Ad Hoc Commission to "purify" the armed forces. Composed of three Salvadoran civilians chosen for their "recognized independence of judgment and unimpeachable democratic credentials," the Commission was charged with evaluating military officers, taking into account their records of observance of human rights, professional competence and capacity to function "in the new situation of peace, within the context of a democratic society."[11] Any officer found deficient in one of these criteria was subject to discharge or transfer.

The origin of the Ad Hoc Commission was the desire of the FMLN to oust the *tandona* class of 1966 graduates of the Salvadoran Military Academy who dominated the army and public security forces. Unwilling to agree to the direct purge sought by the FMLN, the government proposed the establishment of a military commission to perform a "self-purge."[12] The Ad Hoc Commission was proposed by the UN as a compromise, to which the government reluctantly agreed but only on the condition that two members of the military be associated as observers.[13] For its part, the FMLN would have preferred foreigners on the Commission but accepted the compromise on the condition that the UN and the FMLN be involved in selecting the Commissioners.

The Commission issued its report on September 22, 1992, based on its review of 232 of the most senior military officers. By agreement of the recipients of the report – President Cristiani and Secretary-General Boutros-Ghali – it was kept confidential.[14] The recommendations should have been implemented one month later, but intense negotiations between Salvadoran authorities and emissaries of the Secretary-General led to an extension until January 1, 1993. When President Cristiani announced his plan in early January for removal of the named officers, however, the Secretary-General claimed that it did not fully

---

[11] Peace Agreement (hereinafter Chapultepec Agreement), *The Path to Peace,* pp. 49–50.

[12] Center for International Policy, "Salvadorans nearing agreement on armed forces," April 22, 1991, p. 2.

[13] Interview with senior UN official, New York, April 1993.

[14] The Accords do not stipulate whether the report should have been public but upon reading it President Cristiani felt, and the Secretary-General agreed, that confidentiality was necessary. Interview with President Cristiani, El Salvador, January 25, 1994. Although it became an open secret that many senior members of the military establishment were named, including the minister of defense and his deputy, the full list was never publicized.

conform to the recommendations of the Ad Hoc Commission.[15] Two months later, President Cristiani informed Mr. Boutros-Ghali that all officers listed in the report would be placed on leave by June 1993 and retired by the end of the year, which satisfied the Secretary-General.[16] Meanwhile, the Truth Commission released its report on March 15, 1993, naming some of the same officers, including Minister of Defense René Emilio Ponce and Vice-Minister of Defense Juan Orlando Zepeda. Ponce offered his resignation three days before the Truth Commission report was released, and he officially stepped down (with full honors) on July 1, 1993, completing implementation of the Ad Hoc Commission recommendations.

Assessment of the Ad Hoc Commission process

Purging the military was the most sensitive aspect of the entire peace process, precisely because some feared it would provoke a serious backlash in the military if not handled carefully. These fears became acute when the Commission exceeded expectations by recommending discharge of the entire senior military establishment, including officers the government viewed as having been integral to the peace process.[17] Although the need for full implementation was never publicly questioned, it was clear the government hoped to make the process as painless as possible for those purged. The FMLN, for its part, was split on how hard it should insist on complete and rapid implementation. The People's Revolutionary Party or ERP (changed to People's Renovating Expression in 1993) and National Resistance or RN were quite concerned about making President Cristiani's position *vis-à-vis* the military untenable and therefore displayed more flexibility than the other FMLN factions.[18]

---

[15] S/25078 (January 9, 1993). Of the 102 officers identified, eighty-seven were properly transferred or retired, seven were appointed as military attachés to embassies abroad and eight remained in their posts pending appropriate steps in the "period of transition" – i.e. during the remainder of Cristiani's mandate. The Secretary-General accepted the decisions on the eighty-seven, but not the other fifteen and requested President Cristiani to adopt measures "to regularize the situation" as soon as possible.

[16] He reported to the Security Council that the government's plan, when implemented, "would bring it into broad compliance with the recommendations of the Ad Hoc Commission." S/25516 (April 2, 1993). The decisive moment for President Cristiani may have come in February 1993 when the Clinton administration informed him that it would withhold military aid pending full compliance with the Ad Hoc Commission report. Margaret Popkin, George Vickers and Jack Spence, *Justice Impugned* (Cambridge, Mass.: Hemisphere Initiatives, 1993), p. 14, note 8.

[17] Negotiators on *both* sides and UN officials confirmed in interviews that few people expected such a far-reaching report from the Ad Hoc Commission. Interviews with Dr. Oscar Santamaría, El Salvador, August 16, 1993, Ana Guadalupe Martinéz, El Salvador, August 16, 1993, and a senior UN official, New York, April 1993.

[18] Interview with FMLN representative, El Salvador, January 1994. It should be

The Secretary-General accepted that the report should remain confidential and was flexible on the pace of implementation but drew a firm line on the need for full compliance.[19] After the initial delay, he refused President Cristiani's request to let some of the top officers remain in their posts until normal retirement, but carefully refrained from demanding action by a specific date – effectively putting the matter on hold until the Truth Commission reported in March. Thus the UN deftly insisted on compliance with the recommendations, but not in a way that would have destroyed President Cristiani's standing with the military.[20] Although this manner of handling the situation was necessary in the circumstances, it had the unfortunate effect of sending a mixed message to the population as a whole. The military officers named were removed from power, but allowing some to retire only when they were ready – and with full honors – raised doubts about whether the peace process had really cemented civilian control over the military.

Truth Commission

Overview

When the government and FMLN agreed in the April 1991 Mexico Agreements to establish a Truth Commission, "little notice was taken,"[21] because it was seen as secondary to the constitutional reforms agreed to at the time. It was conceived in response to FMLN pressure to prosecute and punish human rights abusers. The government demurred, but did not object to the idea of a commission to uncover the "truth" about the worst abuses committed by *both* the military and the FMLN.[22] The two sides then discussed the possibility of investigations of "sample" cases, leading the UN to propose a commission (composed of foreigners) to investigate past cases, but not to prosecute or criminally

---

emphasized that the Salvadoran military was not necessarily a unified bloc at the time. Some of the younger officers may have seen the purge as a welcome opportunity to supplant the *tandona* that had dominated the military for many years.

[19] The UN, USA and Four Friends all agreed that full compliance was essential but to achieve it; pragmatism was necessary, since it would be counter-productive to push President Cristiani to do the politically impossible. Interview with two UN diplomats, New York, 1993.

[20] Even for those officers who were known to have been included on the list, the basis for their removal was never public. This face-saving device meant none were publicly accused of having committed human rights violations – they could have been removed for the lesser offenses of "unprofessionalism" or "lack of adaptability to the new situation of peace."

[21] UN Press Release, SG/SM/4942. Statement of the Secretary-General on release of Truth Commission report (March 15, 1993).

[22] Interview with senior UN official, New York, April 1993.

punish offenders. In agreeing to the Truth Commission, each side saw it as a complement to the Ad Hoc Commission and therefore compromised a little – the FMLN by accepting its non-prosecutorial character, and the government by accepting foreigners.

The objective of the Truth Commission, as set out in the Mexico Agreements, was to "investigate serious acts of violence that [had] . . . occurred since 1980 and whose impact on society urgently require[d] that the public should know the truth." The Commission could gather information by any means deemed appropriate, interview anybody and visit any place freely. It was authorized to recommend *binding* legal, political, or administrative measures that followed from the investigations, but it was expressly forbidden from functioning as a judicial body. The Commissioners were appointed by the Secretary-General on December 10, 1991, after some difficulty getting the parties to agree on three people who had sufficient international stature, were knowledgeable about the region and had the acumen to pull off such a sensitive assignment. The appointees were Belisario Bentacur, former president of Colombia, Reinaldo Figueredo, former foreign minister of Venezuela and Thomas Buergenthal, United States' law professor and former president of the Inter-American Court for Human Rights. A staff of twenty-two advisors and researchers, plus fourteen forensic and other experts (all foreign) was recruited to assist the Commission, which began its work in July 1992.

To alleviate the fears of potential witnesses about the repercussions of testifying and in line with its non-judicial character, the Commission decided it was neither necessary nor appropriate to grant full due process rights to each accused wrongdoer. Nevertheless, because it felt it had no alternative but to name individuals in its report – not to do so, the Commission stated, "would be to reinforce the very impunity to which the parties instructed the Commission to put an end"[23] – at least minimal procedural and evidentiary guarantees had to be provided. Thus most of the information was gathered on a confidential basis, which meant the subjects of the investigations did not have the opportunity to confront their accusers, although no findings were based solely on the testimony of a single source or witness nor on secondary sources such as reports from governments.

Truth Commission report

The Commission received over 22,000 complaints of extra-judicial executions, forced disappearances, torture, and other acts of violence

---

[23] S/25500 (April 1, 1993), p. 25.

which occurred between January 1980 and July 1991. It focused on individual cases that "outraged Salvadoran society and/or international opinion" and series of cases revealing a "systematic pattern of violence or ill-treatment." The report, released on March 15, 1993, attributed to the government side twelve cases of extra-judicial executions, three of enforced disappearances, three massacres of peasants by armed forces and four cases of death squad assassinations. On the FMLN side, it described the execution of eleven mayors, plus eight other extrajudicial executions (although the Commission could not reach full agreement on responsibility for two of the cases) and one case of kidnapping. Among the most notorious events described were, on the government side, the assassination of Archbishop Romero in 1980, the massacre of over 500 people at El Mozote in 1981, the murder of six Jesuit priests, their cook and her daughter in 1989 and, on the FMLN side, the killing of four US marines in an affluent suburb of San Salvador in 1985. Although the report did not shed much new light on these events, by giving them the stamp of official acknowledgment, debate on whether they occurred and who was responsible finally ended.[24]

More far-reaching were the numerous recommendations made by the Truth Commission, including:

- dismissal from the armed forces or civil service, and disqualification from public office for ten years, of all persons named in the report;
- resignation of all members of the Supreme Court;
- deconcentration of the power of the Supreme Court;
- an investigation of "private armed groups" (a euphemism for death squads);
- new legislation to guarantee due process in the criminal justice system, including measures to make the remedy of *habeas corpus* more effective; and
- ratification of various international human rights instruments and acceptance of the compulsory jurisdiction of the Inter-American Court of Human Rights.

The Truth Commission did not recommend prosecution and punishment of those named because, in the words of the report, "El Salvador

---

[24] Human Rights Watch/Americas *Accountability and Human Rights: The Report of the United Nations Commission on the Truth for El Salvador*, vol. 5, no. 7 (1993), p. 2 (hereinafter *Accountability and Human Rights*). The most important new finding of the Truth Commission report was to attribute responsibility for the murder of the Jesuit priests to Colonel René Emilio Ponce (who became minister of defense), Colonels Zepeda and Montano (who became vice ministers of defense), General Bustillo and commander of the army first brigade Colonel Fuentes. It also revealed that Colonel Manuel Antonio Rivas Mejía, the chief investigator on the case, was involved in its cover up.

has no system for the administration of justice which meets the minimum requirements of objectivity and impartiality so that justice can be rendered reliably. [A] judicial debate in the current context, far from satisfying a legitimate desire for justice, could revive old frustrations, thereby impeding the achievement of that cardinal objective, reconciliation."[25]

The Secretary-General hoped publication of the Truth Commission report would be "a watershed in the process of reuniting Salvadoran society" on the theory that Salvadorans had to go through "the catharsis of facing the truth" in order to put behind them the trauma of the war.[26] The government's reaction to the report, on the whole, was dismissive. The members of Supreme Court denounced it and said they had no intention of resigning,[27] and Defense Minister Ponce called it "insolent." President Cristiani accused the Commission of exceeding its authority and claimed the report "[did] not respond to the wishes of the majority of Salvadorans who [sought] to forgive and forget everything having to do with that very sorrowful past."[28] He called for an amnesty immediately before the report was released to foreclose any possibility of those named being prosecuted, and legislation to that effect was adopted in the Assembly on March 20.

Nor was the FMLN entirely satisfied with the report. In a letter to the Secretary-General, the Coordinator-General of the FMLN stated that notwithstanding a number of reservations, the Frente accepted responsibility for the events reported and pledged to fulfill the recommendations in the report.[29] However, the FMLN conditioned its compliance on compliance by the government, and the leader of the only faction specifically named in the report, Joaquín Villalobos of the ERP, called the ten-year ban on holding public office "absurd and ridiculous."[30] The FMLN leadership as a whole expressed dissatisfaction with the

---

[25] S/25500 (April 1, 1993), p. 178.

[26] UN Press Release, SG/SM/4942 (March 15, 1993). The Security Council for its part issued a statement through its president underlining the need for the parties to comply with the recommendations. S/25427 (March 18, 1993).

[27] Statement signed by 15 Supreme Court officials on March 22, 1993, pp. 1–12 (quoted in Human Rights Watch/Americas *Accountability and Human Rights*, p. 21). Supreme Court President Mauricio Gutierrez Castro, the most vociferous critic of the report, said "only God can remove me from my position – by taking my life." Tracy Wilkinson, "Salvadoran leader blasts UN report," *Los Angeles Times*, March 19, 1993. The president argued that the Truth Commission was created by "an eminently political agreement" between the Executive Branch of the government and the FMLN "from which no impact whatsoever may be derived that subverts the order established by the Constitution . . ." *Diaro Latino*, March 29, 1993.

[28] Quoted in *Accountability and Human Rights*, p. 20.

[29] S/25812 (May 21, 1993), para. 54.

[30] FBIS, March 22, 1993, p. 14 (quoted in *Accountability and Human Rights*, p. 23).

"politics" that went into preparation of the report, although they were less critical than the government of its findings.[31]

The UN's first response to the report was the Secretary-General's expression of displeasure with the hasty amnesty, which in his view should have come only after a broad degree of national consensus had been created in favor of it.[32] Regarding the recommendations, as with the Ad Hoc Commission report, the UN was in the awkward position of having to decide whether it should push for full compliance more assertively than the parties themselves. It moved cautiously by first conducting a detailed analysis of the recommendations and the measures needed to implement them.[33] And in the end, ONUSAL refrained from pushing forcefully for implementation of the most controversial recommendations, such as the resignation of the Supreme Court and the dismissal or disqualification from public office of those named in the report.

Assessment of the Truth Commission process

The impact of the Truth Commission report was mixed. The first and most obvious outcome was to end debate on some of the incidents described in the report, which were well-known but never officially acknowledged. Furthermore, assigning "intellectual" responsibility for those acts to senior officials or leaders was a step in breaking down the wall of impunity that had developed as Salvadoran society became more militarized. The too hasty amnesty, however, undermined the significance of that step. The "catharsis" the Secretary-General hoped the Truth Commission would generate was not possible with so little political or public debate about the implications of the report.

The recommendations were perhaps more important than the findings. In March 1995, the Legislative Assembly finally ratified the optional Protocol to the International Covenant on Civil and Political Rights, and accepted the jurisdiction of the Inter-American Court of Human Rights. A group to investigate death squad activity was established, and certain steps were taken to improve the administration of justice. However, even the relatively mild personal sanctions were not fully implemented: the members of the Supreme Court did not resign,

[31] Interview with FMLN representative, El Salvador, January 1994. Americas Watch reports that the ERP felt it was unfairly singled out because it leaders were the most forthcoming, but that it was not clear evidence of ERP abuses came only or even primarily from "confessions" by the faction's senior leaders, or that the ERP provided more information than the other factions. *Accountability and Human Rights*, p. 12.

[32] UN Press Release, SG/SM 4950 (March 24, 1993).

[33] The outcome of the analysis is contained in S/25812 (May 21, 1993), add. 3 and annex.

various named civil servants remained in their posts, and members of FMLN faction named in the report participated in the elections and won seats in the Assembly. The UN belatedly began pushing hard for implementation of the structural recommendations, but those requiring constitutional amendments were not adopted before the end of that legislative term. As a result, the deepest reforms recommended by the Truth Commission, including deconcentration of the power of the Supreme Court, cannot be implemented until at least 1997, because constitutional amendments require ratification by two successive legislatures.[34]

Joint Group for the Investigation of Illegal Armed Groups

Overview

The Truth Commission reported that "one of the most horrendous sources of the violence which swept the country in recent years was the activity of private armed groups which operated with complete impunity."[35] The activities of death squads peaked during the war and subsided throughout the peace process, although few doubted that the squads still existed when the Truth Commission issued its report. From 1991 until the middle of 1993, overt death squad activity was rare. From August to November 1993, however, ONUSAL received forty-seven complaints of possible political homicides, prompting it to announce in its ninth report that the death squads had been reactivated.[36] The Secretary-General, therefore, instructed the Director of the Human Rights Division of ONUSAL to assist the government of El Salvador to carry out the investigation recommended by the Truth Commission.[37] Following a trip by Under-Secretary-General Marrack Goulding to El

---

[34] For a full discussion of this issue, see pp. 332–34.

[35] Truth Commission report, p. 180.

[36] S/1994/47 (January 18, 1994), para. 97. In the Human Rights Division's own investigation of the phenomenon, it found no indication of state involvement in the killings. The political violence was directed at the "democratic political system" rather than particular social sectors or political groupings, ONUSAL concluded, reflecting "the intransigence of fringe elements attacking the Salvadoran nation as a whole, all national political forces and the democracy proposed in the peace agreements". S/1994/47 (January 18, 1994), paras. 15 and 16.

[37] S/26689 (November 3, 1993), Letter from the Secretary-General to the President of the Security Council. In October, the government had created an Interinstitutional Commission and an Interinstitutional Investigation Group to investigate the possible resurgence of illegal armed groups, but ONUSAL deemed it insufficiently independent. S/26790 (November 23, 1993), para. 11 and S/1994/47 (January 18, 1994), para. 21. The Commission was composed of the Minister and Chief of Staff in the Office of the President, and representatives of the Office of the Attorney-General, the National Civil Police, the Criminal Investigation Commission, the State Intelligence Agency, and the

Salvador, "a Joint Group for the investigation of politically motivated illegal groups" was established, composed of two independent nominees of President Cristiani, the El Salvador human rights ombudsman and the Director of ONUSAL's Human Rights Division. The Group was formally established on December 8, 1993, with a mandate to investigate the activities of "illegal armed groups" from January 16, 1992 (when the Peace Accords were signed) to the present.

The Group issued its report at the end of July 1994. Relying heavily on documents declassified by the US government in 1993, the Joint Group was able to uncover abundant information about the connections between the death squads and Salvadoran public security forces during the years of conflict.[38] It confirmed that squads still existed after 1991 but, on the whole, the organs of the state were not involved. Nevertheless, the Joint Group found that illegal armed groups continued to operate under the protection of *some* members of the armed forces and National Police, and that the justice system "continued to provide the margin of impunity these structures require." Individuals were not named publicly because the Group decided the data in its possession did not "have the force of full evidence that would make it possible to point to specific responsibilities."[39] Its main recommendation was the creation, within the Criminal Investigation Division of the National Civil Police, of a special unit to continue the investigations. It also requested the human rights ombudsman to monitor the investigation of murders in which a political motivation seemed to exist, and recommended a "purification" by the Supreme Court of all magistrates and judges who, according to the evaluations of the National Council of the Judiciary, were involved in legal infractions or professional misconduct.

Assessment of the Joint Group process

The fact that the Group was established at all is significant given the sensitivity of the issue and the suspected past links of death squads to state officials and members of the wealthy elite.[40] Furthermore, it did

Presidential Commissioner for Human Rights. It was assisted in its investigations of some of the cases by police bodies from the USA, UK, and Spain.

[38] Report of the Joint Group for the Investigation of Politically Motivated Illegal Armed Groups, S/1994/989 (October 22, 1994), p. 19 (hereinafter, Joint Group report).

[39] Instead, the evidence gathered was turned over, in a restricted annex, to the competent Salvadoran authorities, the National Counsel for the Defense of Human Rights and ONUSAL. Joint Group report, p. 29.

[40] The ONUSAL Human Rights Division called its establishment "a wholesome example of political transparency, commitment to law and order and an institutional will to carry out an effective and independent investigation, which should be assessed in a positive light by domestic political forces and the international community". S/1994/47 (January 18, 1994), para. 100.

seem to have a dissuasive effect, at least during the election campaign, given that a major resurgence of death squad activity did not materialize, as feared. Beyond that, assessments of how "successful" it was depend on how success is defined. When the Group began its work, it was generally thought that the death squad phenomenon was more manageable than in the 1980s, primarily because the purge of the army and disbandment of the other security forces meant there was less "institutional cover" for these groups.[41] Nevertheless, there was considerable doubt that the Joint Group would be able to go much further than the Truth Commission in rooting out the problem. Optimists hoped individuals would be named, while skeptics would have settled for an "honest effort" that succeeded in promoting "reflection and thought."[42] In the end, the Group did not meet the hopes of the optimists but exceeded the expectations of the skeptics by drawing firm conclusions about cases of death squad activity which were "directed, backed, covered up or tolerated by members of the military or police, the judicial organ or the municipal body."[43]

Uncovering the truth: lessons from El Salvador

The combined experience of these human rights investigative commissions provides a number of important lessons. First, it illustrates some of the advantages and disadvantages of leaving sensitive issues in peace talks to be dealt with by ad hoc bodies after the negotiations have been completed. On the positive side, the decision to create the Ad Hoc Commission broke the deadlock in the negotiations on the purge of the military. Also, empowering the Truth Commission to make binding recommendations opened the door to broader judicial reform than the parties specifically agreed to. On the other hand, as Timothy Wilkins argues elsewhere in this volume, these post-agreement devices can be risky if their mandate is not clear.[44] The Accords were negotiated between the FMLN leadership and the executive branch of government, but in consultation with those affected by the terms of the agreement. Referring some of these details to ad hoc bodies produced some unexpected results which, though not necessarily bad, nearly threw off the equilibrium the parties sought to establish in their negotiations.

A second more fundamental issue raised by these commissions

---

[41] Interview with Salvador Samoyoa, El Salvador, January 20, 1994. Interview with ONUSAL official, El Salvador, January 1994.
[42] Interview with FMLN representative, El Salvador, January 1994.
[43] Joint Group report, p. 27.
[44] See Timothy Wilkins, "The El Salvador Peace Accords", chapter 11.

concerns the complex relationship between uncovering human rights abuses and promoting reconciliation. Some would argue that the best way to promote peace and reconciliation following conflicts characterized by massive human rights violations is to avoid dwelling on the past. Others claim that true reconciliation is not possible unless the truth about the past is revealed and the responsible individuals prosecuted and punished.[45] What happened in El Salvador fell between those extremes: the truth about the past was uncovered, individuals responsible were identified and some were sanctioned, but none were prosecuted or criminally punished.

Does this strike an appropriate balance? In the context of El Salvador, the answer is probably yes, even though the manner in which the recommendations of the Commissions were implemented left something to be desired. A purpose for prosecuting human rights offenders is to reinforce the principle of accountability by demanding an official accounting for wrongs that occurred.[46] Judicial proceedings are one way of achieving that goal,[47] but it can be served in other ways if individual responsibility is assigned and the wrongdoing is acknowledged – at least by those who have responsibility for ensuring it does not happen again.

[45] This is part of the rationale for the establishment of a war crimes tribunal for the former Yugoslavia, a conflict characterized by summary executions, "ethnic cleansing," torture, and rape. It also motivated calls for a war crimes tribunal in Rwanda, where the UN leveled accusations of genocide. For an interesting discussion of the problems inherent in trying to prosecute war criminals while simultaneously negotiating a peace settlement, see A. D'Amato, "Peace versus accountability in Bosnia," *American Journal of International Law*, vol. 88, no. 1, 1994, pp. 500–6. See also, T. Meron, "The case for war crimes trials in Yugoslavia," *Foreign Affairs*, Summer 1993, pp. 122–35. For legal analyses of the mandate and jurisdiction of the tribunal, see T. Meron, "War crimes in Yugoslavia and the development of international law," *American Journal of International Law*, vol. 88, no. 1, 1994, pp. 78–87; J. O'Brien, "The International Tribunal for Violations of International Humanitarian Law in the former Yugoslavia," *American Journal of International Law*, vol. 87, no. 4, 1993, pp. 639–59. The former Yugoslavia situation has generated renewed interest in the establishment of a Permanent International Criminal Court. See Report of the Working Group on the draft Statute for an International Criminal Court, annex to Report of the International Law Commission on the work of its 45th session UN/GAOR, 48th Sess, supp. no. 10 at p. 255, UN doc. A/48/10 (1993). See also, M. Cherif Bassiouni and Christopher L. Blakesley, "The need for an International Criminal Court in the New International Order," *Vanderbilt Journal of Transnational Law*, vol. 25, 1992, p. 151.

[46] Another reason of course is to deter future offenders, which is perhaps less important in the context of a peace process like El Salvador's where the reforms to the justice system are designed to provide that future deterrent.

[47] Amnesty International takes the position that cutting off judicial proceedings with preconviction amnesties undermines the goal of "healing the wounds and revealing the truth in a society." However, it takes no position on pardons granted after a conviction, "recognizing that [post-conviction pardons] may be deemed in the interests of national reconciliation after a period of violence and repression." Amnesty International, *Peacekeeping and Human Rights* (New York: Amnesty International USA, 1994), p. 25.

Despite the delays in purging the military and the fact that amnesty was granted to those named in the Truth Commission without any political or public debate, a deep dent was made in the impunity that plagued Salvadoran society. The "finger-pointing" by these commissions did not provide complete justice for crimes of the past but, combined with the institutional reforms to the public security and justice systems that were recommended, went a long way towards ensuring those atrocities would not recur.

Finally, the experience of these commissions raises important questions about the dilemma the UN faces when neither party is pushing hard for implementation of a particular aspect of a peace agreement. The government and the FMLN were ambivalent about the merits of aggressive implementation of the recommendations contained in the Ad Hoc and Truth Commission reports, genuinely worried that some of the far-reaching measures would generate a backlash and jeopardize the entire peace process. In those circumstances, how forcefully should the UN insist on implementation? Normally, the UN should not second-guess the apparent will of the parties in a consent-based operation. But, for three reasons, there may be exceptions to the rule. First, as a peace process progresses, the bargaining power between the parties shifts. Implementation of complex agreements should not turn on which party happens to have leverage on a particular issue at a given time. In the case of El Salvador, once the FMLN disarmed, it had little bargaining power left and therefore had to rely on the UN to maintain pressure on the government to fulfill its obligations. Secondly, the "parties" themselves may change over the life of a peace process. In El Salvador, a new president and a new administration were installed before the Accords were fully implemented, and the cohesiveness of the FMLN gradually eroded. In those circumstances, whose will should count when deviations from the Accords are contemplated? Third, the signatories to complex peace accords are not the only relevant actors in a process designed to transform a society. In El Salvador, other political parties, other government organs, and civil society all had a stake in the peace process. It would be perilous for the UN to endorse deals that suit the interests of the parties but are opposed by other actors on whom the success of a peace process depends. Nevertheless, the UN cannot be unduly rigid in the name of "loyalty to the mandate." Because circumstances can change, flexibility is sometimes required. When to show this flexibility is a matter of political judgment but a good rule of thumb for the UN is to seek as broad a local consensus as possible when deviations from the letter of peace accords are contemplated, or gaps need to be filled. "Deals" to that effect should be struck within representative bodies rather than between the parties narrowly defined.

Institutional reforms

Electoral participation

Expanding electoral participation, one of the rights enumerated in the Universal Declaration of Human Rights and other international instruments,[48] was an important element of the Salvadoran peace process. Although not intended to be the centerpiece of the Accords, the Secretary-General hoped the March 1994 elections would be the culmination of the peace process. They were called El Salvador's "elections of the century" because votes for president, the legislative assembly, municipalities and the Central American parliament all came (coincidentally) at a key moment in the history of the country.

Calderón Sol, leader of the ARENA party, won the presidential race, by a substantial margin over Rubén Zamora, who ran for a coalition composed of the Democratic Convergence, FMLN, and National Revolutionary Movement. Of the eighty-four seats contested in the assembly elections, ARENA won thirty-nine, the FMLN twenty-one, and the Christian Democratic party eighteen. ARENA's thirty-nine seats combined with the four that went to a smaller right-wing party gave the right a very slim majority in the assembly. ARENA also won 206 out of 262 mayoralties, with only sixteen going to the FMLN.

In retrospect, the elections were not the culmination of the peace process, but the significance of converting the FMLN from a military force to a legitimate political party should not be underestimated. It meant that the insurgent movement would operate within rather than outside the constitutional framework and, after a decade of bitter civil

---

[48] See Universal Declaration of Human Rights, art. 21; International Covenant on Civil and Political Rights, art. 25; and American Declaration of the Rights and Duties of Man, art. XX. Thomas Franck, in making the case for an emerging right to democracy in international law, argues that the right to self-determination, at least since the adoption of the International Covenant on Civil and Political Rights, has become a "principle of inclusion": the right of "peoples in all states to free, fair and open participation in the democratic process of governance freely chosen by each state." T. Franck, "The emerging right to democratic governance," *American Journal of International Law*, vol. 86, no. 1, 1992, p. 58. He also argues that the recent developments in the General Assembly, though non-binding, strengthen "the normative requirement of a participatory electoral process" by specifying the content of the right (at pp. 64–5). See GA Res. 45/150 (February 21, 1991) and GA Res. 46/137 (December 17, 1991). See also Franck's discussion of legislative and jurisprudential developments at the regional level in Latin America, Europe and elsewhere (at pp. 65–77).

war, could legally challenge the government in an election campaign on relatively equal footing. The elections themselves, however, came in the middle of the peace process (not at the end as called for in the original timetable), and they were marred by controversy surrounding registration and voting. Problems in registration meant that of the 2,700,000 names on the electoral lists, only some 2,350,000 were in possession of voting cards on election day.[49] Of those, the UN estimated that at least 25,000 people with voter cards were unable to vote; other observers estimated as many as 87,000.[50] Taking into account the 74,000 people whose applications for voter cards could not be validated, some portion of the 350,000 discrepancy between those on the electoral lists and those with voter cards, and as many as 87,000 people who showed up at the polls but did not vote, a figure of 300,000 is not an unreasonable estimate of those who wanted to vote but could not – which represented 20 percent of those who actually voted.[51] Moreover, of those who could have voted, a surprisingly large percentage chose not to. Voter turnout was 55 percent in the first round and 46 percent in the second, when the two top presidential candidates squared off against one another. These figures were an improvement over the 1991 elections but a lower turnout than either the 1982 or 1984 races.

The irregularities in the elections prompted ONUSAL (and later MINUSAL) to use its good offices to promote electoral reforms, the most important of which was the establishment of a national registry based on a single identity document. Despite recommendations to that effect by a presidentially appointed commission and pressure from the international donor community, little progress has been made and it appears unlikely they will be adopted in time to have an impact on the 1997 legislative elections.

Thus the 1994 elections did little to restore the confidence of the citizenry in the electoral system, confidence that had been shaken by many years of limited suffrage, electoral fraud, and violence. Nor did

[49] S/1994/304 (March 16, 1994), para. 7. According to one report, approximately 300,000 of the 350,000 disparity between names on the lists and holders of voting cards were people who followed all the procedures to get cards but never received them. "El Salvador elections 1994," New Jersey Observer Delegation report. The figure cited in a New York Times editorial is 340,000. "El Salvador's messed-up elections," *New York Times*, March 23, 1994, p. A14. The remainder are deceased persons whose names were never taken off the list and people who were registered twice.

[50] An Argentinean polling firm estimated that 6 percent of voters with cards, or 87,000 people, had attempted to vote and failed. This estimate is judged to be reasonably accurate by Hemisphere Initiatives, who had their own delegation of observers there and who consulted with other observers. *Elections of the Century*, pp. 6–7. See also, Steve Cagan, "El Salvador tries to vote," *The Nation*, April 18, 1994, p. 526.

[51] *Elections of the Century*, p. 7.

they advance other aspects of the peace process, because the Peace Accords were not a major issue in the campaign.[52] They were, however, the first elections in which all political forces in the country participated, marking a tentative step towards effective multiparty democracy. How big a step was taken should become clearer in the lead up to the presidential election in 1999. As a key figure in the peace process, David Escobar Galindo suggests, that may be El Salvador's true "election of the century," when Salvadorans must vote for a new president after five years of *peaceful* political struggle, in the context of a society transformed by the peace process.[53]

Thus for UN peace operations, the experience illustrates the importance of not becoming focused on elections to the exclusion of all else. In El Salvador, when the "electoral moment" took over, the attention of the parties turned away from the Accords, and elements in the country suggested there would be less need for the UN to monitor compliance after the formation of a new government. In this era of scarce resources, it is tempting for the UN to accept this logic and use elections as a convenient exit point from peacekeeping operations. In El Salvador, the UN wisely resisted this temptation.

Human rights ombudsman

An important element of the April 1991 agreement on legal and constitutional reforms was the creation of a National Counsel for the Defense of Human Rights (the ombudsman), with a mandate to promote and ensure respect for human rights. Though lacking judicial or legislative competence, the power of the office, at least on paper, is broader than most such institutions in other countries.[54] Among other things, the ombudsman in El Salvador can investigate cases, promote judicial or administrative remedies, monitor state organs, recommend legislation, and propose systemic reforms.

In its early stages, the ombudsman's office struggled to live up to its broad mandate. Financial constraints meant the work was slow to get started and slow to develop. By June 1994, only five regional offices had

---

[52] According to polls, the main concerns of voters were – in descending order of importance – reducing crime, creating jobs, dealing with inflation and eliminating poverty. *Elections of the Century*, p. 11. Human rights came much further down the list and campaigners found it difficult to run on the abstract platform of social and economic peace

[53] Interview with David Escobar Galindo, El Salvador, January 25, 1994.

[54] S/25521 and A/47/912 (April 5, 1993), para. 245. Its terms of reference are set out in art. 16 of the constitutional reform law (new article 94 of the Constitution), annexed to the Mexico Agreement, *The Path to Peace*, p. 23.

been opened (three in the preceding two months), and the target of one office in each of El Salvador's fourteen departments was not reached until early 1995.[55] To complicate matters, non-governmental human rights groups were half-hearted in their support for the first ombudsman, concerned that he would not be able to stake out an independent role for the office.[56] He, in turn, acted with "extreme caution"[57] and tended to view his mandate to promote "peace and reconciliation" as being as important as the protection of human rights.[58] Even more seriously, the stature of the office with other organs of the state was low, illustrated by the fact that as late as March 1995, just before ONUSAL's departure, most officials felt free to ignore the ombudsman's non-binding recommendations.[59]

Fortunately, as the peacekeeping mission neared its conclusion, the UN upgraded efforts to strengthen the ombudsman's office. Relations were not always easy, although from the beginning ONUSAL provided technical support and advice on human rights procedure, techniques of police and judicial investigation, and legal reasoning. More active efforts to actually transfer experience and raise the profile of the ombudsman began in the summer of 1994, when joint verification began, marking a turning point for the office as its level of activity (and access to international funding) increased.[60] Meanwhile, the ombudsman's participation in the Joint Group and continuing responsibility, in conjunction with the PNC, to investigate potential death squad activity, thrust the office into the middle of El Salvador's most serious human rights challenge. Moreover, in March 1995, Ms. Victoria Maria de Avilés, a

[55] Even then, the branches were underfinanced and lacked qualified personnel. A/49/888-S/1995/281 (April 18, 1995), para. 22; A/50/517 (October 6, 1995), para. 12.
[56] While favorably disposed to Dr. Molina personally, some the human rights organizations questioned whether he had adequate experience and firmness for the job. Interviews with representatives of human rights organizations, El Salvador, August 1993 and January 1994.
[57] S/1995/281 (April 18, 1995), para. 11.
[58] Interview with Dr. Molina, El Salvador, August 17, 1993. In dealing with other organs of the state, the ombudsman said he believed in carrying out his role "discreetly" rather than through public confrontation. Second report of the independent expert of the UN Commission on Human Rights. E/CN4/1993/11 (February 9, 1993), para. 128.
[59] S/1995/220 (March 24, 1995), para. 33.
[60] Before the summer of 1994, the ombudsman's office was concerned about appearing too dependent on ONUSAL and the UN did not want to appear to be abandoning its verification responsibilities. Fortunately, they were able to work out an operational approach that respected the independence of both institutions. S/1994/886 (July 28, 1994), para. 106. The idea behind joint verification, according to an ONUSAL regional coordinator in San Vicente, was to replicate the successful mentor relationship the Police Division had established with the National Civil Police. By serving as a model to the staff, introducing them to the population and advising and assisting on investigations, the ombudsman would progressively acquire ONUSAL's responsibilities and respect. Interview with Hector Contreras, El Salvador, August 14, 1993.

legal expert whose commitment to human rights was widely recognized, was elected the new National Counsel for the Defence of Human Rights. Unfortunately, her personal commitment has not been matched by the government, and she must still rely largely on international funding.

Judicial system

One of the most important but least developed aspects of the Peace Accords concerns the administration of justice. Prior to the peace process, the judicial system in El Salvador suffered from two major defects: the judiciary's lack of independence from organs of the state and political parties, and the over-concentration of power in the Supreme Court.[61] In an effort to deal with these problems, some critical constitutional and judicial reforms were agreed to in the April 1991 Mexico Agreement, including a new procedure for electing Supreme Court judges and the restructuring of the National Council of the Judiciary (the body that nominates Supreme and lower court candidates). These reforms marked a breakthrough in the negotiations,[62] but alone were not enough to overcome the deep defects in the system. To fill the gaps, ONUSAL's Human Rights Division and the Truth Commission made numerous supplementary recommendations, the most important of which sought to "depoliticize" the Supreme Court and remove some of its near total control over the administration of justice.

The new manner of electing the Supreme Court, namely by a two-thirds majority of legislators from a list drawn up by the NCJ, came into effect in June 1994, at the end of the term of the sitting members of the Court. However, there was a four-week delay caused by a bitter partisan struggle in the National Assembly, during which there was no Supreme Court.[63] The new president, José Domingo Mendez, was eventually

---

[61] The weaknesses of the system are well-described in the report prepared by Pedro Nikken, Independent Expert of the UN Commission on Human Rights. A/47/596 (November 13, 1992), paras. 151–9. See also, the Truth Commission report, Part V Recommendations, pp. 172–3.

[62] In an interview with the author, President Cristiani said that the constitutional amendments enacted pursuant to the Mexico Agreement were critical because they put in place "the basic foundations for reform," which would bind future governments as well as the signatories to the agreement. Interview with President Cristiani, El Salvador, January 25, 1994.

[63] In fact, in early 1994, the government began pushing for appointment of the new Supreme Court magistrates after the elections but before the new Assembly was installed at the end of April. Although this procedure would have been constitutional, ONUSAL publicly took the position that the new Assembly should elect the Court, based on the spirit of the Accords. (Interview with senior ONUSAL official, El Salvador, January 1994.) In the end ONUSAL's position won the day, but the new

elected by consensus as a compromise candidate and the Court quickly signaled its intention to modernize the judiciary.[64]

However, efforts to scale back some of the administrative power of the Supreme Court ran into considerable difficulty. Before the 1991 constitutional reforms, the Court appointed and dismissed all judges of first and second instance, justices of the peace, forensic physicians, and court employees, and it licensed and disciplined all lawyers. The only significant dent in this concentration of power brought about by the constitutional reforms was to authorize the National Council of the Judiciary (NCJ) to provide the Court with three candidates from which it would make each lower court appointment. Dissatisfied with this minimal step, the Truth Commission recommended granting the NCJ the power to appoint (not just nominate) and remove judges, and establishing a special independent body to license and discipline lawyers.[65] A draft law on these recommendations submitted to the Legislative Assembly generated little interest prior to the elections. A push from opposition political parties and non-governmental organizations after the elections led to the adoption of reform package in April 1994, which partly met one of the recommendations by assigning power to suspend lawyers to a new National Council of Lawyers and Notaries. However, no action was taken on the most important recommendation – granting to the NCJ the power to appoint judges – which requires amendment of the constitution and therefore ratification by two successive legislatures.

Moreover, the National Council of the Judiciary itself has not acquired the institutional independence envisaged in the Peace Accords, a potentially significant failing since, in addition to nominating judicial appointees, it evaluates the performance of magistrates and judges for promotion and disciplinary decisions made by the Supreme Court, and it oversees the Judicial Training School. Because the NCJ was effectively controlled by the Supreme Court prior to the peace agreement, the parties agreed to restructure it "so that its composition [would] guarantee its independence from the organs of State and from political parties and its membership [would] include not only judges but also sectors of society not directly connected with the administration of

Court was appointed only after an intense battle in the legislature over the presidency pitting David Escobar Galindo against Abraham Rodriguez.

[64] S/1995/281, April 18, 1995, para. 76.

[65] Truth Commission report, section V.III.A.2, 3 and 4, p. 181. These recommendations were essentially endorsed and reiterated by the Human Rights Division of ONUSAL. S/25521 (April 5, 1993), para. 224.

justice."[66] Much effort went into draft legislation but the Act eventually adopted, in the view of most outside observers, conflicted with the Mexico Agreement, primarily because it left the dismissal of some members of the Council to the discretion of the Supreme Court and none of them represents "sectors of society not directly connected to the judicial system."[67] Constitutional reforms initiated in April 1994 changed the procedure for dismissal but fell short of the recommendations of the Truth Commission in that no change was made to the composition of the NCJ or the manner of selecting it.

To make up for this lack of headway in direct challenges to the centralized justice system, ONUSAL encouraged bottom-up efforts to improve the quality and integrity of lower court judges and justices of the peace.[68] The first was the creation of a Judicial Training School, which was brought under the authority of the National Council of the Judiciary in late 1993, to enhance the professionalism of judges and other judicial officials. At that time ONUSAL began providing the school with technical support and a guiding vision, efforts which are still carried on by the UNDP and MINUSAL.

[66] Mexico Agreements, II.2.a, *Path to Peace*, p. 15; Chapultepec Agreement, chapter III.1.A., *Path to Peace*, p. 75

[67] These provisions were criticized by Pedro Nikken (E/CN4/1993/11, February 9, 1993, paras. 170 and 222), by the Truth Commission (section V.I.D.(a), p. 177), and by the Human Rights Division of ONUSAL (S/25521, April 5, 1993, para. 222). Some independent observers are even more critical, arguing that the manner of selecting the National Council of the Judiciary ensures that its composition will continue to be controlled by the Supreme Court. The new Council has eleven members: two lawyers proposed by the Supreme Court, one appellate magistrate, one trial judge, three practicing lawyers, one law professor from the University of El Salvador, two law professors from authorized private universities, and one member of the Public Prosecutor's Office. Critics worry that the Supreme Court, given its hold over the entire justice system, will be able to insure that at least six of the eleven members are loyal to it. Interview with Francisco Díaz (CESPAD), El Salvador, January 25, 1994. Interview with Benjamin Cuéllar (IDHUCA), El Salvador, January 20, 1994.

[68] It should be noted that the flaws in the El Salvador justice system relate more to bad officials than bad laws. The law on the books has always been quite good, and some important new legislation on criminal justice has been initiated since the peace process began. For example, important changes to the law of habeas corpus, the Penal Code, and the Code of Criminal Procedure were proposed by the Ministry of Justice, which are well-described in various reports of the Human Rights Division. See, in particular, S/26033 (July 2, 1993), paras. 250–8; S/26416 (September 15, 1993), paras. 76–81; S/26581 (October 14, 1993), part IIA; S/1994/385 (April 5, 1994), paras. 97–100 and 139; S/1994/886 (July 28, 1994), paras. 82 and 95. Unfortunately, much of the legislation remains stalled in the legislature, including constitutional amendments relating to the law of habeas corpus, which were passed by the last legislature but await ratification For a review of legal reform efforts sponsored by USAID and the UN prior to and in the early stages of the peace process, see Lawyers' Committee for Human Rights, *Underwriting Injustice: AID and El Salvador's Judicial Reform Program* (New York, 1989); and Lawyers' Committee for Human Rights, *El Salvador's Negotiated Revolution: Prospects for Legal Reform* (New York, 1993).

Secondly, ONUSAL pushed for implementation of the provisions in the Mexico Agreement designed to guarantee the competence, impartiality and freedom of "the career judicial service." The quality of judges began to improve with the new procedure for their appointment (i.e. following nomination by NCJ), and when the Supreme Court began "purging" corrupt or incompetent judges, based on evaluations by the NCJ. The purification of the judiciary was recommended by the Truth Commission and Joint Group, and the Human Rights Division of ONUSAL provided information about judicial performance to the NCJ.[69] The systematic but very slow process adopted meant that by March 1995, after almost a year in office, the Court had removed only eleven judges for professional misconduct. The pace had not picked up by the end of the year. Aware that much more must be done for El Salvador to overcome the "culture of impunity" described by the Truth Commission and Joint Group, ONUSAL and then MINUSAL have been pushing the Court to expedite this work.

The challenge of institution-building: UN strategies

The mixed results in efforts to promote institutional reforms reveal how difficult it is for the UN to overcome sustained resistance from the various organs of the state. Even if the executive branch, as the signatory of a peace agreement, is committed to political and institutional transformation, bringing other branches of the government along requires a sustained effort. Direct pressure from the UN sometimes works – not least because it gives the signatories to the Accords (in El Salvador, the executive branch and the FMLN leadership) leverage in their internal negotiations. Thus starting in 1993, the Human Rights Division of ONUSAL tried to push for deeper reforms to the administration of justice by applying an expansive interpretation of its power to make recommendations in the San José Agreement and insisting on compliance with the recommendations of the Truth Commission.[70] The UN in

---

[69] Ibid. S/26581 (October 14, 1993), annex, I.E. According to an ONUSAL official, the information is provided only if 100 percent reliable and it points to corruption or inefficiency of the judges. Interview with ONUSAL official, El Salvador, January 1994.

[70] In mid-1993, ONUSAL adopted an elaborated methodology called "active verification." Described as a "systematic investigatory procedure," active verification entailed a three-step procedure – complaint, investigation, and recommendations – plus the use of "good offices to contribute to the transparency and efficiency of police investigations, due process, safety of witnesses, etc., and its power of initiative to assist in overcoming existing situations of human rights violations." (A/47/912 and S/25521, April 5, 1993, para. 41.) The notion of active verification, therefore, signaled a conscious decision to push more assertively for individual and structural remedies. At the same time, ONUSAL began publicizing the records of the parties in implementing

effect, did the "dirty work" for the signatories who shared an interest in seeing the peace process through but who found it difficult to put direct pressure on their constituencies.

When direct pressure did not work (or was seen as inappropriate), the UN employed less threatening techniques, which produced some results, though slowly. It established "consultative mechanisms" with the government to evaluate recommendations of the Human Rights Division. It provided courses for judges, prosecutors and other officials in the justice system, and cooperated with the Judicial Training School to enhance the competence and professionalism of judges. It escorted individuals through the judicial system, putting pressure on officials to act. It provided information on the performance of judges to the body responsible for evaluating their professionalism. It undertook joint verification activities with the human rights ombudsman in order to transfer ONUSAL's stature and experience to the new office. And "on-the-job training" for PNC officers by the Police Division and the Human Rights Division were a way of preserving the civilian character of the new police force.[71] The UN essentially made itself a factor in the administration of justice – not always appreciated by the authorities, but seen by the parties as a tolerable degree of interference with domestic processes.

Observations and lessons

Human rights and peacemaking

The San José Agreement is not a revolutionary document but its adoption and the subsequent deployment of ONUSAL were a milestone for UN peacemaking. Ironically, an issue that would have been sure to

the recommendations of both the Truth Commission and the Human Rights Division. Although the former are binding, the parties pledged only "to give their earliest consideration" to the latter. (San José Agreement, article 15 (d), *Path to Peace*, p. 11.) Applying an expansive interpretation of this pledge, ONUSAL argued that the only effective means of ensuring that active verification would have an impact on the situation was to have its findings reflected in concrete and specific recommendations *to be implemented by the parties* (emphasis added). A/47/968 and S/26033 (July 2, 1993), paras. 324 and 325. In other words, the power to make recommendations would be meaningless unless the parties felt some obligation to implement them.

[71] After graduating from the National Public Security Academy, recruits received what amounted to on-the-job training from ONUSAL's Police Division, which allowed the UN to mold the attitudes and practices of the new recruits without directly challenging the authority of the public security hierarchy. This was done pursuant to a six-month agreement that terminated in October 1993. From then on, the Human Rights Division tried to pick up the slack with special courses and programs for the PNC. See S/1994/886 (July 28, 1994), paras. 121–6.

raise red flags about sovereignty in the past, and which was not a priority for either side in El Salvador, was the first on which it was possible to reach agreement and paved the way to the broader political settlement that followed.

That it is now a legitimate and potentially effective function of the UN to push for human rights accountability in the context of a peace process reflects important changes in global attitudes.[72] The San José Agreement is symbolic of an evolving "normative climate" that stems back to the 1948 Universal Declaration on Human Rights, and culminated in Latin America in the 1991 Santiago Commitment to Democracy and the Renewal of the Inter-American System,[73] and globally in the 1993 Vienna Conference on Human Rights. Since the El Salvador break-through, human rights promotion and protection have been linked to peacemaking efforts in the former Yugoslavia, Haiti, Guatemala, Burundi and Rwanda.

Human rights and peacekeeping

Although UN Human Rights Commission rapporteurs and experts have been reporting on human rights for years, ONUSAL marks the first time the UN has deployed a mission to engage in continuous human rights verification in the context of a broader peace process. Furthermore, it did this before a ceasefire was achieved, without loss of life – a precedent that has since been followed in Guatemala. There was some tension between the UN's "finger-pointing" and "honest broker" roles, but when one considers the broad range of activities the UN undertook in the name of "active verification" – from investigating cases to un-covering structural defects in the justice system and promoting remedies

---

[72] In his analysis of early peacemaking efforts in Haiti, Ian Martin argues that they failed because, unlike El Salvador, the human rights situation was not treated as central to the political process. Ian Martin, "Haiti: mangled multilateralism," *Foreign Policy*, Summer 1994, p. 87. Some human rights groups go so far as to suggest that the UN should put human rights on the negotiating table even if the parties to a conflict do not, and should refuse to monitor an agreement that has inadequate human rights provisions. Amnesty International, *Peacekeeping and Human Rights*.

[73] The Santiago declaration committed the Organization of American States to hold Latin American governments accountable to the organization for the means by which they came to power. An OAS resolution accompanying the declaration commits the Organization to convene a meeting and adopt decisions "deemed appropriate" to deal with "occurrences giving rise to the sudden or irregular interruption of the democratic political institutional process or of the legitimate exercise of power by the democrati-cally elected government ... " GA Res. 1080 (XXI-0/91). For an interesting discussion of the significance of the Santiago Commitment, see D. Acevedo, *The OAS and the Protection of Democracy*, prepared for the Inter-American Dialogue Project on Reconstructing Sovereignty in a Democratic Age, December 31, 1993.

– it is clear that the two can be mutually reinforcing. Conversely, separating the functions could undermine both the status of human rights monitors and the moral authority of the rest of a peacekeeping mission. The monitors would be less effective if perceived as separate from and secondary to the political mission; and the political mission would lack credibility if it were perceived as indifferent to human rights concerns.

Institutional reform

The extent to which the UN can or should attempt to reform governmental institutions is central to debates over the evolution of UN peace operations. Although the issue is sharpest in a case like Somalia where there is no functioning state,[74] it has also arisen in Mozambique, Haiti, Cambodia and other places where a state apparatus exists but is in need of renovation. In El Salvador, the parties agreed to major overhauls of the military, police, judiciary and other institutions, as well as the conversion of an insurgent military group into a political party. But agreement between the executive branch of the government and the guerrilla leaders did not guarantee that all those affected would automatically comply. Direct pressure by the international community was often necessary and it sometimes worked, not least because it gave the immediate signatories to the Accords leverage in their internal negotiations. Even if the signatories desired the institutional changes they agreed to, they could not always publicly say so for fear of alienating important constituents and generating a backlash. The UN, in a sense, did their dirty work.

But direct pressure did not always succeed. Fortunately, the San José and other agreements provided openings for the UN to employ less threatening means of reforming and strengthening institutions. Through technical support, training, joint human rights verification, and evaluations of professional conduct, the UN sought to strengthen various institutions critical to civil peace in El Salvador. These efforts were carried on by the small political office that was left behind (MINUSAL), in collaboration with the UNDP and other agencies,[75] illustrating how

---

[74] Gerald Helman and Stephen Ratner, "Saving failed states," *Foreign Policy*, vol. 89, 1992–3, p. 3.

[75] For an excellent discussion of the need for sustained and coordinated peacebuilding during and after comprehensive peace operations, see Alvaro de Soto and Graciana del Castillo, "Implementation of comprehensive peace agreements: staying the course in El Salvador," *Global Governance*, May/August, 1995. See also Alvaro de Soto and Graciana del Castillo, "Obstacles to peacebuilding," *Foreign Policy*, vol. 94, 1994.

post-conflict peacebuilding in the political as well as economic realm can be carried on beyond the life of the peacekeeping operation per se.

Managing rights and reconciliation

Related to the peacemaking, peacekeeping and peacebuilding role of the UN are the three extraordinary commissions established to investigate El Salvador's human rights past – the Ad Hoc Commission, the Truth Commission and the Joint Group. They have generated great interest as the international community struggles to strike the delicate balance between peace and justice in dealing with other conflicts characterized by gross human rights violations, for example in Burundi, Guatemala, Haiti, Rwanda, and former Yugoslavia. In El Salvador, the balance struck was to investigate and uncover the truth about the past, to identify individuals responsible and sanction some, but not to prosecute or criminally penalize anyone. The aim was not to punish but to produce a "catharsis" in which Salvadoran society as a whole would come to terms with its past. Although it is not clear that a true catharsis has taken place, the El Salvador model reveals that, in circumstances where international criminal prosecution is not feasible, for political or other reasons, there are alternatives to simply burying the past. Tempting as it may be for those whose first priority is reconciliation, ignoring a history of human rights abuses poses grave dangers, especially when the systematic denial of that history is a continuing source of tension. In the context of negotiated peace agreements, commissions that investigate and publicize the truth can at least send a signal that impunity will no longer be tolerated. Though a step short of criminal accountability, they provide a measure of justice *if* accompanied by official acknowledgment of the wrong-doing, removal from power of those responsible, and institutional reforms to prevent or deter a recurrence.

On being more royalist than the king

At various stages in the Salvadoran peace process, the UN has been confronted with a dilemma that goes to the heart of its role in consent-based multidimensional peacekeeping operations. How hard should it push for implementation of a particular aspect of a complex peace agreement when the parties themselves are not pushing? Is it ever appropriate for the UN to be "more royalist than the king" by insisting on strict compliance when the parties themselves strike "deals" (tacit or open) that contravene the Accords. There is no simple answer to the question. On the one hand, it is risky for the UN to second-guess local solutions in consent-based operations, crossing the line from facilitator to protagonist. On the other hand, as a peace process unfolds, the bargaining power of the parties shifts and the "parties" themselves often change – in El Salvador the presidency changed hands and the FMLN essentially fell apart. Furthermore, actors other than the signatories often have a stake in and capacity to disrupt these complex processes. In transformed societies, new actors, institutions and political alignments are forged, to whom an equal, and perhaps greater, responsibility is owed.

A way out of the dilemma is indicated by the El Salvador experience. In executing its mandate to oversee the implementation of complex peace agreements, the UN must act flexibly, but in exercising that flexibility, it should seek as broad a social and political consensus as possible. It can do this by relying on bodies that give expression to that consensus, like COPAZ, which was composed of two representatives of the government, two from the FMLN and one from each of the political parties represented in the National Assembly. The UN was never more than an observer in COPAZ, so its power of initiative was limited. But referring controversial matters to it – such as implementation of the Truth Commission recommendations on dismissal and disqualification from public office – ensured broader participation in the deliberations and the UN was not left with the impossible choice of either condoning questionable revisions of the Accords or setting itself in opposition to the very parties who invited its intervention in the first place.

Conclusion

UN peacekeeping has gone through a period of profound experimentation in recent years – not all of it successful. ONUSAL, as a multidimensional operation, has proven to be one type of mission the UN can do well. Its role in monitoring human rights, reforming institutions and promoting reconciliation illustrates how the UN can help bring about the social and political transformations often required for the settlement of internal conflicts.[76] In the El Salvador operation, firmly based on consent, the UN did not seek to impose a settlement, but took an active role in trying to address some of the root causes of the conflict. The parties were ready to make peace but only on terms that were so complex, the UN was needed to facilitate, support and guarantee the agreements reached. The UN in effect became a junior partner in the process of creating a less militarized and more open society. Human

[76] T. Farer and F. Gaer, "Human rights," p. 290.

rights was central to the process because, by tackling that problem head on, it was possible to root out some of the political, social and institutional conditions that gave rise to the conflict in the first place. While not uniformly successful and still incomplete, ONUSAL's efforts provide important lessons for future operations and illustrate that the era of UN activism is far from over.

14   The arms-for-land deal in El Salvador

Graciana del Castillo

Introduction

Perhaps the most daunting challenge of post-conflict peacebuilding,[1] and the one for which national governments and the international community still lack adequate mechanisms and proven strategies, is the reintegration of groups marginalized during years of conflict into productive, civil, and institutional life. These groups include not only former combatants and war-disabled, but often a large number of returning refugees and displaced persons.

El Salvador is rather a unique case in that the United Nations has been involved not only in peacemaking and peacekeeping but in post-conflict peacebuilding as well, where the parties to the peace agreements gave the UN a clear mandate of good offices and verification in the implementation of all peace-related programs. A series of UN-sponsored agreements culminating with the signature of the Chapultepec Peace Agreement in January 1992 (hereafter referred to as the Chapultepec Agreement) provided for reintegration to take place through three channels. These were participation in political life, admission to the National Civil Police and access to productive activities. As envisaged in the agreements, the agricultural sector would absorb not only the bulk of ex-combatants of both sides but also a large number of civilian

The views expressed here are entirely those of the author and should not be attributed in any manner to the United Nations. I am grateful to Alvaro de Soto for his contagious interest in El Salvador and for the many comments and suggestions on this paper. I am also grateful to Gert Rosenthal, Rafael Moreno and Teresa Whitfield for comments and to Melanie Redondo for invaluable assistance.

[1]   This term was coined by UN Secretary-General Boutros-Ghali in his *An Agenda for Peace* (New York: United Nations, 1992). The concept has been more recently elaborated in his "Supplement to *An Agenda for Peace*" (New York: United Nations, 1995). For an in-depth analysis of this concept, the many activities it involves and the implications for the UN, see G. del Castillo, "Post-conflict peace-building: the challenge to the UN," *CEPAL Review*, vol. 55, April 1995. Translated into Spanish as Consolidación de la Paz Después de los Conflictos, *Revista de la CEPAL*, vol. 55, April 1995.

supporters of the Frente Farabundo Martí para la Liberación Nacional (FMLN) – the so-called landholders (*tenedores* in Salvadoran parlance) – who had taken over and worked the land in conflict areas throughout the war years. Land was not to be "given away"; credit for purchase would be provided to potential beneficiaries. In spite of this it has been said that the peace agreement in El Salvador consisted of an "arms-for-land" exchange.[2]

It is not surprising that land became the main vehicle for reintegration. Because of the dismally inequitable distribution of land in El Salvador and its importance to the overall economy, land had been one of the root causes of the conflict. However, notwithstanding the prominence given to land in the agreement, it stopped short of attempting to solve the overall problem of land tenure or distribution as such. Though it was quite restricted in its objective, the land agreement has proved to be the most difficult to implement of all the peace agreements. The reason for this has not only been its short-run cost and the complex technical, administrative, and legal issues involved, but also the reluctance of many, including public employees, to increase the economic and political power of the FMLN, the difficulties of the FMLN itself to satisfy many of the requirements of the program, and the problem of converting former young combatants into agricultural producers overnight, when the overall trend for young people is to move away from rural into urban centers.

Since other chapters of this book focus on the political process in general and on military and police aspects in particular, our purpose is to take a critical look at the Salvadoran experience with reintegration of former combatants through the land program. That we do so is especially relevant and timely in light of the increasing involvement of the United Nations in post-conflict peacebuilding, and the realization that purely military police peacekeeping operations might turn out to be costly and ineffective unless a solution is found to the non-military issues which are often root causes of conflict. In this regard, the improvement of the economic and social condition of those that played an active role in the war as well as the strengthening of national institutions to facilitate peaceful resolution of future problems are particularly relevant in ensuring that the conflict will not recur – the overall objective of post-conflict peacebuilding.

The analysis will be divided as follows. Following the introduction, the second section will focus on the land problem in general. The third

---

2   See Alvaro de Soto and Graciana del Castillo, "Obstacles to peacebuilding," *Foreign Policy*, vol. 94, 1994. Translated into Spanish as "Los obstáculos en la construcción de la paz," *Revista Tendencias*, vol. 32, 1994.

section will analyze the agreements themselves as they relate to land and the limitations they have imposed on the implementation of the land program. The fourth section will present an overview of progress or lack of it in the implementation, focusing on the problems and difficulties that have arisen and the solutions that have been sought. The objective of analyzing both the agreements and their implementation is to build a body of evidence – both good and bad – from which to draw lessons that could help the UN in future peace negotiations and facilitate its role in good offices and verification. This is the subject of the last section.

The land problem

El Salvador has a geographical area of barely 8,620 square miles (21,000 square kilometers).[3] It is the smallest country in the continental Americas. With a population that more than doubled in thirty years to close to 5.5 million in 1994, El Salvador is by far the most densely populated country in all of Latin America.[4] With a gross domestic product (GDP) of over $7 billion in 1994, average income per capita was approximately $1,300.[5] This has made El Salvador ineligible for most concessional programs of the international financial institutions involved in the country, mainly the Bretton Woods institutions and the Inter-American Development Bank. Income and wealth of the country are highly concentrated. It used to be said that about 85 percent of the land belonged to fourteen families.[6] In spite of an agrarian reform program that started in 1980,[7] it is estimated that there are about 300,000 families[8] of *campesinos* (small farmers) that still have no land. Whether or not these figures are accurate, they are illustrative never-

---

[3]   According to official data, agricultural lands account for 40 percent of the total, grazing lands for an additional 5 percent, and 36 percent of the land has been forested.

[4]   The United Nations Economic Commission for Latin America and the Caribbean (ECLAC, 1993) reports that there are in El Salvador 260 inhabitants per square kilometer as compared to 27 in Nicaragua and 47 in Costa Rica.

[5]   Unless otherwise specified, macroeconomic data is taken from various IMF and World Bank publications and staff estimates.

[6]   According to Walter LaFeber (1993, p. 10), "fewer than 2 percent (the 'oligarchs' or 'Fourteen Families') control nearly all the fertile soil and 60 percent of all the land."

[7]   According to the ECLAC (1993), the agrarian reform program distributed more than 415,000 manzanas (1 mz is equivalent to 0.7 hectare) to 82,000 families. Although this had some impact on land distribution, 78 percent of production units are smaller than 3.5 mz and account for only 12 percent of the land.

[8]   Families in El Salvador have on average seven to eight members. According to R. Rubén, "El problema agrario en El Salvador: Notas sobre un economía polarizada," *Cuadernos de Investigación*, vol. 7 (San Salvador: Centro de Investigaciones Tecnológicas y Científicas, Año II, 1991), the total number of landless peasants has increased since 1950, accounting in the early 1990s for over 50 percent of the rural population. J. Strassma, "Land reform in El Salvador," University of Minnesota, mimeograph,

theless of the high degree of land concentration and economic power existing in the country.

Rapid economic recovery[9] followed the implementation of a rigorous economic stabilization and structural reform program adopted at the inception of the Cristiani administration, but agricultural production has lagged.[10] The most important external shock affecting the country during this period was the dramatic fall in the price of coffee,[11] particularly after the breakdown of the International Coffee Agreement in June 1989. This has imposed serious constraints on government finances.[12]

In an economy widely perceived as agricultural, this sector accounted for only 28 percent of GDP in 1980, as compared to 21 percent for industry and 52 percent for services. Agriculture was much more important, however, in terms of employment (over 40 percent) and export revenues (well over 60 percent). Coffee has been of primordial importance to the economy of El Salvador, accounting in the 1980s for about 8 percent of real GDP, 37 percent of real value added in agriculture and 50 percent of exports.[13]

With one of the most diminished natural resource bases in Latin America, serious ecological problems in El Salvador were aggravated with the fall in the price of coffee. A 1993 Inter-American Development Bank report points out that as a result of problems of misallocation and

1989, estimated that about 12 percent of the total rural labor force passed from being wage workers to being owner-operators as a result of the agrarian reform.

[9] One of the big achievements of President Cristiani was to put the country back on a path of growth which created a large number of jobs. Reintegration of large numbers of former combatants, refugees and internally displaced is bound to be far more difficult in a country like Mozambique, with a per capita income of $80 and a paralyzed economy.

[10] The share of agriculture has fallen from 28 percent in 1980 to less than 9 percent in 1993.

[11] The price of coffee fell from $120 per quintal (100 lbs) in the 1980s to $58 in 1992. An international market price of $70–75 is said to cover only the cost of coffee production in El Salvador. The quantity of coffee exported fell by 30 percent from 1980 to 1992. As a result of price and quantity changes, revenue from coffee exports fell from $615 million in 1980 to $220 million in 1991. The percentage of tax revenue from coffee exports, which averaged 24 percent annually in 1980–86, fell since then and by 1991 it had plunged to only 5 percent.

[12] The non-financial public sector deficit increased from 0.4 percent of GDP in 1990 to 2.4 percent in 1991, 3.5 percent in 1992 but approached 5 percent by the end of the year, a figure significantly higher than the program target, partly because many peace-related projects had not been incorporated into the original projections. The deficit reached 4.5 percent in 1993 and fell to 4 percent in 1994.

[13] Because there are no natural forests, half the energy requirements, particularly for cooking, come from wood from coffee trees which are trimmed once a year. The fall in the price of coffee discouraged producers from investing in trimming coffee plants.

land overuse, almost half the agricultural land in El Salvador is used in a manner that downgrades its productive capacity.[14]

The land program

The purpose of the land program was to provide demobilizing combatants with a viable livelihood and a stake, however tiny, in the country's wealth. For this, credit was to be provided to potential beneficiaries to purchase land. The land program was to be supplemented with credit programs for agricultural production and technical assistance. The agreement contemplated short-term (agricultural training, distribution of agricultural tools, basic household goods and academic instruction) and medium-term progams (credit for production purposes, housing and technical assistance).

The land situation in the areas of conflict was very complex. Production had been virtually paralyzed during the war and the infrastructure was seriously damaged. As landowners abandoned or were forced off their land during the conflict years, landless peasants had moved in. During the negotiations the FMLN had insisted on the legalization of the landholders' precarious tenure as a reward for their crucial support to the FMLN's largely rural-based guerrilla movement. The landholders were also expected to provide electoral support for the FMLN's post-conflict political ambitions. Moreover, regardless of the FMLN position, the problem had to be addressed in any case, lest it remain as a potential source of instability as landowners tried to recuperate their land.

Curiously, the implementation of the agreements was made more difficult by provisions of the agreements themselves. While the sections of the Chapultepec Agreement dealing with legal and institutional reforms were negotiated in great detail, negotiations on economic and social issues, of which reintegration was a crucial part, took place literally at the last minute, when negotiators came under pressure to strike a deal before the expiration of Secretary-General Javier Pérez de Cuéllar's term in office at midnight on December 31, 1991. The inadequacy of the agreement in this regard also reflected the lack of technical expertise of the FMLN on these issues as well as the reluctance of the government to make major concessions on socioeconomic issues.

On certain land transfer issues, the Chapultepec Agreement was excessively precise, creating serious constraints to its implementation. It stipulated that private land to be transferred should be "voluntarily

[14] Cited in UNDP, *Launching New Protagonists in Salvadoran Agriculture: The Agricultural Training Program for Ex-Combatants of the FMLN* (San Salvador: UNDP, 1993), p. 30.

offered for sale by its owners"; that transactions should take place at "market prices"; that beneficiaries would repay government loans in accordance with the agrarian reform terms of payment (over thirty years, with a four-year grace period for principal and interest, and a fixed annual interest rate of 6 percent); that preference would be given to ex-combatants of both sides; and that landholders would not be evicted until a satisfactory legal solution for their land-tenure problem was found somewhere else.

Under normal agrarian reform programs land is expropriated and owners are usually paid with government bonds.[15] The fact that the Chapultepec Agreement stipulated that owners had to offer their land voluntarily for sale at market prices created tremendous difficulties for both the acquisition and the financing of land purchase. Repayment terms, which were similar to those of the 1980 agrarian reform program, also created difficulties for financing. The situation was aggravated by the fact that the government had not honored some of the bonds of the agrarian reform in the past and hence the possibility of financing this program through the issuance of bonds was nil.

The important differences between the Chapultepec land program and that of the 1980 agrarian reform have been missed by many serious analysts; this continues to be a source of confusion and misunderstanding. It is precisely these differences that have made this agreement particularly difficult to implement.

The Chapultepec Agreement stipulated that the FMLN would submit an inventory of affected lands in the conflict zones within thirty days of the signing of the agreement, and that the legalization of land tenure in these zones was to be completed within six months, that is, by July 31, 1992 (this date was later put off till August 31 in the context of an overall rescheduling). Before land could be transferred, the multiparty National Commission for the Consolidation of Peace (known by its Spanish initials, COPAZ) would set up a special unit (CEA-COPAZ) to verify the inventory of lands presented by the FMLN to determine, among other things, the number of landholders occupying them.

Despite the precision of the Chapultepec Agreement on certain issues, it completely ignored certain crucial parameters: the total number of potential beneficiaries; the size of the plots to which they would be entitled; and the amount of government credit that would be made available to them. Nor did the agreement determine the practical arrangements under which the transfer of land would take place.

The vagueness of the agreement on these issues gave rise to contra-

---

[15] The Agrarian Reform Law of 1980 established that landowners would be paid for their land at the value they had declared for land tax purposes.

dictory expectations on the part of the many players. By the end of September 1992, the lag in implementation was so wide that land transfer had become one of the most contentious issues in the implementation of the Chapultepec Agreement. In early October the FMLN unilaterally halted the third phase of its demobilization (out of five phases each demobilizing 20 percent), holding the government responsible for not having started the land program.

More worrying, however, was the hardening of positions and the widening gap between the FMLN's demands and the government's offers. The government insisted that the acreage to be transferred should be determined by the availability of land and of financing, and that a ceiling in domestic currency (*colón*) was to be imposed on the amount of credit that it would provide to ex-combatants and landholders. This implied that if the *colón* depreciated or the price of land rose during the implementation of the program, the size of plots which beneficiaries could afford would be reduced. Predictably, the transfer of land to the FMLN and its supporters was resisted by the land-owning class. It was viewed by many as a way of increasing the political appeal of the FMLN, which was certainly the FMLN's intention.

The FMLN contended that arguments about the availability of land and finance were irrelevant and that both could be found if the government had the political will to do so. In their view, the government had agreed to facilitate the transfer of land in exchange for their demobilization and was simply under an obligation to deliver. The negotiating capacity of the FMLN was strengthened by the fact that they were occupying the land in question and the Chapultepec Agreement protected them from eviction.

As an indication of the significance of the lack of progress in the land program, it is worth noting that a national survey conducted in October 1992 – at a time when the purification of the armed forces and the demobilization of the FMLN were still pending – revealed that 37 percent of Salvadorans considered the transfer of land to be the most difficult agreement to implement while only 20 percent thought that it was the demobilization of the FMLN. Thirteen percent responded that it was the purification of the armed forces.[16]

Thus, since the Chapultepec Agreement stipulated that the demobilization of the FMLN was itself linked to the reduction and purification of the armed forces, the land program abruptly became one of the most contentious issues in the implementation of the Agreement and

[16] Ten percent responded that other issues were most important and 20 percent did not know (National Survey conducted by the Institute of Public Opinion of the University of Central America, UCA).

threatened the collapse of the entire peace process. Finding a solution to this complex problem took on great urgency. After intensive consultations with the two parties, the Secretary-General drafted a program, within the constraints imposed by the Chapultepec Agreement, which he judged to be a fair compromise. Although he anticipated the difficulties associated with the implementation of such a program and was aware that it was not fully satisfactory to either party, on October 13, 1992 he asked them to accept it, as a package and without amendment. With its acceptance by the parties a few days later, the so-called October 13, 1992 draft became in effect a supplement to the Chapultepec Agreement.[17] A major impediment to the demobilization of the FMLN and hence to the implementation of the peace agreements as a whole had been removed.

In the Secretary-General's compromise proposal as accepted by the parties, while the size of plots to which beneficiaries could aspire was smaller than the FMLN expected, the government agreed not to press for a ceiling on the amount of credit to be granted to beneficiaries.[18] In practical terms this meant that the government was assuming both the foreign exchange risk and the risk of land price speculation. The bottom line was that under the October 13 program beneficiaries were guaranteed a fixed amount of a particular type of land, irrespective of its price or possible foreign exchange fluctuation.

The program was designed to insure the early and rapid transfer of substantial quantities of land to ex-combatants of the FMLN and the armed forces and the legalization of tenure or, if necessary, the relocation of landholders in the conflict zones. It provided for a maximum number of 47,500 beneficiaries, consisting of 7,500 ex-combatants of the FMLN, 15,000 from the armed forces and 25,000 landholders in the former zones of conflict. The amount of land to which each ex-combatant was entitled was determined by the agrarian reform criteria of the Instituto Salvadoreño de Transformación Agraria (ISTA) according to the different types of soil.[19]

---

[17] For a full analysis of this program see the reports of the Secretary-General on the United Nations Observer Mission in El Salvador to the Security Council (UN, 1992, 1993a, 1993b, 1993c, 1994a, 1994b, 1994c, 1995a and 1995b) and the reports to the General Assembly on the situation in Central America (UN, 1995, 1996). See also ECLAC (1993) and Alvaro de Soto and G. del Castillo, "Implementation of comprehensive peace agreements: staying the course in El Salvador," *Global Governance*, Spring 1995.

[18] The decision on the size of plots was the result of long and difficult deliberations and negotiations. It was determined that, even taking into account the serious land constraints of El Salvador, any smaller size would not even allow production at a subsistence level.

[19] The viability of the program has been questioned on many grounds. In an interesting

If owners of land occupied were willing to sell, the landholders would remain on their plots with a maximum size of land equal to that of ex-combatants and a minimum size of half that amount. If owners did not sell, relocation of landholders to land in comparable conditions would await the end of the program. Since landholders could not be evicted, relocation was to be left for the end. Landowners thus had to face the following dilemma: sell their occupied land for cash at current market prices (obviously below the market price of unoccupied land) or not sell and wait until the landholders currently occupying their land could be relocated by the government somewhere else. Given the government's lack of financing to complete the land program and the existing land constraints, relocation could well take a long time. Thus, putting off relocation was intended to encourage owners to sell and thereby to put downward pressure on prices.

Assuming that beneficiaries would receive on average 5 mz of an average type of land that would cost an average of $600 per manzana (mz),[20] it was estimated that between 175,000 and 235,000 mz would be required at a total cost of between $105 and $143 million.

The program was divided into three phases, reflecting the availability of land and financing. For the first emergency phase resources would be made available between October 1992 and January 1993 when the government would provide state lands and USAID would donate financial resources to cover the needs of over 15,000 beneficiaries. In this phase priority was to be given to former combatants from the FMLN as they demobilized and to landholders on the transferred lands. It was anticipated that, although required resources would be available, the implementation of this phase would take significantly longer because of the practical and legal difficulties involved.

A second phase had to be identified due to the fact that during that period additional financing was to be made available by the European

---

analysis of the microeconomic viability of the land program, an ECLAC (1993) study (internal document for discussion, April 13, 1993) found that production of basic grains could only be considered an emergency solution, until the country was in a position to finance the modernization of the agricultural sector as a whole. ECLAC calculated that if 80 percent of the transferred land was dedicated to the production of basic grains, this would significantly increase supply in a market where low prices already resulted in insufficient income to satisfy the needs of peasant families. The same study concluded that for an ideal diversification of the land transferred under the program, close to $300 million to be spent over five to ten years would be needed, and the gross value of expected annual production would be about $150 million.

[20] The assumption of $600 per mz of an average type of land for calculation purposes has created serious confusion. The UN, the government, and sometimes both have been accused by landowners and the press of "fixing the price of land." This was clearly not the case. This price reflected the average at which comparable occupied land was sold through the Lands Bank up to August 31, 1992.

Union (EU), which imposed different conditions for the implementation of the program. The EU program was to benefit former combatants of the FMLN and the armed forces in equal numbers. Since it excluded landholders, this phase was to take place simultaneously with the first one so that landholders could also be legalized. For the EU phase, resources would be made available between February and March of 1993. It would finalize only when enough land could be negotiated for about 4,000 beneficiaries.

The third phase, which was to cover the needs of about 60 percent of the beneficiaries, was open-ended in time since there were neither financial resources nor land available to satisfy the requirements of about 28,000 remaining beneficiaries and it was not possible to predict with any degree of certainty when these would become available.

Implementation of the program

Once the parties had accepted the October 13, 1992 program, the urgency of implementing it was dramatized by the occupation by peasants and FMLN ex-combatants of properties in former conflict zones, some of them part of the FMLN land inventory. The former combatants asserted that they were simply returning to land that they had occupied previously and had to leave for concentration zones at the time of the ceasefire, as agreed at Chapultepec. An incident near Ciudad Barrios in November 1992, which prompted the dispatch to the site of a contingent of recently demobilized troops in the guise of the National Police personnel, almost led to a breach of the ceasefire. A clash was eventually defused through the intervention of the UN Mission in El Salvador (ONUSAL) and the Archbishop of San Salvador.

Although the logistical difficulties of carrying out the transfer of land were never underestimated, many unforeseen problems also contributed to distortions and long delays. The Chapultepec Agreement had contemplated that landholders would be given agricultural credit to reactivate production even before their land tenure was legalized. Since this only happened in isolated cases, because of the high risk it implied for the agricultural bank, many missed the planting seasons in 1993 and 1994, requiring greater international food assistance than originally planned.

Both the government and the FMLN as well as some conditions imposed by donors rendered the implementation of the program extremely difficult. The Lands Bank was to act both as intermediary between buyer and seller and financing agency. The original legal procedures consisting of seventeen steps were extremely time-consuming and difficult to satisfy by both the FMLN beneficiaries and the land-owners. Problems with the measurement, appraisal, and negotiation of properties also contributed to long delays. The repayment terms in the original Lands Bank contracts did not conform to those specified in the agreements and had to be changed. Although administrative, technical, and legal difficulties resulted from bureaucratic inefficiencies common in developing countries, many of these reflected the unwillingness of lower ranking government officials to facilitate the transfer of land to FMLN ex-combatants and their supporters.

A further problem was that the entitlement to land was much easier to determine in the case of FMLN former combatants[21] than in that of landholders. This turned out to be critical. Under the agreement those who had been verified by CEA-COPAZ as being on lands which were part of the FMLN land inventory would be entitled to credit for the purchase of the land they were occupying (or to relocate to other plots if owners did not want to sell). However, the FMLN questioned the way the CEA-COPAZ verification was conducted[22] and argued that its deficiencies had unjustly left many landholders out of the program. Furthermore, when the government designed the first phase of an operational plan to accelerate the implementation of the program,[23] this acted as an additional filter.[24] The program could not advance since the so-called "non-verified" landholders, who in general refused to be relocated since they did not want to be separated from family and friends, occupied many private properties that had already been ear-marked. They could not however be legalized since it was not possible to do so selectively. This situation dragged on for a long time, particularly since the government did not want to discuss any solution[25] until it

---

[21] ONUSAL issued identity cards to demobilizing FMLN combatants.

[22] The CEA-COPAZ records of the verification (*actas*) often included board members of cooperatives but not the rank and file or absentees. Many worked the land but did not live there because of lack of housing. The FMLN argued that these people, who had filled in forms for verification purposes (*boletas*), had been excluded and that therefore the verification underestimated the total number of landholders.

[23] The first phase of the Acceleration Plan was presented in August 1993 and was supplemented in mid-November by operative guidelines, which spelt out how the Plan was to be implemented.

[24] In October 1993, forty-two government offices of OCTA (Oficina Coordinadora del Tema Agrícola) were established in the former zones of conflict and potential beneficiaries had to be "reverified" by presenting themselves to these offices and claiming the specific property to which they aspired. Since only those who were in the CEA-COPAZ verification were eligible and many of those did not attend, the number of potential beneficiaries was further reduced.

[25] The government was under no obligation to include non-verified landholders since at a September 8, 1993 high-level tripartite meeting (government-FMLN-ONUSAL) the government had proposed to leave them for the end of the land program, as resources became available, a proposal which the FMLN had accepted.

knew the exact number of people involved and the FMLN failed to provide the list of names. Only in April 1994 did the magnitude of the problem become known when the FMLN provided a list of 7,285 people (the aggregate total of potential FMLN beneficiaries to the overall program remained below the maximum 32,500 stipulated in the October 13 agreement). This problem paralyzed the program from December 1993 to May 1994 when, at the request of the Secretary-General, who also interceded with donors to make financing available, the government agreed to include the bulk of the non-verified along with the others. This unquestionably removed one of the main impediments to the implementation of the program.

In spite of this agreement by the government, which was thought of as a breakthrough at the time, the program remained at a virtual standstill until late in 1994. Progress reported in the land program from the end of April to mid-October allowed us to calculate that at this rate (slightly over eight beneficiaries a day) it would have taken nine-and-a-half years (114 months or 3,420 days!) to complete.[26] The lack of progress in the transfer of land was seriously delaying other reintegration programs such as those for agricultural credit, technical assistance and housing, for which legalization of land tenure was a prerequisite.

A second phase of the government's Acceleration Plan adopted on February 1994 created new problems. The operational plan provided for the issuance of credit certificates by the Lands Bank so that potential beneficiaries could negotiate terms for the purchase of land directly with landowners. These certificates were at odds with the agreements on two grounds: first, they had an expiration date (April 30, 1995) and second, they had a ceiling specified in *colones* for the maximum allowable credit. The probability that all potential beneficiaries would have purchased land by that date was, as time has confirmed, very low. As pointed out by the Secretary-General himself in his report to the Security Council of May 1994, the possibility that those who had not received land by then would lose their rights was (and continues to be) quite disturbing. As a result of the Secretary-General's concern, the May 19 recalendarization specified that the expiration date of the certificates could be extended. The fact that the government had imposed a credit ceiling was also worrisome since in the negotiations leading to the October 13 agreement, the FMLN had accepted smaller plots than it had originally

---

[26] Excluding human settlements, there was agreement that potential beneficiaries of the FMLN and landholders amount to 28,648 and former combatants of the armed forces amount to 12,000 for a total of 40,648. The Secretary-General reported that by the end of April 11,585 had received title to land and this figure had climbed to only 12,942 in mid-October. These 12,942 beneficiaries had received 51.303 mz, which is on average slightly below 4 mz (2.8 hectares) per beneficiary.

demanded in exchange for the government guaranteeing a certain physical amount of land according to the type of soil. At 1995 prices and exchange rate, the 30,000 *colones* ($3,500) stipulated in the credit certificates continues to suffice to purchase the amount of land specified in the October 13 agreement. However, it would not be sufficient if land prices increased[27] or the domestic currency depreciated.[28] Although this is admittedly not a likely scenario in the short run, the Secretary-General has recommended that provision be made for this eventuality.[29]

The second phase of the government's acceleration plan did not have the operational impact expected. Although the government opened several regional offices to decentralize implementation of the program, they lacked the legal and administrative capacity needed to facilitate the measurement, appraisal, negotiation, and legalization of properties. At the same time, the FMLN has been unable to mobilize its people to facilitate the process by being present with the necessary documentation at every stage and to insure that all of them receive the land certificates and sign the deeds as required. The FMLN and their supporters have also slowed down the process by their inability to honor previous commitments to stop putting new people on the land and refrain from relocating them from one property to another.

In mid-August 1994 the government presented what would be the third phase of its Acceleration Plan. It proposed to strengthen the regional offices of the executing agency and to wage a local radio campaign to inform potential beneficiaries of their rights and obligations if they wanted to benefit from the program. It was hoped that this would improve the chances that potential beneficiaries would be at the right place at the right time with the appropriate documentation. On October 11 the Legislative Assembly approved Decree 150 to accelerate the legal procedures and solve other problems related to the land program.[30]

---

[27] The average price of land has not increased since the October 13, 1992 program was adopted. As stated earlier, it was calculated at that time that the average price of the type of land for which 5 mz could be purchased would cost $600. The average plot of land transferred has been of 3.8 per manzana/beneficiary at an average price of $685 *colones* per manzana. Thus, the average cost of land per beneficiary has been $2,600, even lower than the $3,000 assumed by the program.

[28] Because of large inflows of capital in the form of remittances, long-term loans and reversed capital flight, this has not happened in spite of instability created by the Mexican crisis. Although the type of capital has been longer term than inflows to Mexico, the 1994 crisis in the latter was nevertheless a reminder of how easily investors' confidence in an economy can be lost, particularly in the presence of political instability.

[29] See report of the Secretary-General on the United Nations Observer Mission in El Salvador: UN, S/1994/561), paras. 74–5.

[30] In many cases, because beneficiaries had not signed, land deeds could not be finalized and landowners could not be paid for their land (as a result of restrictions from

With slightly more than 30 percent of potential beneficiaries having been able to title their land, and with the remainder of the land to be transferred considered "problematic cases," the government adopted the fourth phase of the Acceleration Plan in October 1994. The president of the Lands Bank was replaced and a new government institution (Instituto Libertad y Progreso or ILP) was added to the already numerous list of institutions involved in the land program. It was the position of the government that the Lands Bank had done all it could in transferring land that had no legal problems. The ILP, which until then had been in charge of titling properties (mostly urban) that were not in the census of real properties, assumed executing powers for the land program from the Lands Bank. The latter transferred the files "as they were" and the public notaries under sub-contract from ILP became the managers/promoters of those cases. By subcontracting sixty-five public notaries ILP claimed that it could do "massive titling."

High expectations raised by the assignment of the ILP to accelerate titling have gone largely unfulfilled, with concomitant resentment and impatience on the part of potential beneficiaries. Further administrative changes in the Lands Bank in early January 1995, which included the replacement of key employees closely involved in the land program, problems of coordination between the Lands Bank, OCTA, and ILP, and the lack of capacity at the regional level of ILP contributed to the land program coming to a standstill once again in early 1995.

Although the program experienced problems in the transfer of land to both the FMLN and former members of the armed forces, the latter was even more delayed and underfinanced. As of the end of 1994, land had been transferred to only about 3,400 people and additional financing was needed to cover more than 8,000 remaining potential beneficiaries. As pointed out by the Secretary-General, the situation had been aggravated by delays in indemnifying demobilized members of the armed forces and their link to the land program, and the increasing threat of an organization representing disgruntled former military personnel called ADEFAES (Association of Demobilized Members of the Armed Forces). In September 1994, for the second time, members of ADEFAES occupied the National Assembly, taking some of its members hostage. They also occupied the Lands Bank and ISTA to press the government to yield to their demands, which consisted mainly of extending entitlement to paramilitary forces demobilized pursuant to the peace agreements.[31] Encouraged by the results, ADEFAES used the

donors). Decree 150 allowed the Lands Bank to purchase a share of up to 25 percent to replace those who had not yet signed.
[31] These forces have been roughly estimated between 50,000 and 250,000, including

January 16, 1995 date (celebration of the third anniversary of the signature of Chapultepec Agreement) to take forceful action in pursuit of their objectives, occupying land in the Department of La Paz which belonged to the Banco Centroamericano de Integración (BCIE). On January 24, 1995 they took the National Assembly again as well as another government building. Although the violent crisis was again defused, with ONUSAL playing a very active role, the favorable terms received by ADEFAES for their demands are likely to create further confrontation in the future. Pressured by the situation, the government accepted to include in their regular social programs 5,000 former members of paramilitary bodies, 3,000 of whom would also have access to state lands.

Action by ADEFAES in late 1994 and early 1995 deflected attention from the real problem which was the serious delays and distortions that had plagued the implementation of the land as well as other reintegration programs. Furthermore, because of the scarcity of available land and finance, the more resources are committed to this group, the more difficult it will be to complete peace-related programs, particularly the land program. More worrisome as a precedent is that by resorting to forcible action, ADEFAES received ostensibly better terms than those peacefully negotiated by the FMLN and FAES.

By the end of 1994, only 17,200 titles had been issued, covering slightly over 40 percent of potential beneficiaries. The October 1994 Plan accelerated appraisals, negotiations and measurement of properties but issuance of titles continued to lag behind. Coordination problems among different government agencies continued to seriously disrupt the program. Delays in payments discouraged owners from selling, thus exacerbating the scarcity of acceptable land and increasing the need to relocate landholders. Most worrying, remaining potential beneficiaries were problematic cases, with one or more of the following characteristic: the *minifundio* land tenure system (with the problem of dealing with numerous owners and titling a large number of properties); legal problems (lack of title to the land, inheritance and other problems of owners); and land whose owners did not want to sell and therefore created the need to relocate landholders to other acceptable land.

Because of delays in the land and other programs and the need for the UN to complete verification of compliance with pending peace-related programs, a small team was set up to replace ONUSAL after its Security Council mandate concluded in April 1995. The new mission, which

former members of paramilitary groups, and hence could never be included in the program that contemplates a maximum number of 15,000 beneficiaries of the armed forces.

enables the Secretary-General to report to the General Assembly and keep the Security Council informed, continues to provide good offices and verify the implementation of remaining programs, although with considerably less visibility than before given that it is not under the magnifying glass of the Security Council.[32]

From April until June some acceleration in the titling of land took place. By the end of June, 24,500 beneficiaries (60 percent) had received title to their land. It was only in July, however, that it became apparent that such an acceleration had taken place at the expense of failing to register the titles in the national land registry. In fact, only about 20 percent of the issued titles had been registered. This presented a serious problem of which the UN had not been aware before. Furthermore, the legal procedure followed by many of the people that the UN had already verified as full beneficiaries of the PTT was incomplete since titles issued had not been filed with the national land registry and unregistered land could not be sold. Thus, beneficiaries under such conditions had incurred a debt without having the possibility of selling the asset should they desire to do so or were forced to by failing to service their debt.

Slow progress in the PTT continued throughout 1995. Although the Chapultepec Agreement contemplated that the legalization of land tenure in the former zones of conflict would be completed by July 31, 1992, by the end of the year 15 percent of potential beneficiaries had not yet received title to land. Furthermore, of the 85 percent who had title, only 34 percent had their title filed with the national land registry. Thus, the PTT has only been completed for less than 30 percent of potential beneficiaries.[33] Titles have been issued to almost 31,000 people (76 percent of total) amounting to 121,000 mz – an average of 4 mz per beneficiary.

Lessons for the future

Although unfortunately still far from complete, the arms-for-land deal in El Salvador allows us to draw some lessons which could help parties to a conflict as well as the international community – particularly the United Nations – in the negotiation, design, implementation and verification of future such deals. An analysis of this rich and complex experience would also help in tackling the myriad problems of post-conflict (or even post-

---

[32] For an analysis of this problem see de Soto and del Castillo, "Implementation."

[33] These percentages will likely increase insignificantly given the parties' January 1996 agreement to slightly reduce the universe of potential beneficiaries of the FMLN (from 28,648 to 28,513) and the fact that beneficiaries from FAES are also likely to decrease since many have not complied with the requirements or are not interested in purchasing land.

chaos) peacebuilding in countries such as Haiti, Angola, Mozambique, Guatemala and others in which the UN is, has been or may become involved to a greater or lesser degree.

The experience of El Salvador clearly points to the importance as well as the difficulty of post-conflict peacebuilding. Ceasefire agreements may be negotiated at a high cost in terms of time and resources but they will not necessarily last if an effort is not made to create mechanisms to deal peacefully with some of the causes that led to the conflict in the first place so as to decrease the likelihood of its recurrence. With increasing frequency the maintenance of peace requires not only traditional peace-keeping operations composed of observers and interposition forces but also multidisciplinary operations. These involve a number of non-military functions including the establishment of civilian police forces, monitoring and promotion of human rights, electoral assistance and monitoring and a wide variety of socio-economic activities ranging from emergency humanitarian relief to rehabilitation and reconstruction. These activities can play a critical role in the consolidation of peace, an area of activity for which the affected countries and the international community are still ill prepared.

One of the most important aspects of post-conflict peacebuilding is the strengthening of national institutions to facilitate the peaceful resolution of disputes and respect for human rights. Another key aspect of post-conflict peacebuilding is the systematic and long-term reintegration of demobilized combatants and other groups estranged from society and marginalized from productive activities during conflict years: if disaffected groups are not brought back into the mainstream, the job has quite simply not been done and the seeds of strife remain.

The experience of El Salvador with reintegration – and in particular with the arms-for-land deal – allows us to discern a number of issues to which special attention should be paid to insure that such an experience is indeed a success. Among these, the following are worth pointing out.

Need to design peace agreements carefully

An important lesson from the Salvadoran experience is that the design of a peace agreement is critical to its successful implementation. For this reason, careful thought and the right kind of expertise can facilitate implementable peace agreements.

Peace agreements should explicitly contemplate reintegration of previously marginalized groups. It is often the case that these groups are those more used to violence and therefore more likely to resort to banditry or to take up arms if promises to them are not kept. Post-

Sandinista Nicaragua is relevant in this regard. Peace processes will only be irreversible if they include serious reintegration mechanisms which go beyond mere cash handouts. Some desirable features of peace-related programs will be described below.

Peace agreements should not build up expectations about what peace will bring which are unrealistic and difficult to satisfy. Unfulfilled expectations of disgruntled groups can seriously endanger an entire peace process.

It could be argued that in the case of El Salvador targeting land as the main venue for reintegration was not the optimal choice. This decision was justified by the importance that land had as one of the root causes of the war and the principal livelihood of Salvadorans. There is room to query this, however, having regard to the scarcity of land; the difficulties in financing land purchases (because of donor restrictions); the existing tenure problems and the likelihood that they would give rise to a variety of legal difficulties in transferring land; and the fact that in spite of their rural origin, many former combatants were not naturally inclined toward farming, or lacked training after long years of war. Given the renowned inventiveness and entrepreneurial capacity of the Salvadoran people, perhaps a much larger percentage of people could have been given the opportunity to reintegrate through credit for mini- and micro-enterprises. A lesson from this experience is that it is important to analyze carefully the viability of implementation and the financing implications of different options before deciding on a particular channel for reintegration.

It is clear that the letter of the peace agreements themselves can determine the ease or difficulty with which the resulting programs will be implemented. Many lessons can be drawn from the operational difficulties encountered in the implementation of the land program. The specificity of the Chapultepec Agreement with regard to the price of land and the way in which it was to be sold prevented the option of land expropriation paid with government bonds. This has unquestionably been the main constraint on the implementation of the program. On the other hand, the vagueness of the agreement with regard to many other variables including the number of beneficiaries, the size of plots and the availability of credit led to diverging expectations by the two parties. This delayed the inception of the program, stopped the demobilization of the FMLN and threatened the implementation of the peace agreements as a whole. Thus, a proper balance between specificity and vagueness of agreements is critical to their implementation.

If agreements are drawn with a certain logic, they should be implemented accordingly. At the time the land program was adopted in

October 1992 many analysts observed that the price calculation for the entire program, based on average prices of transactions that had taken place during the previous year, was unrealistic because prices were likely to increase significantly once the program started and demand for land jumped. The logic of the October 13 program to defer relocation of landholders on lands whose owners did not want to sell to the end of the program was to induce owners to sell and thus put downward pressure on land prices. For different reasons both the government and the FMLN flirted with early relocation. The government was under pressure from landowners who wanted to recover their land after long years of conflict; the FMLN was under pressure, from landholders on plots whose owners did not want to sell, to relocate as soon as possible so as to legalize their land tenure and receive credit. In May 1993, the Secretary-General warned that a reversal of the sequence and an alteration of the logic of the program could well compromise it. ONUSAL also objected to the relocation of landholders and the end result was that relocation only took place on a very small scale. Because of this, average prices did not change much.

Need to facilitate implementation of peace agreements

Both domestic and foreign factors will be critical in determining the ease or difficulty with which agreements are implemented. Both the government and the international community have a crucial role to play in facilitating their implementation.

The success of reintegration programs is often dependent on post-conflict economic recovery and foreign financing. Reintegration becomes particularly difficult in stagnant economies and in countries undergoing necessary but rigorous economic stabilization and structural reforms programs. This is so because the financial implications of peace-related programs are often in conflict with the objectives of stabilization. In this regard, it is particularly important that the UN, the international financial institutions and bilateral donors work closely together in support of the economic program, particularly to insure domestic and foreign financing for all peace-related programs. Efforts by the Cristiani and Calderón Sol administrations at macroeconomic management and also to finance part of the peace-related programs domestically through expenditure reallocation facilitated foreign financing. A lesson from this experience is that donors are much more likely to support countries that do their best to help themselves.

The legal difficulties to the transfer of land resulting from the land tenure system in the country were but one of the problems encountered.

A number of administrative, technical, and logistical difficulties also affected the program at different stages. Among the most important were the inadequate capacity of the executing agency, particularly at the regional level, and the inadequate organization and lack of resources of the FMLN to comply with what proved to be quite complicated requirements of the land program. Potential beneficiaries have often lacked information about their rights and about the different things they have to do to take advantage of the program. Notices were often made through the press – to which many rural people have no access – rather than through local radio stations. A proper evaluation of potential difficulties in implementing the peace agreement should be made early in the process, not only to avoid building unrealistic expectations about its potential rewards but also to try to find solutions to the main constraints from the very beginning.

Donors' preferences and requirements as well as their own financing restrictions may create serious constraints to the implementation of peace agreements. Foreign financing is sometimes selective (one program and not another, one group to the exclusion of another). In the case of the land program in El Salvador, the conditions imposed by donors with regard to measurement and appraisal of properties have often proved costly and time-consuming. One of the most serious problems has been the inability to pay landowners until all beneficiaries have signed the deed for a property. Since missing signatures have been the rule rather than the exception, payments to owners have been unnecessarily delayed and this has discouraged some of them from selling. Early awareness of these constraints may allow time which can be used to persuade donors of the need for changes. As with the other difficulties discussed above, addressing this problem from the very beginning may also avoid building unrealistic expectations.

Equity considerations become a serious problem in reintegration. From the Salvadoran experience it can be observed that it was politically expedient to target groups directly affected by the war for preferential treatment right after the ceasefire agreement. As time goes by, it often becomes more difficult to justify adopting preferential treatment for these groups, when there are others in similar conditions of poverty and need. Moreover, leaders who negotiated the peace agreements may change. It was President Cristiani who signed the peace agreements and was committed to their implementation. President Calderón Sol, though openly supportive of the peace agreements, has made social development the top priority in his agenda; as such, it will be difficult for him to discriminate among groups, particularly since poverty is widespread. Because of this, it should be expected that the problems of implementing the land and other reintegration programs in El Salvador may be more difficult to solve with time. Similarly, it would perhaps have been easier to negotiate a solution to the related problem of human settlements soon after the ceasefire than over two years later when the government was less likely to make preferential concessions for these communities: given the scarcity of resources, preferential treatment for some necessarily implies less for others. The policy of the FMLN of postponing certain decisions with the expectation that further efforts at negotiation would yield better results might – in retrospect – have been misguided; as time goes by targeted groups are likely to receive less rather than more.

Need to plan, coordinate and finance peace-related programs

To insure consistency and effectiveness, peace-related programs need to be well designed and coordinated and proper financing should be targeted.

A global strategy, designed to deal with the different problems in an integrated way and flexible enough to adapt to rapidly changing circumstances is required to insure that different programs are well planned and structured to cover the wide-ranging needs of peace consolidation. This is preferable to a step-by-step approach, as has mostly been the case in El Salvador. At the same time, appropriate coordination should take place among the different bodies of the UN system, bilateral donors and NGOs so as to maximize their impact and minimize their cost.

The experience of El Salvador shows that while short-term reintegration programs (which are all completed by now) served an important purpose in providing demobilized soldiers with an alternative to banditry as a means of survival and in facilitating respect for the ceasefire, these were neither well planned, properly coordinated or synchronized with demobilization dates. As a result, short-term programs were used more for short-run economic gain than as a first step in the process of developing a viable, longer-term occupation. Short-term programs should be designed not only to satisfy emergency needs but also as a first step in longer-term reintegration. Building on the short-term emergency and training programs, medium-term programs should aim at ensuring proper productive reintegration.

One important lesson from the Salvadoran experience is that providing credit for reintegration through the purchase of land is not sufficient. Unless well coordinated training, technical assistance and credit for agricultural production as well as housing is provided, reintegration will not succeed or be sustainable. Although medium-term programs are far from being completed in El Salvador, they have already proved to be inadequate in terms of their scope and breadth. Given the lack of agricultural experience of most beneficiaries and the small size of the plots to which they can aspire, it has become clear that even the maximum amounts of agricultural credit and technical assistance contemplated in these programs may only allow them to produce basic grains for subsistence, which will be insufficient to allow them to repay their debts. Medium-term programs should always be complemented by adequate credit and technical assistance facilities so as to insure their success and long-term viability. Unless production becomes profitable, those for whom the purchase of land was facilitated might end up worse off than they were before: in the past land did not belong to them, but they had no debts; after the program is finalized they will own the land but they will also be indebted to the government; unless they service their debt, they will soon be ineligible for any further credit, making future production difficult. The international community should play a crucial role in providing adequate credit and particularly technical assistance in support of medium-term programs. In the case of El Salvador, for example, the sustainability of the land program in the longer term will very much depend on the ability of UN programs and agencies (including the World Bank), as well as bilateral donors and NGOs, to support producers both financially and with technical assistance. It should be kept in mind that the cost of doing so would be but a pittance by comparison with the cost to the international community of maintaining a peacekeeping operation, let alone the cost if war were to break out once again.

Need to define clearly the role of the UN and the resources it requires

There is a need to define clearly the role of the UN and how this is to change over time, not only because of changes on the ground which require fine-tuning, but also as a result of new agreements entered into by the parties.

Parties' informal agreements which depart from formal agreements make UN verification more difficult. In the case of El Salvador, departures from the October 13 program agreed to informally by the two parties (letters to ONUSAL of December 1992 and February 1993 and further informal agreements resulting from tripartite meetings government–FMLN–ONUSAL) have made insistence by ONUSAL on compliance with the letter and the spirit of the peace agreement much more difficult and often ineffective. This has certainly been the case with the credit ceiling specified in the land certificates, in clear violation of the October 13 agreement.

Strengthen the UN to carry out multidisciplinary peacekeeping operations

The new multidisciplinary peacekeeping operations, in which the UN is asked to use good offices and verify agreements in wide-ranging areas, require expertise which is seldom available to the UN. In this regard the experience of El Salvador with reintegration allows us to make the following points.[34]

Peacemakers should start early on in the peace process to think about and plan for the requirements and constraints of post-conflict peace-building. Thus, peace negotiators should always be supported by a well-qualified advisor (or team depending on the case) on post-conflict peacebuilding, particularly as it refers to socio-economic issues. As we mentioned earlier, experience, particularly relating to the case of El Salvador, has shown that stipulations in a peace agreement relating to these issues are likely to have an important effect on its implementation, either by facilitating it or by making it more difficult.

Multidisciplinary peacekeeping missions with post-conflict peace-building responsibilities should have a unit headed at a high level to deal solely with these matters. Such a unit will in most cases survive the peacekeeping operation itself and could be an important factor in facilitating the transition from the strict surveillance by the Security Council of the peacekeeping operations, to the more general support provided by different bodies of the UN system to development activities of the country.

Verification of the land program in El Salvador has shown that there is a clear need for an "institutional memory" within a peacekeeping operation mission and also at headquarters. Unless such a memory exists the parties might find it to their advantage to wriggle out of or distort previous commitments to which they sometimes agreed only reluctantly. A serious effort should be made in future missions to recruit qualified experts from the beginning of the operation so that they do not need to be changed, and to recruit them with the clear understanding that they will remain in their posts throughout the duration of the mission.

Systematic evaluations during and following completion of such

---

[34] Many of these points were made in del Castillo, "Post-conflict peace-building."

operations are greatly needed: they can facilitate drawing of lessons and cross-fertilization.

For all these things to happen and to deal with and support post-conflict peacebuilding activities both at the peacemaking and peace-keeping phases as well as in the post-conflict peacebuilding phase itself, responsibilities need to be clearly assigned at headquarters. Given the Secretariat's present structure, there is no self-evident place for it. The political department would probably have to play a prominent role, particularly at the planning stage, since the central purpose – the consolidation of peace – is inherently political. The department of peacekeeping operations would need to be strongly involved given its own responsibilities during the implementation phase. It would also make eminent sense to draw on the economics departments and the regional economic commissions. Furthermore, if the required expertise were not available within the UN, the Secretary-General should have the flexibility to request that experts be seconded from the agencies, including the Bretton Woods institutions. This would be a first step toward an integrated approach to the problem of human security encompassing the UN system as a whole.

The presence of a peacekeeping mission in a country often over-shadows the work of the development programs and agencies of the UN system in that country, despite the fact that these might have been there from much earlier and will be expected to remain much longer. Because of this, it is very important that, as the peacekeeping operations winds down, a smooth transition is worked out with the UN agencies led by the Resident Representative of the United Nations Development Programme (UNDP) as resident coordinator. This will be extremely important in El Salvador. Many of the peace-related programs have been receiving the constant support of ONUSAL/MINUSAL which has used its good offices and verification role to insure their implementation. Once the UN verification role is completed, the long-term viability of many of these programs will depend on whether the UN agencies as well as NGOs and bilateral donors can provide technical and financial support in the post-MINUSAL phase.

The Salvadoran experience with reintegration is extremely rich and would allow us to draw many more lessons. If the basic principles it gives rise to can be kept in mind in future peace negotiations, in the drafting of agreements and in the formation of peacekeeping operations, the implementation of new agreements would be eased and the chance of success and long-term viability of peace-related programs enhanced.

Conclusion and chronologies

15   Strategies for peace: conclusions and lessons

Michael W. Doyle, Ian Johnstone, and Robert C. Orr

Introduction

The problems of peace enforcement manifested so signally in Bosnia and Somalia were avoided in Cambodia and El Salvador. Recognizing the continuing political significance of national sovereignty, the UN sought out a consensual basis for a restoration of law and order in Cambodia and El Salvador and tried to implement its global humanitarian agenda in a way that produced less friction and more support. As our authors have shown, UNTAC and ONUSAL contributed to the UN's commendable record of success in multidimensional peace operations established in conflicts as diverse as those in Namibia (UNTAG), and Mozambique (ONUMOZ).[1] After summarizing the results of UNTAC and ONUSAL, we will now draw lessons concerning ways in which the international community can enhance the UN's role in peacemaking, peacekeeping and peacebuilding and thereby succeed in managing these complex multidimensional operations that are increasingly likely to be the hallmark of the UN's contribution to international peace and security.

The record of successes and failures

Defining success and failure in complex peace operations is far from an exact science. Should one measure the extent to which the agreed mandate was fulfilled, article by article? Or should one focus on whether peace and reconciliation – the operations' fundamental purposes – were achieved? Or perhaps how much order or justice improved, and what credit – or blame – the UN should be given for the change? Each measure would lead to a different judgment, each of which would lead one to consider whether the results could have been achieved at less cost

---

[1] For a valuable collection of case studies see William Durch (ed.), *The Evolution of UN Peacekeeping: Case Studies and Comparative Analysis* (New York: St. Martin's Press, 1993).

or more efficiently. No one of these measures seems to us to be sufficient, and each is dependent on the others. We have chosen – admittedly, unscientifically – to consider all of the above in an eclectic approach.

Cambodia

The picture of the UNTAC operation at its conclusion was highly complex and, despite the many difficulties, surprisingly successful. Considering that the main antagonists in Cambodia – the Vietnamese-installed government and the radical Khmer Rouge – were pressured by their big-power sponsors to sign the 1991 Paris Peace Accords and never fully cooperated with the UN, UNTAC's accomplishments before and after the May elections were remarkable.

Failures

If we look at UNTAC's official, initial mandate, two major areas of failure become clearly visible. The first lies in the failure to achieve a ceasefire and then canton, demobilize, and disarm 70 percent of the four factions's military forces; the second in the failure to achieve control over civil administration and subsequent breakdowns in law, order, and political neutrality.

First, the failure to achieve a ceasefire (phase 1) and then canton, demobilize, and disarm 70 percent of the four factions' military forces (phase 2) had a dehabilitating effect on the operation of the original mandate. As initially planned, the May 1993 elections were supposed to take place in a secure – cantoned and disarmed – political environment in which the relative military weight of the factions would play little direct role in either the electoral campaign or the voter's choice. When the Khmer Rouge refused to canton, SOC and other factions that had partially cantoned almost 55,000 soldiers refused to demobilize and disarm. Most of the soldiers that were cantoned then went on "agricultural leave," with clear results: during the election campaign, the continuing civil war and occasional armed intimidation prevented the emergence of the "neutral political environment" called for in the Paris Accords.

Second, UNTAC also failed to establish control over Cambodian civil administration. The Paris Agreements specified that UNTAC would control essential areas of administration and do so over each of the four factions. By controlling them – so it was anticipated – UNTAC would be able to insure that the political environment was neutral, and that no faction – and especially the predominant faction of the State of Cambodia – would be able to employ sovereign resources to tilt the electoral contest in its favor.

Successes

First, although the country was temporarily subject to the UN's "transitional authority," it also enjoyed – for perhaps the first time – the prospect of true independence from the control of any foreign power. Having endured French and Japanese colonialism before 1954 and American, Chinese, and Vietnamese competition for influence thereafter, Cambodia experienced national self-determination (and Southeast Asia, regional self-determination). During the peace process, disturbing foreign presences continued to complicate Cambodia's future. Thai generals in the west and Vietnamese interests in the east allegedly participated in the illegal export of Cambodia's logs and gems. Many thousand Vietnamese entered the country to take advantage of the economic boom created by UNTAC's presence. But as of September 1993, for better or worse, Cambodia was in the hands of the Cambodians.

Second, the mere presence of UNTAC had an impact. Its arrival signaled the end of full-scale civil war. The country became mostly peaceful. True, some provinces were very tense, but skirmishes were limited in duration and the pitched battles of 1990 and earlier ended. The UNTAC presence also opened up the political system, helping opposition parties to compete against the incumbent regime. They acquired offices, held meetings and had access to the media. Harassment continued, but not enough to undermine the electoral process. The jails, once crammed with political prisoners, held a vastly reduced population of inmates, all of whom seemed to have had some – albeit sometimes exaggerated –criminal charge laid against them. UNTAC even made a dent in the most blatant corruption.

Third, more than 370,000 refugees were peacefully repatriated from camps in Thailand. In what became UNHCR's "most complex, best funded and most visible refugee repatriation," the repatriation component of UNTAC (staffed by UNHCR, with the cooperation and support of the military component, the Cambodian Red Cross and other humanitarian and relief organizations) organized a massive undertaking. In addition to overcoming the formidable logistic difficulties of transportation and supplying a start-up resettlement package, UNTAC ensured that the refugees were repatriated voluntarily to a location they found acceptable.

Fourth, UNTAC organized an election in a country with a shattered physical infrastructure. The UN has monitored and supervised many elections, but Cambodia's was the first election that the UN directly organized from the planning stages through to the writing of an electoral law and the registration for and conduct of the poll itself. Hundreds of foreign volunteers in nearly every village registered voters and spread information. Voters walked considerable distances and braved threats of physical harm. UNTAC passed a comprehensive electoral law – over the initial opposition of the Supreme National Council – and began to educate Cambodians about human rights and elections, employing an imaginative range of techniques that included traveling acting troops, Khmer videos, public rallies, debates among candidates, and extensive radio coverage. Nearly all eligible Cambodians – almost 5 million – registered to vote. The May election rewarded their efforts by affirming the determination of the Cambodian people to have a voice in their future. Despite months of attempted intimidation by some of the parties, 90 percent of the electorate turned out to vote.

As we noted, the "peace" in Cambodia produced a legitimate sovereign government, but civil war with the Khmer Rouge persists. The failures to build the long-term foundations of a civil peace have moreover resulted in repeated erosions of civil liberties.

El Salvador

If UNTAC achieved a few striking successes despite significant failures, ONUSAL achieved many significant successes despite a few striking failures. Perhaps the most important factor in determining ONUSAL's greater success rate was the fact that the Salvadoran parties were more prepared to make peace than the Cambodian parties. Because the parties still mistrusted one another deeply and had trouble agreeing on the precise terms of their peace, they still needed the UN, but on the whole ONUSAL was asked to do relatively less than UNTAC. Thus ONUSAL became one of the most successful post-Cold War UN peace operations. While not all aspects of the peace Accords have been fully implemented and problems of violence, weak institutions, and social and economic tensions remain, the UN was instrumental in bringing an end to the longest civil war in Latin America in the twentieth century.

Successes

In contrast to Cambodia, the military element of the UN mission in El Salvador was a significant success. The armed conflict was brought to an end, the FMLN was fully demobilized and disarmed (if with some difficulty), and government forces were dramatically reduced, restructured, and, after great resistance, purged at senior levels. Although structural changes were not as deep as originally envisioned, unregistered military weapons remain in the hands of civilians, and the military still participates in internal security affairs – despite the new constitution's clear restrictions on such action – Salvadoran society has been significantly demilitarized.

The human rights dimension of ONUSAL also stands out as an important success story. While human rights violations persist in El Salvador, the level of terror has reduced dramatically and some measure of accountability for past abuses was established through the Truth Commission, Ad Hoc Commission, and the Joint Group. Though a step short of criminal accountability and less effective than might have been hoped in generating a "catharsis" in which Salvadoran society would come to terms with it past, they sent an important signal that impunity would no longer be tolerated.

A third area of success – though mixed – is that of promoting institutional reform. The peace process generated a range of constitutional and legal reforms that have opened the possibility of a new political framework for El Salvador. Of primary importance is the conversion of the FMLN into a legal political party, enabling El Salvador's first inclusive, democratic – if somewhat flawed – elections in 1994. A new National Civilian Police (PNC) and civilian police academy were created from scratch and have done relatively well despite attempts to politicize the force, problems with some internal abuses, and a serious post-war crime wave. The National Counsel for the Defense of Human Rights has established itself as a viable and trusted institution. The election of a new Supreme Court, albeit after great partisan wrangling, has created the opportunity for real change in a previously farcical judicial system. Moreover, these changes might stimulate progress in other areas of judicial reform, and help create a truly independent and professional justice system.

Failures

The most striking set-back of the Salvadoran peace process thus far has been the inability to bring the initial stages of the reintegration process to a satisfactory close. The first major problem has been that of land distribution. As del Castillo points out in this volume, by March 1996, long after the program was scheduled to be over, only 49.6 percent of the potential beneficiaries have received land and completed the titling and registry process. Even those beneficiaries that received land were saddled with debt and not given necessary credit and technical support, raising serious questions about their ability to pay off these debts and hold on to the land. A second major problem, in part because it has detracted attention from the critical land issue, was the violent protest of demobilized members of the armed forces and the subsequent decision to grant these forces more favorable terms.

A second area of difficulty has been that of public security. Not only has the new PNC been unable to cope with the crime wave in post-war El Salvador (including renewed death squad activity), there are numerous indications that criminality has taken root in the PNC itself, including such serious offenses as assassination, participation in illegal armed vigilante groups, and dramatic rises in the excessive use of force and other violations of due process. Equally serious has been the increasing use, and institutionalization of the use of the military to address internal security concerns. On one hand there appear to be few options to deal with pronounced lawlessness in parts of the country, especially given the insufficient numbers of PNC, their inexperience, and lack of specialized training. On the other hand, this precedent seriously challenges one of the most critical aspects of the constitutional reforms resulting from the entire peace process, that of permanently removing the military from internal security functions. Efforts to address this problem continue, both by the UN and bilaterally by the USA and others. As of early 1996, however, lawlessness and use of the military for internal security functions remain a problem with little hope of any significant change in sight.

A third failure of the Salvadoran process was in the area of social and economic development. The parties not only attempted very little in the social and economic arena, but they failed on the few measures they undertook. Even if the highly problematic land transfer program were successful, the scope of the program would do little to affect the fundamental inequities in land distribution in the country. The Forum for Economic and Social Consultation was designed in part to make up for the lack of attention to such issues in the Peace Accords, but it made little progress other than in the area of labor rights, and this only after the USA threatened to revoke Generalized System of Preferences privileges.

The roots of semi-success

If the UN missions in both Cambodia and El Salvador can be called qualified successes, it is important to identify the roots of their success.

On a basic level success, and to a great extent failure, can be seen as a product of consent, or lack thereof. The mobilization of political will embodied in consent, when combined with the wide array of dimensions of implementation, has proven to be crucial to the success of multi-dimensional operations. Nonetheless, although non-enforcing, these operations are far from harmonious. Consent is not a simple "bright line" demarcating the safe and acceptable from the dangerous and illegitimate. Peace treaties may themselves depend on prior sanctions, threats of sanctions, or loss of aid, all imposed by the international community.

But enjoying consent is not enough. Multidimensional operations work best when they actively enhance consent,[2] usually through three independent channels. The first is through pressured consent. Parties often agree to a settlement and abide by its terms only under pressure from the international community. Achieving the peace treaty itself will often require heavy persuasion by outside actors. In Cambodia, the USSR and China are said to have let their respective clients in Phnom Penh and the Khmer Rouge know that ongoing levels of financial and military support would not be forthcoming if they resisted the terms of a peace treaty that their patrons found acceptable. In El Salvador, the shift from the Reagan to Bush administrations and the collapse of the Soviet Union produced similar though less direct pressures. The second channel is "active consent," in which artificial bodies are created in the peace process to embody, sustain and develop the consensus of a peace agreement. The third is "open-ended" consent, by which the parties agree to a proactive UN presence, the parameters of which are not fully delineated in the peace agreement and the outcome of which is not pre-ordained in every detail. The parties in a sense agree to a UN-guided process, delegated to and directly administered by the UN, as in Cambodia, or administered by the parties but monitored by the UN, as in El Salvador.

Each form of enhanced consent reflects an important innovation in the UN's strategy of peace – peacemaking, peacekeeping and peace-building – all of which were outlined in the Secretary-General's *Agenda for Peace*. These innovations will be examined next, along with other pertinent lessons learned, in the context of the UN's overall strategy for peace.

---

[2] On this and subsequent points see Michael Doyle, *The UN in Cambodia: UNTAC's Civil Mandate* (Boulder, Col.: Lynne Rienner, 1995).

Lessons learned

Peacemaking

The UN has developed a set of crucially important innovations that help manage the building of peace on a consensual basis. First among them is the diplomatic device that has come to be called the "Friends of the Secretary-General." This is a multinational leverage for UN diplomacy to help make and manage peace. Composed of ad hoc, informal, multilateral diplomatic mechanisms that join together states in support of the Secretary-General's initiatives, it legitimates, with the stamp of UN approval and supervision, the pressures that interested states can bring to bear to further the purposes of peace and the UN. In El Salvador, the Four Friends of the Secretary-General were Venezuela, Mexico, Spain and Colombia, and were frequently joined by a "fifth Friend" – the United States. Together they played a crucial role in negotiating and implementing the Peace Accords. So too did the Extended P5 in Cambodia. The device has been employed, with variations in Haiti, Guatemala, Georgia, Cambodia, Angola, Rwanda and elsewhere.

Playing a crucial role in the Secretary-General's peacemaking and preventive diplomacy functions, these groups serve four key functions:

First, the limited influence of the Secretary-General can be leveraged, multiplied, and complemented, by the "Friends." The UN's scarce attention and even scarcer resources can be supplemented by the diplomacy and the clout of powerful, interested actors.

The second value is legitimation. The very act of constituting themselves as a group, with the support of the Secretary-General, lends the diplomatic activities of interested states a degree of legitimacy that they might not otherwise enjoy. It allows for constructive diplomacy when accusations of special and particular national interest could taint bilateral efforts.

The third value is coordination. The mechanism of the Friends of the Secretary-General provides transparency among the interested external parties, assuring them that they are all working for the same purposes, and when they are doing so, allowing them to pursue a division of labor that enhances their joint effort. It ensures that diplomats are not working at cross purposes because they regularly meet and inform each other of their activities and encourage each other to undertake special tasks.

Fourth, the Friends mechanism provides a politically balanced approach to the resolution through negotiation of civil wars. It often turns out that one particular "Friend" can associate with one faction just as another associates with a second. In the Salvadoran peace process, it is said that at the beginning Mexico was a particularly close interlocutor with the FMLN, just as Venezuela played a similarly close role with the government of El Salvador (as did the "fifth Friend," the USA). The Friends open more flexible channels of communication than a single UN mediator could provide. The process works best when the "Friends" are well coordinated and subordinate to the lead mediator – often, but not necessarily, the UN. Without such a commitment to play a supporting role, at least in principle, the Friends allow themselves and the UN to be played off against one another by the competing parties. They also run the risk of forging an unworkable peace agreement which the UN will then be asked to implement.

In Cambodia, the process proved crucial both in design of the peace agreement and the later management of UNTAC, as Jin Song and Michael Doyle have both noted. In Cambodia the Extended P5 provided key political and financial support to UNTAC and helped organize almost $1 billion of ICORC aid while also providing special funds for various projects. But the Extended P5 lacked a fixed composition. It, of course, included the P5, but also included – or excluded – others on an ad hoc basis, depending on the issue or topic to be covered and the "message" to be sent. For example, Thailand was excluded from certain meetings in order to send a signal of concern about its lack of support for the restrictions imposed on the Khmer Rouge. In Cambodia, moreover, there was not a sovereign government to monitor or support. Much of the Extended P5's diplomacy was therefore directed at UNTAC itself, protecting, for example, the interests of national battalions.

In El Salvador, this Friends role was if anything even more important. Formally recognized and defined as Four Friends by the Secretary-General, with the USA playing the special but informal role of "fifth Friend," they served as the managing board of directors of the entire peace process. As Mark LeVine points out, this Friends mechanism was perhaps the single most important international factor in obtaining a successful outcome in El Salvador. The mechanism on one hand built successfully on previous regional efforts, and on the other provided the Secretary-General with the necessary clout to effectively manage the peacemaking process.

A second, more mundane lesson that arises from a comparison of the Cambodian and Salvadoran experiences is that successful peacemaking can be done in a variety of ways. As Jin Song points out, the Cambodian process was successful at least in part because it was an overall package of Accords that were agreed upon not only by the parties to conflict, but also by the global and regional powers that took an active and direct interest. As Mark LeVine notes in his chapter on El Salvador, however, peacemaking efforts were successful at least in part because they were actively led by the UN Secretary-General and his representatives, and in part because they were piecemeal, using agreements in individual areas as building blocks for future agreements.

Peacekeeping

The traditional part of peacekeeping is observing the implementation of a ceasefire and the cantonment and demobilization of military forces. In Cambodia and El Salvador, these functions proved to be more challenging than usual. As Metrikas and Kim point out in their chapter, the Cambodian peacekeeping mandate was compromised principally by the unwillingness of the Khmer Rouge to abide by agreements which they had already signed. At the same time, they note, the peacekeeping mission was undermined by lack of sufficient advanced planning, excessive UN bureaucracy, very slow deployment, and an insufficient command and control structure. In El Salvador the process of obtaining a ceasefire and disarming and demobilizing troops proceeded much more smoothly than in Cambodia, though, as David McCormick reveals, there were plenty of problems that had to be overcome, including major logistical obstacles and attempts by both sides to renege on parts of the agreement.

As both cases suggest, political will is the key to achieving the goals of the peacekeeping missions. Perhaps the first lesson to be learned about the peacekeeping phase of multidimensional operations is that the UN needs a political strategy to win and maintain popular support and create – and not just enjoy – the support of local forces of order. To do this, the UN must discover new ways of mobilizing voluntary consent.

Peacekeeping experiences in Cambodia and El Salvador have suggested that one effective way to do so is through an ad hoc, formally instituted, semi-sovereign mechanism designed to manage a peace process. It has often been remarked that chapter VI presents the United Nations with too little authority and chapter VII offers too much; and that chapter VI is associated with too little force, chapter VII too much. The value of ad hoc, semi-sovereign, artificial bodies is that they provide a means of encouraging and influencing the shape of consent. Indeed, these semi-sovereign artificial bodies can help contain the erosion of consent and even manufacture it where it is missing. Created by a peace treaty, they permit the temporary consensus of the parties to be embodied – constitutionalized, incorporated – in an institution with regular consultation and even, as in the Cambodian Supreme National Council, a semi-autonomous sovereign will. They can represent the once warring parties and act in the name of a preponderance of the "nation" without the continuous or complete consent of all the factions.

This type of mechanism has proved crucial in Cambodia, where the Paris Agreements constructed the Supreme National Council to "enshrine" Cambodian sovereignty. The Council, composed of the four factions and chaired by Prince Sihanouk, offered a chance for the warring parties to consult together on a regular basis and to endorse the peace process. It also lent special authority to Prince Sihanouk, who was authorized to act if the Supreme National Council failed to achieve a consensus. Beyond that, it empowered the United Nations, represented by Special Representative Yasushi Akashi, to act in the interests of the peace process if Sihanouk failed to do so. Artificially created, the Supreme National Council thus established a semi-sovereign legal personality designed to be responsive to the general interests of Cambodia (when a complete consensus was lacking among all the factions) and to the authority of the United Nations special representative.

The Commission on the Peace (COPAZ) in El Salvador played a related – although much less authoritative – role in the Salvadoran peace process, serving as a forum for consultation among the FMLN, the government and the other political parties, with the UN and Catholic Church serving as observers. Designed as a "mechanism for the monitoring of and the participation of civilian society in the process of changes resulting from the negotiations," it was the only political institution that embodied the full scope of Salvadoran politics, the only institution that could legitimately speak for "El Salvador." Its minimal role in the peace process was unfortunate, but it did serve two useful purposes beyond mere "talk." First, its existence facilitated the negotiations leading to the final Chapultepec Accords, providing the parties with a place to refer some of the details they could not work out in their initial talks. Second, during the implementation phase, it was used for consensus-building on matters not covered by the Accords.

An item to note in the design of these semi-sovereign, artificial bodies, is that one should try (to the extent that one's freedom of negotiation allows) to "preview" the peace that the parties and the international community seeks. For the Paris Peace Agreements for Cambodia, seeking a "pluralist democracy" should have meant adding to the Supreme National Council advisory bodies, such as one for civil society. It might have included, for example, Buddhist monks, non-governmental organizations, and other representatives of society outside the state. These supplementary bodies, it should be noted, need not perform executive or legislative functions. The important point is that civil society participate in the decision-making process, at a minimum through formally recognized consultative channels.

The UN must try to avoid the trade offs between too much force and too little, another area in which advisory bodies can play a crucial role. The dangers of chapter VII enforcement operations lead many observers to doubt whether states will actually provide troops for them unless vital national interests are at stake; the risks are much more costly than the member states are willing to bear for humanitarian purposes. But even in chapter VI operations, consent by parties easily dissolves under the difficult processes of peace. Given those options, the semi-sovereign artificial bodies offer the possibility of mid-course adjustments. They artificially but usefully enhance the process of consent in the direction of peace while simultaneously avoiding the dangers associated with attempts to implement a forced peace.

A second important lesson for peacekeeping is that the use of force is even more problematic in a multi-dimensional operation than in a traditional peacekeeping operation; the critical political and humanitarian activities of a multi-dimensional mission are likely to be compromised if force is used other than in self-defense. The case of Cambodia makes this point quite eloquently. Instead of responding to Khmer Rouge ceasefire violations with force – as it was being pressured to do from many quarters – the UN chose to redefine its military mandate to focus on creating a secure environment for the upcoming elections. As Metrikas and Kim point out, this change allowed the military component of UNTAC to contribute to that which defined the success of the operation, even though its original mission was not realized. The caveat concerning the use of force except in self-defense – since 1973 defined to include defense of the mandate – is critical. In Cambodia, a judicious defensive use of force by UNTAC peacekeepers in response to Khmer Rouge attacks played an important role in assuring the integrity of the UNTAC electoral operation and in maintaining the credibility of the operation itself. Equally important, in the crucial weeks leading up to the election, UNTAC successfully called on "all" parties to protect the electoral process. The CPAF (army of SOC) seems to have responded, pushing back the Khmer Rouge from vital electoral sites in the most populated areas.[3]

A third lesson learned by examining the peacekeeping phase of the Cambodian and Salvadoran operations is that a competent police

---

[3] Lieutenant General John Sanderson, cited in *Peacemaking and Peacekeeping for the Next Century: The Report of the 25th Vienna Seminar* (IPA, 1995), Ameen Jan, Robert Orr, and Timothy Wilkins, rapporteurs.

division is a critical element of a peacekeeping mission to resolve internal conflicts, just as a competent civilian police force is critical to the future development of peace and reconciliation in the country in question. In Cambodia a great deal was learned about failure in this area, while in El Salvador an equal amount was learned about success. As Metrikas and Kim argue, failure of the civilian police component in Cambodia was due not only to the abysmal situation on the ground, but also to an unrealistic mandate, poor planning, and problems with the quality of personnel and command and control capabilities. In the end the need for policing and the failure to develop this capability among local forces even impelled the UN to become directly involved, raising logistical as well as ethical quandaries. On the other hand, as McCormick notes, in El Salvador a new civilian police force was successfully created from scratch despite having to overcome some serious problems along the way. This was at least in part due to a serious effort made in this area by the international community from the start. What is common to both cases, however, is the realization that work in the area of police development is not enough, as this is intimately related to the justice system. In both Cambodia and El Salvador serious problems with the justice system as a whole impeded effective policing. Future operations must not only address policing issues early in the process, but also link those issues with equal efforts to improve the administration of justice as a whole. One will do no good without the other.

A fourth lesson to be learned about the peacekeeping phase of multidimensional peace operations is that human rights monitoring and verification efforts can play an extremely important role, even if there is natural tension between being a "finger-pointer" and an "honest broker." This is most evident in the case of El Salvador. While the tension between monitoring human rights and providing good offices was very much in evidence in El Salvador, ONUSAL also demonstrates that when human rights accountability is part of a broader peace process, the two functions can be mutually reinforcing. Conversely, separating the functions can undermine both the status of the human rights observers and the moral authority of the rest of the mission. In Cambodia, human rights concerns were addressed not so much in a peacekeeping context as in a peacebuilding context. It is to this aspect of peace operations that we now turn.

Peacebuilding

Multidimensional, second-generation peacekeeping contemplates deep collective involvement in areas long thought to be the exclusive domain of domestic jurisdiction. If a peacekeeping operation is to leave behind a legitimate and independently viable political sovereign, it must help transform the political landscape by building a new basis for domestic peace.

Traditional strategies of conflict resolution, when successful, were designed to resolve a dispute between conflicting parties. Successful resolution could be measured by the stated reconciliation of the parties, the duration of the reconciliation, and changes in the way parties behaved toward each other.[4] But successful contemporary peacebuilding doesn't just change behavior; it also, and perhaps more importantly, transforms identities and institutional contexts. More than reforming play in an old game, it changes the game. This is the grand strategy Reginald Austin, electoral chief of UNTAC, probed in the course of the operation when he asked what are the "true objectives [of UNTAC]: Is it a political operation seeking a solution to the immediate problem of an armed conflict by all means possible? Or does it have a wider objective: to implant democracy, change values and establish a new pattern of governance based on multi-partism and free and fair elections?"[5]

In either case, but especially if multidimensional operations have the wider objectives mentioned by Austin, the parties to agreements that call for multidimensional operations consent to a proactive UN presence. They do so because they need the help of the international community to achieve peace. But acceptance of UN involvement in implementing these agreements is less straightforward than, for example, consenting to observance of a ceasefire. It represents the voluntary relinquishing of sovereignty in critical areas for the life of the peace process.

Authentic and firm consent, in the aftermath of such severe civil strife as that endured by Cambodia and El Salvador, is rare. The international negotiators of a peace treaty and the UN designers of a mandate should, therefore, attempt to incorporate as many bargaining advantages for the UN authority as the parties will tolerate. Even seemingly extraneous bargaining chips will become useful as the spirit of cooperation erodes under the pressure of misunderstandings and separating interests. The UN counted upon the financial needs of the Cambodian factions to insure their cooperation and designed an extensive rehabilitation component to guarantee steady rewards for cooperative behavior.[6] But

---

4   See A. B. Fetherston, "Putting the peace back into peacekeeping," *International Peacekeeping*, vol. 1, no. 2, 1994, p. 11, citing a paper by Marc Ross.
5   Dr. Reginald Austin, Chief Electoral Officer's Electoral Evaluation: Summary Report, UNTAC, 1993, p. 14.
6   This link was drawn explicitly by Deputy Secretary Lawrence Eagleburger at the Conference on the Reconstruction of Cambodia, June 22, 1992, Tokyo, where he proposed that assistance to Cambodia be "through the SNC – to areas controlled by

the Khmer Rouge's access to illicit trade eliminated this bargaining chip. And the suspicion of SOC's rivals prevented a full implementation of rehabilitation in the 80 percent of the country controlled by the SOC. Passport and visa control succeeded simply because the UN, as a representative of the international community, had the leverage to persuade the SOC to comply.

A related, second lesson is that the architects of UN operations should therefore design into the mandate as much independent implementation as the parties will agree to in the peace treaty. In Cambodia, the electoral component and refugee repatriation seem to have succeeded simply because they did not depend on the steady and continuous positive support of the four factions. Each had an independent sphere of authority and organizational capacity that allowed it to proceed against everything short of the active military opposition by the factions.

Even in cases of greater reconciliation, such as El Salvador, the implications of accepting UN involvement in implementing these agreements is far from straightforward. Even when genuine consent is achieved, it is impossible to provide for every contingency in complex peace accords. Problems of interpretation arise, unforeseen gaps in the accords materialize and circumstances change. The original consent, therefore, is open-ended and in part a gesture of faith that later problems can be worked out on a consensual basis.[7] Thus numerous "recalender-izations" and variations from the Accords were agreed to in El Salvador. In fact, the UN often found itself in the awkward position of being "more royalist than the king," insisting on full compliance more strenuously than the parties themselves. It was justified in doing so precisely because the transformative nature of the peace process meant the UN owed a duty to Salvadoran society as a whole, and not merely to the signatories of the Accords.

A third critical lesson to be drawn from UNTAC's and ONUSAL's experiences with peacebuilding is that there are various strategies for promoting institutional reform, all of which can work well or poorly depending on the circumstances. The three different strategies can be called pressuring, facilitating, and replacing. In El Salvador the first two strategies tended to work best, while in Cambodia the third was by far

those Cambodian parties cooperating with UNTAC in implementing the peace accords – and only to those parties which are so cooperating." (Press Release USUN-44-92, June 23, 1992.) Disbursing the aid through the Supreme National Council, however, gave the Khmer Rouge a voice, as a member of the Supreme National Council, in the potential disbursement of the aid.
[7] On this and subsequent points see Ian Johnstone, *Rights and Reconciliation: UN Strategies in El Salvador*, International Peace Academy Occasional Paper (Boulder, Col. and London: Lynne Rienner, 1995).

the most effective. In El Salvador, much of the legislation passed in the course of constitutional reform and its aftermath was drafted and adopted under direct pressure from the UN and other important international actors. As McCormick and Johnstone discuss in their chapters, direct pressure of another kind was also exerted – that of human rights and civilian police monitors working side by side on a daily basis with Salvadoran police and justice personnel, ensuring that they comply with certain provisions of the Accords. In El Salvador the UN also played a lower-profile, but perhaps equally important role by simply facilitating change through technical assistance and other non-threatening techniques in a number of areas, including police and judicial training, reconstruction efforts, and reintegration efforts.

In Cambodia, on the other hand, the most effective strategy tended to be replacing Cambodian actors in critical areas at critical points in the process. As Williams and Doyle show, this was certainly the case with two of UNTAC's biggest successes – the elections and the repatriation. It was also the case for human rights education, though in this area important efforts were made to facilitate the creation of Cambodian human rights organizations. At the same time, as Uphoff reveals, direct pressure helped solve some border control problems, while facilitation helped achieve the implementation of important administrative and economic reforms. This is to say that there is no single useful approach in a given case; the most successful UN missions will be those that are able to effectively combine all three types of institutional reform strategies.

General lessons for multidimensional operations

In addition to providing lessons specific to each aspect of peace operations, the missions in Cambodia and El Salvador also provide more general lessons concerning the design of peace operations as a whole.

Comprehensive, agreed upon peace[8]

First, the international community must try to achieve a comprehensive, agreed upon peace among all the parties. The costs of failing to achieve a

[8] The problems of peacekeeping in the midst of a continuing semi-civil war have been effectively explored in Shashi Tharoor, "Should UN peacekeeping go 'back to basics'?," *Survival*, vol. 37, no. 4, 1995–96, pp. 52–64; Marrack Goulding, "The use of force by the UN," Mountbatten-Tata Memorial Lecture at the University of Southampton, November 23, 1995; John MacKinlay and Jarat Chopra, "Second generation multinational operations," *Washington Quarterly*, vol. 15, no. 2, 1992; Adam Roberts, "The United Nations and International Security'," *Survival*, vol. 35, no. 2, 1993; Mats Berdal, *Whither UN Peacekeeping?*, Adelphi Paper 281 (London:

starting framework for peace highlight the value of a peace agreement. Amid the historic animosities of Yugoslavia or the anarchy of Somalia, it found itself without the means to make good on an enforcement mandate. When the UN's peacemaking efforts stall, as they did in Yugoslavia and Somalia, the UN will be faced with difficult alternatives. The options include first, exiting altogether because the United Nations is unwilling to use force; second, delegating authority to a multinational coalition or regional organization to try to make or enforce a peace; and third, dividing the country, separating out those sectors or regions prepared to cooperate with the UN in pursuing the peace while exiting from those unprepared. Each of these options has its own dangers. There may be nothing left to separate, or no single acceptable coalition of willing states may be prepared to accept a delegation to enforce a peace.

But in humanitarian emergencies, the moral consequences of abandonment are so extreme that conscience rebels, as it did in Somalia and Bosnia in the fall of 1992. Under those circumstances there may be no alternative but UN engagement – a limited operation with enforcement powers to provide necessary humanitarian protection. "Good soldiering" for peace then requires, where force must be used, minimum force, especially where non-combatants are involved. The UN should negotiate first, defend itself and its mission when necessary. It is wrong to act otherwise. Military victories will turn into political defeats if UN peacekeepers enter into a war with the people they were sent to protect. National governments, moreover, will refuse to have the blood of their soldiers shed for far away foreign causes, however just.

The UN will find it difficult to stay out of very unpromising, violent civil conflicts. Simple prudence will keep it out of the affairs of powerful states, unless countering international aggression – the UN's first purpose – mobilizes the world community as it did against Iraq. Otherwise powerful states will be free, as they always have been free, to oppress their populations as they see fit. But elsewhere the UN's other purposes – to defend human rights and promote social progress – will be heard. Humanitarian needs will not wait upon the agreement of all the parties and even an agreed peace can fail (as the Addis Ababa agreement among the Somali factions did). The scale of likely human suffering if the UN abandons its humanitarian effort may leave no choice but muddling through.

With popular support, superior force, and diplomatic engagement of the international community, "peace enforcement" may seek to create

Brassey's for the IISS, 1993); and Thomas Weiss, "New challenges for UN military operations," *Washington Quarterly*, vol. 16, no. 1, 1993.

and defend a narrow corridor of continuing humanitarian support, as it did in Bosnia. After the fall of the safe havens and the expulsion of Serbs from the Krajina, NATO then bombed the Bosnian Serbs (represented by Serbian president Milosevic) to the bargaining table. In Somalia peace enforcement had some similarly positive results in terms of supporting a narrowly defined humanitarian mission, but produced much less salutary effects on the overall peace process.

In the end the lessons of peace enforcement are that peace cannot be forced. It must be negotiated, as it was in Geneva under the leadership of the UN and the European Union and in Dayton under the leadership of the USA. The effort to work with the UN should not be abandoned. The UN can and should feed the hungry and protect those driven from their homes, but most of all it can and should try to bring warring parties together through negotiation in order to induce them to begin to make their own peace.

Enhancing consent

Second, the key to effective UN peace operations is thus a strategy that exploits the possibilities of enhanced consent that brings innovative diplomatic and administrative mechanisms to bear to further the process of peace. Friends of the Secretary-General and ad hoc, semi-sovereign entities are but two of the means the UN can employ to promote a negotiated settlement and then steer it through the troubled crises that will surely ensue. Failed states, such as the former Yugoslavia and Somalia, have often been the victims of partition or imperial rule. Unlike the usual partitioner, the United Nations must insist on all-round consent and worry about the precedents such actions will set. Unlike imperial rulers, UN peacekeeping operations have as their goal reconciliation, rehabilitation, and authentic self-determining independence. But self-determination must have indigenous roots if it is to be truly self-determining and stable. In failed states, these roots seem to take at least a generation or so of indigenous order and political success to nurture. Moreover, they often grow in distorted ways in reaction against foreign, imperial, law and order. Even the most well-meaning outside body, the UN, will fail to engender stable national solidarity, bypassing the usual birth pains of nations.

Under these conditions, even the best of UN peacebuilding operations are bound to be patched up affairs, shaky agreements among distrustful parties and elections held in the middle of moderated war, as was the UN-organized election of May 1993 in Cambodia. Their justification is the alternative: a return to unmoderated war. The challenge for the UN in these situations is to secure ongoing consent throughout the peace-building phase, not just between the parties to a conflict but from all political actors with a stake in – or the capacity to disrupt – a peace process. Including all relevant actors requires a determined effort on the part of the UN to reach out to and strengthen civil society. Broad social reconciliation on this level entails the generation of new institutions and new attitudes, characteristic of the transformed (and often more open) society that emerges from the peace process. For the UN, it means community relations, public information, and efforts to engage all sectors of society in the shared enterprise of peacebuilding.

In operations based on enhanced consent, the UN can and should play a major role in rebuilding ineffective state structures. Sovereignty is respected, but the concept undergoes a transformation when the parties to the conflict accept – out of necessity – a high degree of international involvement. Organizing elections, monitoring human rights and re-forming public security bodies, now accepted UN practice, indicate a much wider role for the organization in the administration of social and political transitions required for the settlement of internal conflicts.[9] They also point the way towards meeting one of the greatest challenges the international community faces – devising innovative political and legal arrangements for protecting minorities and peoples within existing states, if necessary with the UN as guarantor.

Multidimensionality as a source of success

A most important lesson is that the multidimensionality of complex UN operations is itself an important factor in enhancing the possibility of success. Complex UN operations are employed in extremely challenging situations, and as such can be expected to experience significant failures, just as those in Cambodia and El Salvador did. As the record in both of these cases shows, however, failures of specific aspects of the program are not enough to destroy the entire mission if various avenues of pursuing peace and reconciliation are available and flexibility is maintained. This is true even when the failure is a central one, as in the case of Khmer Rouge intransigence and the resulting inability of the UN to demobilize, disarm, and canton the factions' troops as specified in the UNTAC mandate. Even in this extreme case, UNTAC was able to advance the cause of peace and reconciliation in Cambodia by sponsoring the national elections which provided the basis for a new,

---

[9]   Tom Farer and Felice Gaer, "The UN and human rights: at the end of the beginning," in Adam Roberts and Benedict Kingsbury (eds.), *United Nations, Divided World* (Oxford: Clarendon Press, 1993), p. 290.

legitimate government. In El Salvador, failure of the land program to move sufficiently rapidly and to benefit the supposed "beneficiaries," while negatively affecting reintegration efforts, did not cause the failure of the entire peace process. Instead, representation through the elections, involvement in other aspects of the reconstruction program, and other avenues prevented even the FMLN supporters for whom land was central from resuming conflict and endangering the peace process as a whole. In both of these cases, multidimensionality kept specific failures from preventing success of the overall mission.[10]

Dynamic processes

In theory, peacemaking, peacekeeping and peacebuilding are conceptually distinct aspects of UN peace operations. Each can be perceived as a sequenced set of phases, with peacemaking preceding peacekeeping, which in turn sets the stage for peacebuilding. In practice, however, the phases overlap and their overlap can become essential for the success of the operation. In El Salvador, enhancing the observance of human rights – a peacebuilding function – was a crucial component of the peacemaking process, building the mutual confidence the parties needed to reach a settlement. In Cambodia, when civil war re-emerged, UNTAC soon found itself engaged in monitoring temporary ceasefire lines –a traditional peacekeeping function – when the mission schedule suggested that it should have been completing its demobilization, demining and other peacebuilding functions. Much of the time of the special representative is spent in continuous peacemaking among the factions, renegotiating the meaning of the peace agreement. UN peace operations, it appears, need to be ready to improvise their functions dynamically.

Mandate design

Despite the fact that a clear mandate is invaluable to furthering mission goals in the implementation stage, mandates tend to be ambiguous. Ambiguous mandates result from two sets of contradictory pressures. First, in order to get an agreement, diplomats assume all parties are acting in good faith. In order to get them to sign on to as much peace as they can, diplomats avoid questioning the intentions of their diplomatic partners. But to implement a peacekeeping and peacebuilding operation, planners must assume the opposite – that the parties will not abide

---

[10] Interview with Miss Hisako Shimura, October 3, 1993

by the agreement or cannot fulfill the agreements made. These two divergent agendas militate against clear understandings. Diplomats seek to incorporate the most that the parties will agree in order to expand the bargains that the parties will demand before they are prepared to sign the treaty. Military officers and UN officials writing the Secretary-General's report implementing the mandate seek flexibility in their obligations, knowing that much of what was agreed to will not be achievable in the field. Confused mandates are an inevitable result of this tension.[11]

Timeliness of implementation

The mandate, like a natural resource contract, is an obsolescing bargain. When a country begins a negotiation with an oil company for the exploration of its territory, the company holds all the advantages. The costs of exploration are large while the possibility of oil is uncertain. The country must therefore cede generous terms. As soon as oil is discovered, the bargain shifts as discovered oil is easy to pump and any oil company can do it. The old bargain has suddenly obsolesced.[12] So with a UN peacekeeping operation. The spirit of agreement is never more exalted than at the moment of the signing of the peace treaty, the authority of the United Nations is never again greater. Then the parties assume that the agreement will be achieved and that all are operating in good faith. They depend upon the UN to achieve their hopes. The UN as yet has no investment in resources or political prestige. The UN, in short, holds all the cards. But as soon as the UN begins its investment of money, personnel and prestige, then the bargaining relationship alters its balance. The larger the UN investment – and these multidimensional operations can represent multibillion dollar investments – the greater is the independent UN interest in success and the greater the influence of the parties becomes. Since the parties control an essential element in the success of the mandate, their bargaining power rapidly rises. Precedents are established. What the UN does not achieve early in the peace process, it may not achieve at all. This is borne out by the experiences of UNTAC in particular, which was severely undermined in many of its goals by long delays in the deployment of both the military and the police components.

[11] Edward Luck has effectively presented this argument.
[12] See Raymond Vernon, "Long-run trends in concession contracts," *Proceedings of the Sixty First Annual Meeting of the American Society of International Law* (Washington, DC: American Society of international Law, 1967).

Sovereignty and a selective UN "trusteeship" role

Multidimensional operations are characterized by rather striking UN involvement in internal, state-like functions – the traditional territory of "sovereignty." Four areas of activity stand out, within each of which there are varying degrees of "intrusiveness": first, demilitarization, in which the UN might be involved in overseeing the demobilization of forces, reforming military establishments, or – on the far end of the spectrum – creating integrated armies; second, elections, which the UN has often observed occasionally provided assistance for and in one case (Cambodia) organized and conducted; third, police work, which could range from monitoring local forces to training and creating new forces and, in exceptional cases, actually performing police functions; and fourth, human rights, where the UN has been involved in verifying ongoing situations, investigating past abuses (and, where international tribunals have been established, prosecuting offenders) and building institutional capacity to prevent or deter future violations. The range of possible levels of effective UN intervention is clearly shown in the difference between the UN semi-"trustee" role in Cambodia and its active, but relatively non-sovereignty infringing role in El Salvador. Whatever the level of UN involvement, a balance must always be struck between respect for sovereignty wherever possible and the potential need for the UN to assume some important "sovereign" functions temporarily. While the SNC and COPAZ represent important innovations in this area (although both should be improved for future use), there are also a number of specific issue areas in which the UN should remain open to taking direct responsibility, as it did in the cases of elections in Cambodia, repatriation in Cambodia, and active human rights monitoring and oversight in El Salvador.

Dealing with recalcitrant parties

Whatever success was achieved in Cambodia was due to a combination of UN flexibility and firmness. Instead of letting Khmer Rouge intransigence destroy the peace process in Cambodia, the UN skillfully managed the situation by maintaining open lines of communication with the KR and keeping them involved in the process to the greatest extent possible, even as it met KR military attacks with firm, defensive military operations. Similarly, in El Salvador, as David McCormick and Ian Johnstone have shown, the UN managed the challenges of the FMLN weapons cache and government attempts to avoid military purges. The key in all these cases, and quite likely in similar situations in future operations, was flexibility combined with underlying rigidity when either the letter or the spirit of the respective Accords was called into question.

Whole mission versus the parts

In both Cambodia and El Salvador compromises in specific issue areas were needed to reach agreements among the parties and make the missions as a whole work. At the same time, many of these compromises have proved to be highly problematic either during the UN mission or after its departure. As Brian Williams pointed out, the UN took a large risk in agreeing to repatriate refugees before elections had taken place. This compromise had to be made, however, to achieve agreement among the Cambodian factions. Luckily for the UN, the unexpected success of the elections prevented this risk from resulting in a terrible outcome. In El Salvador, however, a compromise designed to keep the United States on board – allowing direct transfer of the Special Narcotics Unit and the Special Investigative Unit into the new National Civilian Police – had serious negative consequences that have plagued this essential institution. Perhaps the lesson is that while compromises need to be made in order to secure the overall mission, these must be kept to an absolute minimum to avoid compromising the long-term viability of the processes.

One important subset of this issue is the question of how hard the UN should push for implementation of a particular aspect of a complex peace agreement when the parties themselves are reluctant to do so. On the one hand, it is risky for the UN to cross the line from facilitator to protagonist. On the other, both the bargaining power of the parties and the parties themselves often change. In these situations the UN should work to the extent possible with bodies such as COPAZ and the SNC that express as broad as possible a social and political consensus on the issues at hand.

Even with all of their collective advice, none of these lessons will substitute for dedicated implementation by an expert and courageous contingent of peacekeepers, both civilian and military, or for inspired leadership from a well-chosen group of UN officials enjoying the full support of both New York and the international community. But the challenges today's peacekeepers face will be lessened if the diplomats and officials give them better mandates to implement in the very trying circumstances the peacekeepers will discover in those parts of the world most in need of their services.

Cambodia chronology

1941

French colonial authorities install Prince Norodom Sihanouk as Cambodian king.

1954

Cambodia obtains independence from France.

1955

King Sihanouk abdicates in favor of his father and, as Prince Sihanouk, founds the People's Socialist Communist Party, which wins all the seats in the national assembly. Sihanouk becomes premier in 1957.

1970

Civilian and military officials overthrow the government of Prince Norodom Sihanouk and turn over power to Prime Minister Lon Nol as US-backed general. The Cambodian monarchy is abolished.

1975

Communist guerrillas of the Khmer Rouge seize the capital and oust Lon Nol's government after victories in provincial cities. The Khmer Rouge imposes a brutal reorganization of society; more than a million people die in three years. Prince Sihanouk, a virtual captive, is declared titular head of state.

1976

Prince Sihanouk resigns and goes to Beijing. The shadowy leader of the Khmer Rouge, Pol Pot, becomes prime minister.

1978

Vietnamese troops invade in December.

1979

Vietnam installs a new government in Phnom Penh led by Heng Samrin.

1982

With encouragement from China and the United States, the three Cambodian rebel factions form the CGDK, a government in exile with Prince Sihanouk as president, Khieu Samphan of the Khmer Rouge as vice president, and Son Sann of the conservative Khmer People's Liberation Front as prime minister.

1988–89

The JIM I and JIM II regional peace negotiations are held under the sponsorship of Indonesian foreign minister Ali Alatas.

1989

Vietnam announces that all its troops will leave Cambodia by the end of September. Sponsored by France and Indonesia, First Paris Peace Conference meets in July 1989 and deadlocks on the issue of power-sharing.

1990

The United States, Russia, China, France, and the United Kingdom – the five permanent members of the Security Council – draft a peace plan calling for an interim administration made up of the four factions to run the country under UN supervision until free elections can be organized. The factions form the Supreme National Council and agree in principle to accept the plan, which also calls for mutual disarmament and a UN buffer force.

June 1991

The Supreme National Council agrees to an indefinite ceasefire.

October 1991

Second Paris Peace Conference. Cambodia's warring factions and eighteen nations sign a peace treaty based on the 1990 draft peace plan in Paris, ending the civil war.

November 1991

The UN advance mission (UNAMIC) deploys in Cambodia.

March 1992

The United Nations starts deploying a peacekeeping force of 22,000 soldiers and civilians to oversee the elections. Yasushi Akashi is named special representative, Lt. Gen. John Sanderson, force commander.

June 1992

Cantonment and demobilization scheduled to begin, but the Khmer Rouge refuses to yield weapons.

December 1992

UNTAC electoral component completes the registration of 4.7 million potential Cambodian voters, approximately 90 percent of those eligible. After months of sporadic attacks, the Khmer Rouge begin taking United Nations troops hostage for brief periods. Over the next six months, they kill thirteen peacekeepers and wound at least fifty.

January 1993

The Khmer Rouge says it will boycott the vote. UNTAC establishes control teams to probe SOC violence and intimidation.

April 1993

The Khmer Rouge pulls out of the capital and regroups in strongholds. Clashes escalate. Electoral campaign begins; Radio UNTAC broadcasts human rights and electoral information directly to the Cambodian people. Japanese UNV Atsuhito Nakata is killed in Kompong Thom; UNTAC undergoes a crisis of confidence.

May 23–28, 1993

National elections for a Constituent Assembly are surprisingly non-violent, with 90 percent voter turnout.

June 1993

FUNCINPEC wins a plurality of fifty-eight seats (45 percent of the popular vote) in the Assembly; CPP (SOC), fifty-one (38 percent of the popular vote); BLDP (KPNLF), ten (3.8 percent of the popular vote). The Constituent Assembly begins its work, following a brief secession by the eastern provinces led by SOC hardliners. A provisional national government is formed, with Ranariddh and Hun Sen as co-prime ministers. The Committee of Assembly begins drafting a constitution.

September 1993

Sihanouk signs the constitution and accepts his restoration as king, creating a parliamentary democracy. UNTAC departs Phnom Penh. Prince Ranariddh (FUNCINPEC) becomes first prime minister, Hun Sen (SOC), second prime minister. CPP continues to exercise dominant influence over the bureaucracy and army.

January 1994

Following the failure of negotiations with the Khmer Rouge, the Royal Cambodian Army begins an offensive.

March 1994

The royal government at first seizes, then loses Pailin, a Khmer Rouge stronghold. The civil war stalemate continues.

October 1994

Sam Rainsy, Minister of Finance, resigns amid controversy. He later accuses the government of engaging in pervasive corruption. Rainsy later forms Khmer Nation Party in opposition.

November 1995

Prince Norodom Sirivuddh, foreign minister, is forced to resign and sent into exile, after he is accused of plotting against the government. Violence and threats against the press raise concerns of the international community.

February 1996

Justice Michael Kirby, UN Special Representative for Human Rights, resigns after noting signs of progress, including the growth of civil society, and of danger, including mounting restrictions on political parties, the electronic media, and the privileges of the National Assembly.

Spring 1996

Rivalry between FUNCINPEC and CPP ministers in the royal government escalates with accusations of favoritism and financial corruption.

El Salvador chronology

December 1931

A young group of military officers crushes Farabundo Marti and his army of peasants and workers frustrated with the concentration of power in El Salvador. The officers then seize power for themselves; Marti becomes a symbol for Salvadoran revolutionaries.

December 1980

The outbreak of civil war in El Salvador.

March 1981

Led by Roberto D'Aubuisson, the radical right forms the Nationalist Republican Alliance (ARENA).

August 7, 1987

The presidents of Costa Rica, El Salvador, Guatemala, Honduras, and Nicaragua sign the Esquipulas II Agreement, committing themselves to peace in the region and pledging to prevent the use of their territory for the destabilization of other nations.

September 15, 1989

The government and the FMLN agree to initiate a dialogue to end their armed confrontation through political means.

April 4, 1990

The government and the FMLN agree on a framework for negotiations under the auspices of the United Nations. The two sides outline four goals of the peace process: to end the armed conflict through political means, to promote democratization, to guarantee unrestricted respect for human rights and to reunify Salvadoran society.

July 26, 1990

The government and the FMLN sign the San José Agreement on Human Rights, which calls for the United Nations to deploy a verification mission to monitor the human rights situation in El Salvador as soon as a ceasefire is reached.

April 27, 1991

Meeting in Mexico City, the government and the FMLN agree on constitutional reforms affecting the armed forces, the judiciary and the electoral system. They also agree to establish a Commission on the Truth to investigate human rights abuses that occurred during the civil war.

May 20, 1991

The Security Council establishes the United Nations Observer Mission in El Salvador (ONUSAL) for an initial period of twelve months to monitor all agreements concluded between the Government and the FMLN. ONUSAL's initial mandate is limited to verification, by a Human Rights Division, of the July 1990 San José Agreement on Human Rights.

September 25, 1991

The government and the FMLN sign the New York Agreement, agreeing on a "compressed" agenda for negotiations and on a series of measures including purification and reduction of the size of the armed forces; organization of a new National Civilian Police force; institution of a land transfer program; and establishment of a National Commission for the Consolidation of Peace (COPAZ) to oversee implementation of all political agreements reached by the parties.

December 31, 1991

The government and the FMLN sign the Act of New York which, combined with agreements previously signed at San José, Mexico City, and New York, completes the negotiations on all substantive issues of the peace process.

January 14, 1992

The Security Council broadens ONUSAL's mandate and increases the Mission's strength, adding military and police divisions.

January 16, 1992

The Peace Agreement is formally signed at Chapultepec Castle in Mexico City in a ceremony attended by the Secretary-General. An informal ceasefire comes into force.

October 15–16, 1992

The government and the FMLN accept the Secretary-General's compromise solution for the transfer of land to ex-combatants and others.

December 15, 1992

Following the final demobilization of the FMLN's combatants and the FMLN's legalization as a political party, the armed conflict between the government and the FMLN formally ends at a ceremony in San Salvador.

March 15, 1993

The report of the Commission on the Truth is made public. It contains the results of the investigation into human rights violations committed during the civil war and the Commission's recommendations for preventing a repetition of such acts.

May 23, 1993

An explosion at an automobile repair shop in Managua, Nicaragua, leads to the discovery of an FMLN weapons cache; investigations by ONUSAL conducted with the cooperation of the FMLN reveal the existence of 114 previously unknown weapons deposits in El Salvador, Nicaragua, and Honduras.

July 7, 1993

The Secretary-General informs the Security Council that the government has removed from active service all army officers identified for dismissal so as to fully comply with the recommendations of the Ad Hoc Commission on Purification of the Armed Forces.

August 18, 1993

The destruction of the FMLN's weapons and equipment under ONUSAL verification is completed.

December 7, 1993

A joint group for the investigation of politically motivated, illegal armed groups is formed, as recommended by the Truth Commission.

March 20, 1994

Presidential, legislative, and mayoral elections are held. With no candidate in the presidential contest obtaining more than 50 percent of the vote, a run-off is required between the two parties winning the most votes – Alianza Republicana Nacionalista (ARENA), with 49.26 percent, and the Coalition Convergencia Democrática/FMLN/Movimento Nacional Revolucionario, with 25.29 percent. Observers document some irregularities and shortcomings, but ONUSAL states that the elections, in general, took place under appropriate conditions in terms of freedom, competitiveness, and security.

April 24, 1994

The ARENA candidate, Armando Calderón Sol, wins the presidential run-off election.

March 1995

The government initiates Plan Guardian, creating joint commands of military and police personnel to conduct patrols in rural areas of El Salvador. This institutionalizes the increasingly common use of military for internal order functions, in violation of constitutional procedures established under the Peace Accords.

April 27, 1995

The parties to the Chapultepec Peace Agreements sign a program of work for the completion of outstanding areas of the peace accords, including public security, land transfer, human settlements, reinsertion programs, Fund for the Protection of the Wounded and Disabled, and legislative reforms.

May 1, 1995

ONUSAL is terminated and replaced by MINUSAL, a small mission responsible for providing good offices and verifying implementation of the outstanding provisions of the peace agreements.

December 1995

President Calderon Sol announces the formation of a Public Security Council to address the many issues raised in MINUSAL's second evaluation of the public security sector, including increasing problems with the excessive use of force, alleged assassination, and membership in illegal armed groups within the newly created National Civil Police.

March 1996

Eight-seven percent of total land has been transferred by this point, though only 11,987 of the total 32,700 approved beneficiaries, or 36 percent, had received registration and completed the transfer process.

Spring 1996

The UN General Assembly (A/RES/50/226, May 22, 1996) has decided to establish the United Nations Office of Verification (UNOV), a smaller version of MINUSAL. UNOV is mandated to verify the implementation of the following aspects of the Peace Accords: the public security sector, the process of constitutional and legal reform, the land transfer program, and the transfer of the rural human settlements. The resolution will be in effect until December 31, 1996.

Bibliography

GENERAL

Amnesty International. *Amnesty International Report*, London, Amnesty International Publications, 1987.

Amnesty International. *Peacekeeping and Human Rights*, New York, Amnesty International USA, 1994.

Baehr, Peter R. and Leon Gordenker. *The United Nations in the 1990s*, London: Macmillan, 1994.

Ball, Nicole. *Pressing for Peace: Can Aid Induce Reform?* Washington, DC: Overseas Development Council, 1992.

Development Aid for Military Reform: A Pathway to Peace. Washington, DC: Overseas Development Council, 1993.

Berdal, Mats. *Whither UN Peacekeeping?* Adelphi Paper 281, London: Brassey's for the IISS, 1993.

Boudreau, Thomas. *Sheathing the Sword: The UN Secretary-General and the Prevention of International Conflicts*. New York: Greenwood Press, 1991.

Cassese, Antonio. *Human Rights in a Changing World*. Cambridge, UK: Polity Press, 1990.

Chand, D. Prem. "The role of the military and the civilian police." In Heribert Weiland and Matthew Braham (eds.), *The Namibian Peace Process: Implications and Lessons for the Future*. Report of the Freiburg Symposium, July 1–4, 1992, Freiburg, Germany. Co-organized by Arnold Bergstraesser Institut and International Peace Academy.

Chayes, Abram and Antonia Handler Chayes. "On Compliance." *International Organizations*, vol. 47, no. 2 (Spring 1993).

Childers, Erskine and Brian Urquhart. *Renewing the United Nations System*. Uppsala: Dag Hammarskjold Foundation; New York: Ford Foundation, 1994.

Collier, P. "Demobilization and insecurity: a study in the economics of the transition from war to peace." *Journal of International Development*, vol. 6, no. 3 (1994).

Creative Associates International Inc. *Program Options for Reintegrating Ex-Combatants into Civilian Life*. Contract 519-0281-C-00-1014-00. Submitted to USAID, El Salvador, San Salvador, April 26, 1991.

Crocker, Chester. *High Noon in Southern Africa: Making Peace in a Rough Neighborhood*. New York: W. W. Norton, 1992.

de Soto, Alvaro and Graciana del Castillo. "Obstacles to peacebuilding." *Foreign Policy*, vol. 94 (1994).

Diehl, Paul. *International Peacekeeping*. Baltimore: Johns Hopkins University Press, 1994.

Donnelly, Jack. *Universal Human Rights in Theory and Practice*. Ithaca, NY: Cornell University Press, 1989.

Durch, William J. (ed.). *The Evolution of UN Peacekeeping: Case Studies and Comparative Analysis*. New York: St. Martin's Press, 1993.

Evans, Gareth. *Cooperating For Peace: The Global Agenda for the 1990s and Beyond*. St. Leonards: Allen and Unwin, 1993.

Farer, Tom and Felice Gaer. "The UN and human rights: at the end of the beginning." In Adam Roberts and Benedict Kingsbury (eds.), *United Nations, Divided World*. Oxford: Clarendon Press, 1993.

Forsythe, David P. *The Internationalization of Human Rights*. Lexington, Mass.: Lexington Books, 1991.

Goulding, Marrack. "The evolution of United Nations peacekeeping." *International Affairs*, vol. 69, no. 3 (1993).

Helman, Gerald and Steven Ratner. "Saving failed states." *Foreign Policy*, vol. 89 (1992–3).

Henkin, Louis. "The internationalization of human rights." *Proceedings of the General Education Seminar*, vol. 6, no. 1 (1977).

Higgins, Rosalyn. *The Development of International Law through the Political Organs of the United Nations*. Oxford: Oxford University Press, 1963.

James, Alan. *Britain and the Congo Crisis, 1960–63*. New York: St. Martin's Press, 1996.

Liu, F. T. *United Nations Peacekeeping and the Non-Use of Force*. IPA Occasional Paper. Boulder, Col.: Lynne Rienner, 1992.

MacKinlay, John and Jarat Chopra. *A Draft Concept of Second Generation Multinational Operations*. Providence, RI: Watson Institute, 1993.

MacKinlay, John, Jarat Chopra and Larry Minear. *An Interim Report on the Cambodian Peace Process*. Oslo: Norwegian Institute of International Affairs, 1992.

Martin, Ian. "Haiti: mangled multilateralism." *Foreign Policy* (Summer 1994).

Maynes, C. William. "Relearning intervention." *Foreign Policy* (Spring 1995).

Otunnu, Olara A. "Maintaining broad legitimacy for United Nations action," in *Keeping the Peace in the Post-Cold War Era: Strengthening Mulitlateral Peacekeeping*, New York: The Trilateral Commission, 1993.

Princen, Tom. *Intermediaries in International Conflict*. Princeton: Princeton University Press, 1992.

Raman, K. Venkata. *The Ways of the Peacemaker*. New York: UNITAR, 1975.
    "United Nations peacekeeping and the future of world order." In Henry Wiseman (ed.), *Peacekeeping: Appraisals and Proposals*. New York: Pergamon Press, 1983.

Ratner, Steven. *The New UN Peacekeeping*. New York: St. Martin's Press, 1995.

Riesman, Michael. "Comment: sovereignty and human rights in international law." *American Journal of International Law*, vol. 84 (1990), pp. 866–71.

Rikhye, Indar Jit. *Military Adviser to the Secretary-General: UN Peacekeeping and the Congo Crisis*. London: Hurst, 1993.

Ruggie, John G. "The United Nations: stuck in a fog between peacekeeping and enforcement." In *Peacekeeping: The Way Ahead?* McNair Paper 25, Washington, DC: Institute for National Strategic Studies, National Defense University, Washington, DC.

Ruiz, Hiram A. *Left Out in the Cold: The Perilous Homecoming of Afghan Refugees.* Washington, DC: US Committee for Refugees, 1992.

El Retorno: Guatemalans' Risky Repatriation Begins. Washington, DC: US Committee for Refugees, 1993.

Schachter, Oscar. "The development of international law through the legal opinions of the United Nations Secretariat." *British Yearbook of International Law,* vol. 25 (1948), p. 91.

International Law in Theory and Practice. Boston, Mass.: Martinus Nijhoff, 1985.

United Nations. *The Blue Helmets: A Review of United Nations Peace-keeping.* New York: United Nations Department of Public Information, 1985, 1990.

United States. The Clinton Administration's Policy on Reforming Multilateral Peace Operations, Executive Summary, May 1994.

Urquhart, Brian. *Hammarskjold.* New York: Harper and Row, 1984.

Ralph Bunche: An American Life, New York: W. W. Norton, 1993.

Weiss, Thomas G. (ed.). *The United Nations and Civil Wars.* Boulder, Col.: Lynne Rienner, 1995.

Zartman, I. William (ed.). *Elusive Peace: Negotiating an End to Civil Wars.* Washington, DC: Brookings Institution, 1995.

UNITED NATIONS DOCUMENTS

Charter of the United Nations and Statute of the International Court of Justice. In *Yearbook of the United Nations.* Lake Success, NY: UN Publications, 1947, pp. 831–50.

Universal Declaration of Human Rights. GA Res. A/RES/217A, 10 December 1948.

Convention Relating to the Status of Refugees. UNTS 189, July 28, 1951.

International Covenant on Civil and Political Rights. GA Res. A/RES/220A, December 16, 1966.

Protocol Relating to the Status of Refugees, January 31, 1967. UNTS 267, 268. Art. I(2) 60.

Vienna Convention on the Law of Treaties, Concluded at Vienna on May 23, 1969. United Nations Conference on the Law of Treaties, March 26 to May 24, 1968 and April 9 to May 22, 1969, Vienna. A/CONF.39/11/add.2. UNTS vol. 1155:331.

Convention on the Elimination of Discrimination Against Women. UNTS vol. 1249, December 18, 1979.

Convention Against Torture. GA Res. A/RES/39/46, December 10, 1984.

Convention on the Rights of the Child. GA Res. A/RES/44/25, November 20, 1989.

Security Council Resolution. S/RES/688 (1991).

Further Report of the Secretary-General Pursuant to Paragraph 7 of Resolution 840 (1993). S/26260, August 26, 1993.

"Supplement to *An Agenda for Peace*: Position Paper of the Secretary-General on the Occasion of the Fiftieth Anniversary of the United Nations." In Boutros Boutros-Ghali, *An Agenda for Peace*. New York: United Nations, 1992, 1995.

Report of the Secretary-General on the Situation in Somalia, March 28, 1995. S/1995/231.

CAMBODIA

Akashi, Yasushi. "The challenge of peacekeeping in Cambodia: lessons to be learned." Lecture, SIPA, Columbia University, November 29, 1993.

Alagappa, Muthiah. *Political Legitimacy in Southeast Asia: The Quest for Moral Authority*. Stanford, Calif.: Stanford University Press, 1995.

Becker, Elizabeth. *When the War Was Over: The Voices of Cambodia's Revolution and its People*. New York: Simon and Schuster, 1986.

Chanda, Nayan. "Cambodia: in search of an elusive peace." *The American–Vietnamese Dialogue*. February 8–11, Conference Report. Queenstown, Md.: The Aspen Institute, 1993.

Chandler, David. *The Tragedy of Cambodian History: Politics War and Revolution Since 1945*. New Haven, Conn.: Yale University Press, 1991.

  Brother Number One: A Political Biography of Pol Pot. Boulder, Col.: Westview Press, 1992.

Chandler, David P., Ben Kiernan and Chantou Boua (eds. and tr.). *Pol Pot Plans the Future: Confidential Leadership Documents from Democratic Kampuchea, 1976–1977*. New Haven, Conn.: Yale University Press, 1988.

Chopra, Jarat. *United Nations Authority in Cambodia*. Providence, RI: Watson Institute, 1993.

Commonwealth of Australia. *Cambodia: An Australian Police Proposal*. Working papers prepared for the Informal Meeting on Cambodia, Jakarta, February 26–28, 1990. Canberra: R. D. Rubie, Commonwealth Government Printer, 1990.

Cuny, Frederick and Barry N. Stein. "Prospects for and promotion of spontaneous repatriation." In Gil Loescher and Laila Monahan (eds.), *Refugees and International Relations*. Oxford: Oxford University Press, 1989.

Doyle, Michael W. "Lessons from Cambodia." *The United Nations, and US Policy in the Post-Cold War World*. Queenstown, Md.: The Aspen Institute, 1994.

  UN Peacekeeping in Cambodia: UNTAC's Civil Mandate. Boulder, Col.: Lynne Rienner, 1995.

Doyle, Michael W. and Nishkala Suntharalingam. "The UN in Cambodia: lessons for complex peacekeeping," in *International Peacekeeping*, vol. 1, no. 2 (1994).

Fernando, J. Basil. *The Inability to Prosecute: Courts and Human Rights in Cambodia and Sri Lanka*. Hong Kong: Future Asia Link, 1993.

Findlay, Trevor. *The UN in Cambodia*. Stockholm: SIPRI, 1995.

Franck, Thomas M. "The emerging right to democratic governance." *American Journal of International Law*, vol. 46 (1992).

Goodwin-Gill, Guy. "Voluntary repatriation: legal and policy issues." In Gil Loescher and Laila Monahan (eds.), *Refugees and International Relations*. Oxford: Oxford University Press, 1989.

"Voluntary character of repatriation." *International Journal of Refugee Law*, vol. 4, no. 2 (1992).

Haas, Michael. *Genocide by Proxy*. New York: Praeger, 1991.

Heininger, Janet. *Peacekeeping in Transition: The United Nations in Cambodia*. New York: Twentieth Century Fund, 1994.

Human Rights Watch. "Cambodia: the facts." *The New Internationalist*, April 1993.

Landmines in Cambodia: The Coward's War. New York: Human Rights Watch, September 1991.

Jennar, Raoul M. *Cambodian Chronicles (III)*. Joidoigne, Belgium: European Far Eastern Research Center, May 1992.

Cambodian Chronicles (VII): Before it comes too late. Letter to the Members of the Security Council. Joidoigne, Belgium: European Far Eastern Research Center, 15 February 1993.

Kiernan, Ben. *How Pol Pot Came to Power*. London: Verso, 1985.

Cambodia: The Eastern Zone Massacres. New York: Center for the Study of Human Rights, Columbia University, 1987.

"The American bombardment of Kampuchea, 1969–1973." *Vietnam Generation* (Winter 1989).

"The failures of the Paris Agreements on Cambodia, 1991–93." *The Challenge of Indochina: An Examination of the US Role*. Congressional Staff Conference, April 30–May 2, 1993.

Kiernan, Ben and Chantou Boua (eds.). *Peasants and Politics in Kampuchea 1942–1981*. London: Zed Press, 1982.

Kingdom of Cambodia. Constitution. Adopted 21 September 1993.

Koh, Tommy T. B. "The Paris Conference on Cambodia: a multilateral negotiation that 'failed'." *Negotiation Journal*, vol. 6, no. 1 (1990).

Maley, Michael. "Reflections on the electoral process in Cambodia." In Hugh Smith (ed.), *Peacekeeping: Challenges for the Future*. Canberra: Australian Defense Studies Centre, 1993.

Marks, Stephen. "Forgetting 'the policies and practices of the past': impunity in Cambodia." *The Fletcher Forum of World Affairs*, vol. 18, no. 2 (1994).

McAulay, Peter. "Civilian Police and peacekeeping challenges in the 1990s." In Hugh Smith (ed.), *Peacekeeping: Challenges for the Future*. Canberra: Australian Defense Studies Centre, Australian Defense Force Academy, 1993.

McLean, Lyndall. "Civil Administration in transition." ADFA Seminar, Canberra, May 1994.

McNamara, Dennis. "The origins and effects of humane deterrence policies in South-east Asia." In Gil Loescher and Laila Monahan (eds.), *Refugees and International Relations*. Oxford: Oxford University Press, 1989.

Muscat, Robert J. "Rebuilding Cambodia: problems of governance and human resources." In Dolores A. Donovan, Sidney Jones, Dinah Pokemper and Robert Muscat (eds.) (with introduction by Frederick Z. Brown), *Rebuilding Cambodia: Human Resources, Human Rights and Law*. Washington, DC: SAIS Foreign Policy Institute, 1993.

Ratner, Steven. "The Cambodia Settlement Agreements." *American Journal of International Law*, vol. 87 (1993).

"The United Nations' role in Cambodia: a model for resolution of internal conflicts?" In Lori Fisler Damrosch (ed.), *Enforcing Peace: Collective Intervention in Internal Conflicts*. New York: Council on Foreign Relations, 1993.

Robinson, Court. "Still trying to get home: the repatriation of Cambodian Refugees in Thailand." *Refugee Reports*, vol. 13, no. 11 (1992), p. 6.

"Something Like Home Again": The Repatriation of Cambodian Refugees. Washington, DC: US Committee for Refugees, May 1994.

Roos, Klaas. "China and the Cambodian peace process: the value of coercive diplomacy." *Asia Survey*, vol. 31, no. 12 (1991), pp. 1170–85.

Sanderson, John M. "Preparation for, deployment and conduct of peace-keeping operations: a Cambodia snapshot." Paper presented at "UN Peacekeeping at the Crossroads," International Seminar, Canberra, March 21–24, 1993.

Sesser, Stan. "Report from Cambodia." *The New Yorker*, May 19, 1992.

Shawcross, William. *Quality of Mercy: Cambodia, Holocaust and the Modern Conscience*. New York: Simon and Schuster, 1979.

"A new Cambodia." *New York Review of Books*, August 12, 1993.

Solarz, Stephen. "Cambodia and the international community." *Foreign Affairs*, vol. 69, no. 2 (1990), pp. 99–115.

Summers, Laura. "The sources of economic discontent in Sihanouk's Cambodia." *Southeast Asian Journal of Social Science*, vol. 14 (1986).

Sutter, Valerie O'Connor. *The Indochinese Refugee Dilemma*. Baton Rouge, La.: Louisiana State University Press, 1990.

Than, Sina. "Cambodia 1990: towards a peaceful solution?" *Southeast Asian Affairs*. Institute of South East Asian Studies, 1991.

Vickery, Michael. *Kampuchea: Politics, Economics and Society*. Boulder, Col.: Lynne Rienner, 1986.

Warner, Nick. "Cambodia: lessons of UNTAC for peacekeeping operations." In Kevin Clements and Christine Wilson (eds.), *UN Peacekeeping at the Crossroads*, Canberra: Peace Research Centre, School of Pacific and Asian Studies, 1994.

Weiss-Fagen, Patricia and Joseph Eldridge. In Gil Loescher and Laila Monahan (eds.), *Refugees and International Relations*. Oxford: Oxford University Press, 1989.

World Bank. *Cambodia: Agenda for Rehabilitation and Reconstruction*. Washington, DC: World Bank, 1992.

UNITED NATIONS DOCUMENTS

Report of the Secretary-General. The Situation in Cambodia A/40/759, 17 October 1985.

UNHCR, *Durable Solutions*. (UNHCR, 1985).

Enhancing the Effectiveness of the Principle of Periodic and Genuine Elections. GA Res. A/RES/45/150, December 18, 1990.

UNHCR. Tripartite Memorandum of Understanding among the Royal Thai Government, the Supreme National Council of Cambodia and the Office of the United Nations High Commissioner for Refugees Relating to the Repatriation of Cambodian Refugees and Displaced Persons from Thailand. November 21, 1991.

The Agreements on a Comprehensive Political Settlement of the Cambodian Conflict. 23 October 1991. A/46/608-S/23177; Department of Public Information DPI/1180-92077, January 1992.

Report of the Secretary-General on Cambodia. S/23613, February 19, 1992.

First Progress Report of the Secretary-General on the United Nations Transitional Authority in Cambodia. S/23870, May 1, 1992.

Second Special Report of the Secretary-General on the United Nations Transitional Authority on Cambodia. S/24286, July 14, 1992.

Second Progress Report of the Secretary-General on the United Nations Transitional Authority in Cambodia. S/24578, September 21, 1992.

Report of the Secretary-General on the Implementation of Security Council Resolution 783 (1992). S/24800, November 15, 1992.

Third Progress Report of the Secretary-General on the United Nations Transitional Authority in Cambodia. S/25124, January 25, 1993.

Report of the Secretary-General on the Implementation of Security Council Resolution 792 (1992). S/25289, February 13, 1993.

Fourth Progress Report of the Secretary-General on the United Nations Transitional Authority in Cambodia. S/25719, May 3, 1993.

Report of the Secretary-General in Pursuance of Paragraph 6 of Security Council Resolution 810 (1993). S/25784, May 15, 1993.

Security Council. S/RES/826, May 20, 1993.

Report of the Secretary-General. S/26090, July 16, 1993.

Further Report of the Secretary-General Pursuant to Paragraph 7 of Resolution 840 (1993). S/26260, August 26, 1993.

UNHCR. Cambodia Repatriation Operation. August 31, 1993.

Security Council. S/RES/940, July 31, 1994.

UNTAC DOCUMENTS

Roos, Klaas. *Evaluation Report: UN CIVPOL, UNTAC, Cambodia.* Phnom Penh, August 1993, p. 8.

UNTAC. The Secretary-General's Consolidated Appeal. May 1992.

Note sur le contrôle de l'administration civile. August 19, 1992.

Report on UNTAC's Activities: Civil Administration Component. September 7, 1992.

Report on UNTAC's Activities: The First Six Months. March 15 to September 15, 1992.

Information/Education Division Report. September 18, 1992.

Activity Report of Civil Administration, September–October, 1992. November 27, 1992.

Operation Order No. 2 for the Joint Military Component of UNTAC. December 9, 1992.

Briefing Note: Terms of Reference of the Proposed UNTAC Control

Mechanism at the Provincial Level. January 19, 1993 (unpublished UNTAC document).

Notes on the Control Exercised by the Civil Administration Component, September–October, November, December 1992, and January 1993.

Rehabilitation and Development in Cambodia: Achievements and Strategies. February 25, 1993.

Report on the Political Environment in Siem Reap Province. Discussion with Political Parties, UNTAC Memorandum, March 29, 1993.

Final Report of the Civil Administration Component. Phnom Penh, September 16, 1993.

Human Rights Component, Final Report. Phnom Penh, September 1993.

Border Control Unit, Final Report. September 1993.

EL SALVADOR

Human Rights Watch/Americas. *El Salvador: The Massacre at El Mozote: The Need to Remember.* New York: Human Rights Watch, 1986.

   Accountability and Human Rights: The Report of the United Nations Commission on the Truth for El Salvador, vol. 5, no. 7 (1993).

Baranyi, Stephen and Liisa North. *Stretching the Limits of the Possible: UN Peacekeeping in Central America.* The Aurora Papers, Ottawa: The Canadian Center for Global Security, 1992.

   The United Nations Role in El Salvador: The Promises and Dilemmas of an Integrated Approach to Peace. Toronto: York University Press, 1993.

Boyce, James K., et al. *Adjusting Toward Peace: Economic Policy and Post-war Reconstruction in El Salvador.* San Salvador: UNDP, 1995.

Buergenthal, Thomas. "The United Nations Truth Commission for El Salvador." *Vanderbilt Journal of Transnational Law,* vol. 27, no. 3 (1994).

Bulmer-Thomas, V. *The Political Economy of Central America since 1920.* Cambridge: Cambridge University Press, 1987.

Cagan, Steve. "El Salvador tries to vote." *The Nation,* April 18, 1994.

Castro, I. "El Salvador: crime replaces war with a murder every hour." *Inter Press Service,* February 23, 1995.

Center for International Policy. *Salvadorans Nearing Agreement on Armed Forces.* 22 April 1991.

Coleman, Christopher C. *The Salvadoran Peace Process: A Preliminary Inquiry.* Oslo: Norwegian Institute of International Affairs, Research Report no. 173 (1993).

Colindres, E. *Fundamentos economicos de la burguesia salvadorena.* San Salvador: Universidad de Centroamerica, 1977.

Costa, Gino. "Naciones Unidas y la creacion de una policia Civil en El Salvador." *Analisis Internacional: Revista del Internationales,* no. 11 (1995).

de Soto, Alvaro. "The UN operations in Namibia and Central America." Speaker at the Tokyo Symposium on The United Nations Peace-keeping Operations: Recent Experiences and Future Prospects. Co-organized by The United Nations University and The International Peace Academy and supported by the Ministry of Foreign Affairs of Japan, September 3–4, 1991, Tokyo.

"The negotiations following the New York Agreement." In Joseph S. Tulchin and Gary Brand (eds.), *Is There a Transition to Democracy in El Salvador?* Boulder, Col.: Lynne Rienner, 1992.

de Soto, Alvaro and Graciana del Castillo. "Obstacles to peacebuilding." *Foreign Policy*, vol. 94 (1994). Translated into Spanish as "Los obstáculos en la construcción de la paz," *Revista tendencias*, vol. 32 (1994).

"Implementation of comprehensive peace agreements: staying the course in El Salvador." *Global Governance*, June 1995.

del Castillo, Graciana. "Post-conflict peace-building: the challenge to the UN." *CEPAL Review*, vol. 55 (1995). Translated into Spanish as "Consolidación de la Paz Después de los Conflictos," *Revista de la CEPAL*, vol. 55 (1995).

Dunkerly, J. *Power in the Isthmus: A Political History of Modern Central America.* London: Verso, 1988.

El Salvador Proceso. Informativo Semanal del Centro Universitario de Documentación e Informacion, San Salvador: University of Central America.

Garcia, José Z. "The *Tanda* system and institutional autonomy of the military." In Joseph S. Tulchin and Gary Brand (eds.), *Is There a Transition to Democracy in El Salvador?* Boulder, Col.: Lynne Rienner, 1992.

Gordon, Sara. *Crisis politica y guerra en El Salvador.* Mexico City: Siglo XXI, 1989.

Government of El Salvador. *Acuerdos de paz. Costos y deficit financiero.* San Salvador, 1995.

Holiday, David and William Stanley. "Building the peace: the role of the United Nations in El Salvador." *Journal of International Affairs* (Winter 1992–3).

International Monetary Fund. *El Salvador: Recent Economic Developments.* IMF Staff Country Report, no. 94/10, November 1994.

Inter-American Court of Human Rights. *Annual Report of the Inter-American Court of Human Rights, 1988.* OAS/Ser.L/V/III 19, doc. 13, August 31, 1988.

Jiménez, Edgar C., Raúl Benítez M., Ricardo Córdova M. and Alexander Segovia. "The FMLN: new thinking." In *El Salvador, guerra, politica y paz.* San Salvador: CINAS-CRIES, 1988.

Johnstone, Ian. *Rights and Reconciliation: UN Strategies in El Salvador.* International Peace Academy Occasional Paper. Boulder, Col. and London: Lynne Rienner, 1995.

Jones, E. and L. Taylor. *Infrastructure Restoration/Reconstruction Assessment for the Government of El Salvador National Recovery Plan, 1991. Volume II, Appendices.* Development Associates, Inc. consultants' report to USAID, September 1991.

Karl, Terry Lynn. "El Salvador's negotiated revolution." *Foreign Affairs*, vol. 71, no. 2 (1992).

Kramer, Francisco Villagràn. "Understanding the crisis in Central America: essential facts." In Jack Child (ed.), *Conflict in Central America: Approaches to Peace and Security.* London: Hurst, 1986.

LaFeber, Walter. *Inevitable Revolutions.* New York: W. W. Norton, 1993.

Lawyers' Committee for Human Rights. *Underwriting Injustice: AID and El Salvador's Judicial Reform Program.* New York: 1989.

El Salvador: Human Rights Dismissed: A Report on 17 Unresolved Cases. New York: 1990.

El Salvador's Negotiated Revolution: Prospects for Legal Reform. New York: 1993.

Loehr, W. and R. Nunez. *El Salvador: An Assessment of the Impact of Recent Policy Changes on Agriculture.* APAP II Technical Report no. 127. Cambridge, Mass.: Abt Associates, 1991.

MIPLAN. *Consolidating the Peace Through National Reconstruction and Poverty Alleviation: Report to the Consultative Group Meeting, Paris, 1 April 1993.* San Salvador: MIPLAN.

Montgomery, Tommie Sue. *Revolution in El Salvador: From Civil Strife to Civil Peace.* Boulder, Col.: Westview Press, 1995.

Moss, Ambler Jr. "Peace in Central America?" *Survival* (September–October 1990).

Needler, Martin C. "El Salvador" The military and politics." *Armed Forces and Society*, vol. 17 (1991).

Popkin, Margaret. *Human Rights, Development and Democracy: Experience of the UN in Post-Conflict El Salvador.* UNDP Working Paper, April 15, 1993.

Popkin, Margaret, George Vickers, and Jack Spence. *Justice Impugned.* Cambridge, Mass.: Hemisphere Initiatives, 1993.

Rubén, Raul. "El problema agrario en El Salvador. Notas sobre un economia polarizada." *Cuadernos de Investigación*, vol. 7 (1991) (San Salvador: Centro de Investigaciones Tecnológicas y Científicas, Año II).

Schwarz, Benjamin. *American Counterinsurgency Doctrine and El Salvador: The Frustrations of Reform and the Illusions of Nation Building.* Santa Monica, Calif.: Rand, 1991.

Scott, David Clark. "Purge of Salvador's army brass dismantles military clique." *Christian Science Monitor*, July 6, 1993.

Spence, Jack, George Vickers and David Dye. *A Negotiated Revolution: A Two Year Progress Report on the Salvadoran Peace Accords.* Cambridge, Mass.: Hemisphere Initiatives, 1994.

El Salvador: Elections of the Century. Cambridge, Mass.: Hemisphere Initiatives, July 1994.

The Salvadoran Peace Accords and Democratization: A Three Year Progress Report and Recommendations. Cambridge, Mass.: Hemisphere Initiatives, 1995.

Stanley, William. *Risking Failure: The Problems and Promise of the New Civilian Police in El Salvador.* Cambridge, Mass.: Hemisphere Initiatives, 1993.

Toward a Level Playing Field? A Report on the Post-War Salvadoran Electoral Process. Cambridge, Mass.: Hemisphere Initiatives, January 1994.

Protectors or Perpetrators? The Institutional Crisis of the Salvadoran Police. Cambridge, Mass.: Hemisphere Initiatives, January 1996.

Strassma, J. *Land Reform in El Salvador.* University of Minnesota, mimeograph, 1989.

Torres-Rivas, Edelberto (ed.). *Centroamerica la crisis en cifras.* San José: FLACSO-UCA, 1989.

US Department of State. *Country Reports on Human Rights Practices for 1991.* Washington, DC: USGPO, 1992.

Country Reports on Human Rights Practices for 1992. Washington, DC: USGPO, 1993.

University of Central America (UCA). *National Survey.* Conducted by the Institute of Public Opinion, UCA, undated.

Vickers, George. "The political reality after eleven years of war." In Joseph S. Tulchin and Gary Brand (eds.), *Is There a Transition to Democracy in El Salvador?* Boulder, Col.: Lynne Rienner, 1992.

Vickers, George, and Jack Spence. *End Game: A Progress Report on the Implementation of the Salvadoran Peace Accords.* Cambridge, Mass.: Hemisphere Initiatives, 1992.

Weiss-Fagen, Patricia. "El Salvador: lessons in peace consolidation." In T. Farer (ed.), *Beyond Sovereignty: Collectively Defending Democracy in the Americas.* Baltimore, Md.: Johns Hopkins University Press, 1995.

Whitfield, Teresa. *Paying the Price: Ignacio Ellacuria and the Murdered Jesuits of El Salvador.* Philadelphia: Temple University Press, 1994.

Wood, Elizabeth. "Economic change, civil war, and democracy in El Salvador: rural social relations in revolution and reconstruction." Doctoral dissertation, Stanford University, 1995.

World Bank. *Proposed Second Structural Adjustment Loan of US$50 million to the Republic of El Salvador.* Washington, DC: World Bank. Report no. P-6108-ES, August 23, 1993.

  El Salvador: The Challenge of Poverty Alleviation. Washington, DC: World Bank, 1994. Report no. 12315-ES, June 9, 1994.

UNITED NATIONS DOCUMENTS

The Contadora Act. S/16041, October 18, 1983.

Costa del Sol Agreement of February 1989. S/20491.

Tela Declaration of August 1989. S/20778.

Caracas Agreement of May 21, 1990. A/45/706-S/21931.

San José Agreement of July 26, 1990. A/44/971-S/21541.

Mexico Agreements of April 27, 1991. A/46/533-S/23130.

New York Agreement of September 25, 1991. A/46/502-S/23802.

Chapultepec Agreement. S/23504, December 31, 1991.

El Salvador Agreements: The Path to Peace. DPI/1208-92614, July 1992.

Geneva Agreement of 13 October 1992. A/45/706-S/231931, Annex I.

UNDP. *Launching New Protagonists in Salvadoran Agriculture: The Agricultural Training Programme for Ex-Combatants of the FMLN.* San Salvador: UNDP, 1993.

Report of the Commission on the Truth for El Salvador. *Madness to Hope: The 12-Year War in El Salvador.* S/25500, April 1, 1993.

ECLAC. *Economic Consequences of Peace in El Salvador.* August 30, 1993.

Letter from the Secretary-General to the President of the Security Council. S/26689, November 3, 1993.

Letter from the Secretary-General dated 24 May 1994 transmitting the Agreement on a Timetable for the Implementation of the Most Important Agreements Pending. S/1994/612.

General Assembly and Security Council. The Situation in Central America: Procedures for the Establishment of a Firm and Lasting Peace and Progress in Fashioning a Region of Peace, Freedom, Democracy, and

Development: Note by the Secretary-General." Doc. A/49/281 S/1994/886; July 28, 1994.

Report of the Joint Group for the Investigation of Politically Motivated Illegal Armed Groups. S/1994/989, October 22, 1994.

Report of the Secretary-General on the United Nations Observer Mission in El Salvador. Reports to the Security Council of November 23, 1992 (S/24833), May 21, 1993 (S/25812) (The 13 October 1992 land agreement is included in add.2 of S/25812), June 29, 1993 (S/26005), November 23, 1993 (S/26790), May 11, 1994 (S/1994/561), August 26, 1994 (S/1994/1000), October 31, 1994 (S/1994/1212) and March 24, 1995 (S/1995/220) and April 18, 1995 (S/1995/281 or A/49/888).

International Colloquium on Post-Conflict Reconstruction Strategies: The Chairman's Synopsis and Conclusions. Organized by the Reconstruction Unit, DDSMS, and sponsored by the Austrian Federal Ministry for Foreign Affairs; Austrian Study Centre for Peace and Conflict Resolution, Stadtschlaining, Austria, June 23–24, 1995.

Reports of the Secretary-General on the United Nations Observer Mission in El Salvador to the Security Council (UN, 1992, 1993a, 1993b, 1993c, 1994a, 1994b, 1994c, 1995a and 1995b).

Reports to the General Assembly on the situation in Central America. 1995, 1996.

The Situation in Central America: Procedures for the Establishment of a Firm and Lasting Peace and Progress in Fashioning a Region of Peace, Freedom, Democracy and Development. Reports to the General Assembly of October 6, 1995 (A/50517) and February 1996.

Index